W9-CJS-468

BILL DAVIS

BILL DAVIS

A Biography by Claire Hoy

ⓝ METHUEN

Toronto New York London Sydney Auckland

Canadian Cataloguing in Publication Data

Hoy, Claire   *Cat May/85*
Bill Davis

Includes index.
ISBN 0-458-99130-9.

1. Davis, William G., 1929 — .   2. Prime ministers —
Ontario — Biography.   3. Ontario — Politics
and government — 1943 — *   I. Title.

FC3076.1.D38H69   1985   971.3'04'0924   C85-098152-2
     F1058.D38H69   1985

The publisher kindly thanks the people, organizations, and
government departments who gave their permission to
reproduce the photographs that appear in this book. Because
many of the photos came from the Davis family and the Office
of the Premier, it was not always possible to establish the
copyright holders. However, every effort has been made to do
this, and any errors or omissions drawn to the publisher's
attention will be rectified in subsequent editions.

Design by Fortunato Aglialoro

Printed and bound in Canada

1 2 3 4   85   89 88 87 86

To Lydia and my children:
Paul, Kathy, Zachary, and Clayton.
Love is ...

Contents

PART THREE The National Man

Acknowledgments

The first time I heard Bill Davis speak was in 1963. I was on assignment for the *Ryersonian*, my college paper; otherwise, I probably would have left. I was a student, he was the new education minister, and I cannot remember a word he said, but I do remember the image of this chubby guy speaking, no, reading directly from a text, rarely glancing at his audience, and looking more relieved than we were when he finished.

Bill Davis improved over the years to the point where it became a standing joke with his speechwriters that regardless of what they wrote, he wouldn't use it, anyway. While he was never a fiery orator, he could move a crowd, make them laugh, make them feel good about themselves, about their party, their province, and, yes, their country.

One thing Bill Davis never could do, however, was speak about his parents, his family, those things he truly loved, without beginning to show some emotion — something he hated to do — at which point he would deflect it with a joke, or simply change the topic to something more comfortable, something less personal.

It is both the public and the private Bill Davis I hope this book captures. As much as those who have read my columns in the *Toronto Sun* will know I disagree with almost every single major initiative Bill Davis took, I confess I like the man as a person and I thank him here for his co-operation, however reluctant it may have been. And it was reluctant. After an initial two-hour interview, eleven times over a three-month period he cancelled out of a second interview at the last minute. It was only after I threatened to invade his cottage sanctuary in July, 1984, that he agreed to another lengthy session, this time for four hours, just the two of us in his Brampton den. Coincidentally, it was the day John Turner called to say the Queen's visit was cancelled and there would be a fall federal election.

While I have seen the tough side of Bill Davis and write about it freely here, I have also seen the human side. It was Bill Davis who visited my first wife, Beverley, in Princess Margaret Hospital in 1976 when she was dying of cancer, the first time he'd been in that hospital since his own first wife, Helen, had died of cancer in 1962. They chatted about playing the piano, something

Beverley, Helen, and Bill Davis had in common. It was that same Bill Davis who would be literally shattered when marital problems hit some of his personal staff, the same Bill Davis who went out of his way to attend the funeral of the mother of a press gallery reporter when there were no yards in it for him, just an opportunity to show that for all his efforts to hide his emotions, he was never completely successful.

I want to thank him not only for his help but also for telling his aides, his family, his friends and senior staff to co-operate with this project. Indeed, Joe Dobbs, his closest friend, wouldn't even answer my telephone calls until I sent the premier a note asking him to let Joe speak with me. That same hour I received a note that "Joe Dobbs would be pleased to speak with you about the book," and thirty minutes later Dobbs himself telephoned to arrange an interview.

A special thanks to my friend Larry Zolf, who helped me organize the structure of this book and put Methuen on to me in the first place. If I didn't believe the Senate was such a useless organization, I'd wish Zolf success in his historical quest for an appointment.

Another word of thanks for Irene Beatty and her staff for giving me access to the hundreds of thousands of newspaper clippings they kept to chronicle the Davis career. Without that I'd still be buried somewhere in a library trying to sort out this man's achievements and failures.

After twenty years as a journalist I must confess a certain satisfaction in being able to boast that I've never been an editor (unless you count one year as sports editor of the *Ryersonian*). As a result I have always viewed editors with suspicion, although I admit they are, like accountants, a necessary evil, and I have had some good ones. Two good ones I've enjoyed both helped fashion my sometimes disparate ramblings here into a cohesive unit, and I thank Methuen's senior editor Greg Cable and copy editor Stephanie Stone for that.

I also thank the *Sun* for allowing me the time to work on this project and promote it and for giving me the forum from which the whole thing became possible.

There, that's the nicest I'm ever going to be for the rest of my life. Enjoy.

Claire Hoy
Ottawa March, 1985

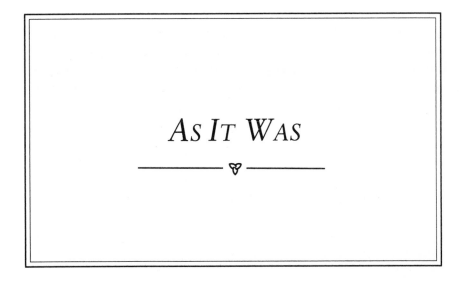

AS IT WAS

Kathleen Davis, slightly bleary-eyed from waiting up late for her husband the night before, shuffles along the grey-white tiles of the long, narrow kitchen in her sprawling, ranch-style home.

She's gone full circle from her carefree days at Berkeley and her "grand tour of Europe," as she calls it, when she and a girlfriend tripped gaily across the Continent with plans to study German at the University of Munich.

One of three children of a prominent, suburban Chicago (Hinsdale) neurologist, Kathleen no longer looks after black slum kids in a trendy drop-in centre in San Francisco. But while she gave up many of the trappings of her free-spirited life — trading her battered old Volkswagen for a life of chauffeur-driven limousines and switching from a Bohemian lifestyle to one befitting Ontario's first lady — she retains the attitudes acquired during her life as a left-wing Democrat, a significant influence on the politics of her husband, Bill Davis.

Pausing briefly to pat Blue, one of the two family mongrels (Thor is the other), Kathleen checks the automatic coffee maker, a recent acquisition from the five children — four from Davis's first wife, Helen McPhee, who died of cancer in 1962, and one by her. The gift replaced the ancient, dented drip coffee pot that Davis preferred and Kathleen insists made better coffee. "But what can you do when your children give you something?"

Wearing her housecoat and slippers, looking every bit your

average Ontario housewife, Kathleen flips on radio station CFRB, wanders over to the fridge, removes the apple juice (domestic, of course), and pours two glasses. In a moment she'll carry them down the corridor to the den, a cosy room overlooking the vast expanse of lawn leading directly to Main Street, Brampton.

But first she glances at the bulletin board where long ago she tacked her favorite cartoon from the *New Yorker*. It shows a man and woman at their breakfast table. He's dressed for work and reading the newspaper. She's telling him that she'd had a dream that night, and at last she had been given the chance to do what she had always wanted—sing the lead in *Madame Butterfly*. In her dream she had asked her hubby if he could attend. He had said he couldn't; he had a meeting. "No, it's not without its message," explains Kathleen.

The telephone rings. It's 7 a.m., Tuesday. Another day at the top of Mount Ontario has begun as so many others have before it.

Kathleen's husband, Bill (actually, she calls him Billy, as his mother did, which still embarrasses him in public), wanders slowly into the walnut-panelled den that once was his father's refuge from the pressures of being the local Crown attorney. He takes his time. The caller will wait.

He may have been premier of Canada's most powerful province for fourteen years and a major player on the national political scene as well, but right now Bill Davis looks anything but the fat-cat boss of the fabled Big Blue Machine. Later he'll shower (he loves showers), shave, comb his hair, and dress in his customary business suit — a standard grey, brown, or blue. The wide pinstripes of his early years have disappeared along with his Cuban cigars, a concession to the poor political image—that fatal, Bay Street, baronesque look—he felt his dress and smoking habits gave him; with Bill Davis, nothing is too trivial to be politicized. But for the moment his feet are bare, he is unshaven, his silver-grey hair is tussled, and his sturdy frame is wrapped in a ratty, old terrycloth robe that wouldn't look out of place at the Scott Mission for indigents.

He arrives on the fourth ring and plunks himself down in the wooden, green-upholstered chair behind his walnut desk, an elegant furnishing, more like a table than a desk, with brass trim and embossed leather on the top. The den is cluttered with me-

mentoes of his office: crossed swords, canes of various shapes, sizes, and inscriptions, and a collection of seven oil colors that Kathleen calls his father's "funny old paintings." They are encased in large, ornate, gilded frames and are mostly close-up portraits of leather-faced European men, nearly all either holding a pipe or smoking one. One features a man at a table, foot propped on a chair, a violin in one hand and a full beer mug in the other; another shows a sad-faced man with a French horn; a third a fishing boat with no people. All have about them a strangely haunting quality of doom.

Like the men in the paintings, Davis habitually smokes a pipe, and his Mac Baren "Symphony" tobacco sits on the desk in front of him. Bill Davis is a man who believes you can never be too careful, so he has three pipes in a wooden holder to his left and another two in an ashtray on the desk.

The den also sports three models of sailing ships, not surprising when boating (although he's a stink-potter, not a sailor) rates along with football and bridge as his main non-political pursuits.

His crowded bookshelves feature such works as *Kingston Before the War of 1812*, Diefenbaker's *One Canada*, *Who's Who in Football*, *Duplessis*, *The Town of York*, and *Muskoka-Haliburton 1615–1875*, reflecting his keen interest in history and sport. He actually loves reading spy thrillers most, but that collection is out of sight in the bedroom and elsewhere, not part of the official bookshelf collection.

It is the kind of den you'd expect Bill Davis to have: traditional, serviceable, solid. Brampton Gothic.

The only surprise is a small, black rubber spider hanging incongruously on a string from the ceiling in the corner above his desk, a "good luck charm" from the children many years ago, he explains, but perhaps a hint that somewhere beneath that studied blandness there lurks a touch of quixotry.

While he talks on the phone, or rather listens, in his peculiarly detached fashion, to the Palace Guard regulars who call with news of fresh disasters or triumphs, he watches the Broadcast News on cable television in the corner, looking as much for last night's sports scores as for news of great political events.

He has few odd habits, but one he does have is dropping ice cubes into his coffee. Not surprisingly, even a premier's coffee is cooled by this action, a scientific phenomenon that prompts him to slip down the hall to the kitchen, pop his coffee in the microwave, and repeat the process several times.

He is, after all, a cool guy, that Bill Davis. Ask anybody.

*   *   *

A few miles to the southwest, in deepest suburban Etobicoke, Edward Stewart, deputy minister in the Davis office and king of all Davis doesn't survey (and much of what he does), has been up for over an hour. He has made his call to Brampton, had breakfast, and, depending upon his mood and the weather, gone for a walk.

Stewart, the most powerful bureaucrat in Ontario, began ruling the premier's office and the senior civil service after Davis plucked him from the education ministry in 1974 to replace businessman-cum-bureaucrat Jim Fleck and his prickly aide, Malcolm Rowan — two men frequently blamed for building an impenetrable wall around Davis during the first four years of his reign.

Because it is Tuesday, Stewart has already reviewed his copy of the agenda, prepared late yesterday, for the regular Tuesday morning breakfast club. He speaks briefly with Davis about a couple of last-minute items, as is the custom, but Stewart is so in tune with Davis and so powerful in his own right that there's rarely a problem with anything he wants to put on the agenda.

When the breakfast routine first began upon Stewart's arrival in the premier's office, there were no cabinet ministers in the group, except for Davis. But then Toronto lawyer Eddie Goodman was recruited to run the inner circle just before the disastrous 1975 election (although he had certainly never been far away), and he insisted that cabinet ministers be included. But only the select few. Other ministers would be summoned only when an issue directly affected their ministry.

Goodman is, of course, a regular at the breakfast, along with long-time Davis confidant Hugh Macaulay, former Ontario Hydro chairman and currently boss of Canadian Tire Corporation.

In addition to Stewart and Davis's principal assistant, John Tory, the contingent from the premier's office includes Davis's resident whirling dervish, his veteran executive assistant, Clare Westcott, a one-eyed high school dropout whose value to the operation was always tragically underestimated and whose feelings about Davis can range, within minutes, from undying devotion to pathological outrage.

Party president David McFadden, who is not an exciting man, also attends, along with Bob Harris, the party's executive director, Brian Hamilton, caucus office director, and party fund-raiser Senator Bill Kelly. They are joined from the wonderful (and lucrative) world of partisan advertising by Norm Atkins and Hugh Segal of Camp Associates and Tom Scott and Rich Willis from Foster Advertising — two firms with noted Tory connections — along with financial analyst Tom Kierans and former deputy minister (and department store executive) Bob Butler.

Rounding out the starting squad are seven powerful cabinet ministers: Deputy Premier Bob Welch, also Minister Responsible for Women's Issues, Intergovernmental Affairs Minister Tom Wells, Treasurer Larry Grossman, Industry and Trade Minister Frank Miller, Agriculture Minister Dennis Timbrell, Attorney General Roy McMurtry, and Education Minister Bette Stephenson.

At one time Davis had a forty-member policy committee, but that became too unwieldy and was chopped in half to become the Tuesday morning group in Suite 1024–25 in Toronto's downtown Park Plaza Hotel.

Stewart is first to arrive for the event, with John Tory in tow. Somebody has to open the door, and it may as well be the guy with the key. Laird Saunderson, the premier's appointments coordinator, has ordered breakfast the day before, usually juice, coffee, scrambled eggs, tea, toast, and muffins.

For all the mystique surrounding the event, the suite itself is nothing extraordinary. Paid for by party funds on a year-round basis, although it's hardly ever used for anything else, it consists of three rooms plus a bathroom (yes, they are mortals, after all). A sitting room, with several chairs and couches, is straight ahead when you enter the suite, with a bedroom off to the right, used periodically by Davis for a brief pre-appearance snooze. The fabled meeting room itself is (naturally) off to the left.

A long, narrow table slashes the centre of the room, with bordello-red chairs on either side. The décor is beige wallpaper, plush, light brown carpet, and a beige couch. On an end wall someone has posted the message from Isaiah: "Come now, and let us reason together." On a side wall the inspiring message reads: "Say it simple — Say it often."

The players change periodically, but not often. Most of the regulars have been there for years. The inner sanctum, political primates love to boast, shows what a skilled leader Bill Davis is because he can have such a select group of insiders and not generate envy among those on the outside of the tent peeking in. John Tory, for example, has said the exercise doesn't upset those who aren't invited because "it's a brainstorming session that doesn't have any real power." Yet many of the outsiders dispute that boast, some privately and others openly, and complain that it reduces the role of most elected members to that of an automatic stamping machine.

Macaulay, one of the premier's oldest and most trusted personal friends, says the influence of the inner circle is highly exaggerated. "I can probably persuade him to have mashed potatoes instead of french fries for lunch, but I could never persuade him against his own mind or his own judgment, against something he proposed to do. Nor in my opinion could anyone else."

Hugh Segal acknowledges that some people in cabinet and caucus who don't get to share scrambled eggs with the premier "may be resentful . . . it's the nature of government." And Stewart says, "It's just human nature that some people are going to feel that they aren't involved extensively enough, and yet it would be next to impossible to consult everybody fully about everything." Besides, "Nothing is decided at these Tuesday morning meetings. It may come to a conclusion, but it's got to be tentative, subject to him [Davis] going to cabinet the next day or caucus the same day to see whether he can get the rest of them to accept that this is the way we're going to go."

Technically, who can argue? It's right there in any political science text you wish to name: Policy positions are advanced first in caucus, then in cabinet, but the decisions are made by the people's representatives in the legislature. In fact, however, most decisions, certainly all the major ones, are made either at the Tuesday morning breakfast club or within an even tighter conclave of Davis's Palace Guard, those eight super-elite troops who have ready access to him.

The decisions that count — such as rent controls, buying a piece of Suncor, the constitutional position, the revised Ontario Human

Rights Code, stopping the Spadina expressway — may be discussed to varying degrees in cabinet, and even less in caucus, but they are never put to the test. Indeed, in many cases caucus and cabinet ministers are as surprised as the opposition and the public at major initiatives.

In short, the Tuesday morning group is anything but a social club. It is where patronage is dispensed with a passion, where careers are advanced or stonewalled, where legislation is hashed out and new directions explored, where the latest laugh and the latest problems are freely exchanged in absolute confidence. All the while Davis, the benevolent patriarch, sucks his pipe quietly and oversees the debate. He says little but keeps the discussion in check by the power of his presence, periodically playing devil's advocate, his Cheshire cat smirk firmly intact, doing what he does best — listening and listening — and creeping interminably to what he does worst — making decisions.

Never mind the legislature, the cabinet, the caucus. The Tuesday morning breakfast club is the real government of Ontario.

PART ONE
THE MAN AND THE MACHINE

———————— ❦ ————————

Bill Davis was born to be a politician. As a young boy he spent countless hours listening to his father and local MP Gordon Graydon discuss the political issues of the day, and in school he would argue the merits of George Drew or John Bracken. At sixteen he became the youngest delegate ever to attend a national Tory convention. He knocked on doors for Graydon as well as for Tom Kennedy, a veteran Tory cabinet minister who became premier briefly between the departure of Drew for Ottawa and the arrival of Leslie Frost.

Part One is about that Bill Davis. About the strict Victorian upbringing that shaped a personality and a political style that turned him into the longest-serving Tory premier in Ontario's history, second overall only to Liberal Oliver Mowat. It is about Tory rule in Ontario and the electoral machine that Davis built to keep the Tory regime in power for a fifth decade.

It traces Davis from his comfortable beginnings in Brampton to the laying on of hands by Kennedy, his first election, his remarkable reforms of Ontario's educational system, his ascent to power, the early years of scandal and secrecy, his impressive comeback from minority government, and his decision to retire at the height of his popularity. It charts his course from a shy, chubby, uncertain young lawyer to pre-eminent position as everybody's favorite uncle.

In March, 1981, after six years of minority rule, Davis drove his famous Big Blue Machine one last time to a crushing seventy-seat shellacking of the Liberals and NDP. For a man who once replied to an opposition taunt about his blandness that "bland works," Bill Davis was walking, talking proof of his own belief.

Journalist Stanley Meisler of the *Los Angeles Times* summed up Davis after his 1981 comeback, writing: "Premier William G. Davis of Ontario, the province where more than one out of every three Canadians lives, has the image of a squarish, competent, avuncular, prudent, and pleasant leader who likes to extol the virtues of family morality and of the monarchy.

"In the view of those who follow politics closely here, the image does not hide anything. The silver-haired, carefully dressed, fifty-one-year-old premier is exactly what he seems, and what he seems is exactly what the voters of Ontario want."

Apparently so.

CHAPTER 1
BRAMPTON GOTHIC

———————— ᛪ ————————

During his first visit to Israel, going up the majestic Masada by cable car, Bill Davis peered out over the still-visible Roman encampments, looked at the rolling landscape, and said, "You know, it's nice. It reminds me of the Caledon Hills."

To Bill Davis the world is measured against Brampton. But *his* Brampton, not the sprawling bedroom community of 150,000 people twenty-five miles from downtown Toronto, with its huge developments in Bramalea and Heart Lake. His Brampton is the small town of his youth where, as he endlessly said in his campaign speeches, "we still have some farmers." His Brampton is the town of five thousand huddled within a few blocks of Queen and Main streets, a quiet, idyllic little place where everybody knows everybody else, especially their politics, and life just flows smoothly on.

It was into one of Brampton's leading families that he was born on July 30, 1929, at Toronto General Hospital, the son of Grenville and Vera Davis. His birth certificate actually shows July 29, but his mother always said that was a mistake. "I believe my mother. She should know better than the registrar — she was there."

For years he held a highly public job, yet he remained an intensely private man. Getting him even to admit he had a childhood was always a chore; thinking of himself running around in diapers and doing all the things normal children do seemed too much for him to contemplate. He always worked hard, with remarkable success, at keeping the two sides apart — premier is public, the person is private — almost as if he wanted Ontarians to think that there was no Bill Davis until he arrived on the provincial political scene in 1959.

But there was a Bill Davis before that, a little boy with two sisters — one older, one younger — who grew up under the Victorian influence of his grandparents and his parents, and who lives today in the home he and his father built over thirty years ago, just a few blocks from the home he was raised in and directly across the street from the home he and his first wife built in the 1950s.

There's a scene in the movie *Atlantic City* where Burt Lancaster walks along the boardwalk with a petty hustler who has never seen the ocean before. Lancaster, romanticizing about the good old days, says, "You should have seen it back then. It was really something."

That's what everybody says about The Castle, built a couple of blocks north of the town's main intersection over a century ago by Colonel George Wright, a local MP and entrepreneur, and bought by Davis's maternal grandfather in 1919. (The railway went right through the property, built there deliberately for Wright's convenience when he had to go off to Ottawa on business.) It is still impressive, a large, white house sitting on the top of a hill, overlooking the flats where young Bill and his chums played football every night. But that was before they covered the red brick with siding and tore down the turrets and the vines. In January, 1976, Davis officially opened the home as a residence for the mentally handicapped. "The banisters were great to slide down," he reminisced that day. "You just had to be careful at the bottom rung."

Indeed, they had to be exceptionally careful everywhere in the house, guarded as it was by the family matriarch, Davis's grandmother Eliza Hewitson.

Davis's older sister, Peggy Dale, says her maternal grandmother "was a very nice lady, but she was definitely Victorian. Children were supposed to be seen but not heard. I remember whenever we had company, if we weren't behaving my mother would look at us with her sharp eyes and let us know we were doing something we weren't supposed to be doing."

The Hewitson clan owned and operated Hewitson Shoes, one of Brampton's largest employers at the time, a red-brick factory just a block from The Castle and now owned by Sisman's, an Aurora-based safety shoe manufacturer.

In addition to their Brampton home, the Hewitsons had a family cottage on Townsend Island in Georgian Bay, about eight miles from Honey Harbour by water. Today that island and most of the other islands nearby all have cottages owned by an offspring of the four Hewitson daughters: Vera Davis, Winnifred Prouse, Edith Cooper, and Muriel Volkes.

Grenville Davis, a local lacrosse star who eventually was inducted into the Canadian Lacrosse Hall of Fame, was a soft-spoken, tuberculosis-ridden young lawyer when he met and fell in love with Vera Hewitson. Grenville was so weak with TB when he and Vera married that they moved into The Castle with her parents. When Bill was born, they actually wanted to call him Grenville, but his maternal grandfather started calling him Bill (after himself), and when he died a couple of years later, the name stuck.

Grenville and Vera were house-hunting and on the verge of moving out when Bill Hewitson died, so they stayed there with Grandmother Hewitson, eventually buying the house from her. Bill lived in that house until he was twenty-two.

Nicknamed "Dutch" because he stuttered when he was young—making him sound like the people in a nearby Dutch settlement — Grenville Davis, who would spend thirty years as Peel Crown attorney, was a strict Presbyterian. Vera, on the other hand, was Methodist, a strong temperance advocate who later joined the United Church. Eventually Grenville also joined; he was upset the Presbyterian minister didn't visit him during his long bout with tuberculosis, while the United Church minister did.

Church remained the centre of their lives, both theologically and socially, and church values and traditions were passed on to the three Davis children, profoundly influencing Bill Davis's approach to political issues. Every Sunday the family went to Grace United Church, then returned home for their main Sunday meal at noon. The whole family would be there for dinner — not just the Davis group but also aunts, uncles, and cousins. The kids went back to Sunday school, and the family sometimes went for a drive in the country before going back to church at night.

Davis says his upbringing was "very strict in some respects but flexible in others. There was no alcohol in the house [he was twenty-seven before he took his first drink and rarely drinks now], and Mother and Father didn't serve it for guests, either. We went through a period when playing cards on Sunday was discouraged, but one of the toughest decision periods was on Sunday sports [in the early 1950s]. I can recall Grandmother had some strong views on that, and Father used to do some legal work for the Lord's Day Alliance, but he was eventually able to rationalize, with my help, that if you went to church Sunday morning, it wasn't bad to see the Argos Sunday afternoon.

"It wasn't so much they were strict—there's an inference there that has the opposite effect of what you mean. They had certain values and lived by them. I never heard my father swear, for example. It wasn't so much they laid down rules as they lived by their own value code or moral code, and they expected us to follow suit."

Even now a glow comes over Davis's face when he speaks of his father. Grenville died in February, 1973, at age eighty. Vera, known as "Gramsy," died in June, 1981, at age eighty-eight; she suffered a stroke just one month after her son regained his majority in the March, 1981, election sweep.

"My father was one of the most highly respected members of the bar; he was one of the fairest Crowns anywhere. He rescued many people from the inadequacies of defence counsel. He was not a person out to convict for the sake of getting a conviction."

There's a trace of bitterness in his voice when he talks of his father's unfulfilled dream of being a judge. "He wanted to go to the county court bench. That's a federal appointment, and there weren't many openings. He'd been offered one in some distant geographic area, but he was pretty well set in Brampton. There was an opening once in a neighboring county, though, when Diefenbaker was in. I would have been a member by then, and there was a feeling because of that it wouldn't be appropriate to appoint him. He was disappointed, and I always felt badly for him. There was always a little sadness with him about that."

Sally Barnes, who went to work for Davis for a year and stayed seven, says the most poignant family scene she ever witnessed was the 1971 election night, when she was a *Toronto Star* reporter covering the Tory victory party at Brampton's 4-H Club hall. "There was pandemonium. Everybody was hugging and kissing, and Davis looked embarrassed by that. But standing by the door was a very tall, extremely handsome man of about seventy. I couldn't help noticing him, but I didn't know who he was. On the way to the press conference Davis stopped and said, 'Hello, Father,' and this gentleman said, 'Hello, Bill.' I think they shook hands, at which point Davis introduced me to his father. There was an embarrassing silence. Other men would have hugged each other in that situation, but here we were, the proudest moment of Grenville Davis's life, and they were just unable to show it. They have as much love and affection as anyone else, but it's all very restrained and proper."

Nick Lorito, Davis's long-time driver, says Davis was "very close to his father. He had a lot of admiration for him but could never show emotion towards him. I never saw him put his arm around him." Near the end of Grenville's life, Lorito was the only person who could get him to go to the cottage. "He became very fragile, and he'd refuse to get into the car. Davis just used to look at me and say, 'Nicholas, what are you doing this weekend? We are having some difficulty.' You'd think, being father and son, he'd do it, but no, I'd put him in the car and hear the same story fifty times. I had to promise to put him in the boat and go with him, and we'd sit there and play cribbage. He'd retire early, but it was quite sad, really. He used to say, 'Why should I go up there? Nobody bothers with me, anyway.' As a family they wanted him there, but they didn't know how to deal with it."

As for Davis's mother, Ron Webb, next-door neighbor, friend, and partner in the law firm of Davis, Webb, says, "She got mixed reviews. I thought she was great, but she was outspoken. She had strong opinions and expressed them. She also lived by them."

Sally Barnes could "never get a handle" on Davis's relationship with Gramsy. "Sometimes I thought there was downright animosity there, because I think she really put him through hell, I really do. At the same time I think he had a great love and affection for her. But again, it would never show in a physical sense." Davis would rarely call her "Mother." It was always either "Vera" or "Gramsy."

"Mother was the disciplinarian in the family," says Peggy. "She did most of the spanking. She broke a brush over my behind one day. My father wasn't well for many years, so she did it. Bill got his share, too. We had this little room where we kept the coats, and when we were acting up at dinner — dinnertime was quite formal — we'd have to go and stand in there and say we're sorry before we were allowed back. I was never really sorry. I always thought that was hypocritical."

Davis agrees that "Mother was the disciplinarian. That's correct. Apart from those traditional forms of punishment, such as being sent to my room and standing in the clothes closet during dinner, I did receive from time to time a modest degree of corporal punishment," he says in his classic circumlocutious style. "One of Mother's great lines was, 'This is going to hurt me more than it hurts you.' I never challenged that, but I always wondered about it."

Peggy describes her younger brother as "a naughty little boy. He was a pest like all young brothers. He'd flick us with tea towels or, if he didn't win a game, turn over the Rummoli board, stuff like that. But I liked him." One summer at the family cottage, when Bill was ten or eleven, Peggy had a group of her teenage girlfriends up. "We were having a pyjama party in the sunroom, and the door was locked. He started pounding on the glass door, and his hand went right through it. He cut his hand, and there was so much blood I thought he was going to bleed to death and it would be all my fault for locking him out. He just didn't want to be left out of anything."

Molly, four years younger than Bill, remembers him as her "protective big brother, although he was a terrible tease. He had a bit of a temper when he was young, especially when he played football, but I never saw him get nasty with anyone."

Davis is not a spontaneous person. Never was. When he was five he once spent several hours sitting on his tricycle trying to figure out how to ride out to a particular rock by the lake. By going around certain trees and over certain ledges, he was able to do it, but, foreshadowing his political style, he charted his course carefully before setting out.

Until the war the family had a live-in maid, and during the war they took in a guest, Russell Crompton, a distant cousin from England who is now an executive with the *Manchester Guardian*. "He was Bill's age," says Molly. "They were very close, like brothers, really. Of course, they argued and fought over things, but he was a member of our family. When the war was over and it was safe to go back home, he didn't want to."

The two daughters eventually went to boarding school — Peggy to Bishop Strachan for two years, Molly to Havergal for three. "They wanted Bill to go to boarding school, but he preferred to stay home," says Peggy. "Brampton was a very small town, and I think they thought it would round him out a bit more. I didn't really want to leave, either, but I'd read boarding school stories at the time, and I thought it would be exciting. It wasn't."

In a 1971 interview Harold Loughlin, a retired school principal who taught Davis in Grade 8 at Central Public School in 1942, said, "He was an honor pupil, better than average, and he always had the ability to cruise along without seeming to work too hard. The one thing I remember very clearly about Bill was that he was never discourteous, and he had a high regard for fairness. He had the ability to get along with people, and this has certainly carried over to his political career.*

Davis was a member of the Trail Blazers, a United Church equivalent of the Boy Scouts, and taught Sunday school for seven years. He used to bribe the kids by promising to take them to the Junior A hockey doubleheaders at Maple Leaf Gardens if they showed up for class.

In high school he played piano in a three-piece band, performing at school dances and church socials, playing the music of the mid-1940s, particularly Glenn Miller, still one of his favorite artists. When he became fairly accomplished on the piano, the local minister let him practise on the church organ. Once, thinking the church was empty, Davis put away the hymn book and switched to "In the Mood," only to discover to his horror that a grumpy church elder was there. He told Davis to stop and reported him to the minister, who in turn told Vera, ending Davis's short career as a church organist.

At Brampton High School Davis was a B student and extremely active in sports — basketball and football in particular. He says there wasn't a sport he didn't try, including hockey, "But I wasn't very good at it. I played for Central school and for west ward in Brampton. I played right defence." He also sang in the high school

---

*Loughlin, incidentally, later shifted to Gordon Graydon school as principal where he taught four of the Davis children — Neil, Cathy, Nancy, and Ian — missing only the youngest, Meg.

glee club, describing his voice as "lousy," and won a high school public speaking contest. "I was always suspect about that, however. It was my third or fourth try, and my father was the one who had donated the medal for the contest."

He also performed in several Sunday school Christmas pageants, usually as a wise man, he says, "And I actually performed a significant role in a drama on drama night in high school, although I can't remember the play." (It was *Nellie McNabb*, and Davis played Rolly Martin.) The same night, December 5, 1947, he received the Brydon Memorial Trophy for best all-round student at Brampton High. Grenville Davis was school board chairman at the time.

Davis says of his academic career, "I got mixed results. If I was interested in the subject I did fairly well. I used to get good marks in history, but I was not good at languages, although I did well in Latin. I was not a great Math scholar in Grade Thirteen, but at university I got in the nineties a couple of times."

Davis enjoyed playing basketball with his church team at the Brampton Training School. "Of course, they were young offenders, but the odd one would have been put there by my father, as Crown attorney. They always confused the term with the American term [District Attorney], and whenever we played they'd heckle, usually in good fun, 'There goes the D.A.'s son. Let's get him.'"

But above all Bill Davis loved to play football. His intense competitiveness, which isn't obvious behind that bland exterior, certainly showed itself on the gridiron. The late Fred Scambatti, for years a well-known sportscaster and referee, twice threw the young high school quarterback out of a game for disputing a call. "I was never a natural athlete," says Davis. "I had to work at whatever I did. I made up for my lack of natural talent with enthusiasm."

He was eight when his father took him to his first Argo game, and it was love at first sight. Night after night, eight or ten of the neighborhood kids would play pick-up football on the lawn of the Davis house. He describes it as "one of the biggest days of my life" when, as a Grade 9 student, with just three games left in the high school schedule, the coach came to his classroom, spoke to the teacher, then beckoned to Bill. "I played my first game, in Mimico. I was one hundred thirty pounds and played end. We lost, but I didn't make too many mistakes. It was quite a thrill."

From the third form (Grade 11) on, Davis was the team quarterback. In those days the quarterback also played defence. The defensive alignment was 6–3–2–1, and Davis, a fast runner, was in the "2" position in the defensive backfield. His speed also won him several races at Brampton High in the 220- and 100-yard dashes, and he was swift enough to compete with some success in the 220 at the Toronto and District Athletic Association meets.

The high school football game he remembers most was when he was in Grade 12 playing a powerhouse Port Credit team that had not only won every game but had also not been scored upon all year. Davis, who was also kicker for Brampton, says they were losing 57–0 with just a few minutes left to play when "we recovered the ball on their thirty-yard line. I just said to myself, 'I refuse to be part of Port Credit's scoreless record,' so I fooled them and kicked a single point on first down. We lost 57–1, but we took great delight out of that small, symbolic victory."

One game he doesn't like to remember is an intermediate lacrosse match against Fergus, where "it got a little rough," and he ended up with eight stitches across his forehead, "the day I was leaving with the family to go to the bar convention in Banff. I decided that was enough lacrosse until I got to U of T." Davis went to the University of Toronto in 1947, earning his BA in 1951. He graduated from Osgoode Hall with his bachelor of laws degree in 1954, was called to the bar a year later, and began practising law in his father's Brampton firm, acting as assistant Crown attorney on occasion.

At university Davis played halfback on the intermediate intercollegiate team. He also hurt his back, an injury that haunts him still. And it was there that he met two people who became senior ministers in his cabinet — Roy McMurtry and Tom Wells — McMurtry on the football field and Wells in the P.C. club.

"We weren't good friends or anything like that," says Wells, "but we used to see each other at the club. Actually, the first time I met him I had gone with a friend to London for the Varsity-Western game. We were hitchhiking back, and this fellow came along in a big Chrysler, which was obviously his father's, and picked us up. It was Bill Davis."

McMurtry met him in the fall of 1950. "I was eighteen at the time, had just started university, and was fresh out of boarding school. He was in his final year, but we had both gone out for the intermediate team. [McMurtry became a star Varsity player.] He was clearly an intensive, highly competitive guy. He wasn't a big guy, yet he was a very determined football player. If there's anything relevant between those days and his leadership, it's that underneath that benign, placid exterior is a guy who is extremely competitive. It's something I don't say he deliberately hides, but he doesn't wear it on his sleeve, and I think that explains a lot of his successes. I don't think you could survive as long as he has if you were just a nice, easygoing, intelligent, decent guy. You've got to have competitive fibre, which I noticed playing football that he had."

Bill Davis didn't spend all his time at university playing football, going to the Conservative club, or studying. It was there that he met Helen McPhee, a beautiful, athletic girl from Windsor. The romance led to the altar in 1955, the same year he started work in his father's law firm. When they started seeing each other, Helen had also been dating a London student, John White, who later became treasurer in a Davis cabinet.

After their wedding in Windsor, the couple moved back to Brampton. By this time Grenville Davis, with some planning assistance from his son, had built the large, yellow-brick home with its massive picture windows overlooking the lawn that leads down to Main Street and its S-shaped driveway that glides up a gentle, tree-lined slope to the side of the house. Bill and Helen turned the basement family room into an apartment and lived there while they had a house built on a short, dead-end street directly across from the Davis home.

Ralph and Eva Manley, who operate a successful pick-your-own strawberry farm just outside Brampton, met Helen and Bill at Grace United Church in 1956 and immediately became fast friends. "Helen got us to join the couples club, and our kids and their kids started chumming around together," says Ralph. Along with Joe and Joan Dobbs, the Manleys are Davis's closest personal friends in Brampton, but it's a measure of his ability to separate his political and private personas that when the author mentioned the Manleys to such senior political advisers as Goodman, Segal, Atkins, and Macaulay, the name didn't ring a bell. It only became familiar when "the strawberry farmer" was mentioned.

Davis soon got on the local school and hospital boards and became active in the Kinsmen Club and in local Conservative circles. And Helen was the perfect political wife for the times — beautiful, outgoing, and anxious to go to all the teas.

While making political speeches is second nature to Davis now, it wasn't at the time. David Haskell, then a reporter-photographer with the *Brampton Conservator*, tells the story of being sent to cover the dedication of a Kinsmen Club wading pool in Gage Park, immediately next to the house where Davis now lives. "I'd never seen this guy Davis before," says Haskell. "He was fresh out of law school, and he showed up wearing a shirt and tie, black shoes, and [with] some papers under his arm. . . . There was nobody else there. Usually these things had the mayor and some other bigwigs, but there was just him and me. So I stood there; he pulled out these notes and started to orate — a formal dedication. Naturally, I'm not taking down every deathless quote, so he stops and says, 'What do we do now?' I had my trusty Crown Graphic, so I said, 'Let's get a picture.' He stood upright by the pool, but I told him I'd need a helicopter to get him and the pool in. I suggested he take off his shoes and socks, roll up his pant legs, and stand in the pool. He didn't want to, but after a lot of hesitation he did. He was so embarrassed he started to shuffle his feet. I suspect he's learned a bit since then."

Bill and Helen had their first child, Neil, in 1956. Nancy was born a year later, then Cathy in 1959, and Ian in 1961.

For a guy with (eventually) five children, Davis is incredibly shy about sex. He turns beet red at the thought, particularly if there are women around. In 1961 he and Helen were with a group of people in New York on political business while Helen was visibly pregnant with Ian. Some of the others noticed that when they walked down the street, Davis would walk well ahead of his wife. "It soon became obvious why," says one witness. "He was embarrassed. If people saw them together they might get the impression that the two of them did it."

Nick Lorito agrees that Davis is uncomfortable about sex and has trouble relating to babies. "That may go back to Gramsy, I suppose. From all I've seen and heard, she was Queen Victoria's right-hand lady. Babies just sort of happened. All of a sudden, look here, there was a baby. . . . With his own wife, you get the impression people aren't supposed to know they sleep together.

It's taboo. In all our conversations it was never mentioned. Mrs. D would talk about things, but not him. This guy doesn't want to hear how *dogs* have babies."

Clare Westcott recalls the 1961 leadership campaign, when Davis was campaign manager for Bob Macaulay, then Westcott's boss. "I got the call that Ian was born, and I knew Davis and Macaulay were going to be in Kingston that night. So I hopped in the car, headed down the 401 to Kingston, and parked my car at the side of the road. When Davis and Macaulay came driving by, I flagged them down to tell Davis he was a father. He said, 'That's good,' and off they went to another meeting."

It was when Ian was born that doctors discovered that Helen had cancer. She was flown for an operation to a small private hospital in New York, where a doctor had had some success with colitis. At the time Peggy and her husband, Bill, lived in New York, so one of the Davis children stayed with them. "It was nice because at least Helen had somebody to talk to every day. She was there about a month. It was a rough time. The doctor said that he got everything, which he obviously hadn't."

In March, 1962, Davis took Helen to Florida with Joe and Joan Dobbs. "It was so sad," says Dobbs. "Such a beautiful girl. And four little kids." Two weeks later Helen died.

On the night of her death, it happened that Bob Macaulay's estimates were being debated in the legislature. At 10 p.m., when the house was adjourning for the night, Macaulay rose and made a two-sentence announcement, adding that the funeral would take place in three days. Normally a death in the immediate family of an MPP prompts expressions of sympathy from all three parties, but not this time. Even the next day nothing was said. But it was not a thoughtless oversight by the politicians — quite the opposite. Davis asked them not to make an issue of it. "I think they knew that I probably wouldn't want very much said," Davis explains, abruptly changing the topic even more than twenty years later. It was his private grief, and he didn't want it shared.

His sister Peggy says, "I think he feels he has to have a guard up. I haven't been around for every crisis, but I was at the hospital when Helen died, and he wasn't so good at hiding his feelings then. Underneath everything he's a compassionate person, a generous person. But he is not someone who shows his feelings. But you see, our whole family didn't show our feelings very much.

We had them, of course, but we were not demonstrative. You just didn't hug and kiss very much at all."

A small group of family and friends took Davis up to the cottage the weekend after Helen died, just to help him get away from it all. "He was right out of it," his brother-in-law Bill Endress recalls. "It was freezing up there, really cold. He wasn't shaven, he wasn't dressed warmly. He wore a suit and ordinary street shoes, and I remember he was walking out on the ice, just wandering around in a fog. But we played cards and we talked, and I think it helped pull him through. But boy, he sure was shaken up."

CHAPTER 2
FAMILY TIMES

———— ❦ ————

"Billy is not direct, it's true," says Peggy. "He's a bit inscrutable, except when he's up at the cottage."

A sprawling structure set on a fist of rock amid a southern cluster of Georgian Bay's Thirty Thousand Islands, the cottage is Davis's best refuge, now and always. His grandfather found the place and built the original shelter on the island nearly sixty years ago. When Bill was growing up, he worked a couple of summers — one at the Brampton Dairy and one at a camp in Haliburton — but most of his school holidays were spent with the family on Townsend Island. It is still the one place where everyone who knows him well says he comes closest to being relaxed.

And it was at the cottage that he first met Kathleen Mackay. She was from Hinsdale, a Chicago suburb, but had been spending her summers right next to the Davis compound in Georgian Bay since she was thirteen. She and Molly Davis, being the same age, got to be good friends. She had seen Bill often enough and admits she "had an eye for him." But while he was always friendly, "He never looked at me in that way at all."

In 1971 she said, "I remember him as being tall and good-looking with a good shock of hair, crashing around with other boys, as boys do. He was a mischief-maker. Once a bunch of us put an old portable pump organ in a boat at night and went out into the lake and tied up at channel-marker. Somebody pounded the organ, and we all sang hymns at the top of our lungs — a marvellous sing-song."

It was a circuitous route that pulled Kathy to Georgian Bay in the first place. Her grandfather was a hellfire-and-brimstone Baptist preacher from Macon, Georgia, who was asked to take the place of a friend at Toronto's Bond Street Congregational Church for the summer of 1921; he stayed five years. He had a beautiful singing voice and was well known as "The Singing Minister."

Kathy's father, Roland, had just finished undergraduate studies in Atlanta, and he enrolled in medical school at U of T. During the years in Toronto, he went to Georgian Bay on weekend trips, and in those days if someone found an island and built a shelter on it, the island was theirs. Actually, the Mackays built cottages on two islands; Kathy's mother still uses one of them.

Roland eventually went to Johns Hopkins, then won a special fellowship to the Mayo Clinic, where he met his wife, Margaret, a nurse. When he left the clinic to go into private practice, they moved to Chicago, where Kathleen was born in 1933.

"Every summer, except during the war, we went up to the cottage," she recalls. "We'd load up the car and toodle on up the highway to Georgian Bay. So I knew Molly well and knew that incredible network of cousins they have up there. Our cottage was about half a mile away, within easy striking distance with a little wooden boat and a five-horsepower engine. I got to know the whole family, which, as circumstances unfolded, was a blessing for me. To go into that family cold and not know those people with all the other complications would have been very difficult."

When Helen died Kathy was in California, but she got letters from both Molly and Gramsy telling her about it. "Things happened the way those things always happen. We went through a garden-variety courtship that summer when I was at the cottage. I went back out West to think things over. He came out to see me a couple of times. I just didn't hold out very long."

In the interim the children had been split up: Ian was in Windsor with the McPhees, and Davis had hired an English nanny to help Gramsy watch the others.

Bill and Kathy were married in Hinsdale in 1962, and Kathleen, whose world as a working woman had already been turned upside down by joining the family of a politician with four young children, was soon pregnant with Meg. "It was very quick. It was legal and all that, but I wasn't very experienced. I always felt it was my doctor in San Francisco who didn't believe in the Pill. I've often thought I should write him a note and say, 'You really have a godchild up here in Canada.' When I found out I was pregnant, oh boy. The nanny wanted to go back home to England, and I didn't even know there was an election campaign coming up in the fall. I just thought, 'I can't do it,' so I went down to Chicago, as young girls are wont to do, and went home to my mother. I was in search of solace and comfort, but she said, 'Now just a minute. You've made this commitment — you can't change your mind now.' She also pointed out that Meg would be sort of the same age difference as the others and would fit in like an old shoe. [Neil, the oldest, was not quite seven then; Nancy was five, Cathy three, and Ian about a year.] That's exactly what's happened. It all worked out so well, but the first few years were really tough."

Part of the problem was Gramsy. She wasn't crazy about Kathleen's child-rearing methods, and being a domineering person, Helen had been more to her liking. After all, Kathleen drank alcohol, wasn't that interested in church, and had been living in a ghetto. "I think Gramsy was delighted when we married. . . . But in the beginning she used to run over and thought she should accompany me when I took Ian out in the buggy. She didn't know whether I knew anything or not."

"Kathleen sure came around at the right time," says Peggy. "At the time, I must admit, I thought it was a bit rushy, but she's made a marvellous mother for those kids. She tried to run a tight ship, which she had to with all those kids, but to begin with Mother and I thought — well, she had taught school, and we kind of thought she was treating the children more like schoolchildren. But I think Mother would have admitted by the end that Kathy had done a good job."

"Mother was a very strong lady, and Kathy is a very strong lady," says Molly, "and of course that takes some adjusting. I think Kathy is just now beginning to realize a sense of freedom."

Eva Manley says Gramsy and Kathleen "had great difficulties adjusting. She had high principles and expected everybody to live up to them, but Kathy in her own quiet way got the confidence of the children, their love and respect, and I think, too, the confidence of Gramsy."

Life in the Davis household was chaotic for Kathleen. Davis had just been named minister of education, the 1963 election campaign came along, and after that he was off almost every day opening a school.

Over the years his efforts to return home to Brampton at night became legendary, but Kathleen was still stuck with all the kids during the day and evening. Daddy was there just for breakfast. "That was our family time," recalls Neil. "Mom would come down and drag us out of bed at seven-fifteen. Our breakfasts were very important to him and Mom because he was hardly home any other time. We'd argue about everything. I think he was somewhat less reserved than he is outside the home. He never raised his voice or yelled, but he'd get more involved in the debate."

Neil, who seems a sure bet to follow his dad into politics some day, says growing up with a famous father had its problems, but they were lucky to be so well established in Brampton. "I was seven when Dad became education minister. When you're in school, of course, people know, especially about the minister of education. But kids at that age don't care. Their dad is just as important to them as mine was to me. I think I grew up with the friendships everybody else had. If we were put in a new place suddenly, you'd probably find two reactions: one from people who thought it was really neat to hang around the family for a while and others who were resentful. But that stuff only occurs with people who don't know you. I don't think Dad's position made any impression on our close friends."

But the impression Davis himself makes on others has always been an overriding concern, to the point where he remains relatively formal even around his house. "When he goes for a walk," says Sally Barnes, "he thinks he can't go in his jeans and sneakers because he's Bill Davis and people will see him. It's his whole life."

Davis always seemed impervious to media stories that attacked either his style or his programs but became terribly upset, so much as anyone could tell by looking at him, about stories he considered personal. "I remember one written about Cathy," says Neil, "when she was going to Indec [an alternative school in

Mississauga]. It gave the impression she was getting special treatment or having great problems, when in fact it's a school for bright kids who just aren't thriving in normal school. It hurt Dad terribly that somebody [the *Globe*] would think about writing about the family that way."

A more innocuous sort of comment that could tick Davis off was something written after an interview at a swanky resort in Maui at the end of an arduous trade mission to the Far East in 1983. The column mentioned that Davis was wearing his "tennis whites" at the time, a reference that really upset him. "I think that's part of the old Protestant work ethic," says Ron Webb. "Most politicians would dismiss such references as inconsequential, but he had that ethic drilled into him by his parents — you know, that it's almost sinful to have fun. Part of it also may be he feels a lot of people out there think the same way, so he's worried about the appearance. But he feels it himself. He really does."

However much he may feel exhuberance to be sinful, his pleasures are indeed the simple ones of a man who is moderate, careful, precise, traditional, gentle, or, in a word, bland.

His eating habits are what you'd expect: He is basically a meat-and-potatoes man who loves beef and lamb, can't abide seafood, and absolutely adores strawberries, particularly strawberry pie. He is more careful now with his diet, for weight and other reasons. "He was at so many functions where the food was awful," says Nick Lorito, "that he developed this amazing technique of appearing to be eating. But if you check his plate closely, he isn't."

He rarely takes a drink. The odd time he'll try white wine with a meal, a Bloody Mary, or maybe a rum and orange juice. When Gramsy was alive he rarely drank in her presence, and when he did he was obviously embarrassed about it. Indeed, her temperance views were not an insignificant factor in Davis's four-year delay in allowing the sale of beer at professional baseball and football games in Ontario.

For all that propriety, he loves to bet on football and baseball games as well as at cards, usually with a $2 limit. When he has to pay up, though, he has to tap whichever friend or aide is closest because neither he nor Kathleen carry much money with them. His Queen's Park secretary, Helen Anderson (Miss A), handled most of their personal bills, which led to an amusing incident a few years back when she began to notice a regular payment of

$200 for corn flakes. "I couldn't figure it out," she says. "But we kept getting this bill, so finally I asked how they could possibly eat so much corn flakes. It turned out that was the name of Nancy's horse, and they were paying the boarding fee."

As for constantly borrowing small sums of money, Joe Dobbs says, "I think that's why some people think he's tight when they see that, but he isn't. He's too generous sometimes." Most of his friends have the odd painting lent to them by Davis from his collection. (His personal taste runs to paintings with sports themes, but the house is filled with oils of every description.) Davis helped his driver, Nick Lorito, buy his Georgetown home in 1967. Lorito had $10,000 to put down on his $26,000 house but was making $5,200 a year and couldn't get a mortgage. He mentioned it once to Davis, and a few days later Davis turned to him in the car and told him to buy the house; he'd speak to somebody who could get him a mortgage, and "If we can't, I'll get you the money." Within weeks Davis sent Lorito to see a man. The meeting lasted three minutes, Lorito got his mortgage, never missed a payment, and has never seen the man since. "You don't forget things like that."

Davis also loves movies, particularly spy thrillers, and books of the same genre. When they were first married, Bill and Kathleen went to the movies regularly, but it became difficult to do that after he became so recognizable. The family got around that problem by borrowing movies from the censor board, then inviting the kids, the Dobbses, and the Manleys into the family room for their own "Saturday Night at the Movies," complete with fresh popcorn. He also attends the opera and ballet at times, but that's mainly for Kathleen's benefit. "Perhaps through exposure he might get to like it," says Eva Manley. "But yes, Kathleen loves it."

Next-door neighbor and close friend Ron Webb says one thing Davis enjoys doing for relaxation is mowing the lawn. "You'll sometimes see him late at night, dressed in an old pair of coveralls, riding around on their little motorized mower by himself. He'll often cut mine while he's at it. [They have about an acre each.] He'll be there alone, smoking his pipe. I think that's one of the few chances he really ever gets to be alone. You can't very well talk to the guy running after the tractor and yelling over the sound of the motor."

Joe Dobbs says one of Davis's greatest pleasures is helping people decorate or redecorate their homes. "He carries a little steel rule around with him, and if one picture is two inches from the wall, the other has to be exactly two inches. He's very fussy about the placement of furniture and pictures and doesn't hestitate to get involved. He's incredibly observant, too. If you move anything, he'll notice it and give you his opinion."

Neil says his father is "famous for his lists. When we lived at home, he used to prepare long lists for all of us with our chores on them. He'd give us all one every weekend for the cottage. He still does his lists, but now we aren't home, so he can't exercise the same control over us. But it's true — he's a great supervisor."

One habit Davis had that Kathy soon stopped was lining all the kids up in a row at the cottage, putting a John Philip Sousa march on the record player, and literally marching them around the room while he led the way. "I guess it beckoned back to his football days or something, but he was the conductor, and he'd be waving a stick or something and we'd all follow along."

The family still lines up in a row, youngest to oldest, for Christmas, however, and sings "Jingle Bells" while marching into the living room. "It sounds a little corny, but it's fun," says Neil. "When we were kids, we'd all have to line up for our stockings, then we'd have breakfast, and then we'd open the presents. My friends would call to see what I got, and we hadn't even started yet. Dad would hand out the presents. You had to open them one at a time. Everybody had to see what everybody else was getting. It took two hours to do it all. It may be formal, but it was a lot of fun. It was tough waiting, but I think we probably enjoyed it more. The expectations were incredible."

The other family tradition is the Christmas carol sing-song every Christmas eve. "My grandmother wanted to carry on the tradition," says Neil. "It's more difficult now, but it's been so important to them for so long, we're going to keep coming as long as they'll have us."

Three of the Davis kids — Neil, Nancy, and Cathy — were married during the hectic summer of 1981: Cathy in May, Neil in June, and Nancy in September. When Davis retired in early 1985 Meg, the youngest, was studying urban geography at Western, Ian was working in the downtown federal P. C. headquarters, Cathy and her cousin Sally Endress were operating an aerobic exercise studio in Aurora called "Stretches," Nancy worked for the provincial corrections ministry, and Neil was with the law firm of Davis, Webb in downtown Brampton.

There's clearly a romantic side to Davis that sneaks through in his genuine love for Brampton, for his condominium in Florida, and most of all for his rock in Georgian Bay. But Brampton is no longer the way he remembers it, and in Florida more and more people stop him, as Bill Kelly says, just "to touch the hem." Only at the cottage is there neither uncontrolled change nor the bother of recognition.

Early in 1984 somebody stole a gas barbecue from Joe Dobbs's house across the street from Davis. "It was chained, and they cut the chain," says Dobbs. "A couple of days later he [Davis] walked over to our place and didn't even lock his door. He just doesn't think things like that could happen in Brampton." But things like that *do* happen. One night a youth even broke into the Davis house. Davis awoke to see him standing in the doorway of the bedroom. "Billy got up and chased him, but the chap ran away, so he called the police. As it turned out, they caught him. He was a young man who lived nearby and had been in the house with the kids at one time."

Shortly after becoming premier in 1971, Davis bought the condominium in a sixteen-storey building in Fort Lauderdale where he regularly escapes for a winter break. He spends most of his time there strolling through shops, particularly Harold's, a huge department store for boats and boating equipment. "He'll browse there for hours," says Kelly, who has his own condo nearby and plays tennis with Davis in Florida. "He loves boats and knows a lot about them. I'm in the business, and he knows more than I do. He devours every boating magazine."

It is a long-standing affection. His cousin Russell Cooper remembers him "as a little tyke, playing with wooden boats in front of the cottage. He always loved boats. Still does."

"I grew up with them," says Davis. "Of course, you need a boat to get to the cottage. I drove a little 3.5 horsepower when I was four and five years old; it was legal then."

There are six boats now on Townsend Island: a sixteen-foot, fifty-horsepower Boston Whaler outboard, strictly for Kathleen; a fifteen-foot aluminum Starcraft; a Laser sailboat; a canoe; a twelve-foot Starcraft; and the flagship, Davis's own boat — a twenty-six-foot, inboard-outboard, fibreglass Wellcraft Nova day cruiser with twin 260s—called "Old Dutch" after his dad. And while the cottage walls are smothered with ribbons won by the kids in local regattas, Davis takes great pride in his own ability to navigate the treacherous, rock-strewn waters of the bay, day or night.

In the early 1960s, when Ron Webb had a cottage on Clear Lake near the Kawarthas, he bet Davis a sports jacket he couldn't get there from Honey Harbour in a day and a half by boat. "He's so competitive he did it, but I've always suspected he made a deal with the lock-keepers along the Trent Canal so he wouldn't have to slow down." Ralph Manley says, "We didn't cheat, but I've never worked so hard in my life. He was captain; Kathleen, Eva, and I were the crew. We drank Jello powders and lemonade all the way down. We left at seven a.m., stayed overnight at a hotel in Roseneath, but I'll tell you, it was all business. He'd hardly give the girls time to go to the john before we'd get back out into the boat and get away."

The cottage is not a place where Davis's political advisers are welcome, although sometimes they go there on urgent business. For the most part it's strictly family, plus the Dobbses and the Manleys. Actually, Dobbs had no intention of ever getting a cottage there. "We had a little cottage, but it wasn't too near his, so he decided we should be on the island with him. I told him I didn't want to live on an island, but he said, 'Too late — I've already made arrangements.' That was twenty-five years ago. He did the same thing with our house on Woodbrook [the one Bill and Helen had built in the 1950s], across the road from him."

Most evenings there are spent playing cards—bridge, cribbage, loo — or singing with family and friends gathered around the piano at Molly's cottage. "He plays all the old standards," says Dobbs. "But our favorite is 'I Don't Know Why.' Anytime he doesn't know what to play next he'll say, 'I haven't played this one before,' and he'll play that."

Giant's Tomb, an eleven-hundred-acre island a few miles from the cottage, is a favorite site for picnics. The island has a beautiful sand beach where family and friends play some pretty rough touch football. "Some people do some fishing," says Dobbs, "others lie in the sun or just explore the island . . . and in the evenings we light a fire and have a shore dinner, usually hot dogs or something. It's very pleasant."

Oddly, while he loves boats and being around water, Davis never actually goes into the water, although he says he can swim. He often goes out fishing with Dobbs, but he rarely throws a line in, preferring just to sit in the boat. He especially loves listening to a baseball or football game while he's out there.

When the ice breaks in the spring, Davis and Dobbs head out in the middle of the night to go smelt fishing in a treacherous channel about six miles from the cottage. They'll get back about 2 a.m. and fry the fresh smelts in butter. "There's nothing like it in the whole world," says Dobbs. "He'll only have two smelts — that's all, two — and you know how small they are. He doesn't like fish, but he wants to be part of things."

Ron Webb says Davis used to love heading out into Georgian Bay around Giant's Tomb "when the winds would come up and the waves would get to eight or ten feet. He just loved heading into that. It wasn't dangerous, but it was invigorating. He doesn't do that much anymore, though."

Now he is more likely to get up at dawn and walk around the island by himself or spend hours just puttering around with the small white pines he has planted among the rocks.

"I think the way he is publicly is largely the way he is privately," says Neil. "He is shy, a private person. He is even private in his own house. He doesn't say how he is feeling a lot. I would say he relaxes at the cottage more than anywhere else, including Florida. I don't know what it is, but you can see the change in him even when he knows he's going that day.

"If he's had a weekend at the cottage, he's a changed individual. Now for him the change is subtle, but that's the place he releases. The swing of his mood is a pretty narrow range, you understand," he says, holding his hands a couple of inches apart, "and somebody else maybe wouldn't notice any difference. But if you're in the family, you know."

CHAPTER 3
TORY TRADITIONS

———————— ⧗ ————————

Clare Westcott just can't stay away from the telephone. He and his wife were holidaying in the Great Smokey Mountains near Gatlinburg, Tennessee, on October 18, 1982, when he thought he'd check in with Queen's Park. It was just after 8 a.m., and while he spoke to his secretary, another line rang in the Toronto office. She asked Westcott to hang on and moments later came back on and said it was Toronto Police Chief Jack Ackroyd. "He wants to know where to get Mr. Davis. John Robarts has shot himself."

Within minutes Ackroyd had called Ed Stewart with the horrible news that Ontario's seventeenth premier had put a shotgun to his head in the shower of his Rosedale home and pulled the trigger, leaving his remains to be discovered by his wife, Katherine. It was the final chapter in a life of great personal tragedy and great public triumph. He was sixty-five.

Ed Stewart immediately phoned Brampton. "Oh no," Davis said, "not that," followed by a long period of silence. Davis then telephoned Katherine Robarts before going to Queen's Park, where he called Intergovernmental Affairs Minister Tom Wells into his office to make arrangements. Wells had already told his protocol section to be on alert, and Davis sent him up to the Robarts home "to talk to her and offer any services we can."

The legislature sat briefly that afternoon, adjourning out of respect for Robarts following tributes from all three parties. Davis, speaking in a halting, choked voice, eulogized Robarts as one

34

who "had a sense of this province and of this country that few could duplicate." He said what was "truly a sad moment" was all the more tragic "as some of us saw him as recently as a few nights ago making what we thought was such great progress in spite of the massive stroke he had some months ago."

Liberal Leader David Peterson, whose father had run unsuccessfully against Robarts in 1955, recalled him as a "man of warmth, friendliness, and humor. A big man in every sense of the word, a man of stature and importance."

Ex-NDP leader Donald MacDonald, who had led his party through two election defeats by Robarts, said, "There's a real mix of a man who lived life to the full and yet throughout life seemed plagued with profound dissatisfaction and unhappiness. . . . I was startled at the word that he had committed suicide, but on sober second thought, it really doesn't surprise me that much."

And Bob Nixon, who as Liberal leader lost to Robarts in 1967, said Robarts's most memorable accomplishment "was to establish the kind of relationship with the government and people of Quebec which was as good as or better than it had been since the beginning of Confederation." Later, in a bizarre turn of phrase, Nixon told a reporter he had always liked Robarts because he was "a straight-shooter."

Later that day a press release from Wells's office announced there would be a "state funeral," the first in the history of the legislature. Two other longtime and beloved premiers—George Drew and Leslie Frost—had died with Davis in office, but neither was afforded such honors. Years later Wells admitted the release had been a mistake. "It wasn't meant to be a state funeral. That is for a head of state, someone in a position at the time. We were merely assisting the wishes of the family (Katherine). . . . The propriety of it didn't bother me."

It did, however, bother some, including the author, who wrote a column about it and was told privately by at least twenty MPPs that they, too, had grave doubts about the propriety of such honors for a suicide. Indeed, concern about it was so widespread that Most Rev. Lewis Garnsworthy, Anglican Archbishop of Toronto, told the thousand mourners in St. Paul's Anglican Church that "the manner of his passing saddens us. But I am not the judge of that, and you are not the judges."

At the time Davis, the quintessential pragmatist, dismissed the theological concerns as "not part of our considerations." But an official in the premier's office at the time said Davis was "incredibly angry" at the column. "He was doubly upset because he was torn on the thing himself. He only did it for Robarts's wife, but really, the column struck to the heart of his most deeply rooted Christian beliefs."

Above all, however, Davis wanted to do the right thing for his political family, in which Robarts was an important patriarchal figure, and he was prepared to set aside his personal religious values for a higher partisan truth. Davis was, after all, not only the product of his own close-knit Brampton family but a child of the Tory dynasty as well, the inheritor of its traditions. From George Drew he learned the value and political popularity of social programs of the progressive school; from Tom Kennedy he acquired his Peel power base and the skills of grass-roots politics at the riding level; from Leslie Frost he grasped the mechanics of shaping an industrial giant and running a successful political machine; and from John Robarts he gained an appreciation of Ontario's brokerage role in Confederation. From all these men Davis learned that to survive means to adapt to the times, and if adapting meant holding a state funeral for a man who had committed suicide, then so be it.

*   *   *

In 1943, about the time Navy Lieut. John Robarts was being mentioned in war dispatches from Salerno, Col. George Drew, the legend goes, was scribbling his famous twenty-two-point Progressive Conservative program on the back of an envelope. Regardless of how the points were actually set down, they worked, ending nine years of Liberal rule and launching the Tories, albeit with a minority government, on a run that seems certain to break the Canadian mark for continuity of forty-three years, set by the Liberals in Nova Scotia and ending in 1925.

Drew, of course, had the good fortune to capitalize on the self-destructiveness of Liberal Mitch Hepburn, the colorful but erratic Depression premier whose eccentricities and bitter feuds with Mackenzie King ultimately did him in. Indeed, the first two

of Drew's twenty-two points — "We will maintain British institutions and strengthen the British partnership" and "We will at
all times work in effective co-operation with the Dominion
government" — were direct responses to Hepburn's actions.

The populist Hepburn's style was far from the staid Tory
tradition. In a 1934 election speech to rural voters near his
St. Thomas home, Hepburn promised to end the position of
lieutenant-governor in Ontario and auction off the government's
limousines.

On the warm, muggy night of July 10, 1934, the premier-
designate left the King Edward Hotel in a rented car and headed
to Chorley Park, the thirty-four-bedroom, twenty-one-bathroom
Rosedale mansion that housed Lieutenant-Governor Herbert
Bruce, his wife, and staff. After the swearing-in ceremony, Hepburn fired all civil servants hired since October, 1933. One of
those who got the axe was George Drew.

Then in August about eight thousand people crowded into
Varsity Arena to watch while the Tories' forty-seven limousines
were auctioned off for a total of $34,000. Responding to a com-
plaint that the event was a circus, Hepburn said, "Regardless of
whether you consider it burlesque or not, I'm telling you this
auction of ours is going to meet with the whole-hearted approval
of the rank and file of taxpayers. You can have too much dignity
in government."

In 1935 Hepburn and his cabinet refused to attend the annual
state dinner hosted by the lieutenant-governor, ending the event
forever, and he dismissed Chorley Park as "a haven for broken-
down English aristocrats who should be paying for their rooms
at the hotels." In fact, Hepburn wanted a friend, Agriculture
Minister Duncan Marshall, to be appointed lieutenant-governor,
but Mackenzie King refused. Marshall, incidentally, was the uncle
of Tory fund-raiser Senator Bill Kelly. Hepburn and King compromised in 1937 when Marshall was named to the Senate, Bruce
resigned, and the new lieutenant-governor, Albert Matthews,
agreed to entertain in the Speaker's quarters at Queen's Park.

But Hepburn's feuds with King were far from over, as were
his feuds with just about everybody, and he quit as leader in 1942
after accusing King of being soft on the Nazis. Gordon Connant
became premier in October, 1942, but he couldn't rally caucus
support, and on May 17, 1943, Harry Nixon took over, called a

quick election, and set the record for the shortest premiership in Ontario history — three months less a day.

While Torontonians lined up at the Imperial Theatre on August 4, 1943, to see Don Ameche starring in "Something to Shout About," Drew and his Conservatives had something of their own to shout about. They had won 38 of the 90 seats, just four ahead of Ted Jolliffe's Co-operative Commonwealth Federation (CCF), forerunner of the New Democratic Party. Nixon's fractious Liberals had won 15, and there were two Labor Progressives (Communists) and one independent Liberal, a chap named Mitch Hepburn. Drew was sworn in as premier on August 17, 1943.

Two years later Drew won 66 seats, leaving 11 for the Liberals and just eight for the CCF. Jolliffe even lost his own York South seat, the same riding held by future NDP Leaders Donald MacDonald and Bob Rae.

The 1945 electorate also chose three Liberal-Labor MPPs and two Communists, party leader Alec MacLeod and Joe Salsberg, who defeated Toronto-St. Andrews Tory candidate Eddie Goodman, then an energetic young man fresh from the war in Europe. Goodman didn't mind so much losing, "but he even beat me in the overseas service vote, for heaven's sake [430–267], and he'd been hiding in Quebec when war was declared, and I'd been wounded a couple of times fighting over there." Salsberg would win another two elections before finally losing a bitterly fought contest in 1955 to Tory Allan Grossman, whose son Larry, over the objections of party headquarters, inherited the riding in 1975.

As for Alec MacLeod, considered a moderate Communist, he was finally defeated in 1951 but ended up doing research for Leslie Frost. When Bill Davis became minister of education in 1962, he also used MacLeod, who, Clare Westcott says, was "a great influence on Davis" in his early cabinet years. John Robarts, as premier, had him writing speeches, including his most famous one, the "hands across the border" appeal to Quebec, which was destined to launch Robarts's reputation as a great Canadian nationalist.*

Drew's bent, especially with such apparent opposition strength

---

*MacLeod's son, David, also worked briefly for Davis but is somewhat better known as executive producer of the movie *Reds*.

on the left, was decidedly on the so-called "progressive" side of the Conservative scale, and such policies as medical and dental insurance, subsidized housing, assumption of half of school costs (instead of 7 or 8 per cent) to lighten property taxes, and conversion of Ontario Hydro from 25- to 60-cycle, took the wind out of the CCF sails and guided Drew safely into port, well ahead of his nearest rivals.

The turning point in the 1945 campaign was a radio broadcast by Jolliffe, without party knowledge, eleven days before the election. He accused Drew of keeping a government spy organization, "a Gestapo" headed by OPP captain William J. Osborne-Dempster, hidden on government payrolls but known to Drew and Attorney General Leslie Blackwell by the code name D-208. The Tories flatly denied it, and two days later Drew ordered a royal commission inquiry into the charges. There was strong evidence to suggest that D-208 had prepared at least forty-one reports with information on thousands of left-leaning Ontarians, including Jolliffe and Hepburn, but Commissioner A. M. LeBel found there was no secret police force, although he said that Osborne-Dempster was engaged in anti-sabotage work. His sole criticism of Drew was to say that he should have stopped his overzealous snoop when he began writing reports on CCF members.

The Tories dropped to 53 seats in 1948, still a comfortable majority. But Drew lost his own Toronto High Park seat by 1,017 votes to CCF temperance fighter William Temple.* The CCF, with 21 seats, were eight ahead of the Liberals. Then, a month after the June election, federal Conservative Leader John Bracken announced his resignation, and Drew headed down the road to Ottawa to defeat Donald Fleming and John Diefenbaker for the leadership.

When Drew first wanted to run, there was no ground swell of support for him, so Elmer Bell, a senior party official, approached a Young Progressive Conservative then becoming prominent in party circles, Clare Westcott. He told Westcott that A. D. McKenzie (who ran both the party organization and the premier's

---

*After 1948 Temple never won again in three tries but has remained the man most responsible for keeping the Junction Triangle in west Toronto one of the few dry areas in Ontario.

office for Drew and later for Frost) wanted him to go on radio and ask Drew to run "on behalf of the youth of Canada." Westcott and a friend, Gerry Godbolt, had never been in a radio station, but they went to CJCS in Stratford. "I was scared shitless, but we did it, and Drew picked up on the stories about it to get into the race."

With Drew in Ottawa, the provincial Tories had to find a leader, fast. They were, after all, still the government party, but because Drew had left with such unseemly haste and there was no time to arrange a full leadership convention, Peel's veteran Agriculture Minister, Tom Kennedy, was chosen interim leader and served a seven-month stint as premier.

Kennedy was first elected in 1919 and in 1930 was appointed agriculture minister by Premier G. Howard Ferguson. He lost in the 1934 Hepburn sweep to Duncan Marshall but won the seat back in 1937 and kept it through five more elections until his death on February 13, 1959, just weeks after a young Brampton lawyer, Bill Davis, had won the nomination to succeed him.

The most commonly told story about that time is that Kennedy brought Davis down to Queen's Park, introduced him to Kennedy's successor, Leslie Frost, and said, "I'd like you to meet a future prime minister of Ontario." Davis says it wasn't exactly like that. "That's been cited many times, but my best recollection is it was said by Tom Kennedy to a group of cabinet ministers in the dining room they used to have on the first floor. I don't think Frost was there."

Leslie Frost delighted in saying he ran Ontario from the perspective of his barber's chair in Lindsay. But for all his homespun folksiness he was a tough, shrewd politician, likely the best of the bunch. He built Ontario's modern industrial economy and is the grandfather of the Tory party machine.

A lawyer, Frost, like Davis, was raised on a heavy diet of fundamentalist religion. His mother was a Salvation Army captain who founded citadels in Belleville and Peterborough, his father a lay minister in the Presbyterian Church. As a youth he would drive with his father to the little villages around Orillia spreading the gospel and fine-tuning the tremendous skills he had in dealing with people.

"Drew set the course and did it with enthusiasm and foresight," said a retired party official who worked through the entire Drew-to-Davis era, "but Frost is the one who put the frosting on the cake. I think the emergence of the Big Blue Machine under Davis is a mistake. Frost would have frowned on it. He ran a personal party. He was very strict with ministers who made mistakes, some people thought too strict; one goof and they'd be out on their ear. But he used to tell me that you have to avoid even the appearance of wrongdoing, and I often heard him say he regarded the Conservative party as an instrument for good."

Leslie Miscampbell Frost was fifty-four when he became premier, and during the twelve years he ran the province he became revered as "Old Man Ontario." His personal popularity was such that his campaign theme was always "Re-elect the Frost government," not the Conservative government. "That way," the retired organizer said, "he picked up a lot of Liberal votes, too. He went through an entire provincial election without once mentioning the Liberal party. His stock in trade was neutralizing the opposition, and he did that by treating them all with respect."

Frost also recognized early on a uniquely Ontarian electoral phenomenon that helps both the provincial Tories and the federal Liberals: the switch voters. Voting pattern studies show that about one-third of the people who vote Liberal federally in Ontario vote Conservative provincially, and another 10 per cent of federal Liberal voters don't even vote in provincial elections. So, to a large extent, the two parties represent the same constituency, which is why Frost refused to involve the provincial party in campaigning federally for Drew. Davis, with the exception of the second Joe Clark election, made a religion out of campaigning for the federal Tory leader. But then Frost never had federal ambitions.

Frost ran the government, period. He often ignored his ministers, preferring instead to go directly to senior public servants, either by phone or memo, and in the legislature he once intervened seventeen times when one of his ministers was trying to answer questions. Whenever his ministers got themselves into a political jackpot, Frost would immediately dump them, thereby showing that while the criticism may have been valid, Leslie Frost was above reproach.

The party chieftain in those days was A. D. McKenzie, who unexpectedly helped Frost upset Leslie Blackwell for the leadership in 1949. McKenzie held court most evenings in the Black

Knight Room of the Royal York Hotel, listening to the complaints and ideas of MPPs, organizers, and supporters, dispensing patronage and advice, and teaching the Tories the fine art of ward heeling. When McKenzie died in 1960, it wasn't long before Frost decided it was time to step down and let a younger man carry on the process of regeneration, a technique the Tories use every decade or so to give the appearance of a brand-new team and so dispel criticisms of a government being in power too long.

Bill Davis, a backbencher just two years at the time, played a large role in helping Frost's Education Minister John Robarts win the leadership on the sixth ballot by 343 votes over the favorite, Kelso Roberts. Davis had been recruited to run the leadership campaign of the mercurial Robert Macaulay. Out of that experience came two enduring relationships: with Clare Westcott, who held the same executive assistant post for Macaulay, and with Bob Macaulay's brother, Hugh, who became one of Davis's closest confidants.

On a rainy October 25, 1961, Robarts led after five ballots, but Macaulay, just dropped, had enough strength to influence the outcome. Kelso Roberts sent backbencher Allan Lawrence to Macaulay's camp between ballots, because Lawrence was a lawyer with Macaulay's firm, even though he hadn't supported him. Lawrence asked for support, but before Macaulay could respond, Bill Davis said, "I'm sorry, Al," and with that Macaulay told his troops to vote for Robarts, left his own seat, and headed to the Varsity Arena box where Robarts quickly stuck his own campaign button on Macaulay's lapel.

Robarts, an immensely popular man during his ten years as premier, was born in Banff, the son of a bank manager. His mother died when he was three, and he lived in many places until the family finally settled in London in the early 1930s. His first marriage to Norah McCormick ended in divorce in 1976, the same year he married Katherine Anne Sickafuse, a divorcée twenty-eight years younger than him, a fact that did not sit well with some of his longtime friends. Nor, it seems, was she particularly fond of some of them. A year later, Norah's and John's only son, Timothy, twenty-one, committed suicide. Norah died in 1981. Their daughter, Robin Hollis, lives in Toronto.

In 1963 Robarts fought his first campaign against Liberal Leader John Wintermeyer in what became the "scandal a day" campaign. Near the end of the Frost regime, a court reporter with the *Globe and Mail* heard a story about organized crime, and the paper assigned two reporters to it, one of them Harold Greer, who ultimately wrote a story claiming that social clubs used for syndicate gambling were getting provincial charters and that the illegal gambling proceeds were financing legitimate businesses. The *Globe*, acting on the advice of its lawyers, refused to publish the story, saying more proof was needed. Greer was so outraged that he quit the paper, took his story to Wintermeyer, and became his speechwriter. In a two-and-a-half-hour speech in November, 1961, Wintermeyer made the accusations public, and Robarts quickly set up a royal commission under Mr. Justice Wilfred Roach, a former president of the Windsor Liberal Association, who could hardly be accused by the Liberals of being a partisan patsy.

After sixty-six days of hearings Mr. Justice Roach essentially dismissed the charge that gambling was ruled by a syndicate, although he found that gambling had increased. He also found no evidence to support the accusation that the attorney general's department had suppressed police investigations against gamblers. He did, however, recommend that two senior OPP officers be fired for turning a blind eye to gambling activities. They both resigned.

"Up until the report came out [in December, 1962] we were doing pretty well," Wintermeyer says. "We really thought we had them on the run, but the report hit us pretty hard. In the intervening year waiting for the report, we had done a lot of policy work and issued a forty-two-point policy booklet, but after the crime report the session began in January, and Robarts implemented ten of our best recommendations, leaving us denuded going into the 1963 campaign."

The Liberals did manage to gain two seats in the campaign, but it was little comfort because redistribution had enlarged the legislature from 98 to 108 seats and the Tories went up six to 77, with 48 per cent of the vote, while the NDP under Donald MacDonald jumped two seats to a total of seven.

The closest thing to a major scandal in the Robarts regime broke in March, 1964, when Attorney General Fred Cass introduced what became known as the "police state" bill, the most controversial section of which gave the Ontario Police Commission power to force anyone to give evidence in secret or be jailed indefinitely if they refused. Cass himself didn't help the furor when he told reporters the law was necessary, but "it's drastic and it's dangerous and it's new and it's terrible legislation in an English common law country." Robarts, who later gained a reputation for his decisiveness, did not distinguish himself in this instance, allowing the debate to rage for days and even defending the bill himself, before finally allowing Cass to be the scapegoat and resign, as well as dropping the bill's most contentious sections. The controversy did, however, result in the commission on civil rights under the former chief justice of the Supreme Court of Ontario, J. C. McRuer, whose work dramatically updated the legal system.

Robarts handily won his second, and last, election in 1967, beating the Liberals under Bob Nixon, son of the last Liberal premier, 69–28, with MacDonald's NDP winning an impressive 20 seats. But there were no great issues, little passion, no scandals. It was as if the province simply sleepwalked through the campaign and woke up on the morning of October 18 to find things pretty much the same as when they'd nodded off. And that was the way it remained throughout the Robarts regime.

Although he allowed the party organization to go to pot through benign neglect during the last few years of his rule, one accomplishment Robarts will be remembered for is his bridge building with Quebec, activities that have painted him for all time as a great national statesman. He spoke often about unity, extended French-language education in the schools, developed a close friendship with Quebec Premier Daniel Johnson, and in 1967 organized the Confederation of Tomorrow Conference, widely credited with sparking the final constitutional debate, which was to drone on another sixteen years before agreement was finally reached. Indeed, even after his retirement Robarts played a major role in the constitutional process. Prime Minister Pierre Trudeau appointed him as co-chairman (along with Jean-Luc Pépin) of the Task Force on Canadian Unity, which toured the country in 1977 and 1978 in the wake of the separatist victory in Quebec.

But while the Robarts years were quiet on the public front, the private side was anything but quiet. Unlike Davis, who took great pains to separate his political advisers from his personal friends, Robarts and his cronies became legends around Queen's Park.

For advice Robarts relied mainly on his old buddy Ernie Jackson from London South. The two shared an apartment with Jim Auld of Leeds in the 1950s. Jonathan Manthorpe, in his 1974 book, *The Power and the Tories*, described their lifestyle this way: "The three of them worked hard, but they played hard as well. There were sports cars, good food and drink, and rollicking evenings listening to Dixie and jazz on the Yonge Street strip. Robarts, looking and living rather like an untormented political version of Ernest Hemingway, enjoyed it all."

Davis was never fond of the Robarts lifestyle of constant late-night drinking and carousing with his friends. "I think Davis liked John," says Clare Westcott, "but I don't think he respected him very much. John wasn't a genius, but he was lucky. The greatest thing about him was not what he brought into that office, because he brought nothing but the suit of clothes he had on, but how he grew in the office. Bob Macaulay used to jokingly say about Robarts, 'If he reads the side of a cereal box for breakfast, he's shot for the day.' He had a physical capacity, though, at the end of the day which saw no limit. Though his mental capacity was limited, and Davis was aware of that . . . he carried it off well. The extracurricular activities he was carrying on would have killed most men. . . . Robarts left London, not to serve the people, but to get away from his wife a few months every year. There's no shit about that. He didn't sit on committees, he didn't really want to be a minister or do anything. He and his friends were just there to have a good time, and they certainly did that."

Former treasurer John White, another member of the London connection and a close personal friend, said that although everybody thought Robarts was a strong person, "He was really a very insecure chap. He pretended to be confident, but when he was elected leader he went out and bought three suits. He told me he was afraid he'd lose the job, and he wanted to have a decent wardrobe to go back to the practice of law."

White, although he came late, was one of a small group of Robarts's friends who dined at La Scala, a downtown Toronto restaurant, one night late in 1975. The others were Darcy McKeough and Charlie MacNaughton, both former treasurers, and John Labatt Ltd. executive John Cronyn, whom Robarts appointed head of a committee on government productivity that reshaped the organization of government.

As White tells the story, they closed the place down, piled into McKeough's car, and went off to the downtown Holiday Inn. Robarts had made the Westbury Hotel famous during his premiership, but he moved because he'd been named a board member of Holiday Inn, one of a couple of dozen appointments he accepted after he left active politics. When they arrived at the hotel, Robarts said good night to everybody and invited Mac-Naughton up to his room. "I invited myself up," says White. "He didn't want me up there, but I didn't give a damn. He had three or four pictures of Katherine, and he showed them lovingly to us and said, 'Now listen, you fellows are good friends of mine. I want some advice. What should I do?'

"MacNaughton walked to the window and looked out, came over to Robarts, stared at him, and said, 'John, you and I have been friends for a very long time, and I've been one of your confidential advisers, and I'm going to tell you right now that whatever you decide to do will be the right thing.'

"That's when I jumped in uninvited and told him to stick by his family," says White. "I said nobody cares if you screw this good-looking young dame. Nobody cares. Have some fun with her, but stick with your family . . . he didn't take my advice. . . . I have the belief that if John Robarts had stayed with his family, that Norah and John and Timmy might be alive today. The young woman couldn't cope with his affliction, but big, fat Norah would have. She'd mother the guy and clean up after him in a way the beautiful young woman was not prepared to do."

His "affliction" was a lot to cope with. In his last years Robarts experienced bouts of depression after suffering a series of paralysing strokes. The first stroke hit in 1981 as he sat alone at the front of an airplane travelling from New York to Houston for a board meeting of Reed Stenhouse Companies Ltd. He had another in the Houston hospital, and although doctors said he'd have to spend the rest of his life in a wheelchair, he was hobbling around on a cane within six weeks.

A few months before his death, Robarts and White lunched at the Ontario Club, and Robarts constantly complained about everything. White invited him to see his new condominium. "We walked over. He walked, without a cane, with great difficulty. He wouldn't let me take his arm. He limped over there; it was a pitiful sight. . . . During lunch he told me that every word he spoke he had to shove up with his diaphragm. He said it was a terrific effort to speak. He said his second marriage had broken down, and he told me he was thinking of taking the same route that Timmy took. . . . I said the only thing I could think of: I just said, 'Well, I hope you don't.'"

His last public appearance with the party was just three weeks before his death, when he sat at a head table with Davis at a large fund-raising dinner in downtown Toronto. Davis referred to that event in his tribute to Robarts in the legislature, saying how well Robarts had seemed. In fact, Robarts almost didn't get to the dinner.

"Robarts called me," says Westcott, "and says there's this big dinner for Davis, and he hadn't been invited. 'Wouldn't I be expected to sit at the head table or something?' So I called Bob Harris, and he said he'd look after it. Then I left on holidays and didn't hear anything more until I called into my office that day and Ackroyd was calling."

In March, 1983, some of his old friends got together to unveil a new portrait of Robarts to hang outside the premier's office on the second floor at Queen's Park. The first portrait, painted by London artist Philip Aziz and unveiled in 1975, showed Robarts wearing a buttonless suit, standing on a ledge outside the premier's office overlooking University Avenue, with Lake Ontario depicted as a giant tidal wave about to consume him. Through White, as chairman of the Ontario Heritage Foundation, the painting was donated to the University of Toronto, where it now hangs in the lobby of the imposing Robarts Library. The new portrait, by Toronto artist Roberto de Seta, shows Robarts sitting comfortably in a chair, looking every bit the impressive figure he was.

When he first became premier in 1961, Robarts said, "I'm a management man myself. This is the era of the management man. . . . I'm a complete product of my times." And when he retired ten years later, he said, "I am a product of my time exactly, and my time is finished."

CHAPTER 4
FLIGHT PLANS

———— ∇ ————

B ill Davis came by his interest in politics honestly. As Crown
attorney, Grenville Davis was forbidden to become actively
involved in politics, but his Conservative sympathies were the
worst-kept secret in town. Peggy Dale, who used to drop by her
father's office for a ride home after her piano lessons and often
saw Tom Kennedy there, admits "he was pretty active for somebody who wasn't active."

Davis's cousin Russell Cooper remembers that "Brampton had
Tory and Grit funeral homes then, Tory and Grit barbers. Bill
used to go to the Tory barber, of course, and they'd scalp him.
They also had Tory and Grit law offices — in fact, Tory and Grit
everything. If you didn't already know a person's politics, which
you probably did, you could tell what they were just by watching who they did business with."

The family used to talk politics at home all the time, and Tory
MP Gordon Graydon was a regular visitor. It was Graydon who
began taking young Bill to local Tory meetings, the first when
Davis was thirteen. And in 1945, at sixteen, Davis went with
Graydon to the national convention in Ottawa, when John
Bracken was elected leader, making him at that time the youngest-
ever delegate to a national convention. At nineteen Davis became secretary of the Peel P.C. Association, and he remained active
in party affairs, both federally and provincially, before plunging
in himself in 1958.

"I'm sure that Daddy was quite glad Billy went into politics," Peggy says. "I remember being at the house after elections, and I think Daddy lived his life through Billy. He would have liked to go into politics, but his health wouldn't permit it. I don't know that Mother was quite as glad [she wanted Bill to be a minister], but I guess any mother is glad when a child makes some sort of success of his life. She became inordinately proud of him as she got older."

Davis's plan was to wait for Gordon Graydon's retirement, then run in his seat. "My initial interest was federal," he says. "You sort of reflect the interests of the people you admire, and Gordon was interested in international affairs and so was I." (While at U of T, Davis won a scholarship to Connecticut's Institute of International Affairs.) On the other hand, a Port Credit lawyer, John Pallett, was more interested in provincial politics and had been waiting for Tom Kennedy's retirement. "In the normal course of events, everybody expected Kennedy to retire before Gordon Graydon," says Davis. "But when Gordon died [in 1954, just as Davis was getting out of university], there was a by-election, and John Pallett won that."

And so it was that Joe and Joan Dobbs were sitting in their Cooksville living room one night in the fall of 1957 when somebody knocked on the door. It was Bill Davis calling.

"You'd never seen a shyer guy," says Dobbs. "He came to the front door alone. It was all he could do to say hello and introduce himself. He came into the living room and sat there uncomfortably while we talked."

Tom Kennedy, the local legend, was thinking of retiring and sent the aspiring politician to visit Dobbs, who was president of the Cooksville P.C. Association. In those days the riding of Peel covered all of Peel County, an area that is now five separate constituencies, and Kennedy sent Davis around to see all the district presidents. The meeting with Dobbs formed a lasting friendship that makes Dobbs today, indisputably, Davis's closest personal friend. "It was Tom who decided Billy should run after he retired," recalls Dobbs. "When this shy guy came to my door, I knew Tom had sent him down to break the ice. It wasn't long after that meeting we started getting together to plan a campaign and play cards, and we just became good friends. That's it."

The only real concern Davis had at that time was getting the nomination when it came up. After all, Peel was one of the most solid Tory ridings in the province, and while the young Brampton lawyer expected a fight at the convention — and subsequently got one — he figured that was the tough part. The rest was just waiting for the Tory votes to flow in. As it happened, one of the most successful political careers in Ontario history almost got untracked before it began. Not because of anything Davis did, but because of Prime Minister John Diefenbaker.

But we're getting ahead of ourselves. Let's go back to Brampton, 1958, and fresh-cheeked lawyer Bill Davis — married, with two children, scion of a prominent family, son of a well-known and much-admired Crown attorney — the kind of candidate political strategists dream about.

Davis says he was "prevailed upon" to run only by friends and party workers. "I think there was a feeling on the part of some that Tom Kennedy may have had a preference," he says. "He may have had, but I didn't know about that. He didn't use whatever influence he had. He was careful about that." But not so careful as to avoid sending Davis around to meet Dobbs and the other district officials, or to pose with Davis and Leslie Frost for a picture that ran the next day in the *Cooksville Review* with the cutline "Past, Present, Future." "Yes, that was sort of embarrassing," says Davis. "I hadn't even decided to be a candidate yet."

Kennedy finally announced in the fall, on his eightieth birthday, that he was going to retire, and Davis made the decision to run. "I had just been two years out of law school, but it's a case that the opportunity doesn't come that often. It wasn't the best time for me in economic terms, either, but the chance was there and I took it."

He wasn't the only one who wanted that opportunity. The nomination was set for December 11, 1958, and Tony Adamson, who had been reeve of Toronto Township and county warden, decided to join the contest for the seat. Adamson, now a University of Toronto historian, made it close.

Russell Cooper nominated him and ran the campaign; Joe Dobbs seconded the nomination. "It was much tougher than people thought it would be," says Davis. "But there was a feeling at the convention that maybe somebody from the north end of the riding should be chosen because by that time Pallett was the fed-

eral member, and he was from the south end. There weren't
enough votes in the north end in those days to win. All the population densities were in the south [in what is now Mississauga].
I didn't know a thing about campaigning or organizing, but the
constitution at that time gave each polling subdivision three or
four delegates, and you didn't dare not shake hands with every
one of them, so I spent a good part of the fall doing that."

In later years the most common complaint heard from Davis
speechwriters was that their man rarely bothered to actually read
the speech they'd written; it became so well known that Davis
usually used it as a joke in his standard, opening Johnny Carson
routine. But it wasn't always that way. "He wouldn't ad lib anything then," says Cooper. "He wanted everything written out,
and he'd just read it."

"He certainly wasn't an extrovert," says Dobbs. "Helen could
wade into a crowd and greet everybody, but he was too shy for
that. He did have a phenomenal memory for names, though. He
still does. That really helped. Kathleen doesn't enjoy the political stuff like Helen did, so from Billy's standpoint he was very
lucky he had a wife like Helen to start him off. She was politically ambitious . . . or maybe that's not the word, but certainly
politically helpful. He was so shy he needed pushing."

Having won the nomination, Davis geared up for the coming
election. The Liberals put up a strong candidate, Brampton
Mayor Bill Brydon, son of a popular local doctor. Even the CCF,
which didn't figure to win, was represented by Bob Williams, a
well-known local veterinarian. But despite the strong opponents,
his lack of experience, and his dreadful stage manners, Davis
began his quest for a seat with "some fairly optimistic feelings.
Tom Kennedy started taking me around and introducing me to
people. And of course my father was well known and highly
respected, and people would tell me all the time, 'Oh yes, I know
your father.' So things were looking good."

But tragedy struck. First, Kennedy's wife died shortly after the
nomination, taking him out of the campaign. "I remember Tom
got me two tickets to the opening of the House, but it was on the
day of his wife's funeral," Davis recalls. "I didn't go to the House
opening; I went to the funeral instead. I remember him telling
me I should have gone to the House." Davis had counted heavily
on Kennedy to help him in the campaign, but it wasn't to be.

Soon after his wife's death, his daughter and son were killed when the roof of a curling rink in Britannia collapsed under the weight of the snow, and shortly after these family tragedies, Kennedy himself died.

While these events were a terrible personal setback for Davis and certainly didn't help his fledgling campaign, it was Diefenbaker who really sent the political shock waves through the riding, almost knocking Davis out in the process. Diefenbaker cancelled the Avro Arrow, and suddenly, in one political stroke completely outside Davis's control, fourteen thousand workers, most of them residents of Peel, were out of work.

"That set the political agenda of Peel like no other event before or since," says Davis. "Nothing like that had ever happened, and here we were fighting a campaign. It wasn't our fault, of course, but these people were justifiably angry, and since we happened to be the first Conservative after the event to ask for their support, many of them wanted to show Diefenbaker what they thought of Conservatives."

Davis was getting worried. All the talk he'd heard about the massive Conservative organization turned out to be people who had been great friends of Tom Kennedy; there was no organization, just Tom's friends.

"I went to see Mr. Frost, and it was a learning experience. He got on the phone to Dief, and the air was fairly blue. He was angry, as it turned out with good reason. Not so much for the decision necessarily, but because it was such a major blow and he hadn't been consulted. His language and his message were very strong on the phone. But then it was done."

People were so angry that clients they had done business with for years stormed into the Davis law office, demanded their papers, "and said there was no way they were going to be represented by us. When I began canvassing I had doors slammed in my face, not only in Streetsville, where a lot of the aircraft workers lived, but in Brampton. I'd try to say, 'It's not me, it's not Mr. Frost.' But they'd say, 'You're a Tory, that's it.'"

So Davis gave up canvassing in his home area—the north end of the riding—and concentrated on the heavily populated areas in the south.

The night he remembers more than any other was late in the campaign, when he and Cooper were driving by the 4-H Club hall on their way to a meeting. "To me it looked like the largest political gathering, Tory or Liberal, in the history of the county. There were cars everywhere. The guest speaker was the test pilot for the Arrow, and it was under the auspices of the Peel Liberal Association. I looked at that and said to myself, 'Well, you'd better not forget all the law you knew. You're going to need a job.' "

On election night, June 11, 1959, Frost and his Tories steam-rolled the opposition, winning 71 of the 98 seats. Davis won, of course, beating Brydon by 1,203 votes. "Under normal circum-stances we could have expected to win by six or seven thousand votes, but you know, we even lost in Brampton. We were for-given next time around, but it sure made the first run tough."

It was one of the few times in his life Davis ever let loose in public. When the votes were finally counted and he'd won, he, Helen, and Russell Cooper jumped into Davis's car and headed for the Manley farm. "It was after two a.m.," Ralph Manley re-calls. "We heard this shouting and a horn beeping, and they came in and we had a party which lasted all night. I don't remember Bill ever doing that again."

Indeed, a look at the 1962 federal election tells you how strong the feelings were three years later. Although Diefenbaker held off the Liberals nationwide, all three sitting Tory MPs affected by the Arrow shutdown lost.

For Davis, it was the first big scare of his life. He'd have to wait until his leadership campaign for the next one.

CHAPTER 5
EDUCATION TO GO

—————— ☙ ——————

When John Robarts began his time as premier in 1961, he remembered the young backbencher who had dispatched Bob Macaulay's forces to his camp at the leadership convention. In return Robarts hung onto the education portfolio until 1962, keeping it open for Bill Davis. With a wife dying of cancer and with four young children at home, Davis was not ready for cabinet. Robarts waited until he was.

By 1966 Davis had become so firmly entrenched as minister that he was the educational equivalent of a fast-food franchise, opening schools in every neighborhood in Ontario. That year marked the 150th anniversary of a $6,000 grant to common schools, the first time public money had been spent for that purpose in Upper Canada. In his 1966 estimates speech, Davis said that grant was cut four years later. "So it is apparent then, as now, that some people were against progress." What was also apparent then, as now, was that Davis equated spending with "progress," and while the nineteenth-century politicians may have cut education spending, Davis certainly did not.

During the 1960s Ontario's population grew 20.8 per cent and its gross provincial product 122 per cent. Total government spending jumped 296 per cent, largely in education. From October, 1962, until Davis became premier in 1971, education spending rose 454 per cent. Health, the big-buck drain of the 1980s, was well below half that, and education spending with Davis as minister was four times what it was with Davis as premier. The 1960s was a time of rapid government growth overall, but nothing outgrew education. In economic terms it was a perpetual summertime, and the livin' was easy. Not for everybody, but certainly for an ambitious minister who had set his sights on higher office and who had been handed the ticket that practically guaranteed the trip.

Not that there isn't plenty to show for it. No minister before or since transformed the educational system the way Davis did. At a Canadian University Press conference in 1969, Davis, looking back, called himself a "moderate activist" — an understatement for a guy who wiped out one-room schoolhouses, fathered community colleges, upgraded teacher credentials, eliminated over three thousand individual school boards, and introduced educational television to Ontario's classrooms and living rooms.

Davis averaged 100,000 miles a year in the province by plane, train, or phone-equipped car, rarely getting home more than one evening a week, and often not even that, treasuring breakfast with his wife and five kids as his only real family time. And until the decade ended with the imposition of county boards, the free-spending minister remained popular with his colleagues, the opposition, and, more important, the taxpayers.

"Money was easier for both the province and the municipalities during the 1960s," he says. "If we would have been faced with the same needs for physical plant in the 1970s, we wouldn't have been able to build them. It would cost too much."

But back then nothing was too much for education. It was promoted not only as a valuable learning experience but also as the way to prosperity for a rapidly expanding population during a time of immense social and technological upheaval.

If a community needed a new school, Davis was there. If it needed a college, a university, a gymnasium, or an addition to an existing school, he was just a phone call and a press release away. By the late 1960s he controlled almost seventy cents of every provincial tax dollar spent.

No wonder he was so popular.

*　　*　　*

Naturally, when the boys returned home from the war, their minds quickly turned to more pleasant matters, with the result a run on weddings and the massive baby boom of the 1950s and early 1960s. To compare: The birth rate in 1962 was 24.6 per thousand population, but by 1982 it had plummeted to 14.2 per thousand. Even the number of actual births was higher twenty years ago despite a population increase of 36 per cent to 8.7 million people.

So while Davis rode the boom years in education, a succession of education ministers under his regime was faced with a decline in elementary school pupils every year since 1971. Only the separate school enrolment increased during the 1970s, and even that just marginally — from 418,433 to 429,946.

During his first year as minister, there were 880,198 elementary school pupils in 5,375 schools, plus 316,831 separate school students. By 1967 public enrolment topped one million. (To put that in perspective, by 1982 elementary enrolment had dropped by over 200,000 in fifteen years.) Despite the exploding student numbers, however, there were two thousand fewer schools in 1967 than in 1964, a stark reflection of the Davis plan to eradicate small schoolhouses and replace them with large, central schools. Kids who used to walk down the street now had to be bused several miles at public expense, but the central schools offered more courses and better equipment, and as long as the taxpayers didn't mind, Bill Davis didn't.

In a 1965 blitz, 480 elementary schools and sixty-nine high schools were built. Not only did Davis sign the cheques, he also showed up to cut the ribbon for all but a few of them.

"The reality is, we're probably given more credit than we deserve . . ." says Davis, typically using "we" to refer to himself. "And if you're one of our critics, we probably got more blame in that a lot of the changes were really related to the style which the minister practised. If nothing else, we provided a measure of focus, public interest, and enthusiasm."

The first thing Davis did as education minister was tackle the thorny problem of chopping the 3,676 school boards, many of which controlled just one school. "It wasn't easy," says Clare Westcott, his executive assistant in education. "People were jealous of their little boards, and anyway, most of the chairmen were Tories, and what you were doing was putting a lot of Tories out of work. But he did it." He certainly did. By 1965 the number of boards was reduced to 1,673. But the big drop—to 192—came two years later, almost costing Davis his leadership bid in the process.

His next major move, likely his most lasting, was to open community colleges—colleges of applied arts and technology, called CAATS. Scarborough's Centennial College, the first of twenty-two, opened in 1966 with five hundred students, 90 per cent of whom were the first in their families ever to go beyond high school.

"We were criticized at the time for setting up a lesser system, but it wasn't that at all," says Davis. "There are many reasons why the university system couldn't accommodate these students, and it's turned out to be a tremendous success."

When Robarts said he approved the community colleges but wouldn't raise taxes for the $600 million they needed, Davis quickly learned the art of lobbying for money from other ministries. "He did a terrific lobbying job," says Westcott. "He knew he was well liked, and he knew how to capitalize on that."

Former minister Darcy McKeough says Davis was seldom in the House and even less in cabinet in the 1960s. "His attendance at cabinet was a laughing stock. He'd wander in two hours after the meeting had started, if he showed at all. He always got there when he had something to put through, and Robarts, being the former minister, was on the same wavelength. Bill never had much of a problem doing what he was trying to do."

A dubious accomplishment was the construction of the Ontario Institute for Studies in Education (OISE), a resource centre for research and post-graduate work near Toronto's Varsity Stadium, but long a haven for radical, left-wing professors who spend much of their time on projects lacking any practical application. Even today, despite annual grants of over $2 million, its accomplishments are few.

But he generated other innovations, too, such as the four-year program for secondary schools, the abolition of Grade 13 departmental examinations, and the launching of educational television, now a province-wide network called TVOntario. He began pushing educational TV by making it part of the curriculum branch in 1965 but two years later set up a separate TV branch. The opposition complained that ETV, as it was then called, was producing programs that reflected the partisan Tory view, so in 1970

Davis set up the more independent Ontario Educational Communications Authority. Now most of the political grumbling is that TVOntario often reflects the NDP view in public affairs. But then so did Davis.

With the administrative structure overhauled and the boom in school buildings almost complete, Davis turned his attention to what was happening inside the schools.

He had come to government with some interest in education. He had kids of his own in school, and he had spent two years as a school trustee in Brampton. Kathleen, of course, had been a teacher and had her own views, a factor that is more important than either will admit. During a 1984 interview about that period, Davis said a major reform was the requirement that elementary teachers obtain a BA. "It's just as hard to teach Grade One kids as it is Grade Thirteen kids. Not everybody agreed, mind you, but Kathleen has strong views on that." Philosophically, her background as a small-l liberal Democrat did not make her a fan of the structured system her husband inherited. A family friend says she may not have been too influential early on, but that changed. "He bounces ideas and policies off her, and she's never reticent about expressing her views, at least not in the privacy of their home."

On June 12, 1968, Davis tabled the Hall-Dennis report, a $250,000 study that had a profound effect on education in the province. It attacked the traditional structure of schools, introducing a wide-open, do-your-own-thing mentality that people either greeted as the dawning of a new age or condemned as the arrival of the devil incarnate in Ontario classrooms. Davis called it "one of the best approaches to a total philosophy of education that has been produced in any jurisdiction." He now says the report was credited with many reforms that had already begun but concedes, "It certainly did generate a focus."

Called "Living and Learning," the report made 258 recommendations, aimed largely at ending discipline, allowing students to choose their own programs and proceed at their own pace, and replacing the yearly grade system with one of accumulated credits for each subject; the latter is about the only concrete proposal still surviving.

At the time Davis, who had already gained national attention as first head of the council of provincial ministers of education and through his work with the Pussycats — a group of politicians, educators, and business people who wanted a national focus on the subject (their code name supposedly meant they operated quietly, sneaking cat-like behind the scenes) — won nation-wide headlines for his daring, innovative initiatives.

The NDP was ecstatic with Hall-Dennis. Their education critic, Walter Pitman, called it "exciting," a recognition for the first time that "education should be a free and open experience. . . . A revolutionary document . . . because it brings into question the entire society in which we live; the end of competitiveness . . ." People who considered themselves "progressives" must have thought they'd died and gone to heaven when they read the report's brutal condemnation of our competitive society.

Lloyd Dennis, co-chairman of the study, was hired by Davis later to help explain and implement it. CBC producer Larry Zolf met Dennis in 1965 during a shoot for the CBC flagship show, "This Hour Has Seven Days," at Dennis's Deer Park Elementary School. Zolf had permission to interview children there, the idea being to ask them about Christmas, then ask a group of go-go dancers and run their reactions. One little girl had just told Zolf that to her Christmas meant Jesus's birthday, "And all of a sudden I hear this guy screaming, and he yanked the cord right out of the camera. I had no idea who he was or what the problem was, but it turned out to be Dennis, and he started yelling at me, 'How dare you ask these children about Jesus? Don't you know we have Jewish children here, and Chinese and Arabs and Muslims?' I was stunned by this. It seemed rather bizarre, especially with my background, but he threatened to kick us out and actually made me sign a paper saying I wouldn't ask anybody about Jesus. That was the only way I could do the item. When I grew up as a Jew in Winnipeg, we were taught to be proud of everybody's culture. I couldn't believe it. I thought he was one of the giant assholes of my career."

In his maiden speech as minister in 1962, Davis spoke of the pendulum swinging in education "in the 1930s and 1940s towards a more gentle, understanding approach towards the learner." He said the feeling in the 1950s was "it had swung too far in that direction, and a demand then arose for a more rigorous education, with more emphasis on scholarship and scientific research," a view reinforced by reaction to Sputnik "and in tidings that reached English-speaking countries of the demanding nature of the program in the Russian school system. Teachers have welcomed the emphasis upon seriousness . . . and increasing attention is being given to attainment of higher standards."

Five years later, sensing the pendulum swinging back the other way, Davis was among the first to hop on and ride with it. In a 1982 interview Dennis said he has suffered "misplaced abuse" in being described as the author of Ontario's permissive education system. Reacting to the release of a major education review commissioned by Education Minister Bette Stephenson, he said he stood by his report but accused Davis of not seriously analyzing it. He said Davis had it bound and left "on the coffee tables of the province" to see which way the wind would blow.

In the 1980s Stephenson began undoing much of what Davis did, bringing back a more regimented program for high schools, reducing choices, and increasing core subjects — the antithesis of the Hall-Dennis approach. Stephenson, trying not to be critical of Davis, says, "The reality of circumstances since those days has probably played a major part in him [Davis] holding a different set of opinions about what should have been done, what needed to be done, and what was appropriate." She said Davis could not have known that student population would decline in the 1970s, for example, something that had never happened since the system began. "There was no indication, none whatever, that there'd be this huge demographic shift which really began in 1972. It's been a terrible shock to the system of education to realize it wasn't growing. It took the educators ten years to understand it. That's a painful realization for them, just awful."

Looking back on his reign as chief principal, Davis says, "Education can't be isolated from the society around it. Educators have to consistently analyze what they're doing and what they're producing. You analyze the budgets over the years, and they do reflect the growth patterns. The problem is, when you have a decline, it only occurs in certain areas. . . . Enrolment declines, but there isn't a corresponding economic decline. . . . You still have the system to support, and while there is a decline in students, the expense doesn't decline by the same proportion."

On his love affair with the permissive system captured in the Hall-Dennis report, he says, "I don't know what — if you ever started analyzing the reforms — what all came out of that, except education does reflect society generally. You reach a point where the degree of self-discipline which is required in a less structured system . . . well, is that really part of human nature? I'm not sure that even with adults, let alone younger people, that it is."

Maybe not, but years earlier, riding a wave of public support and national adulation for his "progressive" thinking, Davis spent hundreds of millions of tax dollars restructuring schools and school programs on the premise that kids do indeed have the necessary self-discipline. Now he says they don't, but then he would have been among the first to dismiss such criticism as Neanderthal nonsense.

*   *   *

During his years in education, Davis also began assembling the group of people whose skills would serve him well throughout his term as premier. Tom Campbell, now Ontario Hydro chairman, was one of the few Young Turks in the ministry then. He was hired by Robarts to streamline the ministry, and Davis liked his suggestions so much he hired him to implement them. He remained a key bureaucrat in the Davis scheme of things ever after.

Another was Davis's personal secretary, Helen Anderson, known fondly as Miss A, a strikingly handsome woman who left Central Commerce in Toronto looking for a summer job with the government in 1931 and never left. When she started, George Henry had just taken over as premier, and Bill Davis was a two-year-old in Brampton — too young even for him to be involved in politics. Davis is the ninth premier the seventy-one-year-old secretary has seen in her own public career.

And as his executive assistant, Davis took on Clare Westcott. Born in Seaforth, west of London, in 1924, Westcott was the son of a jewelry store owner. He left school in Grade 11 and became an Ontario Hydro lineman, but he lost his left eye while working on a hydro pole in 1946 when a piece of bolt flew off and hit him. Married in 1948, he was working in advertising and writing freelance articles when the *Toronto Telegram*'s Ottawa man, Joe "Ham" Fisher, who had boarded with Westcott's grandmother, got him a job at the paper in 1950. He lasted three days, getting fired for asking not to be scheduled on weekends because he had promised his wife he'd return home to Seaforth then. For the next three years Westcott worked in the stock cage at Dominion Securities, living in a one-room flat off Bloor Street, studying journalism at Ryerson at night, and going home to Seaforth on weekends.

Politics had always been a part of his life. His dad was an active Tory, and Westcott recalls getting into fistfights as a kid over elections. "We didn't know what it was all about, but we still fought over it." Because he was alone in Toronto with little money but lots of time, he got involved in party affairs and was elected vice-president of the Ontario Young Progressive Conservatives. Shortly afterward chief organizer A. D. McKenzie hired him as a field organizer at $4,000 a year. Westcott volunteered for the speaker's panel in the 1953 federal election and still has a copy of his first speech (on agriculture) at Niagara-on-the-Lake. He arrived there by bus, but the candidate, a lawyer, met him "in his Cadillac, a big coupe de ville. Black. I thought it was great."

By then he and his wife Virginia had four children (with five more in their future), and they put $2,000 down on a $13,000 Scarborough house. Although expanded many times, the house is still home. "I've probably paid $300,000 for that house. I started with an $11,000 mortgage, and thirty years later I've got it down to $42,000."

Westcott joined Bob Macaulay as executive assistant in 1959, the year Davis was first elected, and joined Davis in 1962 after Macaulay retired from politics. Westcott says he wasn't anxious to work for Davis, but "I had this mortgage to pay off, so I said, 'Great.' Imagine me, a high school dropout, being a big shot in education. God."

The successful Ontario Science Centre was Westcott's idea, and when the ministry was closing the small schools, Westcott got the desks and arranged to fly them on military training flights to the Caribbean. He still does that, only the service has since expanded to include countless items, such as used ambulances, X-ray machines, generators, and schoolbooks.

Westcott says Davis was "dynamite" in education. "He had to do things himself. . . . If there was a decision to be made, he made it and things were done." But not after moving to the premier's office. The problem, says Westcott, is that Davis surrounded himself with so many advisers that "instead of deciding things, you spend your life checking everything" with them. He says Davis did "much more for the province as education minister than he ever did as premier. You can catalogue the things he did. But what are his accomplishments now?"

Another key relationship that came from Davis's education years was with Ed Stewart, who eventually became deputy in the premier's office. Had it not been for a chance meeting in Toronto in 1956, he likely would have become an education official in Windsor, not Ontario's most powerful bureaucrat.

Born in Montreal in 1930, the son of Scottish immigrants, his father came to Canada in 1923, returned to Scotland in 1925 to marry his childhood sweetheart, then moved back to Montreal. When the Depression hit, his father was out of work, so in 1933 Ed and his mother moved back to Scotland for a year while his father went job hunting. He found work in a small auto plant in Windsor and brought the family back to stay. Stewart's brother and sister were born twelve and fourteen years later, after the Depression, when his parents could afford to feed more mouths.

Stewart went to public and secondary school in Windsor, then to normal school in London (later called teacher's college), and at nineteen began teaching Grades 3 and 4 in his old neighborhood school. At one point his own brother was one of his pupils. He enrolled in night and summer school at Assumption College (now the University of Windsor), got his BA there, took his MA across the river at the University of Michigan, and in 1960 earned his doctorate in education at the University of Toronto. He prefers to be called "Dr. Stewart."

A confirmed workaholic whose only passion outside his job is the Detroit Tigers and U.S. college football, his career changed course in 1956 when he was sent by the Windsor Teacher's Association to the annual Ontario Educational Association conference in Toronto. He chanced to meet two friends from his Michigan class on the subway steps near the Royal York Hotel. They invited him to join them, and there he met Harold Blanchard, one of two principals at Toronto Teacher's College. Shortly afterward Stewart got married, took a job offer from Blanchard, and moved to Toronto. Four years later it led to a job in education's professional development branch, and he was on his way.

In 1964 the operating and capital branches of the ministry topped $100 million. "That looks like chicken feed today [it's now well over $5 billion], but it was a momentous occasion then." Before the 1960s universities had been primarily supported by private funds and tuition fees, but then the province moved in with the big dollars, and Stewart was in the university affairs branch when it was small.

Stewart first met Davis at Christmas, 1962, when the minister was making the rounds to wish his staff a merry Christmas. A few years later the branch became a separate ministry, and Stewart was named assistant deputy minister, university affairs. Then in 1967 Davis made him deputy minister. He was thirty-six.

* * *

Davis didn't spend much time at Queen's Park in the 1960s, but then neither did most delegates to the upcoming leadership campaign. "He got to be popular out on the road," says Darcy McKeough, "and in caucus, too, because if you wanted a minister to appear at your local riding function, Bill was always the guy, and people liked him. He could always explain things well, and calmly."

A scene duplicated across the province was witnessed by Bob Harris, later the party's executive director, who was in high school in 1965 when his parents invited Davis to their couples club at Victoria Presbyterian Church in Toronto's west end. "He was a well-established minister by then, but they invited him and he came. There were maybe forty couples there." Davis chatted informally with Harris's mother, who mentioned she had a daughter in Grade 13. "He had talked to everybody, had dinner, given a speech, and on the way out he turned to my mother and said he wished Jane good luck and hoped she got her scholarship. It really impressed them that he could remember something personal like that and take time to mention it. After that you couldn't say enough about Bill Davis in our house."

But all the credits he accumulated as the well-travelled minister, throwing money and soothing words as he went, almost counted for nothing over a politically disastrous event that wasn't even his fault. Davis was in Europe when John Robarts asked deputy minister J. R. McCarthy to give him an education speech for a testimonial dinner in Cambridge for veteran Speaker Allan Reuter, a speech with some "zip" in it. McCarthy had been pushing for county school boards, but Davis, having already felt the sting of reducing school boards to a township or larger, recognized the political dangers. The Ontario Committee on Taxation had encouraged more school board amalgamation, and while Davis didn't disagree in principle, he wanted to move cautiously.

But there was nothing cautious about Robarts that night in November, 1967, when he simply announced the system of county school boards. Davis returned from Europe faced with the task of working out the details and bearing the brunt of the political fallout. In 1968 Davis called for thirty-eight county boards in southern Ontario, the five existing local boards and the Metro board in Toronto, plus separate boards in Hamilton, London, Ottawa, and Windsor. "They were an enormous upset and worry," says Darcy McKeough. "Bill used to say he needed another $80 million to make it work, but [treasurer Charles] MacNaughton cut him back, and that created a lot of the problems."

So many problems that they nearly derailed the Davis leadership express.

CHAPTER 6
ESTABLISHMENT MAN

A t 2:30 a.m. on February 13, 1971, amid the pandemonium at Toronto's Maple Leaf Gardens, John Robarts shook hands with Bill Davis, patted him on the shoulder, and said, "Billy boy, I'm proud of you. I have now achieved my objective: I am a has-been."

And so the Davis era began.

It almost didn't. Davis, the man everybody figured only had to show up at the convention to win, took four ballots to do it and even then just made it by a heart-stopping forty-four votes over the onrushing Mines Minister Allan Lawrence. The shock waves from that experience were to have a profound effect on the new premier, providing the spark to ignite the legendary Big Blue Machine and transforming Davis from a baggy-pants kid from Brampton to boss of the slickest political machine in the country.

It shouldn't have been close. Davis had been a hero during the halcyon days of the 1960s and was, next to Robarts, by far the most widely travelled and best-known politician in Ontario. He was popular with his caucus, the opposition, the media, and the public. He had such a handle on his complex ministry that once, taking part in an open-line radio show, the department had twelve experts connected to him by telephone in case he was asked something he couldn't answer. He didn't need them.

So why was it close? Two reasons, really: county school boards and Davis's lacklustre campaign. Lawrence's campaign, despite the shortcomings of the candidate, was brilliant.

Tom Wells supported Lawrence, one of only four cabinet ministers who didn't go with Davis. For him, "It was one of the most difficult decisions I ever had to make. I knew him well. I'd worked with him . . . but the big thing at the time, it was not an anti-Davis feeling, but just a feeling that the whole thing looked so stacked. It was as if every member of caucus was expected to sign up and be on his side, which almost all of them did. But they used to continually bring out this list. It was like we were marching down to a coronation. I just didn't like that . . . but the whole thing turned out well; it caused the shock that led to necessary changes. If it had gone ahead in the lackadaisical, ho-hum coronation style, the complacency which had set in might have been a disaster later on in the election."

Davis was the first candidate in the race, making it official on December 21, 1970, two weeks after Robarts had announced his retirement. Lawrence was almost first out of the gate; his aides had told the press gallery their man would hold a press conference right after Robarts ended his, and Lawrence was actually seen hanging around outside the studio while the premier met with reporters. But a Robarts aide took him aside, told him "This is John's day," and Lawrence, who later claimed he had only meant to congratulate Robarts, cooled his heels until after Christmas.

Davis was the Establishment Man going in. No doubt. He was twenty-five pounds heavier then, a chubby-faced, cigar-puffing man who was seen essentially as an extension of Robarts's "chairman of the board" management style. Not that Robarts wasn't admired; he was. But some Tories, quite a few as it turned out, were looking for something different, some sizzle to go with their steak. And there were other rumblings outside the Establishment about the heir apparent.

Davis's move to abolish tiny school boards in the early 1960s had stirred up some discontent, but nothing compared to the rage he'd caused by centralizing the county school boards. Nobody did a survey, but one Tory official at the time estimated that 80 per cent of the township school board officials displaced by the larger, centralized county boards were Tories. Many of them were delegates to the convention and were not inclined to reward the man who had plucked their local plum.

Another powerful figure in cabinet then was Municipal Affairs Minister Darcy McKeough. Davis was so concerned about McKeough's candidacy that he approached him personally about it. "He came back to my little apartment on Walmer Road . . . a very difficult thing for Bill," says McKeough. "He doesn't ask for things easily. He even had a drink, which really amazed me, and he sort of blurted out that he was going to run and asked if I'd support him. I didn't know at the time what I was doing, so I really didn't give him an answer."

McKeough, scion of a wealthy Chatham family, was at thirty-seven the youngest man in cabinet. He had all the credentials of a blue-blood: right family, right schools (like Ridley College), and right marriage, to Joyce Walker, daughter of Conservative Senator David Walker. He was also perceived as a blustery right winger, a no-nonsense guy who might just be the one to turn around the Davis penchant for free spending. McKeough, known as the "Duke of Kent," duly entered the race at a Sunday evening press conference on January 3, 1971, in his office at Bay and College. He didn't have much cabinet or caucus support, but he did enlist media moguls Douglas Bassett and Ted Rogers, Toronto developer Murray Webber, and former Manitoba Premier Duff Roblin's executive assistant, Joe Martin.

Next day Bert Lawrence, forty-seven, an eastern Ontario favorite son who held the financial and commercial affairs portfolio, also joined the race. He was personally admired and respected, but was never seen as a serious threat to the front-runners.

Except for student Robert Pharand, a nuisance candidate, Provincial Secretary Robert Welch, forty-two, was the last of the candidates to declare, jumping in on January 8. He was immediately accused of being too much of a "consensus candidate" for his refusal to discuss policy issues on the odd grounds that if he were elected on the basis of particular policies, it would undermine the authority of cabinet to make decisions. Welch, a dynamic speaker and Anglican lay preacher, also lacked official support, but put on a surprisingly credible show.

Two days earlier, in a large, decorated room at the Westbury Hotel, jammed with dozens of sparkling young men and women and complete with beautiful hostesses pouring coffee for reporters, Allan Lawrence and his wife, Moira, arrived to the staged applause of a large "rent-a-cheerer" section, clearly signalling the American-style tone of his leadership run. "Winning is just the beginning" was the catchy campaign theme.

The key man in the room with him was known nationally for running Robert Stanfield's successful 1967 leadership campaign: Norm Atkins, the soft-spoken president of Camp Associates and brother-in-law of the fabled Dalton Camp.

It was Atkins more than any other man — certainly more than Lawrence himself — who made the leadership fight what it was. Ironically, Atkins had first asked to work for Davis. "They knew we were interested," Atkins said. "Maybe they thought they didn't need us, or maybe it was just basically that the people behind Davis had their own ideas." Whatever the reason, Davis's troops didn't invite Atkins and his friends into their confidence.

Shortly after Robarts had announced he was leaving, Atkins and several friends, including Lawrence and Paul Weed, who ran a collection agency at the time, met at the Albany Club to discuss the situation. It was a meeting of what Atkins called the "Eglinton Crowd," some high-powered Tories who were feeling left out and looking for a project that would channel their energies. It included such people as Don Guthrie, a lawyer who had acted as Stanfield's personal representative in Ontario, stockbroker Ross DeGeer, insurance broker Chad Bark, and investment counsellor William Saunderson. Camp pretty well stayed out of the contest except to show up and vote for Lawrence on the last ballot. The group had met originally at Guthrie's North Toronto house to talk about getting involved, but that was before Robarts announced he was leaving and before the Davis team rebuffed their overtures.

While the Lawrence team was made up of the Young Turks of the party, the Davis team represented the Entrenched Establishment. Treasurer Charles MacNaughton chaired his campaign organization, and John Latimer, who had worked with Davis in the 1961 Macaulay campaign, was campaign manager. Bill Kelly and Hugh Macaulay raised the money and were about the only part of the Davis team that excelled. The committee included Paul McNamara, owner of the Ports of Call restaurant, Ron Webb, Davis's neighbor and former law partner, and John Gillies, who took leave as a communications man in education to handle press liaison for Davis. There were also two men from James Lovick Advertising, Robert Byron and Ab Mellor. Both took a leave of absence from their firm to help out and for their troubles ended up losing the lucrative government ad accounts to Atkins.

"It was just one of those campaigns where everything started to take off," said Atkins. "We got the momentum going, everything fell into place, and it made [Lawrence] a credible challenger. It developed into a kind of 'challenge the Establishment' thing."

Indeed, at the first all-candidates meeting, Allan Lawrence hammered away at education spending and painted himself as the hope of the future. Davis, with the silly slogan, "The New Wave," hated the all-candidates meetings. As the clear favorite, he was the one who had to look like the next premier. (The seven meetings — the first time the Tories had tried the format — were organized by Arthur Harnett, executive director of the party. When Davis won, Harnett's days were numbered.)

Alan Eagleson, who later gained fame as a hockey agent and promotor of the Canada-Russia hockey series, was in charge of the convention. He had been elected in a Toronto riding in 1963, but had lost to New Democrat Pat Lawlor in 1967. Always the hustler, Eagleson had bucked the Establishment to become party president.

Eagleson consistently bragged that this would be the most open, democratic convention in the party's history, and for the most part it was, although there were a dozen or so cases of not following the clear-cut party constitution on choosing delegates. Each riding was alloted ten delegates and ten alternates, to be chosen at an open delegates meeting, and each delegation had to include four men, four women, and two YPCs, or, failing that, two delegates under age thirty. Most ridings complied, but some didn't, notably Lorne Henderson's Lambton riding where "Lorno," a massive hulk of a man, held his riding's delegate meeting privately in the kitchen of his farmhouse. In other ridings delegates were chosen by the party executive. Overall, the YPCs were underrepresented, sparking a convention-floor fight that, given the youth appeal of the Lawrence campaign, undoubtedly helped Davis and hurt Lawrence.

"Davis had almost everybody in his camp," says McKeough.

"I don't think anybody took me or Bobby Welch or Bert Lawrence very seriously, and there was really an awful lot of worry about Al Lawrence. There was a lot of negative feeling about him which turned into support for Bill. . . . [Lawrence] was always a little wild. He really led the revolt internally on the police bill thing, and when the smoke cleared away from all that, Arthur Wishart came in and essentially put through practically the same bill. It embarrassed a lot of party people, many of whom thought Al had overreacted. But Al is very much an overreactor . . . and therefore is a person not to be trusted with leadership, a person to be kept on a short leash."

During the campaign, no one said anything particularly radical. Lawrence continued to attack education spending and centralization of power, and Davis . . . well, his speeches were horrid.

"He said absolutely nothing," recalls McKeough. "He gave incredibly bad speeches. He made only one good one, in Thunder Bay, but that was it." Before that speech the Davis camp, increasingly worried about the onrushing Lawrence, had hired Bill Gold, a former reporter then with the public relations firm of Hopkins Hedlin Ltd. The speech marked the first time Davis had replied to Lawrence's attacks on education, but more important, it was the first public indication of just how worried the Davis people were.

On February 4, six days before the convention opened, the *Toronto Telegram* published a poll of delegates showing Davis ahead with 392, Lawrence next at 197, Welch 187, McKeough 146, and Bert Lawrence 81. The other 745 delegates were undecided, a psychological blow to Davis, who had assumed from the outset he would win handily. But to do that, he would need over 800 of the expected 1,600 delegates. While the poll showed him leading, it was a far cry from the numbers he needed to win.

During the campaign Lawrence travelled to more ridings than any other candidate, was more aggressive — some delegates complained he was too brash — and easily put on the best show at the convention itself. Atkins conducted several polls of party attitudes in the last few weeks of the campaign and structured Lawrence's speeches to coincide with party desires for a new image, although not a radical departure. Atkins also discovered that Lawrence wasn't as well known as Davis, so to compensate he ordered the largest number of posters and put them up first, in the best spots. He also scooped everyone else with a giant calypso bash at the Royal York Hotel on the eve of the convention, catching the other candidates off-guard. They hadn't planned anything because of the tribute for Robarts that night, so delegates arriving in the big city looking for some action had nowhere else to go.

Lawrence was much better on television than Davis, probably because he spoke in short, clipped sentences, while Davis rambled on so long that by the time he got to his point, the news item was over. To take advantage of this skill, Atkins stationed television monitors around showing clips of Lawrence responding to an interviewer (paid, although the viewer wouldn't know that) and coming across extremely well.

There were the usual efforts to entice delegates — meetings and heart-to-hearts in hotel rooms and at the Gardens — and other techniques like picking up room tabs and supplying hookers, things nobody will admit to but were being done just the same. And there was booze everywhere, even in the hospitality suites of the temperate Davis. One Toronto reporter, renowned for his consumption of the stuff, was sent to cover the convention. He didn't file anything for two days, although he was seen at one point sitting fully clothed in a bathtub of ice and Baby Duck in McKeough's Royal York hospitality suite.

The nomination speeches went off as scheduled on the Thursday evening, with about eight thousand people on hand to hear them. When the delegates arrived on that cold, blustery Friday, the chairs had been removed from the arena floor and replaced by twelve voting machines, another innovation by Eagleson and Harnett that the Davis people did not like.

Each candidate was given a block of seats and a telephone and headsets connected to their headquarters bunkered beneath the stands. Again Atkins was ahead of the pack with his sophisticated system of phone banks and transmitter-receivers, overseen by Wells from a balcony high above the floor, giving him a strategic view of who was lobbying whom on the floor itself.

The delegates had gone through several dry runs on how to use voting machines. The American machines were rented from a well-known Liberal, Thomas "Windy" O'Neill, who had the Canadian franchise for them. They were supposed to save at least an hour for each ballot, and the convention was set for a dramatic, prime-time ending televised live across the province.

The gods, alas, were not in the mood to co-operate. Voting began shortly after 3 p.m. and took about an hour. While everyone awaited the results, it soon became obvious that something had gone wrong. Key members of each campaign were seen scurrying to the back of the stage and then to their candidate's box, prompting animated discussions and more rushing back and forth.

Harnett, who co-chaired the convention with Eagleson, had made the deal with O'Neill for the twelve machines. Not only did the Davis people not trust the machines, but for reasons never explained they also suspected Eagleson and Harnett of being in league with the Lawrence camp. They weren't, but as Harnett explained, "Emotions run pretty high at these things. We were getting the machines ready for the second ballot when one of them broke down. Just one. MacNaughton challenged the whole system. He literally grabbed me by the throat backstage and said, 'You son of a bitch, if those machines don't get working and I find out you cooked those goddamn machines, you're finished.' To this day Bob Welch feels he didn't get the support he should have because northern delegates had to catch a plane to go back home. In fact, there were just eleven delegates who didn't vote on the final ballot."*

In any event, the convention had to be told. Eagleson went onstage and announced the machines weren't operating properly, and the candidates, campaign managers, and scrutineers went off to the board room at the west end of the arena to hammer out their next move. In the meantime, word had slipped out about the results of the first ballot, and although obviously not accurate, they did serve as an indicator that Davis by no means had it locked up. The results, later nullified, were: Davis 502, Allan Lawrence 379, McKeough 251, Welch 239, Bert Lawrence 152, and student Robert Pharand 13.

While the candidates and their camps exchanged recriminations in the board room, Ontarians across the province watching the convention on television were likely not impressed by

---

*Actually, 1,657 voted on the first ballot compared to 1,580 on the fourth, a drop of 77 delegates.

the spectacle. If the Tories couldn't run their own convention, how could they run the province? The NDP, taking advantage of this mood, sent Eagleson a telegram offering lessons in operating the machines, and Tory Senator David Walker told a television crew that given the political affiliation of O'Neill, the whole thing was probably a Liberal plot. Walker later had to apologize publicly in order to avoid a lawsuit. As for O'Neill, it took him several months to collect his $6,000 rental fee, which he received only because he settled for less than the original amount.

At about 6:15, three hours after voting had begun, a sheepish Eagleson announced that the first ballot had been cancelled and another one would be held, without machines, in about an hour. "We had to go and print the ballots," said Harnett. "We had to get typewriters in, hire people to type out the names. It was a horror show. We printed the ballots behind the stage on a Gestetner. It took about an hour and a half to print about 6,000 ballots. It could have been an utter disaster, but Eagleson saved it."

Finally, at about 7:40, voting resumed. When the numbers were posted on the giant scoreboard at the back of the stage, they read: Davis 548, Allan Lawrence 431, McKeough 273, Welch 270, Bert Lawrence 128, Pharand 7.

According to the rules, the low man was automatically dropped, which meant Pharand, but Bert Lawrence quickly told Eagleson that he, too, was dropping out. Davis walked over and shook hands with him, but when he tried to give him a campaign button Lawrence refused it. Allan Lawrence, sitting right next to his namesake's section, made no move himself, but many of his supporters moved in and mixed with the Bert Lawrence people, waving placards to make it appear that Bert had gone over to Al. He hadn't.

It was 10 p.m. when the second ballot began and after 11 when the results were posted: Davis 595, Lawrence 498, McKeough 288, Welch 271. Welch and McKeough held an emergency meeting at McKeough's insistence in Welch's headquarters under the stands, but Welch took the position that he wasn't making any deals, thereby killing any hope McKeough had of coming up the middle. While McKeough was inside, Lawrence and Davis both waited out in the hall, but neither man got to meet with him. He just left the room and went back to his box, without acknowledging either of the front-runners.

On the next ballot Davis gained only 74 votes for 669, while Lawrence gained 108 for a total of 606 — just 63 votes behind Davis. McKeough got 346 and had obviously become the kingmaker. "When I was going off the ballot then, Davis phoned and said, 'Can I talk to you?' I said, 'We've got nothing to talk about,' and for an instant he was really shaken. Then I added, 'We settled all that the night before Christmas in my apartment. I'm on my way over.'"

That ended it. When McKeough walked over to Davis and locked arms with him at 12.45 a.m., there was still one ballot to go, but everybody knew the battle was over. Witnessing McKeough's move, Clare Westcott, who had nine children already, shouted, "I'm naming my next four kids Darcy."

Lawrence's people had tried to get to McKeough, but he wasn't interested. About five minutes before his show of support for Davis, Lawrence and his key workers headed to the McKeough box behind their envoy, John McLean, Lawrence's assistant floor manager. It was McLean's fourth attempt to strike a deal with McKeough, and this time he approached Energy and Resources Minister George Kerr, McKeough's only cabinet supporter. He asked Kerr if he wanted to see Lawrence or Wells, both of whom were swiftly approaching the McKeough camp. Kerr replied, "I don't especially want to see either of them." McLean turned and relayed the message to Lawrence, who turned back without speaking to McKeough.

McKeough's band suddenly showed up in front of the Davis box, and while McKeough and Davis held their locked arms in the air, everybody sang "For He's a Jolly Good Fellow," and many McKeough workers slapped Davis stickers on themselves. At the north end of the Gardens, the Lawrence troops tried gamely to out-sing the Davis troops, but their balloon had been pricked. For all that, Lawrence still had a slim chance, but the final tally was Davis 812, Lawrence 768.

Lawrence, as is the custom in these affairs, moved it be unanimous. Davis, in a brief speech, thanked all his workers and his opponents and said, "I make no promises tonight except this — to maintain the principles, the integrity, of our party, to recognize the necessity to move forward, to adapt to those changes that are necessary for our society and, most important, to recognize the needs of it . . ."

Gramsy Davis took her five grandchildren home, with little Meg clinging to her "Vote for Daddy" placard, while Bill and Kathleen headed to the Ports of Call.

It was 4:20 a.m. before Davis danced with his wife. He danced with a couple of campaign workers, too, and then, with Kathleen carrying two dozen red roses, the couple went out the door through the heavy snow to their waiting limousine and headed off for a restful weekend in Brampton.

David had won, but that's all. It was over for him now. But it had really only just begun.

CHAPTER 7
THE BIG BLUE MACHINE

In addition to a university football team, law degrees, and a political party, Roy McMurtry and Bill Davis have something else in common: bad backs.

It was McMurtry's back that kept him from playing an active role in the leadership bids of either Davis or Allan Lawrence, making him the perfect person to bring the two sides together for a truce. He was at the convention but spent most of it lying on a bench in the director's lounge. With close friends in both camps, a spinal operation saved him from choosing sides.

After the convention, Davis holidayed briefly in Florida, using the apartment of his friend Gerhard Moog (about whom more later). Davis knew enough about the realities of politics to understand the need for burying hatchets, and so it was, two weeks after the convention, that the night of reconciliation — or, if you were on the other side, the night of the long knives — began at the National Club.

McMurtry was closer to the Lawrence camp, something that no doubt affected the outcome. But it was clear to him that the Lawrence people bore no ill will toward Davis and that it was in Davis's interest to get them aboard his team. Davis had asked McMurtry to arrange the dinner as quickly as possible. Lawrence wasn't on the guest list, but his key workers were.

"It was an interesting experience," said McMurtry. "Here you had five or six guys from each camp who came to have dinner, just a couple of weeks after the convention. It was not easy to get them to sit down at the same table together; that's one of Bill Davis's great strengths, you know. He had these guys . . . who'd nearly cost him his leadership, and he just had the sort of capacity to put that behind him or at least appear to put that behind him. If anything, I expect a few of the Davis loyalists were pretty annoyed. Those guys had worked hard to get him elected leader, had been involved in the key positions, but Davis had the good judgment and maturity to know that in politics, you can't afford the luxury of continually waging these battles."

Norm Atkins, who three days after the convention publicly called on Davis to make Lawrence his "second in command," said there wasn't "a lot of hostility" at the dinner, although there was more from the Davis supporters than the Lawrence troops. Davis told them the convention was over, an election was coming, and he needed everybody's help to win. "That's how he started," said Atkins. "It really broke down the barriers. . . . He was pretty impressive, and it certainly encouraged me to be supportive. I found out that night we had a number of areas of common interest — football, boating. And the other thing I found out that night was that he's a great admirer of Stanfield, and of course, I was. It was just after the War Measures Act [Atkins helped sponsor a book by Flora MacDonald against it], and I said to Bill Davis, 'I was one of the fifteen per cent who opposed it,' and he said, 'So was I.' That did it for me."

The amazing thing about that night is that Davis enjoyed it so much that afterward he actually went with the others to Stop 33 at the top of the Sutton Place Hotel, saying, "I'm not going to have many opportunities to do things like this once I'm sworn in."

And it was, after all, an occasion to celebrate: It was the birth of the Big Blue Machine.

*   *   *

Norm Atkins likes to call himself "just a poor boy from Jemseg, New Brunswick, Queen's County." He's a bit more than that. But he's not really what you would expect for a guy who has managed so many slick campaigns.

A squat, husky man, he speaks softly, avoids the jargon of

the advertising industry, and lives in the modest home in suburban Markham he and his wife, Anna Ruth, A.R. for short, bought twenty years ago because they couldn't afford Toronto prices. They could now, but Atkins enjoys the drive to his office in a trendy, grey-stone office development at Yonge and Davisville. His licence plate reads NORMAN, a gift from his three sons.

Like Davis, Atkins is a private man. "Who wants to be discovered completely?" he asked during a break as national campaign chairman for the awesome federal Tory sweep in 1984. "I don't, do you? Neither does Bill Davis."

Atkins was born in 1934 in Glen Ridge, New Jersey. His father, George Spicer Atkins, like so many Maritimers, had left Spencer's Island, Nova Scotia, looking for work, moving eventually to his mother's place on Brooklyn's Flatbush Avenue, within earshot of Ebbett's Field. When he was a boy his father took him regularly to the Polo Grounds to watch the Giants play. Atkins's father was a timekeeper on the piers, then opened a chocolate company but lost the business during the Depression. Atkins's brother George lives in New Jersey; his sister Linda is Dalton Camp's ex-wife.

When Atkins was twelve, he was sent to Appleby College in Oakville, graduating from there and going on to Acadia University. He was an American citizen then, and he was drafted, serving in Fort Benning, Georgia, and Schweinsberg, West Germany, before being discharged as a corporal in August, 1959. The next month he became production manager of Camp Associates, which he took over in 1968. Camp himself remained active in the firm until 1972.

Atkins's first political activity was running errands for Camp in the 1952 New Brunswick election when Hugh John Flemming upset veteran Liberal premier John B. McNair. And as a student at Acadia University in 1953, he helped in Nova Scotia when Bob Stanfield ran against Liberal legend Angus L. Macdonald. Three years later, after Macdonald had left, he helped again when Stanfield won. He also worked with Camp in New Brunswick on the "Carry on Hugh John" campaign (Camp's slogan). In 1957 he and Camp worked the Maritimes for Diefenbaker, but he missed the 1958 campaign because of army duty.

In 1960 Atkins again worked for Stanfield—his first full-time effort — and went right from there to another New Brunswick campaign. But Flemming lost to Liberal Louis Robichaud over the issue of health premiums, which the Tories favored. "There probably is a lesson there," Atkins later said.

Atkins was active in the 1962 and 1963 federal elections, helped Camp with the national Tory presidency in 1964, and was Camp's campaign manager in Eglinton in 1965 and Don Valley in 1968, both losing efforts to entrenched Liberals. During the 1967 federal Tory leadership campaign, Atkins was convention chairman for Stanfield. In between he worked on provincial elections in Nova Scotia in 1963 and 1967 and for Manitoba's Duff Roblin in 1962. In 1970 he ran George Key's losing campaign in Prince Edward Island, a campaign he says taught him more than any other. "We did it without research, by instinct." He's never done that again.

Atkins's first foray into Ontario politics was the Lawrence leadership bid. He had met Davis briefly in the basement of the Park Plaza in 1963 when Davis was getting his shoes shined, but their next meeting was an all-candidates affair in January, 1971. Their third meeting was the National Club dinner two weeks after the convention. After that the relationship, both personal and business, was mutually beneficial. Atkins orchestrated the 1971 Davis sweep, was campaign manager again in 1975, was one of three co-chairmen (along with Hugh Macaulay and Eddie Goodman) in 1977, and was campaign chairman in 1981.

During that time Davis prospered politically. Camp Associates didn't exactly suffer, either. In the 1960s the province's tourism accounts, by far the most lucrative, had been handled mainly by Baker Lovick BBDO Ltd., which had inherited them from James Lovick Advertising. Many Lovick staffers had worked for Davis, but even though they had backed the winning horse, they didn't collect. Atkins did.

In 1971–72 Camp Associates had a $50,568 contract with Tourism and Information. A year later the Davis government's appreciation for its work grew, and Camp received $15,114 in work from Transportation, $56,137 from Natural Resources, and $1,429,278 from Industry and Tourism. The agency, of course, just keeps a percentage, but its share of government advertising has never stopped climbing: from $50,568 in 1971–72 to $7,905,996 in 1982–83, plus a $2 million-plus Bicentennial package. Atkins did so well that he set up a subsidiary called

Advance Planning, headed by Hugh Segal. In 1982–83 Advance received a $249,770 contract from Citizenship and Culture plus $29,153 from Labour and in 1984 submitted the winning proposal for a $400,000 campaign to promote women's issues.

Atkins says Davis had "almost total recall," was folksy on the hustings, and, yes, had "charisma . . . his tends to be more eclectic, though, not the awe-struck kind." Atkins considers Davis a personal friend, but "I don't know how anybody really knows him well, because he's too private a person to know well." Asked about Davis's shortcomings, Atkins said, "It's pretty hard for me to criticize Bill Davis."

We shouldn't wonder.

*   *   *

Two other key mechanics of the Big Blue Machine were Bill Kelly and Hugh Macaulay, both of whom shared an intense personal loyalty to Davis and a disdain for personal publicity.

At about the time Bill Davis became premier, Macaulay ran his yacht aground on a shoal about two hundred yards off the Davis cottage on Townsend Island. No one could hear his shouts for help, so Macaulay, who'd forgotten the cottage's unlisted telephone number, contacted Honey Harbour by marine radio. The message was relayed to the premier's Queen's Park office, then back to the cottage, so Bill and Neil Davis could rescue him.

Hugh Macaulay has not hit many such shoals in his life. He was just forty-four in 1969 when he sold York Mills Pontiac and a related car leasing firm for a reported $3 million and decided to retire from business. Two years later the new premier sent a confidential memo to party workers saying simply: "If you have any problems, see Hugh Macaulay." He has held a senior position in each election, and when Davis was looking for someone to take over Ontario Hydro — a perennial political problem — he tapped his friend Macaulay, who served as chairman from 1978 to 1983. He has also served on the Ryerson board of governors, the Ontario commission on post-secondary education, and more recently as head of the Toronto domed stadium study committee.

An intensely private man, Macaulay briefly wrote a column for the *Toronto Sun* but is not noted for his love of the media.

Early in the Davis regime he advised Davis against granting interviews to reporters who had been critical, advice that helped create an image of Davis as isolated and aloof. Macaulay was called "Mr. Balls" in those early days because, unlike Davis, he could make tough decisions.

Known to his close friends as "Chalky," a reference to his milk-colored pallor, he is a tall, handsome man, a former navy officer, and a 1948 graduate of the University of Western Ontario, where he was editor-in-chief of the student newspaper. His father, Leopold, was in the cabinets of two premiers, Howard Ferguson and George Henry, and twice ran for the party leadership, losing once to George Drew, the man who began the Tory dynasty. His brother, Bob, one of the stars of the Frost regime, ran for the leadership in 1961 with Bill Davis as his campaign manager. It was then that Davis and Hugh Macaulay became friends.

Macaulay scoffs at claims that he and some others had great influence on Davis. "Everybody has influence, and in the long run the decisions are his, good or bad. . . . He's his own man."

He says the Davis most Ontarians never saw is a warm, sensitive guy with a terrific sense of humor. "I remember a political meeting in the basement of his house in the 1971 election. There were eight or ten people there, the room was full of cigar smoke, and Cathy, his middle daughter, poked her nose in the door and kind of stage-whispered something to her father. So he said, 'Come in.' So while all this hot political storm was going on, she comes over and he puts his arms around her and she whispers in his ear and you see a big smile on his face and he sort of looks at her, and in a voice that can be heard all over the room he said, 'You want an increase in your allowance?' Well, the kid just went absolutely purple, but before it was all over he had her laughing and had everybody else in the room laughing, and the tension that was in the room before was all gone. You know, 99.9 per cent of the people of Ontario never see that side of Bill Davis. I think it's a marvellous quality."

One of the qualities of the Davis machine the public did recognize was its amazing success in raising money. There was one major reason for that record: Senator Bill Kelly.

Not long ago, a young boy knocked on Kelly's door in Ottawa requesting money for the Canadian Cancer Society. Kelly asked him how much he wanted, and the boy said, "Whatever you want to give." Kelly said he wanted to give a nickel. The boy said, "That's not very much," and Kelly asked again how much he wanted. "Give me an amount." So the boy said most people were giving $5 to $10, some up to $50. "He then said to me, 'Will you give me twenty-five dollars?' I said 'Yes,' and I told him, 'Son, the next door you go to, ask for an amount, and you'll be surprised how well you do.' "

That's the Kelly method: Be specific. It was one he made famous — or infamous, depending upon your point of view — in the early 1970s before donations had to be made public. Kelly said the only fund raising he'd ever done before was taking the collection in church. "It's true; I asked corporations for specific amounts. On the other hand, I showed the party's balance sheets to contributors. . . . I've always believed in asking for an amount. If they say it's too much, at least you've got something to work with."

Kelly was born in Georgetown in 1925. He had two brothers and two sisters, and his father, an executive with Abitibi Paper, was an active Liberal. "I was sixteen before I knew that 'damn Tory' was two words." His uncle was Duncan Marshall, the man who beat Tom Kennedy in Peel in 1934 and then became a senator.

Kelly wanted to become a professional soldier and left home in 1944 to join the infantry, serving at Camp Borden and Brockville and marrying his childhood sweetheart, Betty Paul. Kelly's grandfather, Col. A. E. Carpenter, commanded the Royal Canadian Regiment in 1915, so Kelly planned to attend the Royal Military College. But he gave up the idea after the war, "because at that time the military was pretty heavy with guys full of decorations, and I didn't have any."

He left the army in 1946, took engineering at the University of Toronto, business at the University of Illinois, and the advanced management program at Harvard Business School. He joined Consumer's Gas in 1950, moved quickly up the ranks to senior vice-president, and left in 1971 to run his own firm. "One thing I learned very early was: No matter how high up you are in a big company, it's a consensus decision. I found that frustrating, so I got the board's permission to start my own business on the side so I would not have to do the endless consultation. If there was a business decision to make, it was mine to make."

He certainly did that. He bought what was a piece of swamp in Port Severn in 1960 and transformed it into a major marina storing two hundred boats in the winter with facilities to repair boats up to fifty feet long. He also has a fleet of fifty school buses to keep his marine mechanics busy year-round. In addition to Port Severn Boat Haven, Kelly operates W. M. Kelly Associates, Kelco Management Ltd., Health Assistance for Travellers Inc., and the PC Ontario Fund. He has a home near Davis in Fort Lauderdale, and his marina is within easy boating distance of Townsend Island.

He moved to Toronto in 1950 and began working for the Tories, getting involved in Bob Macaulay's 1961 leadership bid, where he met both Davis and Hugh Macaulay.

He raised over $100,000 for Davis's leadership campaign in 1971, an enormous sum then, and has since become a legend in the fund-raising business, the man who originated the toll-gate method and turned it into a year-round, full-time affair. John Robarts had paid no attention to financing, and when Davis took over, the party was broke. "In those days the parties used to operate on the basis of 'You crank up once every four years.' The NDP learned right from the start you don't do that. You run a good organization all the time, not just before elections."

Kelly was not surprised that he quickly became the bad guy in the piece. "Sure, it goes with the turf. It's a rocky road, but I haven't known a party fund-raiser who hasn't known some rocks along his road."

In those early years Kelly had a healthy share of rocks. He figured prominently in several controversial issues during the first Davis term, including the Fidinam and Shouldice affairs, and his name came up during the Hamilton dredging scandal when excerpts from the diary of a defendant contained references to both Kelly and Davis. In July, 1977, a retired Ontario Supreme Court judge investigated suggestions that political influence was sought to win Ontario Hydro contracts, and Kelly also testified at a 1978 royal commission inquiry into Waste Management Inc.'s controversial $35,000 donation to the Tories while the company was applying for a permit to operate a landfill site north of Toronto. The commission concluded there had been no wrongdoing.

Kelly raised about $5 million for the 1971 election campaign. In the 1975 campaign the party spent about $1.6 million, in 1977 $2.3 million, and about the same amount in 1981. He pushed for an end to confidentiality but met great resistance from the party. "People don't like secrets," he says, although heaven knows he's kept more than a few.

"Stephen Lewis used to love to say that if the Tory party ever disclosed its source of funds, Bill Kelly would be the first to go. That's why it was important to me that when disclosure came in, it showed how wrong Lewis was. The things we were being accused of just weren't true. I wanted disclosure, but a lot of businessmen didn't, and some of the party people thought donations would fall off."

Kelly says political parties have an obligation to spread their message in the best possible way, but "somebody has to pay for it. A political party has no God-given right to run up bills and not pay for them. Since somebody has to pay, somebody has to collect. Canvassing for bucks is the same type of responsibility as canvassing for votes. You can't win without them both."

*　　*　　*

When Atkins arrived at his office the day after the National Club dinner in 1971, there was a message to call Hugh Macaulay. The two men met later that day, and Macaulay asked Atkins if he'd help on the next election campaign. A week later Macaulay looked at a conceptual plan Atkins had drawn up, and a few days after that they showed it to Davis. Within a month Atkins was campaign manager.

Two weeks later the Monday morning breakfast club began (not to be confused with the Tuesday club). The originals were Atkins, McMurtry, Macaulay, and Westcott, meeting in the Royal Hunt Room at the Sutton Place Hotel, then changing venues to Theodore's, a steakhouse at Yonge and Eglinton. The group eventually got too large, and meetings were held every two weeks in a room at the Westbury Hotel listed in the hotel directory as "Hugh Macaulay's meeting room."

Out of the breakfast club came the decision to sell Davis as leader in the style in which Richard Nixon had been sold on television in 1968. It wasn't an easy task. American pollster Robert Teetor told the group that Davis was seen as ministerial grey. He found that 80 per cent of Ontarians knew Davis but didn't know much about him, so he suggested Davis do extensive travelling to generate media coverage and make some dramatic moves to show that he was not as dull as the public thought.

The members of the strategy group quickly resolved that they were going to run a television campaign, beaming Bill Davis into the living rooms of Ontario as an informal family man, a man who liked being with the kids at the cottage and going to football games and who, of course, had a dog. Often they invited key experts to their meetings from fields such as television, radio, the press, riding associations, films, and promotion. They were leaving nothing to chance or to instinct — as Atkins had done in P.E.I., only to discover his instinct was wrong.

Atkins was talking about a campaign that would cost $4.5 million, two and a half times Robarts's 1967 campaign budget and an enormous figure for the day. Bill Kelly, faced with a depleted treasury, promptly went out and raised over $5 million. Obviously, he was a hard man to say no to.

Kelly knew how much a company had been giving, and he knew how much the Tories needed, so he'd go to the company executive and show them two things: the party's budget and how much he felt the company could give. Johnathan Manthorpe later maintained that it went a bit further than that, although Kelly denies it. Manthorpe wrote in *The Power and the Tories* that a junior bagman who was responsible for about 250 Ontario companies — Kelly obviously couldn't go to them all — showed him a list given to him by senior Tories working with Kelly.

"Down the left-hand side of the lists were the names of the companies. Down the centre of the pages was a column headed 'Business Record,' and there were entries after about 15 per cent of the company names. The fund-raiser explained that this referred to the amount of government business the companies had received. . . . On the right-hand side of the pages was another column headed 'Donation Record,' and there were entries for nearly all the companies. The entries in this column were in code, but they set out what the company had given at the last election and what it was expected to give this time."

Kelly did his job so well that most candidates were guaranteed

$12,000 from the party to help them in the election, an unheard-of figure until that time and more than double what candidates could have expected from the Robarts machine.

Out of the Westbury sessions was born Ad Hoc Enterprises, a secret advertising agency originated by Atkins. It eventually set up shop at 461 Church Street in downtown Toronto and involved experts from five different advertising agencies, all sworn to secrecy. The office was directly above the studio of Film Arts, which handled the campaign's extensive film work. The firm created brochures, posters, matchbooks, commercials — everything needed to run an American-style campaign, not just for the leader but for every candidate.

In the spring Ad Hoc film crews followed Davis everywhere, poking their cameras in on his "meet the people" excursions, filming him with his family — great stuff for the free-time broadcasts TV stations offered to help them meet their Canadian content rules. The campaign that emerged featured such scenes as Davis walking pensively beside a lake or reacting warmly to his children.

The opposition and the media criticized the Tories for creating a leadership cult, but Macaulay told the *Toronto Star*, "The news media has been responsible for producing leadership-oriented voters. Whether we like it or not, it is a fact of life. The media will say, 'Davis did that,' when it may well be the whole government . . . behind a decision. On television news all the focus is on the individual leader."

The other man who became active on the Davis team over that first year was the Great Guru, Dalton Camp. He had pretty well stayed out of the leadership race, but after the ballots had been counted, he showed up to collect some of the gravy, a good portion of which was already spilling over to Camp Associates.

McKeough says Dalton Camp's influence during the early going was enormous. "I was summoned over to Bill's office during my first budget, and Camp was there. He was going to tell me how to write a budget. I didn't take too kindly to that. He was telling me what was going to be in it. I remember him saying there's a lot of money in lotteries, which of course came ten years later. He had a lot to say at that point, especially on Spadina."

The Spadina expressway, that is. Two major events marked Davis's first year: his refusal to extend aid to separate schools and stopping the Spadina.

Acting on Teetor's advice to change his image to that of a modern sophisticate, a man leading the parade of concerned citizens on the environment and saving the cities for the folks, Davis first banned logging in Quetico Park. That pleased a few naturalists, but it annoyed loggers in the north and didn't really catch on as a sexy political issue.

Spadina did. Metro Toronto had been building the expressway from Downsview in the northwest to the downtown area since the early 1960s. It was proceeding all right until it got within sight of the City of Toronto limits, when it became a rallying point for every lefty, ten-speed environmentalist in town, provoking a war between the city and North York that is still raging.

The Stop Spadina Save Our City Co-ordinating Committee had been actively fighting the proposed expressway for a decade. The people in the 700,000 cars and 100,000 trucks who came and went from the suburbs to downtown every day were agitating for the expressway, but as usually happens in citizen movements, the opponents were organized and vocal, while the proponents were not. Those who favored the expressway had a few effective representatives, particularly Esther Shiner (who later became a controller in North York on the strength of her showing), but most of them assumed it was going to be built. After all, Metro Council had ended a bitter debate on it by voting overwhelmingly to build the damn thing, and after a long hearing the Ontario Municipal Board had voted 2–1 to build it. Until then cabinet had never overturned a major OMB decision.

Years earlier the Conservative government — many of the same ministers, in fact — had signed a deal with Metro concerning the Yorkdale shopping centre. The province had agreed to build a combined expressway and rapid transit line, so the huge "spaghetti junction" was built beside the shopping centre at Highway 401, and construction began on the Spadina expressway. The OMB had approved the expressway initially in 1963, when Davis was in cabinet, and no one had objected.

Davis claims politics did not enter into the decision. "I have never had to make an important decision that went against my personal convictions. I honestly didn't know whether this was good politically or not." He did once say that the decision was "not made because of its technical merit," quickly adding that if he were quoted, "I'll deny it." He *was* quoted, several times, but never denied it.

The strategists knew what the political impact of Spadina would be. Teetor had convinced them they needed a move to transform Davis into a decisive, modern, ecology-minded leader. There weren't many issues with that potential, but Spadina had it and they knew it. And so Davis stood in the legislature on June 3, 1971, and made what is now an historic "people versus cars" speech, as if cars were going to be coming down the expressway without people in them. "The streets belong to the people," he said. "The city does not belong to the automobile."

When the announcement was made, Darcy McKeough was in London, England on business and found himself at a cocktail party with John Robarts, George Kerr, and H. Ian Macdonald, then deputy minister of economics and later president of York University. "Kerr came in and said he'd just been talking to his home, and Spadina was just turned down. I remember Robarts saying, 'Jesus Christ.' We were just amazed," said McKeough. "When we left a few days earlier, it was going ahead. Camp certainly wrote the speech, and they had that Teetor poll. If you could have polled the day before and the day after all over Ontario, Davis would have gone up enormously. I remember during the election campaign saying, 'Davis is the guy who told Toronto they couldn't have the Spadina.' That was just great around the province, although one day it will have to be built at ten times the cost."

Spadina had been discussed by cabinet regularly in March and April, the last time on a Friday morning in late May. "We concluded we shouldn't overturn the OMB," said McKeough. "That was the first major one. Now, of course, they do it all the time. But Al Lawrence had gone into the House, and I was sitting right beside Davis. [Allan] Grossman was beside me. He'd been fighting it, but he leaned right across me, right across my gut, and said to Davis, 'Okay. We're prepared to accept it reluctantly, but don't make it final until Al Lawrence is here and you get his name on the line.' It was really a question of announcing it that morning and getting it out of the way, or waiting. Bill said, and I remember this, 'We've made a decision, but we'll reflect on it and won't announce it for a while.' Then the next thing I hear, they stopped it."

Camp was so impressed with the decision that he wrote in his *Toronto Telegram* column that he was "one of the last to enlist in the Stop Spadina movement," but they hadn't expected to win, because they didn't know "what the measure of the man [Davis] truly was." He pooh-poohed critics who "alleged . . . the premier was playing politics" and congratulated Davis for his fine decision and fine words. He did not feel obliged to tell his readers that he had played a major role in the decision and had written those words.

Naturally, the voters in 1971 had no idea how costly the Spadina decision would be. Except to those commuters and truckers still fighting traffic—wasting gas and clogging up residential streets in the process — it seemed like a good idea at the time. Although a few years later the unpaved roadbed between Lawrence and Eglinton, popularly known as the "Davis Ditch," was in fact paved, the Spadina still ends at the city limits, a four-lane arterial roadway to nowhere.

The decision certainly broke the mould for Davis, making him appear the modern sophisticate. But that's not all he and his aides did to change his image. They bought him new suits. Gone were the baggy pants, the pregnant lapels, even the wide pinstripes. When Bill Davis arrived for his swearing-in ceremony on March 1, 1971 — the first time the public had been invited to such an event—he wore a new blue-striped, grey suit. And it wasn't long before hair stylist Stan Anderson was brought in to get rid of that old cowlick and the boyish wave in his hair.

Davis's first cabinet, sworn in the day he became premier, included his four leadership opponents in senior portfolios: Allan Lawrence became attorney general, McKeough treasurer, Bert Lawrence minister of health, and Bob Welch minister of education.

Davis's next move was to announce a $25 million lawsuit against Dow Chemical for mercury pollution, settled years later for what amounted to a promise of good behavior but good for lots of glowing headlines at the time of the announcement.

Then he started bopping around the province insisting everybody call him "Bill," although none of his closest advisers ever called him that. It was either "premier" or "sir" or "Mr. Davis." Hugh Segal remembers calling him "Bill" once: "The silence taught me what death must sound like to an atheist."

You could barely turn on the news at night without seeing Bill Davis skippering a tugboat in Hamilton harbor, eating corn at a picnic in Verona, falling off a buckboard in a parade in North

Bay (they can't all go the way they're supposed to), wearing a cowboy hat in Belleville, using a cross-cut saw and driving a pair of Percheron horses in La Passe, and, if you can believe it, donning a blond wig and pedalling around a racetrack in a girls' bicycle race in Windsor.

During an election-style trip to Sudbury in July (although no election had yet been called) Davis had twelve organizers, headed by former Lawrence man Ross DeGeer, to import four thousand schoolkids from area schools by bus, hand them Canadian flags, and encourage them to wave them while they sang "Ontari-ari-ari-o." Later that day a group of union leaders refused to meet Davis because he was surrounded by the Ad Hoc camera crew and they didn't want to be part of the Davis campaign. Aides dogged his every step, taking notes to suggest refinements. They even brought a portable podium along because they liked the way he projected from it. He was so orchestrated for media and public effect that Clare Westcott once quipped, "They even advance him when he goes to the bathroom." They probably did.

That same July night he told a large Tory gathering, "If pragmatism is all we want in Ontario, then we should hire a provincial manager, give him the keys to our purses and our institutions, and then go home and wait for him to empty the first and fill the second." He now boasts of his "pragmatism," and friends call it his greatest strength. But in 1971 he wasn't pragmatic; he was avant-garde, don't you know.

Davis would drop by Queen's Park periodically to make grand announcements, like the one on March 30 when he promised a $500 million housing program to create 30,000 homes and 132,000 jobs, targets the government never came close to matching.

In April he reorganized the office of the premier, making Westcott his special assistant and downgrading Keith Reynolds, who had been chief executive officer under Robarts. Reynolds lost his role as secretary of the cabinet but remained as deputy minister in the office. Davis split his office in two — one part dealing with cabinet matters, the other with general office duties. Carl Brannon was moved from secretary of the treasury board to secretary of the cabinet, and Tom Campbell, who had been secretary of the committee on government productivity, was brought in to work with Brannon. Whether these steps made the Davis office more efficient is hard to say, but it sure increased the staff and the cost. When Robarts became premier in 1963, he had a staff of twelve that grew over the years to thirty-eight. Davis added another dozen and bumped his budget by $264,000, a 60 per cent increase in one year.

On July 18 Davis introduced a bill giving eighteen-year-olds the right to vote, hold elected office, serve on juries, sign contracts, and drink legally (the last part was later upped to nineteen), a move that added 412,000 new voters in the fall election.

He also quietly established a powerful, thirteen-member inner council of cabinet designed to streamline cabinet business, weed out less pressing matters, and advise him on policies. Called the Policy and Priorities Committee (P and P), it was modelled after a federal cabinet group. Davis was chairman, and his four leadership opponents were on it, Allan Lawrence as vice-chairman.

He also hired a historian to determine which of the two terms, "prime minister" (which is what Robarts used) or "premier," was historically more accurate. University of Toronto historian Maurice Careless said it could be argued either way, so Davis opted for "premier," and the next day a man was outside Davis's office changing the sign on the doors to "Office of the Premier."

During Davis's first session as premier, his government introduced 137 bills, making it tougher for those sixteen to eighteen to go on welfare, instituting a detoxification program to help chronic drunks, lowering beer prices, providing a government air service (Nordair) for Northern Ontario residents, stopping the sale of Crown lands and giving preference to Canadians in leasing them, giving preference to Canadian-owned firms seeking government loans and grants, setting up a ministry of the environment, and stopping extra-billing by doctors (a measure that was never proceeded with).

Finally, in September, Davis set the election for October 21. At dissolution there were 68 Conservatives, 27 Liberals, 21 New Democrats, and one Independent. In case people hadn't noticed the presidential style, Davis said it would be a highly personalized campaign. Asked what the major issue would be, he said, "A question of leadership."

The polls looked good for Davis, but it didn't escape Tory strategists that governments had been thrown out in six of the eight provincial elections since 1969, most recently three weeks earlier when Peter Lougheed upset Socred Harry Strom in Alberta.

The Davis campaign used the largest airplane (a forty-eight-seat Viscount) and the most advance men (fourteen) in Ontario's political history. Two catering trucks followed the tour, stopping to make sandwiches or hot meals on the spot to save time and squeeze in more campaign stops. There were more pancake breakfasts and brief concerts by their band, Jalopy, than anyone could count. The tour began in Belleville, covered the entire province — including a Toronto visit to announce a 3 per cent provincial income tax cut — and wound up in Brampton on election night.

With the exception of the separate school protesters who dogged his footsteps, it was clear sailing for Davis. His main message at every stop was, "Hi there, I'm Bill." Then off he'd go again for more pancakes, more handshakes, and more songs — "Davis will make it go, go, Ontario, Davis will make it grow, come on, Ontario" — with one of those bouncy tunes that once you've heard you can't get out of your head.

All the while Atkins and Macaulay and their Big Blue Machine were busy churning out advertising and fine-tuning campaign slogans. Composer-arranger Ben McPeek was told to delete all references to the party from the campaign song: It had to "sell the man, sell Davis."

Everything was *Davis*, not the Conservative party. Local billboards, for example, exhorted, "Joe Blow for Bill Davis"; the party got a tiny credit line. Everything came in the red-and-blue-on-white color combination, including the goodies sent to local riding associations — pins, doorknob cards, sample brochures, calling cards, "vote at" cards, balloons, matchbooks, and T-shirt designs.

The television ads showed a windblown, casual, carefree Davis walking with his wife and dog along pollution-free lakefronts. A slick, full-color brochure devoted one of its thirteen pages to his family — six color shots of his wife in jeans and cardigan, his children, and his dog. Davis said in the text, "I guess you could say we are a political family. They'll campaign with me, and they'll be knocking on doors. They'd like me to win. Every family needs a dog. So do politicians. Ours is Thor. He cost $2.25 new. He's worth a million or so now." Funny. For a man with "a political family" in 1971, a few years later he would go to great lengths to

explain why and how he kept his family out of politics. Whatever sells.

The political family obviously sold, because when the votes
were counted, Davis had scored a decisive personal victory, winning 78 seats, a gain of nine, cutting the Liberals down from 27
to 20 and the NDP from 21 to 19. It was the largest number of
Tory seats since 1955, and the 72 per cent voter turnout was the
highest in forty years. It was Ontario's twenty-ninth election since
Confederation and the seventeenth Tory win, the ninth in a row.

Liberal leader Bob Nixon, who had predicted he would win
forty seats, experienced his second loss. The Liberals ads, created
by Jerry Goodis, posed the question in posters and on radio and
television: "Had enough?" and proposed the answer: "Vote Liberal." Apparently the voters hadn't had enough. Or perhaps
they thought about the answer and didn't like it.

It was the first try for NDP leader Stephen Lewis, more radical
then and much more suited to the role Davis set out for him as
the "socialist menace." At thirty-three Lewis showed his lack of
experience early in the campaign when, travelling through Hastings County in Tory eastern Ontario, he was asked why he would
waste his time campaigning in an area where New Democrats
were hard to find, let alone elect. Lewis said he had come "to
throw a few crackers at the animals." He improved considerably
next time out.

Davis was definitely on a roll. In November he attended a
federal-provincial economic conference and repeated over and
over that he was always an "optimist," while Ottawa kept turning down his proposals. However, when the last communiqué
was written, it included just about everything Davis had sought,
including a committee of finance ministers to review long-term
trends in the economy, a review of proposed taxation on international income, examination of federal credit proposals, and
a look at opting-out procedures in health and post-secondary
education. "I feel better today," he said when the conference
wound up. "I'm going away relatively content. I've retained my
traditional optimism."

Davis wrapped up what was a good year by unveiling the final
report of the committee on government productivity (COGP), recommending a major facelift for the government. The committee, set up by Robarts and chaired by John B. Cronyn, a director

and executive vice-president of John Labatt Ltd., churned out three interim reports on government structure during a two-year study, the final one in December, 1971.

In what amounted to major surgery for an ailing structure, the reports recommended cutting the size of the cabinet from twenty-three to twenty; creating three ministries in charge of policy development in broad groups — justice, social development, and environment and resources; setting up a ministry of finance and intergovernmental affairs with powers sweeping enough to make it the Number Two job in the cabinet; creating a management board with a chairperson who would be a cabinet minister and act like a general manager of government; setting up a new ministry of revenue; and assigning police functions to a ministry separate from the attorney general, leaving that post responsible for the judiciary. There were other proposed changes, too: At least six departments would be absorbed into others, and there would be no more ministers without portfolio, although the committee did recommend that cabinet ministers have parliamentary secretaries, culled from the government back benches.

Davis said he accepted "the general spirit and principle" of the changes and that he would be looking "very closely" at the report. All in all, he said, he was pleased. Indeed, he should have been pleased, not only with the report but also with 1971. Now all he had to concern himself with was Christmas at home with the family and a January holiday in their newly acquired Florida condominium.

Yes, things were looking good for Bill Davis. Very good. Too good to last.

CHAPTER 8

YEARS OF SCANDAL

The new year began on a happy note. Davis spent the post-Christmas season in Florida pondering his new cabinet and deciding to implement the COGP report. Then on January 5, 1972, with Davis still holidaying — Transportation Minister Charles MacNaughton filled in, the only time a premier has ever missed a full cabinet shuffle — he named his four major leadership challengers as "super ministers," a term Davis hated from the outset. As it turned out, the jobs weren't that super, but then neither were the next three years.

Darcy McKeough, at thirty-eight still the youngest man in cabinet, was the Number Two man, named to a powerful post called treasury, economics, and intergovernmental affairs (TEIGA), although he wasn't sworn in that day because legislation setting up his empire hadn't been approved. Allan Lawrence became provincial secretary for justice, Bob Welch provincial secretary for social development, and Bert Lawrence provincial secretary for resources development. In theory the three were in charge of groups of ministers within specified policy areas. But they soon became disenchanted, finding themselves sitting through question period without being asked anything while the ministers with traditional line jobs, supposedly their underlings, got all the media coverage.

Davis never did concede that the secretariats flopped, but in later years he often used the positions for ministers being punished, like Gord Walker, or for ineffective ministers whom he liked but couldn't bring himself to dump, like Margaret Birch.

The shuffle chopped cabinet from twenty-four to twenty, as the COGP had recommended, and involved several departmental amalgamations and a shift of deputy ministers.

The first omen of evil days ahead came on February 2, when veteran journalist Eric Dowd revealed a secret memo from Davis to all Tory MPPs ordering them to drop anything that could become a conflict of interest: "It is important that public confidence in the Party is not seriously reduced by the appearance of a conflict of interest . . ." The memo followed a rash of conflict charges involving municipal Toronto politicians in property deals with the city and rumblings that some Tories owned land in areas under study for a proposed Toronto-area airport. Davis said if members had doubts, they should see him personally. But at the time, that would have been hard to do.

When Davis became premier, Clare Westcott had stayed briefly in education because he didn't like Keith Reynolds, who had been deputy in Robarts's office. "Davis knew that, and I'd spent nine fucking years killing myself for him, but do you think he'd go and tell Reynolds I was coming and that was that? No way." Eventually Westcott did come, however, and he urged Davis to hire Ed Stewart to run the premier's office, but Davis named Stewart deputy in education, listened to others, and hired the duo of Jim Fleck and Malcolm Rowan. They soon built a wall around him.

Fleck, a millionaire manufacturer, was also a university professor and the incoming president of a world-wide organization of company presidents. Just forty years old, Fleck was six foot two, weighed two hundred pounds, and loved wearing fancy hats and flowing capes. He became chief executive officer for Davis, having been executive director of COGP, which in turn had recommended the establishment of the job he got. While Westcott, shuffled further away from Davis by the Fleck regime, had lobbied for Ed Stewart, John Robarts, on behalf of his friend and COGP head John Cronyn, had pushed for Fleck.

It was a bad decision. According to Westcott, Davis "just couldn't withstand the pressure" from Robarts. He says Fleck "wasn't a bad guy, but he brought in a kind of paper control that was way overdone. What he was doing was isolating Davis." It was important for the premier to keep in touch with cabinet, but ministers couldn't get to him. Instead they were sent to Fleck and Rowan, "a very compulsive, hard-working guy, but a real bureaucrat. And what you had was a combination of a federal bureaucrat like Malcolm and a political neophyte like Fleck . . . and suddenly Davis wasn't controlling the situation; they were."

It reached the point where Rowan began editing Brampton constituency letters Westcott wrote for Davis. Westcott complained, and Davis "just said quietly, leaning forward, 'You keep doing it, Clare, but don't send it through the system. Send it to Miss Anderson . . . but don't tell Jim.' Can you imagine? He was premier, and he was afraid to tell Fleck."

Westcott says Davis still worries about criticism of Fleck because "he feels you're being critical of him. He hired him. He can't stand to admit to himself he made a mistake. He likely even looks in the mirror when he shaves in the morning and says, 'What I did was right,' even though he knows it was wrong." And when people tell him he is wrong, "he quickly changes the subject." In an Ottawa hotel, Westcott waited until Davis was shaving before telling him Fleck was "screwing things up, and we had to get rid of him. Davis was really angry about that, but he had shaving cream all over his face, so he couldn't go anywhere."

Darcy McKeough agrees the atmosphere was dreadful. "Bill was aware of it, too, but he's very loyal. People were telling him, but it took him a hell of a long time to do anything about it." McKeough said they used to joke that Rowan "must have caught Bill in bed with somebody else's wife, but since that's, of course, impossible with Bill's standards," they surmised that Rowan's success in obtaining answers from Ontario Hydro when nobody else could made Davis "grateful."

Cam McDonald, who left his University of Western Ontario public relations job in 1972 to run communications in the premier's office and stayed two years, calls Cronyn a principal adviser then on structural matters and Macaulay "a daily confidant" politically. McDonald had some access, "but nobody could see the premier unless they had Fleck's permission." He used to smuggle notes from cabinet ministers in to Davis, and he once sneaked veteran Agriculture Minister Bill Stewart through a side door, "but Fleck intercepted us and Stewart went beet red. A lot of ministers suffered great frustration at that time."

McDonald says Fleck and Rowan didn't like the press and didn't trust press secretary Don Beeney because they thought he was too close to journalists. Some of that attitude rubbed off on Davis, too. At a 1975 campaign stop during a train tour in Windsor, Beeney was giving background information to reporters when Davis walked up. Asked for his views, Davis glared at Beeney and said, "We often wonder whose side he's on," an unusually cruel comment for Davis and a cheap shot at Beeney, an efficient and respected press secretary who moved to agriculture shortly afterward, then retired early to his farm east of Toronto.

The Fleck-Rowan duo also tried to dump Irene Beatty, the office administrative director who had been with the government since Drew's regime. "Finally they just gave up, but they didn't like her way of running the office," McDonald says. "They wanted to make the premier's office swing. They wanted unquestioned authority to do anything that they wanted . . . but Irene Beatty wouldn't let them get away with it. She stood up against them and said, 'You've got to have authorization, and it has to be clearly things for Mr. Davis as premier of this province, not Bill Davis, citizen.' Every expense had to be accounted for. They just wanted to write a blank cheque, but she prevailed, God bless her. Despite all the problems, she kept Davis clean."

To speechwriter John Harvey Miller, who signed up in February, 1972, the activities in the premier's office reminded him of the Robert Redford movie *The Candidate*, where Redford and his campaign manager compromised everything to win, then at the victory party wound up in a washroom. The manager said, "Well, we made it," and the candidate replied, "Fine, Joe. What do we do now?"

"That was the feeling," says Miller. "There was a drift there in a very politicized office that they'd won the 1971 campaign — now what? Davis never really got out of that until minority government." He says they copied the "imperial presidency" style of Richard Nixon, borrowing "certain attitudes from what they saw happening in Washington. Davis had fifteen advance men with him everywhere he went, and that started to affect media coverage. They couldn't get near him."

Tom Campbell, who was deputy of policy and priorities then, agrees Fleck had problems, "but I always thought he got a bit of a bum rap. He wasn't experienced at all in politics . . . he was a

textbook management type. It had always worked for him before, but of course government is different. There seemed to be
a lot of vituperation toward him. I never understood that."

Fleck was asked for an interview for this book and promised
to arrange a time, but he never did. Rowan, however, agreed
immediately. President of the Ontario Energy Corp., he's a wiry,
hyper little guy who draws charts and graphs during interviews.
The interview followed lunch with Dennis Timbrell, a Davis type
who rarely criticizes people in public. Rowan was Timbrell's
deputy in energy, and when I mentioned the upcoming Rowan
meeting, Timbrell quipped, "Don't give him my best regards."
Everybody agrees Rowan is competent, but nobody seems to like
him.

"Listen," he says, "there were some people he [Davis] didn't
want to see, and I was the one who got to tell them. That doesn't
always make you a popular guy." Rowan, a fourteen-year foreign service veteran before joining Davis, estimates there were
about six hundred requests for public appearances by Davis in
1972, 1,100 for meetings, and 52,000 pieces of mail. "I was the
guy who set up the system to deal with it. It didn't make everybody happy, but you're dealing with more requests for his time
than there is time." Rowan denies editing Westcott's letters, although McDonald remembers the "great flap" over it at the time.
He says they revamped the office, set up the businesslike correspondence system and appointments register that is still used,
and initiated policy meetings that brought people in from outside
government. He concedes they overlooked "the political side."

Davis, looking back, says, "The perception is I was isolated.
I'm not sure that is fair. I learned to increasingly trust my own
instincts and judgments. People were very genuine in trying to
be as helpful as they could . . . . Listen, I'm responsible. I made
my determinations, good or bad. It was a difficult period, but
you learn from those things. Other personnel would have been
my first choice, but I was relying on the judgment of other people who had more experience in these things that I had. But I
sorted it out eventually."

And even if they made Davis inaccessible, says Rowan, "Would
all this access have avoided the things that happened—Fidinam,
the Hydro building, the airplane problems? I have to think it
would not have avoided them happening." But happen they did.

The first minor embarrassment came when three MPPS—Tories Claude Bennett and Tom Wardell and NDP Michael Cassidy—wouldn't quit their municipal council seats, forcing Davis to introduce legislation banning concurrent tenure.

The second came in March, 1972, when Liberal Leader Bob Nixon asked a seemingly innocuous question: Was Pat Saunderson, president of Fidinam Investments Ltd., a Swiss-based development firm, a "fund-raiser" for the Tories? Nixon wondered why the company received a $15 million loan from the Workmen's Compensation Board (WCB) for a large complex at Yonge and Bloor streets in downtown Toronto. The Tories said it was a good deal that included Fidinam's purchase of the old WCB headquarters for what Labour Minister Gordon Carton called "better than market value." Davis told Nixon he had "no idea" whether Saunderson was a fund-raiser. Seven months later Davis would learn the connection.

But first other troubles were in the air. Bert Lawrence saw his career die of self-inflicted wounds when he used a government Kingair turboprop to take him, his wife, and two of his children, along with his deputy minister, Keith Reynolds, and his wife and child, to Havana on what he claimed was a "trade mission" but which looked suspiciously like a holiday junket. Lawrence arrived in Cuba on March 17, 1972, as a guest of Fidel Castro. The trip had not been announced, but Lawrence said he had arranged to meet six Cuban cabinet ministers and had four receptions to attend. Besides losing his suitcase, Lawrence ran into holidaying *Kitchener-Waterloo Record* reporter Robert Sutton. He told Sutton he was going skin diving at one of the Caribbean's best-known beaches, and Sutton filed a story to his newspaper about it. It was picked up by The Canadian Press and quickly became a full-blown scandal over abuse of government aircraft. The trip cost the government $3,600, about $1,000 more than commercial rates for the eight of them. When reporters called the premier's office for reaction, they discovered he was on a skiing holiday, having used a government Twin Otter to fly his wife and children to Stowe, Vermont.

Rather than simply tough out the "Cuban Caper," Lawrence was reduced to waving his itinerary in the legislature during a pathetic forty-minute speech on March 27, trying vainly to reason with howling opposition MPPs. Davis returned from his trip a day later, but instead of explaining or apologizing, he said he could see merit in buying a million-dollar, British-made BH125 jet for executive travel, a project he would announce several times over the years only to back off each time under public pressure.

In August, with Davis at the premiers' conference in Halifax, the *Globe* broke a story about Attorney General Dalton Bales and two associates buying a ninety-nine-acre site for $252,000 just east of Markham, an area designated by the Toronto Centred Region Plan as a growth area. Bales, an Osgoode classmate of Davis's and one of his few personal friends in cabinet, flatly denied inside knowledge, saying the purchase was just a long-term investment.

Five days later Davis told the legislature that Bales hadn't used "insider" information, and he promised tougher rules governing such matters. Then Bales told a press conference that he wouldn't resign — he had offered, but Davis said no — but he would sell his share of the land to a trustee and donate any profit to charity. Bales said he couldn't have known when he bought the land in 1969 that Ottawa would pick the area for a proposed airport two years later or that Ontario would plan to expropriate the area for Cedarwood, a planned community of 200,000 people near the airport.

The Tories were just nicely getting over that problem when a man walked into the *Globe* office with a story about Darcy McKeough. Reporter John Zaritsky was assigned to check it out, and in a copyright story on August 28, the paper reported that McKeough, as municipal affairs minister in 1969, had approved a seventy-five-acre subdivision for South Chatham Estates Ltd., even though his older brother Stewart was secretary and one of four company directors. The source told Zaritsky that McKeough also had money in the company.

Davis was away again in London, England. He told The Canadian Press: "Of course I have confidence" in McKeough, but he wouldn't comment further until he returned to Ontario in five days. A few days earlier McKeough and Davis had discussed the land holdings over breakfast in Munich, where they arranged a $31 million loan from a West German bank. Press secretary Beeney told reporters the two men had discussed McKeough's assets before Davis left for Europe, but Davis said Beeney was wrong. He said all ministers had been asked to provide a list of their property holdings, but McKeough's hadn't arrived until August 22, "just as I was getting ready for my European trip, and I had no time to read it."

In any event, it looked bad for McKeough. On August 30, back at his Chatham home, McKeough said he had no immediate plans to quit. "It's not the first time my resignation has been called for."

In 1984 McKeough said he "knew in Munich that bastard Zaritsky had tried to get me before I left. . . . I really didn't think it was that important." When the story broke, McKeough was in Zurich, then discussed it with Davis the next day in Munich. "He'd already heard about it from Westcott and wasn't terribly concerned." But John Robarts was. When McKeough arrived back, Robarts called him for a meeting at the Westbury Hotel. "I remember walking from my office through those bloody tunnels (under Queen's Park) to avoid people. I had a drink with Robarts, and he said I should resign." After that lawyer Eddie Goodman, cable television executive Phil Lind, and some others met with him in his office. McKeough left about 11 p.m. after Lind gave him a statement. "I remember reading it on the can the next morning." And in a late-morning press conference in his Toronto office he resigned, saying, "I am satisfied that I have personally done nothing wrong."

McKeough, who says he had "a little chip on my shoulder" because Davis hadn't sided with him publicly as he had with Bales, had an aide phone Zaritsky the day before the resignation to tell him the press conference would be held the next day at 10 a.m. in Chatham. "So Zaritsky went to Chatham, and he heard the news on the radio. We got the bastard. That was the one really fine piece of work we did that day. He wasn't there for the kill." Perhaps not, but McKeough's cabinet career was buried for eighteen months.

On September 14 Davis ordered his ministers to disclose their financial affairs, stop speculating in land, and divest themselves of any full-time business or professional holdings and turn them over to a trustee. (These business restrictions also applied to ministers' wives and children under the age of eighteen.) Ministers were also ordered to file reports, available to the public, listing all their holdings except their homes, cottages, or vacation retreats. It was the toughest set of rules in Canada, but Davis, still reeling from the Bales and McKeough affairs, said, "It is not too prohibitive." He gave ministers a month to either comply or quit.

At about that time NDP Leader Stephen Lewis slipped the *Globe* some information about Fidinam, the company Nixon had asked about earlier, and on November 2 the newspaper reported that Fidinam (Ontario) Ltd. had donated $50,000 to the Tories in 1971, about a month after cabinet had approved its property deal with the WCB.

Saunderson, the company president, confirmed the donation but said a telex message by a company official relating the donation to the deal was an error. The telex, dated November 23, 1971, was part of an exchange between Fidinam and its Swiss parent: The message from head office had asked for an explanation of "a cheque issued to M Kelly July 23 for $50,000"; the reply from Betty McDonald, Fidinam (Ontario) secretary-treasurer, called it a "political donation, related to UCP/WCB . . ." The acronyms meant Upper Canada Place (the Fidinam development) and the Workmen's Compensation Board; "M Kelly" was Tory bagman Bill Kelly.

The company hotly denied any connection between cabinet approval of their development and the donation, claiming that McDonald had "made a mistake." Davis insisted there was no connection, either. Kelly says Davis called him about it, and "I said to him, 'Billy, that's not your affair.' He said, 'I have reason to ask. The *Globe* has been calling.' I said at the time, in error as it turned out, 'Why is that of interest to anyone?' "

But the Fidinam affair was of great interest to many people, including a group of angry Tory backbenchers led by Frank Drea, a feisty former newspaper columnist, who told a stormy caucus meeting that if "we're to keep our name as a party that cannot be influenced by political contributions" they had to cancel the deal. But Davis said no; the deal was not improper.

At a press conference that day, Davis said as "head of the party . . . I just don't want to be involved in who does or who does not assist the party in a financial way." He didn't say he had already talked to Kelly about this deal and knew the details; he did say he was satisfied with Kelly's public statement that "as a matter of general policy," contributions were "not related to involvement in government business — past, present, or future."

Davis may have been happy, but the opposition wasn't. When

the legislature opened on November 21, Davis read a five-page statement, saying "absolutely no improper influence" had been put on cabinet. His speech was constantly interrupted by shouts of "nonsense" and "shame" from the opposition, and fiery Owen Sound Liberal Eddie Sargent was tossed out when he refused to sit down after being ruled out of order for demanding a full judicial inquiry. Nixon called it "bloody shocking . . . the crassest kind of political corruption," while Lewis demanded a law to limit donations and make them public. Davis continued to stonewall.

Ottawa Liberal Albert Roy accused Bales, still attorney general, of shirking his responsibility by not checking a Criminal Code section prohibiting donations to parties in return for favors, and finally, on November 30, Bales said his officials would investigate. At the time the Liberals were planning criminal charges of their own, but Lewis pushed for a legislative debate to allow broad discussion of the issue and not restrict it to specific points of criminal law.

That same day Davis told caucus that the Ontario Commission on the Legislature (set up in June, 1972) would study the Election Act over the matter of making political donations public. The commission was chaired by Dalton Camp and included journalist Doug Fisher and former Liberal leader Farquhar Oliver. It issued five reports up until October, 1975, profoundly reforming legislative procedures, granting MPPs more money, bigger expense allowances, and better secretarial, research, and constituency office help, revamping the administration in the legislative building itself (switching jurisdiction from government services to the Speaker), and allowing television and radio into the legislature, the first chamber in Canada to do so. Its green-covered third report on party financing, released in September, 1974, disagreed with Oliver, who wanted ceilings on party and constituency election spending. That report formed the basis of fundraising reforms, introducing public disclosure, limits on contributions, and rules limiting the value of campaign advertising as well as the time—to the final three weeks of an election campaign.

In the meantime, however, the Fidinam investigation promised by Bales was handed to Clay Powell, a Crown counsel, assisted by J. E. Grubb of the OPP criminal investigation branch and Brian McLoughlin, a chartered accountant with Touche Ross and Co. The inquiry team concluded that "there is no evidence to indicate" the donation breached the Criminal Code. Bales released the report on January 5, 1973. Technically the Tories were clean, but the political odors lingered on, to grow even stronger during the year.

Bales was also the subject of a bizarre accusation by former Toronto coroner and millionaire NDP member Dr. Morton Shulman of being linked with criminal elements because he had been seen at a Conservative fund-raising dinner at the palatial home of a construction contractor linked to price-fixing attempts and bombings. Bales denied it and later, wielding affidavits from the contractor and a private investigator, told the legislature he was "physically disgusted" that Shulman, with "his own twisted record," could "embark upon a reckless, wanton attack on the character and integrity of another." Shulman withdrew his charge and said he'd resign his seat if Davis called an immediate by-election to fill it. Davis said he was not prepared to bargain with Shulman, adding he should resign, no strings attached. The fact is, Bales had not been at the party, but Dr. Matthew Dymond, the Ontario riding Tory MPP, had.

The Tories, because nothing had been going their way in a while, milked the incident. Shulman had even become a pariah in his own caucus, and Davis said, "We are not prepared to bargain [with Shulman] where the honors and principles of this House are at stake." Those honors and principles had been wobbling noticeably anyway, but for a while the Shulman caper helped the Tories shore them up again.

Not for long. A week later news broke that Agriculture Minister Bill Stewart had received two grants totalling $3,000 from his own department for improvements to his cattle farm. Stewart said there was no conflict because he had checked with Crown legal experts before applying, and the grants were available to any farmer who qualified. Nixon, who owns a Brant County farm, said he couldn't say "the minister is doing something wrong, but it is a personal judgment, and personally, I feel it is a conflict." Nixon, by the way, had announced he was quitting as Liberal leader, and a leadership contest was underway. But the way things were going for the Tories, his hopes were getting higher, and he didn't like front-runner Donald Deacon that much anyway, so he entered the race himself and ended up winning when he was already leader, something only Ontario Liberals would understand.

Davis, then, staggered into 1973 less enthusiastically than he'd stormed into 1972. In February he told fourteen hundred delegates at a party convention in Toronto that he wanted "the processes of politics and government in this province to be open and beyond criticism," adding that it was better for the party and democracy "if we remove this cloak of secrecy."

But the heaviest cloak seemed to be covering the premier's office. Many backbenchers openly grumbled that Davis ignored them. When he decided to introduce donation disclosure, he told the opposition leaders and his key advisers but not cabinet or caucus. John MacBeth said his confidence in his own government was shaken because Davis "had not taken me into his confidence." Dennis Timbrell complained that caucus "does not meet often enough to give the government members an opportunity to really consider proposed legislation or give them time to consult with their own expert contacts." In response Davis said Tory whip Doug Kennedy, the nephew of Davis's patron, Tom Kennedy, could attend cabinet as an observer and liaison between caucus and cabinet.

Globe columnist (now editor-in-chief) Norman Webster summed the Tories up well when he compared that February convention with an NDP one shortly before. He wrote, "Policy is the guts of an NDP meeting," but when the Tories held a policy session, "almost no one came." The NDP "came with beards and parkas and blue jeans and babies and settled in for some good, acrimonious political debate." And the Tories?

"The Conservatives are a slick party. When they registered, delegates received Expo-style passports which admitted them to the various expensive functions. Monogrammed PC beer steins and cuff links and a whole range of other gewgaws were for sale. A Tory could buy his or her sweetheart a lollipop in red, white, and blue for only seventy-five cents (later slashed to fifty).

"It is a party that looks comfortable in a waistcoat, and there are gowns for the ladies in the evening. The most decorative element at the convention was a squad of leggy girls in red blazers and blue skirts. They ran errands, took tickets, shepherded delegates around, and just stood around looking pretty. Any NDP convention trying that would spend the whole weekend debating sexist exploitation of women.

"Life, for New Democrats, is serious—a time to draft amendments, right wrongs, and fight the good fight.

"The Conservatives are content to govern."

They had been doing that, of course, for thirty years, but they hadn't looked so shaky since the first two years of the Tory reign with Drew's minority government. The appearance of public discontent turned into reality on March 15 when the party lost two by-elections in ridings previously held by high-profile cabinet ministers Allan Lawrence (Toronto-St. George), who had left to run federally, and Charles MacNaughton (Huron).

In Huron, a traditionally Tory rural riding in southwestern Ontario, MacNaughton had smothered the Liberal by a 3–1 margin two years earlier, but this time, largely through fears of Tory regional government, Liberal Jack Riddell won by three thousand votes. Even more personally devastating to Davis, however, was the solid loss of his friend Roy McMurtry in St. George to Margaret Campbell, a well-known municipal politician. She had been interested in the Tory nomination but had been told by the Big Blue Machine that the seat was hand picked for McMurtry, so she got the Liberal nod and beat McMurtry by two thousand votes.

Then on March 26, 1973, Nixon charged in the legislature that Gerhard Moog, a "close personal friend" of Davis, had received untendered, multi-million-dollar government contracts. Moog was president of Swiss Granada Holdings, Transortium Realty, and Canada Square Corporation Ltd., three companies Nixon said had been awarded contracts under the government's "proposal method" on construction. The contracts were for Ontario Hydro's new head office, the Ontario Institute for Studies in Education building, and the TransAmerica Building, which houses the Ontario Educational Communications Authority. The Hydro building was the latest agreement, involving a complex lease-back arrangement with four separate leases, whereby Canada Square would invest $6 million in construction loans over three years and be "rewarded with a rental income of almost $6.1 million every year for thirty years." Nixon said the company would recover its investment in less than two years, double its money in less than four, "and continue to pile up profits over the thirty-year life of the lease."

For the moment Davis was silent. His new treasurer, John White, was about to introduce his 1973 budget, which would create even more headaches for Davis. White proposed a 7 per cent energy tax, saying, Marie Antoinette-style, that if people were cold, they should turn down their thermostats and buy sweaters. A determined Tory revolt forced Davis to rescind the tax, on April 25, one of the few times caucus ever won a battle. All but four Tories showed up for caucus, and none supported the tax. The meeting came after several Tories had failed to attend first reading of the budget to show their displeasure and after Hamilton Mountain representative John Smith had actually voted against the tax bill.

Five days later, with the revolt out of the way, Davis ordered a select committee probe into the $44-million Hydro deal, refusing Nixon's demand for a royal commission and the suspension of Hydro chairman George Gathercole pending the outcome. The select committee began its inquiry in May, and although it ultimately cleared Davis of impropriety, it did prove embarrassing, forcing Davis to become the first premier ever to testify before an investigative committee of the House.

Davis consistently denied influencing Hydro in the choice of Moog. But Gathercole testified that he had spoken with Davis in February, 1972, at the opening of Hydro's Pickering generating station and had told him his officials were studying a new office building and had been impressed by OISE, another Moog deal. That July the Canada Square deal was approved in principle, and twelve days later Gathercole sent a letter to Jim Fleck seeking "the premier's judgment" on an announcement. That letter, sent to Fleck's home, contained a proposed press release on the deal, naming Moog's company in the first sentence.

There were other letters to cabinet ministers and government officials as well, all about two months before the agreement was signed. Gathercole said he never mentioned Moog's name, even when talking to Davis about OISE, but the fact remained that Davis and Moog were close friends. They had holidayed together at the Davis cottage, and Davis had stayed at Moog's Florida apartment just after winning the leadership. In addition, OISE was Davis's project when he was education minister, so he would have known who built it.

Having publicly contradicted the Davis version of events, however, Gathercole went back to the committee the next day and reversed his testimony, saying he had no knowledge of the Davis-Moog friendship. "My evidence in that respect must have been mistaken," he said during three hours of intense questioning. A day earlier he had said he was told of Moog's friendship at a Hydro Electric Power Commission meeting in July, 1972, when the Canada Square contract was signed.

Davis testified in late July, 1973, that he, his wife, and the Moogs spent a one-week holiday in Europe in 1971, and said the Moogs were on the aforementioned Vermont skiing holiday, although they had not travelled on the government plane. "I have never attempted to hide the fact that Mr. Moog and I and our families have been friends," he said. "I have endeavored, in spite of some difficulties, to lead a relatively private life in my private capacity. I have not made a conscious effort to tell anyone who my friends are."

It had already been shown that Moog *did* get preferential treatment from Hydro, being called in to discuss the project with Gathercole, so the issue had become whether this had anything to do with his friendship with Davis. Davis said it did not.

Davis testified that when the two families went to Europe, he had told Moog he might have "a general discussion with representatives of the banking community in Munich" and had suggested to Moog he might like to sit in. That meeting never did take place, but Davis had a hunch that the U.S. was about to impose restrictions on Canadian imports (it did a few days later), so during a three-day trip through the Black Forest, he asked Moog if he had any banking contacts in Zurich. Moog arranged an appointment the next day.

Moog's account of the trip to Zurich is one of the most colorful in Queen's Park history. It was, after all, Friday the thirteenth, a pleasant day, but they somehow forgot about the appointment. Moog testified that he had enjoyed some wine and, "fortified like that," had rushed with Davis in a borrowed Mercedes to try to reach Zurich in time. They made a wrong turn, and alas, the car had a flat tire, which he and Davis had to fix, but still, "by testing the capability of the machine" and not stopping to change out of tourist clothes, they made it to Zurich and met with two of the senior bankers of one of Switzerland's largest banks. Moog said that when Davis was engrossed in conversation with one banker, he struck up a conversation in German with the other, enquiring whether the Swiss bank would be interested in financing Canada Square. One can only guess how impressed the banker was that Moog would show up in the company of Davis. In any event, the banker told Moog that eighty million Swiss francs — about $20 million — could be made available at 6 1/2 per cent interest. Davis, who does not speak German, said he knew nothing of the conversation, but a few weeks later Moog mentioned to him at the Davis home that he had been "approached" by Hydro about the project, and Davis had replied, "Fine."

Under the deal Hydro agreed to a maximum rent with the understanding that if Moog could arrange financing at less than 8 per cent, the going rate then, the rent would drop accordingly. In his submission to Hydro in January, 1972, Moog said he had access to Swiss money at 6.5 per cent (Hydro officials testified that he continued to indicate he could get the Swiss money right up until the contract was signed in November, 1972) and U.S. money at 7.75 per cent. But Moog told the committee he had to pay 8 per cent interest on money promised him by U.S. sources, a rate that meant Hydro would not get the rent reduction it could expect to get by dealing with Moog instead of other developers.

The committee, chaired by Tory John MacBeth, reported in October that Moog was guilty of misrepresentation in his dealings with Hydro and concluded that his well-known friendship with Davis may have been a factor that influenced Hydro; Davis was cleared of any involvement. It said the contract was financially sound, but Hydro had not met corporate business standards in negotiations with Moog and had erred collectively in not ensuring that proper competition occurred. In fact there was no competition. It found that Moog had impressed Hydro's chief architect with his friendship with Davis and that his claim of acting as a financial adviser to the premier was untrue and had created a false impression.

Years later Clare Westcott said Davis was loyal to Moog "because he was convinced Moog was right. And Moog was. There was nothing wrong with that deal." He also says taxpayers would be happy if Moog did more work because his building operates for one-third the cost of comparable buildings nearby. "I don't particularly like the guy, but he's good," said Westcott. "And because he was a friend of Davis, that made it a scandal."

Neil Davis says the affair hurt. There was considerable innuendo but "no wrongdoing. But just the fact it was reported that way for thirty-seven straight days, the end result didn't matter any more. It hurt their relationship . . . it made it difficult for Dad to be seen with people he'd been friends with for some time. That hurts him."

The affair certainly gnawed at Davis. In August he told two hundred Tories at a YPC meeting that Conservatives should stop knocking his reforms. "This party has always been known for its internal constructive criticism. That's not always bad, but it's not always good, either."

And in September a public opinion poll indicated that Tories weren't the only ones upset with Davis. He was still top choice for premier—at 31 per cent, with Lewis 20 and Nixon 15—but a whopping 46 per cent said their opinion of him had dropped. Asked if they had heard or read anything about charges of political favoritism in Hydro contracts to a Davis friend, 61 per cent said yes—80 per cent in Toronto—and 38 per cent of those felt the charges were justified.

Finally Davis started to fight back. He began a series of town meetings—grandly called "Ontario: a New Awareness"—which took him and a group of ministers to various cities on Saturdays for open meetings, local press conferences, interviews, and open-line shows. "I'm here to listen," Davis would say. It worked well in Cornwall, Sudbury, Thunder Bay, and into the new year in Hamilton, Kitchener, Ottawa, Kingston, and London. McKeough, who had been returned to grace as Ontario's first energy minister, visited Timmins as part of the plan; Bales went to Peterborough, Tom Wells to Thunder Bay, and John White to Cornwall. As part of the effort by the Tories to make themselves visible, Davis even began bi-weekly press conferences.

On December 4 Davis announced 20 per cent pay hikes for MPPS, the first since 1969, plus a new accommodation allowance for those from outside Toronto, a better mileage rate, and a more liberal allowance for MPPS using all forms of transit between their ridings and Toronto. Naturally, the opposition didn't object to that.

On the eighth he named former attorney general Arthur Wishart as his special adviser on legislative matters; this, translated, gave Wishart the task of transforming the Tories' stinky image by mending fences with disgruntled MPPs.

Then Davis shuffled his own staff. Hugh Macaulay was sent to tell Fleck he would be moving sideways, opening a spot for Ed Stewart. The mood changed overnight. Stewart cleaned house, fired some people, and shifted others. He took charge and never let go.

Paul Weed was named appointments secretary, Westcott was elevated at least partly to his old status of personal adviser, and public relations man Jim McPhee, a veteran royal tour organizer, was hired to put some princely punch into the operation. McPhee tried hard to introduce Davis to senior media people — editors, managing editors, and news directors — and introduced some fireside chats between reporters and Davis. "Not just the set-piece stuff — long talks. But it was ruined by the electronic buggers . . . god, they made a circus out of it."

Around the same time, like so many other Tory leaders when they were in big trouble, Davis turned to an adviser who would remain a key member of the Big Blue Machine throughout the Davis years — Eddie Goodman.

* * *

The first thing noticeable about Goodman was that he never waited to be summoned by Davis. If he wanted an audience, he just went to his office, knocked on the door, and charged in. "I assert myself," he says, "to the despair of everybody. If I waited until he called me or we worked out a formal appointment, I'd never see him."

No one ever accused the ebullient, white-haired, successful Toronto lawyer of being shy. He's held offices in the Conservative party federally and provincially since he was vice-president of the Macdonald-Cartier Conservative Club at the University of Toronto in 1938.

An excitable man, he has a slight lisp that gets more pronounced as his fever pitch rises. He is not noted for ducking tough political advice. Indeed, shortly before the 1975 campaign, he told a group of prominent Tories: "A few more reforms, and we will be reforming ourselves out of office." Despite his bluntness, or because of it, his skill as a political negotiator is legendary. He was national chairman of the party during the Camp-Diefenbaker war, chaired the convention that chose Stanfield, and was probably the only major party figure to come out of it without any visible injuries. Darcy McKeough calls Goodman, admiringly, "a cagey son of a bitch." He says Goodman encouraged him to run in 1971 and pledged to raise $5,000 for him, even though he was supporting Davis. "I'm sure he urged Mulroney to run the last time, and he supported Clark. . . . He has a good relationship with everybody. People get mad at him sometimes, but everybody likes him."

His first foray into politics was during the 1930 federal campaign. He was eleven, and his father was a campaign agent for Col. Reginald Geary, a former Toronto mayor who became minister of justice. "I spent a lot of time putting signs in store windows for him, things like that." He ran himself in 1945 after returning home from the war, where he was wounded twice, but lost badly to Communist Joe Salsberg in St. Andrews, one of only two Toronto seats the Tories lost.

He was a provincial organizer under both Drew and Frost and became active federally when Frost asked him to represent Ontario on John Diefenbaker's organizational committee. In 1956 Diefenbaker asked him to be Ontario organizer for the federal party, which he was until 1963. He quit but then came back to run Dief's 1965 campaign.

It was Goodman who convinced John Robarts, a childhood friend, to become active in politics, and he got to know Davis at the Montmerency policy conference leading up to the 1967 leadership convention where, as chairman, he asked Davis to chair a session. "I can tell you — the Bill Davis of that time and the Bill Davis today are two different people. I thought in those days he was a good minister, but he wasn't nearly as fresh and sophisticated as I thought he was. I had to really guide him through, tell him how to answer questions."

Goodman worked for Robarts in the 1961 leadership campaign, but Bob Macaulay was a good friend of his law partner, so Goodman saw Davis often and came to know him as someone who "was in politics practically from the time he got out of his mother's womb."

Goodman resigned as national chairman in 1971, did some work in the 1972 campaign, then sat out until October, 1973, when Hugh Macaulay came calling. Goodman changed the make-up of the Tuesday morning breakfast club, trimming some non-elected people and inviting cabinet ministers for the first time.

Because he is so active professionally in front of government boards and commissions, Goodman is subjected to constant charges of abusing his influence. "It's not easy for me. There aren't many guys who are as high profile as I am. . . . I never sue anybody for what they say about me politically, but if they attack my integrity as a lawyer, then fuck 'em. I go after them. That's the rule I have." He is often a target because "the minute they hear my name, they figure they're going to do a number. I could have as much chance of bringing political influence to bear on the Ontario Muncipal Board as I could jumping out this window successfully. These boards now are no different than working in front of the courts, except that in the public mind there's some difference. The only solution to this is to give up something. I'm not going to give up law; it's been my life. And secondly, I've got to earn a living. I would hate to have to give up my activity in politics. I think I've made a contribution. But if that was the choice, I would."

*   *   *

Davis was hoping all these changes would revitalize his ailing political fortunes, but 1973 couldn't end without more problems. Just after Davis chided reporters for being too negative — accusing them of ignoring accomplishments and concentrating on "confrontation and criticism" — Davis discovered some other critics: 7,800 teachers in sixteen school board areas who were submitting mass resignations on December 31. To fight them, Davis and Education Minister Tom Wells introduced emergency legislation to block their resignations and send the contracts to compulsory arbitration.

The teachers, and of course the NDP, were outraged. The debate was so wild that when Wells introduced the bill, the Speaker called a recess for a cooling-off period, the first time in the legislature's history. The next day Nixon, who had supported the bill on first reading a day earlier, sparked another uproar by asking the Tories to withdraw it and require compulsory arbitration — period. Lewis called it "crass expediency," and when the Tories began heckling Nixon, Lewis called out, "This is too delicious for words. Let me rub it in a little."

On December 17 Davis announced the bill would not be withdrawn because the government's first priority was "the school system and the kids." His comments followed a meeting with representatives of Ontario's 105,000 teachers a day after Wells had accused them of trying to "intimidate" the government by planning a one-day walkout and mass protest rally.

The next day twenty thousand teachers crowded into Maple Leaf Gardens, where Ontario Teachers Federation president Geoffrey Wilkinson began, "Friends, Ontarians, teachers, lend me your ears. I come to bury Davis, not to praise him." That set the tone, and on their way to Queen's Park the teachers were joined by other supporters, some of whom hadn't been able to get into the Gardens, it was so full. When they arrived on the front lawn they were thirty thousand strong, still the largest demonstration in Queen's Park history.

While the army of teachers was marching up the front steps, Wells and Ed Stewart were in Davis's office overlooking the battlefield. Wells remembers how cool Davis was, at least outwardly, as they watched through the window. "He just sort of puffed slowly on his pipe and watched silently, and the only thing he said, really, was, 'Oh my goodness, there are a lot of people there, Tom.' "

The teachers weren't quite as laid-back when Wells went out to speak to them. Sticking doggedly to his written text, looking up periodically when drowned out by the din, Wells told the mob the bill was just an interim measure to keep the schools open in January and that another bill, to be debated in the spring, would allow "many months of free collective bargaining, using binding arbitration only as a final resort." The reaction was bitter. The crowd sang "No Wells" to the tune of the Christmas carol, booed him, shook their fists, showed thumbs down, and waved thousands of placards denouncing the Tories.

It was an awesome display of strength, and as always with

Davis, it worked. On December 20, after intense negotiations at the Royal York Hotel, Davis and Wells reached an agreement with the six top federation leaders. The Tories agreed to recess without passing the emergency legislation, while the OTF agreed to urge teachers to postpone their resignations until January 31. Wells literally moved into the hotel for January, brought in a team of mediators, and worked almost around the clock to settle fifteen of the sixteen disputes. "We had maps up on the wall," said Wells, "and every time we settled one we checked them off. It felt great to do that."

On February 3 Davis said he was going to introduce a permanent ban on teacher strikes, standing firm despite their show of strength. But standing firm was always a tough business for Davis. He managed for only eighteen months, until July, 1975, when Wells introduced Bill 100 that — you guessed it — gave teachers the right to strike, set up the Education Relations Commission to oversee teacher-trustee negotiations, and called for a fact-finder if bargaining talks reached an impasse. Teachers and trustees could take their dispute to either voluntary or binding arbitration or final-offer selection, and while strikes were prohibited during the life of a collective agreement, they were allowed afterward. It was a complete capitulation by the Tories.

Back in early 1974, with the walkout averted, things were starting to turn around for Davis. But then the *Star* reported that Solicitor General John Yaremko, a minister for sixteen years, had subdivided property he owned on the Niagara Escarpment only three days before the law was changed to prevent the practice without municipal approval. Nixon and Lewis demanded that Yaremko resign, but Davis defended him as an honest man, saying he'd discuss it with him before anything was decided.

The government planned to turn thousands of escarpment acres into a green belt, and Yaremko owned more than four hundred acres there. He said he would declare a conflict when the escarpment plans were discussed but insisted he had done nothing wrong. He even donated a piece of land assessed at $35,000 to a government agency to turn into public parkland, a donation that made him eligible for a $35,000 deduction on his taxable income.

Davis did nothing then, but when he shuffled his cabinet a month later, Yaremko was gone, as were Bert Lawrence and Dalton Bales. "It was the most difficult job I've ever had," said Davis. "These men are all my friends."

The shuffle came just after Housing Minister Bob Welch announced the end of another Tory pipe dream—Cedarwood, the new town of 200,000 near Pickering—after spending $70 million, originally the total budget, acquiring just half the 25,200 acres. Welch blamed escalating land values and said the government planned to scale down the project and expropriate another 8,695 acres for about $60 million, but eventually the scheme was completely abandoned, and the province and some of the expropriated landowners got into a squabble that is still not resolved.

Nixon, citing the Yaremko affair and setting the tone that he maintained for the next year and a half, told a Hamilton riding association meeting early in 1974 that the Tories lacked moral fibre. They certainly lacked something, for on October 3, 1974, the Tories once again lost two by-elections in ridings vacated by cabinet ministers. In Carleton East, Ottawa Mayor Pierre Benoit finished third in a riding Bert Lawrence had won easily in 1971, and in Stormont (Cornwall), the fiefdom of the former labor minister Fern Guindon, Tory Guy Léger, a Roman Catholic priest, lost to New Democrat George Samis. The retiring Guindon didn't help matters any when he warned voters they'd better vote Tory if they wanted to get anything from the government for their riding, nor did Léger help himself when he refused to show up at all-candidates meetings, only to be represented by an empty chair.

Davis announced sweeping reforms of political financing in November, but already Nixon was openly predicting the end of Davis. "People are fed up with his policies," Nixon told a Niagara Falls rally. "We see it everywhere we go in the province. Our chances have never been better than right now."

In January, 1975, McKeough returned as treasurer in the twenty-six-member cabinet, restoring the aristocratic forty-one-year-old to his place just below Davis in the pecking order. John White, who had been treasurer, was dumped, but he had announced he wasn't running again.

By this time pressure was beginning to mount for rent controls (about which more in the next chapter), and resentment was building over the Davis-McKeough regional government plans for a host of southern Ontario counties. It had been so long since something went right, a Davis aide lamented, "If we do get a break, we won't believe it, anyway. We'll figure it's a plot of some kind to suck us in, then zap us."

Finally they did get a break, although at first blush it looked like the *Globe* had found another scandal. On January 27, 1975, the paper reported that bagman Bill Kelly had denied receiving a letter offering the Tories $30,000 if the government would buy almost one hundred acres of land needed for a highway link near Oakville. The offer was made in a November 23, 1971, letter to Kelly from Ross Shouldice, a party fund-raiser and former Sudbury real estate agent. The newspaper had copies of letters seized from Shouldice's files by government investigators looking into his Sudbury dealings; one letter was written to Davis on November 11, 1971, about problems he was having as a fund-raiser in the Sudbury area.

As it turned out, the story pumped air into the deflating Davis balloon. This time the *Globe* had gone too far. Unlike previous stories, this one was shaky, and Davis, shark-like, sharpened his political teeth and went directly for the throat. He issued an angry denunciation of the story and newspaper, so sure of his facts that he called a press conference to debunk the story. In case it wasn't noticeable by the flush in his cheeks or the squint in his eyes, Davis inserted into the text the words "I am angry." With most people you could tell.

Davis said Kelly severed Shouldice's connection with the party in November, 1971, which wasn't quite true, and categorically denied that Shouldice had received preferential treatment, which apparently was true. He said the suggestion was "total nonsense. It's not supported by any factual documentation." It wasn't.

Shouldice lived in Orlando, Florida, then. He and another man had been charged in 1973 with eleven criminal counts, including forging Ontario Housing Corp. documents and defrauding creditors of $28,000 and OHC of $158,000. The charges were dismissed in 1974, but Shouldice was told in July, 1973, that the government would not renew his real estate broker's licence.

Davis, on a roll, next surprised sixteen hundred guests at the annual Metro Board of Trade dinner, who had expected a speech on the economy, when, his face scarlet with anger, he called reports of patronage in the Oakville deal "sinister, sordid speculation . . . baseless rumors. Bill Davis has only begun to fight, and fight we shall." Davis drew a standing ovation by accusing the *Globe* of "an attempt to destroy a government through sheer weight of ink, baseless innuendo, containing allegations and suggestions from supposed evidence that is unproven, unreliable, and unfounded." *Globe* publisher and editor-in-chief, R. S. Malone, a head-table guest, joined in the ovation. Davis continued, "There's a difference between a vigilant press and a vigilante press or between the honorable journalistic tradition of muckraking and the other of mudslinging." He said readers were being asked to believe that several government officials "could be suborned, and conspired to buy land they did not want, for a highway that did not exist, in order to gratify a man that no one knew. . . . That's a crock of sheer nonsense."

And so it went. The story was revived briefly in late January when Kelly said he hadn't actually fired Shouldice — "You can't fire people you never formally hire" — but there was little substance to it.

Those close to Davis saw a sharp reversal of form from that point on. For the first time since 1972, he was on the offensive. He was still in trouble, and he knew it. But it was a different, more aggressive Davis after Shouldice.

Davis did hit one more bump along the road to partial recovery when Solicitor General George Kerr resigned on February 21 to fight allegations that he had asked for and got a $10,000 campaign donation from a man involved in the Hamilton harbor scandal. Kerr said the allegations against him were "a complete fabrication . . . absolutely untrue," but he resigned because it brought an "unfortunate cloud" over him and his office. As the province's top cop, Kerr said he had to resign "so as not to leave any questions." After meeting with RCMP commissioner M. J. Nadon, federal Solicitor General Warren Almand said Kerr's name was mentioned several times in preliminary hearing testimony, but there was no evidence to warrant charges against him. And at the trial of former Hamilton harbor commissioner Kenneth Elliott in July, Mr. Justice P. Callon said there was no evidence that Kerr was "involved in any impropriety." Davis, welcoming Kerr back into cabinet, said, "I was confident it would happen all along. There was never any question of his integrity. . . ."

But the question of Tory integrity wasn't so easy to dispose of.

Davis had lost all four by-elections since 1971 in solid Tory seats; he was trailing the Liberals in public and private opinion polls; he'd been under constant attack for three years; and even many in his own party were publicly unhappy with his leadership.

But in August, 1975, just days after the Tories clamped a ninety-day freeze on prices of petroleum products (long enough to get them through a campaign), Davis said, "Nothing has prepared me so much for a second term in office as premier of Ontario as has my first term in that office."

Everybody agreed. Things couldn't get any worse.

CHAPTER 9
RENT ASUNDER

—————— ☙ ——————

The big issue for Brampton city council on February 11, 1975, was a letter from Bill Davis. The council had asked for tough rent control laws a few months earlier when a large developer, Peel-Elder, had made noises about increasing its apartment rents by 40 per cent.

But Davis had written, "Information we have gathered from other jurisdictions indicates that rent review boards, for example, generally do not resolve the underlying problem of inadequate supply," adding that rent controls often meant that existing rental units were allowed to deteriorate. "In addition to discouraging supply, such boards also tend to be cumbersome . . . and lead to frustrations on both the part of the tenants and the landlords." He said talks between the housing ministry, developers, and landlords had often tempered proposed rent increases — as they had with the Peel-Elder proposals — and the real problem was that the high cost of mortgage financing and increased construction costs had reduced the rental supply. To combat this the province planned to increase its supply of lower-interest mortgage money and boost housing programs generally.

But first there was an election to win. The political landscape of Ontario was quickly heating up with election speculation, particularly from the Liberals who sensed, with immense justification, that 1975 might be their year. In January, 1975, Nixon said of the Tories, "I don't believe they've ever been in a more precarious state." He had cause for such optimism. A Gallup poll released the same day had set Nixon's popular support at 41 per cent, up 13 points from 1971, while the Davis Tories had dropped from 45 to 33 per cent. The Tories had surveys of their own that didn't give them any more comfort, except that they showed that Nixon personally was less popular than his party, a key factor that prompted Tory strategists to concentrate on attacking him. In 1971 Stephen Lewis and the socialist hordes had been the villains, but now the hot-headed Nixon was targeted. The Tories were convinced that voters would never elect an NDP government, but they were worried about the Liberals.

In a speech on Valentine's Day wrapping up a stormy, eleven-month session, Davis said, "I listen to the leader of the Opposition talking about being the party of the seventies, and if the Liberal party, with its present posture, its lack of policy, and its total contradictions, is the party of the seventies, then heaven help the people of Ontario." The thirty-minute speech was interrupted several times by Liberal catcalls and Tory desk thumping, while the NDP, virtually ignored by Davis, sat silent. Davis was outraged at comments made a few days earlier by the Ontario Liberal party president, who described the government as "grasping, cringing, and corrupt." "What sewer did . . . [he] come from with some of the observations he made?" asked Davis, setting a tone that was to be closely observed by both him and Nixon throughout the coming year.

Davis then introduced a bill setting ceilings on campaign advertising of twenty-five cents for each registered voter, requiring full disclosure of all contributions over $100, and limiting donations by individuals, corporations, and unions to any one party or its riding organization in a single year to $4,000. The legislation was the government's long-awaited response to the uproar caused by the Fidinam scandal. It also set up an all-party Commission on Election Contributions and Expenses to oversee registration of political parties and release annual audited statements of party finances. It was tough legislation, even though it allowed parties to salt away a secret pot that they couldn't add to but never had to disclose. Davis boasted that it gave Ontario "the most open political system in the country" and said he wouldn't tolerate people who questioned "the honesty of this administration. Not without a fight." But Nixon kept hammering away at his theme of integrity, and not just in general terms: He questioned Davis's personal integrity as well.

The legislature resumed sitting in March, and a few weeks later Darcy McKeough's budget lowered the provincial sales tax from 7 to 5 per cent and chopped 450,000 low-income families from Ontario's tax rolls. The sales tax cuts were temporary — just until the end of 1975 — but long enough to get an election out of the way. The budget also promised an $83 million program to give grants of $1,500 to buyers or builders of their first home, and it added a $15 million plan for "free" drugs for senior citizens, a program that by 1984–85 cost $278 million—an 1,800 per cent increase.

A week later Davis unleashed another election-year scam, setting up a royal commission on the effects of movie and television violence headed by former federal cabinet minister Judy LaMarsh at $250 a day. Lewis dismissed the commission as an election gimmick and said Davis should drop the idea and save taxpayers "several hundred thousands of Ontario dollars." Actually, Lewis's estimate was low. The commission ran until June, 1977 (nicely timed for yet another election), and ran up $2.2 million, making more news by its lavish spending than by any recommendations on a subject outside provincial jurisdiction to begin with. LaMarsh earned $93,000 at a time when she had regular television and radio shows of her own and was frequently critical of government spending, and she and the other commissioners, Judge Lucien Beaulieu and writer Scott Young, tooted about the world first-class, spending $124,000 travelling to sixteen countries, running up hotel bills of $150 a day, and using cabs and chauffeur-driven limousines lavishly.

In April Ross DeGeer, then the party's executive director, and Hugh Macaulay met the federal Tory caucus. Shortly afterward a Liberal MPP produced a letter written by federal Tory Gus Mitges complaining that the Davis government was "alienating practically every segment of the people of the province due to policies regarding teachers, public servants, organized labor, rural people, . . . municipal reeves, mayors, and councils regarding zoning and land severances." Tory MPs told Davis he should shed the "Big Blue Machine" image, be more available to the "man on the street," be a people's premier, forget regional government, admit mistakes, and instead of taking cabinet around the province, go by himself as Frost did.

In early May it was revealed that the Tories had set up a high-level, twenty-four-member group three months earlier to restore morale, recommend policies, and get ready for the election. Called the Progressive Conservative Policy Committee ("PC squared" in party circles), and chaired by Davis himself, the group set out election strategies and organizational flow charts, dividing the province into seven regional subcommittees under the aegis of cabinet ministers, and each regional group in turn involved about fifty people, including MPPs, riding presidents, nominated candidates, and campaign managers. The law-and-order campaign, which began with the LaMarsh commission and also involved crackdowns on Toronto film and body-rub joints, came out of this group-think.

All this frantic political activity, plus Revenue Minister Arthur Meen's planned $400,000 campaign to advertise home-buyer grants, prompted Kitchener Liberal James Breithaupt to say Davis was trying to become "the greatest Tory ever sold."*

Before May was out, Management Board chairman Eric Winkler tried to kill widespread fears about the regional government schemes of Intergovernmental Affairs Minister Darcy McKeough by pledging that there wouldn't be any more "unless the people ask for it." (Winkler would lose his own seat in the election, largely on that issue; indeed, many current southwestern Ontario Liberals owe their careers to the plan.)

McKeough acknowledges the issue hurt the party badly but says some of the blame lies with Davis. "Robarts was very committed to regional government, but Bill never really was, which pissed me off. He'd gotten his way in the county school boards. . . . The other mistake I made, which Bill didn't make, was he was pretty rough in dictating the terms to the school boards, telling them what they could do, who the administrators were, even though the mill rates went sky high. We said nobody would be fired in the regions, and they could sort out themselves who they wanted. We named all the chairmen — and most of them

---

*In 1984 Breithaupt left the Liberals to become Ontario Law Reform Commission chairman at $70,000 a year.

were good—but looking back on it, we should have been tougher and more authoritarian, like Bill was."

Davis's next unofficial election move was to name broadcaster Betty Kennedy, former federal auditor general Maxwell Henderson, and General Foods president Robert Hurlburt to "review all future spending by the provincial government."

Then Davis hit the road, delivering his "law and order, God save the Queen" morality speech everywhere and dropping election goodies along his path. He drew two thousand people to Lorne Henderson's Petrolia picnic, passing out $200,000 while he was in the neighborhood and announcing an $11 million local highway project. Culture Minister Bob Welch came along to give Victoria Playhouse $40,000 to restore the former opera house, and Henderson, uttering a line that has become a Queen's Park legend, handed officials of the Charlotte Eleanor Englehart Petrolia Hospital a $160,000 cheque and said, "Me and the premier brung you this cheque." Nobody ever gave Henderson marks for grammar, but when it came to working the system for his constituents' advantage, he had few peers.

By early July the activities seemed to be paying dividends. A Gallup poll showed that Davis's popularity had risen by 6 points and Nixon's had fallen by 3, leaving him just 3 points ahead, 39–36. The NDP reached 25 per cent, mainly on the strength of its stand on rent controls.

That same week Housing Minister Don Irvine announced a five-point tenant-protection package, including $2 million to help low-vacancy areas set up boards to study rent increases. The boards would have no power to alter rent increases, just to publicize increases they considered excessive to embarrass landlords into cutting back. Irvine also promised to increase rental supply by ten thousand family units that fiscal year and amend the Landlord and Tenant Act to provide for one-year leases, two months' notice for rent increases, and three months' notice for non-renewal. It wasn't much, but it was a crack in the door. It was followed by a promise of $30 million more for housing in McKeough's July 7 mini-budget, which also froze civil service hiring, pledged a 10 per cent cut in government operating costs, and took the sales tax off most North American-built cars bought before the year ended.

After criminal lawyer Arthur Maloney was sworn in as Ontario's first ombudsman and legislation granting teachers the right to strike was passed, the session recessed for the summer on July 18. Then, finally, after months of running an unofficial campaign, Davis announced the September 18 election, promising a "no nonsense" campaign. Nixon made it clear that integrity was his top priority, saying, "The Davis government is the issue in this election — its record, its leader, its friends." Lewis likened the Tory decline to a Shakespearean tragedy. "The whole province can see it and sense it," he said, "this almost Shakespearean decline of the government," adding that Davis, whom he described as "a very generous and decent person, . . . could be Hamlet if he lost a little weight."

The first thing Davis did was fly to Sault Ste. Marie to challenge Nixon to either "put up or shut up" on integrity. He accused Nixon of unloading "his arsenal of innuendo, . . . mud, and hot air . . . The phrase 'integrity' in government is nothing more than an obsequious, evasive slander," adding that Nixon was being "deliberately misleading, deliberately dishonest, and deliberately dishonorable."

Nixon responded, "When I talk about integrity, I'm talking about the need for a government that respects the taxpayer's dollars. If Mr. Davis believes that his government's integrity is not an issue, let him deny that Gerhard Moog contributed $35,000 and was awarded, without contract tender, a $44 million contract for the new Ontario Hydro headquarters. I'm not talking about Mr. Davis's personal affairs [although he clearly was] . . . that's not dirt, that's not innuendo. Those are the facts that have come forward on the record during the Davis years."

Things weren't about to improve. Throughout the campaign Nixon and Davis savagely attacked each other, and because neither thought Lewis was much of a threat, they both tended to ignore the NDP. In mid-August Lewis offered Nixon some advice, which wasn't accepted, when he said the Liberal "lust for extinction" was showing by trying the integrity campaign in the light of the post-Watergate connotations of political integrity. "I have never seen evidence of corruption. . . . I have no evidence of a dishonest premier who lacks integrity."

Stung by criticisms, especially from within, the Tories decided not to repeat the Big Blue Machine approach of 1971, when Davis held daily pancake breakfasts and giant evening rallies complete with all the U.S.-style hoopla imaginable. In 1975 the brassiness was replaced by a more casual pace, a studied casualness to be sure, and instead of concentrating almost exclusively on Davis, the emphasis was more on the individual candidates, all given their handy guidebooks on how to deal with the media, special-interest groups, and local issues. The party also did more direct mailing to voters than ever before, buying lists from magazine publishers and obtaining addresses of driver's licence holders from the transportation ministry.

Stephen Lewis hammered relentlessly away on rent controls from the opening bell of the campaign, trotting out almost daily, with the help of the media, dramatic horror stories of innocent tenants victimized by ghoulish landlords. Who could withstand the heart-wrenching tales of lonely widows being forced to eat dog food because of huge rent increases, or the tragedy of single mothers unable to clothe their children because some unfeeling lout had jacked the rent up 75 per cent? Rent controls soon became the only issue in the campaign — other than Tory integrity.

On August 19 Davis said he would legislate against landlords charging excessive rents, the first time he'd promised that. (Not surprisingly, a survey of five hundred North York tenants had just found that 92 per cent favored controls.) And on September 2 he promised to amend the Unconscionable Transaction Act to allow rent review boards to apply to courts to stop a landlord they thought was gouging tenants. Davis said the court route wouldn't be followed often because "the fact that it is in the act will be a sufficient deterrent." Lewis called it "ludicrous," saying landlords and their lawyers could delay forever. "You'll be retired by the time you get a settlement. You'll start at the age of thirty, you'll get your first judgment when you're forty, it'll be appealed when you're fifty, it'll go to the Supreme Court when you're sixty, and your kids will inherit the settlement."

The next day Lewis outlined eight specific cases — with names, dates, addresses, and rent increases — which he said illustrated the inadequacy of the Davis scheme. One was of a forty-year-old single working mother, forced to leave her Mississauga apartment because of a 53 per cent rent increase (from $209 to $319) that would have taken 41 per cent of her monthly income of $780. Another was of a seventy-year-old widow in Willowdale whose fixed total monthly income was $299. Her rent was increased by $43 to $230 — a 23 per cent hike. And so it went. Later some of his examples proved suspect, particularly because some seemingly large hikes were the first increases in several years, but it didn't matter. He had made his point.

A few days after the Lewis salvo, Davis announced a special subsidy program of up to $25 a month to help pensioners whose rent went up more than 12 per cent in a year, and at the same time he increased the standard monthly pension supplement (GAINS) to 300,000 seniors by $6.02 a month.

Then on September 8 Consumer and Commercial Relations Minister Sid Handleman walked into his Carleton campaign headquarters just as the phone began ringing. It was Housing Minister Don Irvine calling, the no-nonsense Conservative from Prescott. "Did you hear they've brought in rent controls, Sid?" asked Irvine. No, Handleman hadn't heard, which struck him as odd because it would affect his and Irvine's ministries the most. "It had been discussed several times in the past," he said years later. "It came up briefly in 1974, was argued down, and we thought it had died, we really did." Irvine hadn't known, either. He'd been called that morning by the premier's office and told that rent review boards would be given power after all to roll back excessive rents, but just those set since July 30.

In 1984 Davis said, "There's no reason Sid and Don should have been surprised. They disagreed, yes. I understand that. But it was brought in along with the federal government's AIB [anti-inflation board]. It had been fully discussed many times in cabinet." That's not quite how Handleman and Irvine remember it. Both men opposed rent controls and have since left politics, largely because of that issue. Irvine said he doesn't know "where the decision was made, but it was not made in cabinet. It was a mid-campaign decision, there's no doubt about that. It may have been a good decision at the time politically, in Toronto, anyway, but the facts have shown since that rent control did not help the tenants, nor did it help the industry."

But the Tories were desperate. They had closed the gap between themselves and the Liberals, but with only ten days left in the campaign, their own polls still showed them lagging behind by three points. It didn't matter that many of Lewis's horror stories didn't stand up under later scrutiny or that those that did weren't the norm. Nor did it matter that to the extent there was a problem, it was confined pretty well to Toronto, with some spillover in Ottawa and Hamilton. No, everybody had to have rent controls whether they needed them or not. This was no time for details. There was a campaign, and the Tories were losing. Nothing else mattered.

The fact was, Davis was so confused about his rent control scheme that on September 11, while campaigning in London, he said during a taped news conference that new tenants might be covered by rent review. *London Free Press* reporter Pat Crowe, who'd been on the campaign bus with Davis, asked him about this on the way to the next event, and Davis said he hadn't meant to imply that new tenants would be covered, even though that was what he'd just said. Crowe was filing this story from a phone booth outside a hall where Davis was speaking when Davis aide Larry Steinman came over and said he'd been talking to Norm Atkins in Toronto, and Davis may have been right the first time: that new tenants could be covered. Crowe, who was on deadline, began filing the new version, but moments later Steinman came running back and said he'd been talking to Toronto headquarters again, and new tenants hadn't really been part of the plan. Crowe, a laid-back, mild-mannered type, told Steinman, "I'm filing what Davis told me *his* policy is. You guys figure out *your* policy later." Crowe's story said, "New tenants will not be able to appeal to the planned rent review boards."

With tenants looked after, on September 12 Davis announced a mortgage subsidy scheme, a $25 million plan to grant tax credits of up to $500 a year if Ottawa didn't protect homeowners from rising mortgage rates. Davis gave the federal government thirty days to lower or subsidize the rates; if it didn't, his government would offset three-quarters of mortgage interest costs above 10¼ per cent.

At the same time large advertisements by the ministry of housing began to appear in newspapers heralding rent review, even though it had no legal status. It was just another election promise.

The new spending laws restricted campaign advertising to the last three weeks of the campaign, and the Tories planned to blitz Ontarians with a media avalanche. They had tried so hard to avoid the backroom wheeling-and-dealing image of machine politics that with two weeks left, Atkins complained bitterly that their low-key campaign wasn't having much impact. He said

Davis was announcing things regularly, "something positive and responsible, but some of it's not getting through." The Tories were leaving as little as possible to chance or good news judgment. They set up Tory Central Radio News Bureau, giving away free tapes to all radio stations. These reports were used extensively, especially by smaller stations always searching for fresh news clips and only too happy when they didn't have to pay a reporter to get them.

While Tories were unhappy with the media coverage of their campaign, the NDP was ecstatic. The rent control horror stories, combined with the constant Davis-Nixon bickering, were beginning to make Lewis look better and better.

It all came home to roost on the television debates, a round-robin series on CFTO-TV hosted by journalist Fraser Kelly. The first debate on August 31 featured Nixon alone. Lewis refused to participate because the station would not let the travelling media in to cover the event. Nixon, too, had pledged to reporters a day earlier that he wouldn't go in under those terms, but he didn't keep his promise. Asked by Kelly if he was questioning the integrity of the government or Davis's personal integrity, Nixon replied, "The premier and the government." One of those anxiously watching Nixon's appearance was Eddie Goodman. "I saw that and I said, 'Now we'll get the bastard.'"

The Liberals had made an error in calculating federal and provincial deficits, prompting an Oakville Liberal candidate to run an ad in his local paper disowning his own party's claims. "Out of that came those advertisements of the windcock going around and around to show Nixon didn't know what his positions were on anything," said Goodman. Nixon had also miscalculated a scheme to save money for school boards, and the Tories ran an ad showing Nixon saying, "$500 million is going to be saved — oops, only $50 million."

The Tory strategists all met in Davis's basement on Labor Day weekend when a Teetor poll showed Nixon just three points ahead. "Gallup had him 13 points in front," says Hugh Segal. "We knew the NDP vote was hard, but the important thing tactically was Nixon's vote was soft. From then on the strategy was to put together the best election-day machine that ever existed up to that time. We had to get our voters out, every one of them. And we did."

For his debate with Davis, Lewis abandoned his principled view about not letting CFTO dictate campaign coverage. After all, the segment with Nixon was shown at 10:30 p.m. on a holiday weekend, but with Davis as his opponent and in a better time slot, ratings would be considerably higher. The debate itself was cordial but dull. Lewis got into trouble over his plans for a higher minimum wage, which Davis said would hurt the tourist industry, but people were still underestimating the Lewis campaign, so this round was seen as a tune-up for the main bout with Nixon five days before voting day.

After the Lewis debate, Davis left for a four-day, old-fashioned, train-stumping tour of southwestern Ontario, stopping at little stations to greet loyalists and going off by van to meetings in nearby towns—an unusually relaxed pace for so late in the campaign—and doing nothing to detract from growing excitement about what was being called The Great Debate.

It had come down to this. Both men knew it, both camps felt it, and heaven knows the media reported it. The months of growing hostility, of intense, personal animosity, had come down to one thirty-minute TV debate, when just the two of them, moderated by Kelly, would be up there, head to head.

Tory strategists held a pre-debate confab at the Park Plaza suite. They were all nervous. They were losing, and this was their one chance to survive. Throughout the campaign they'd tried to bait Nixon, to ignite his lightning temper, and that was the plan for the debate. Make him mad. Force him to lose his cool and, they hoped, lose votes with it. "The premier was saying he didn't want the debate to become personal," says Segal. "Can you imagine? I said to him, 'Premier, Bob Nixon is going around this province making you personally responsible for everything but brain cancer. That's pretty personal. He's calling you corrupt. He's calling you dishonest. I don't know how much more personal it gets.'" Goodman was growing more excited by the minute, jumping up and down, egging Davis on, trying to get him charged up for the most important event of his political career.

When Davis arrived on the set for taping, he was so nervous he first went to the wrong desk, then dropped his papers on the floor. During the debate itself, even though he'd known Fraser Kelly for years, he kept calling him "Mr. Fraser."

The debate lived up (or down) to expectations. Both men were angry and vicious. Tight-lipped and clearly tense, Davis called his opponent "Mr. Nixon" (a formality he used on reporters when he didn't like their questions); Nixon, adopting a cool, smirking style, called him "Bill."

Nixon opened by welcoming the debate, saying it had been a good campaign and predicting a Liberal victory. Davis returned, "It has not been a good campaign," calling the Liberal effort "one of the worst that I have ever seen in my history in politics. It has been founded on misrepresentation, inaccuracies, and, on occasion, deliberate falsehoods. . . ." Davis accused Nixon of a $10 billion fabrication — a reference to his claim that Davis had built up a $5.3 billion deficit, compared to Ottawa's $2.3 billion. In fact, Ottawa's was $11.5 billion, but at one point Nixon said he stood by his charges. Nixon chided him later for using such words as "untruth" and "deliberate falsehood" instead of "lie."

At the end the Tories were delighted. Davis hadn't really won, but they thought Nixon, by being disrespectful and by dodging direct challenges to his figures, had lost. A year later, after quitting as leader, Nixon admitted as much, too.

When Tories across Ontario woke up on September 19 to a minority government, the first in thirty years, they still must have been thankful for the seats they did hold. The NDP, in second place after doubling their seats from 19 to 38 with a mere 2 per cent hike in their share of the popular vote and picking up seven new Metro Toronto seats, were ecstatic, prompting Lewis to say, "It's wonderful to have for a change a political victory rather than a moral victory." For Nixon, in last place, it was small comfort that he had increased his party's popular vote by 6 per cent over 1971 and had gone from 20 seats to 36. His time was done.

Davis had plummeted from 78 seats in a 117-seat legislature to 51 seats out of 125. His share of the popular vote had plunged from 44 per cent to just over 35 per cent, a working example of the advantage to the government party in Ontario, the only three-party system in the country. There are, after all, only so many anti-government votes, and despite four years of valiant effort to alienate his traditional constituency, even Davis had fallen slightly short of turning everybody off.

As for rent controls, on a partisan level they didn't even win seats for the Tories — tenants in west Toronto, where the issue was strongest, weren't conned by Davis's death-bed repentance, and with the exception of Larry Grossman's St. Andrew-St. Patrick riding, they voted NDP, anyway. Yet ten years later the "temporary" measure imposed by Davis and his machine in a desperate bid for votes continues to cause headaches and cost taxpayers millions without doing anything to address the problem of supply.

John Harvey Miller, the gifted speechwriter who toiled for Davis from 1972 to 1977, says Davis is "fundamentally a very decent man, but when you come to principle, ideological principle, no. I'm always reminded of an article written in the early 1960s by the late Adam Clayton Powell, which began, 'The first duty of an elected politician is to be re-elected.' If Bill didn't read that article, then by osmosis he absorbed it, because that's the way he operates. . . . They were philosophically and intellectually opposed to rent controls, but you get into a campaign and you're getting hammered, so what do they do? They bring them in. I don't know if they teach that in political science, but that's what happened."

Eddie Goodman sees the 1975 campaign as the watershed for Davis. "I have a theory that was the turning point when he got that minority. You know what it's like — it's like a boxer taking a hell of a punch on the jaw, shaking his head, and then realizing he's taken the very best the other guy had and he's still on his feet. . . . It's not the end of the world, you know, to get the shit kicked out of you a bit."

In his quiet, sober speech on election night, with his mother, his wife, and five kids surrounding him, Davis thanked his supporters and congratulated Stephen Lewis for a clean campaign. He never once mentioned Nixon.

Davis had won, or, more accurately, he had survived. But as he stood there under the glare of the television lights looking out into the living rooms of Ontario, he didn't look very proud of himself.

CHAPTER 10
THE TWO PER CENT SOLUTION

—————— ❦ ——————

Having survived an election he should have lost through a combination of a brilliant NDP campaign and Liberal stupidity, Bill Davis shifted direction. Margaret Thatcher and Ronald Reagan were already heralding a resurgence of the right, and Davis, always ready to go with the flow, thought he'd hop on the bandwagon himself. Many defeated Tories blamed the free-spending, centralized Davis style for their electoral losses, the most celebrated being London's Gordon Walker, who wrote a letter complaining that the party had moved too far left and had lost touch with the public. Davis publicly dismissed the complaints, but the proof of Walker's pudding came in a highly publicized "restraint" program and the appointment of two right wingers — Frank Miller and Jim Taylor — into major social portfolios.

Taylor was summoned to the Park Plaza and given social services. "I said, 'Bill, you're talking to Jim Taylor, you know,' and I asked him why. . . . It seemed odd to me." But Davis told Taylor it was because of the restraint program and upcoming federal-provincial negotiations on the Canada Assistance Plan. Miller was thrown into health as part of the same slash-government-spending fad and tried to close ten hospitals to show that the Tories meant business with restraint. Miller soon learned they didn't really mean business. Davis did what he saw as being popular, and when Taylor and Miller did their jobs and upset too many lobby groups, he hung them out to dry. Miller, who had snowballs thrown at him and who became an object of vilification for months, ended up with a heart attack for his troubles. Taylor ended up in energy.

"I became a focus and a lightning rod," says Taylor. "I did what I was told to do. It wasn't pleasant. When you're getting protest after protest of people claiming you're hurting the poor, they've got to put a face on that anger, and the face was mine." The social services budget had increased 20 per cent each year for the previous five years, and "that couldn't continue, obviously, but if I had any regret, it's that I felt I wasn't being supported around here. I had support privately from backbenchers, but the premier never gave me any public support. Yet I can recall him going to a meeting of the Yorkville businessmen and supporting Frank Miller's efforts on the hospital closings."

One of the more bizarre cabinet ministers appointed was a tiny, deeply religious Hamilton Mountain teacher, John Smith, given correctional services mainly because there were no other Tories left in the Hamilton area after the election. He ran into problems, too. A former president of the Canadian Bible Association, Smith not only wore his fundamentalist beliefs on his sleeve, which was fine, but he also mixed them with his ministerial duties.

Under the Fleck regime, ministers' speeches were vetted by the premier's office to avoid conflicts or statements that would compete against each other for news. Smith had already made some controversial speeches — one called for mandatory teen identification cards, with picture, signature, and Social Insurance Number on them and fines for parents who didn't know where their children were — when John Harvey Miller asked Ed Stewart to reconstitute the old system to avoid embarrassments and suggested to Stewart and Davis that they should speak to Smith. They agreed but did nothing.

One Friday night a Smith speech arrived on Miller's desk for a Tory function in Hamilton the following Monday. Among other things, Smith was advocating that prisoners have regular Bible reading to improve their souls. Miller made what he calls "an executive decision" and told Smith's officials to go ahead. Miller was at the corner of Yonge and College streets on Monday evening to get the *Globe*'s bulldog edition, and "as expected, this embarrassment was on the front page." At 7:15 a.m. Stewart buzzed the intercom in his office, told him to "get your ass down here," threw the paper at him, and said he'd never seen Davis so upset. Davis finally spoke to Smith that day — Smith apologized in the legislature for going too far — but he didn't speak to Miller for three weeks.

But while the public saw the higher profiles of ministers from the right, the key addition to the Palace Guard was a new recruit from the left.

*   *   *

Hugh Segal was relaxing on the beach at Cavendish, Prince Edward Island, just two weeks after the election when a phone call came through from Ed Stewart. The inner circle wanted Segal to work full-time for Davis because he had experience working with Stanfield during the 1972–74 federal minority. He was hired as the premier's legislative secretary, but right from the start he not only had Davis's ear, he also had the ability to make him laugh.

A rotund, witty, articulate (some say glib) man, Segal was thrown out of Grade 8 in 1962 at an orthodox Jewish rabbinical school in Montreal after putting John Diefenbaker stickers on his books, including three or four biblical and talmudic texts. "The rabbis went through the roof. They considered that blasphemy."

Segal was born in a working class Montreal area in 1950, the youngest of three sons: His oldest brother, Seymour, is a successful Montreal artist, and brother Brian is president of Ryerson Polytechnical Institute in Toronto. His mother was born in Canada, the daughter of an Austrian baker who started the first kosher bakery in Montreal in the late 1880s. His paternal grandfather was a refugee of the Russian revolution, a supporter of social democrat Alexander Kerensky, who was hated by both the Bolsheviks and the czarists. He had his eyes crossed, literally, from fear when during a pogrom he witnessed the Cossacks raping and murdering people. While he was proud of his grandson when he ran for office in 1972, Segal's grandfather viewed the Tories as "the bosses' party." He spent much of his life fighting the bosses and, as an activist with the International Ladies Garment Workers Union, sparked one of the first strikes in Montreal's garment industry. It took him nine years, saving every penny, to bring his wife and son (Hugh's father) over from Russia. He'd often send money, but the Soviets would open the envelopes and take it.

Hugh's father, Morris, was "a great success as a father and a bust as a businessman" who spent most of his working life driving a cab. He was also campaign manager for Liberal Milt Klein when much of the community supported Communist Fred Rose, "until he got busted as a commie spy, and my father's crowd, who had been refugees of commie rule, weren't anxious to support them here."

Diefenbaker visited Segal's school in 1962 and presented the principal with his bill of rights. Segal's enthusiasm for the Chief was not applauded at home, so after a dispute the young Segal wrote letters to each party leader. The others sent him form letters or pamphlets, but Diefenbaker replied with a five-page, handwritten letter. Segal's enthusiasm grew to the point where he led the PCs three times in high school model parliaments, the first to "a crushing defeat," the second to "heady opposition status," and finally "to a crushing victory, at which point I became just like Dief and fired ministers every day. It was terrible."

In 1967 he won the $500 city-wide debating contest, putting the money toward his $600 University of Ottawa tuition in 1968. He couldn't have managed without that money, but even still he was living on student loans from Quebec. He chose that university because it had a good history department, and he wanted to escape the "English-language ghetto" in Montreal and improve his French. He was eventually elected university president and says his group was considered "the right wingers of campus . . . which tells you something about the others." He successfully fought a strong move by the student council in 1970 to condemn the War Measures Act, saying the council "shouldn't get into that stuff."

Soon afterward the radical, left-wing Ontario Union of Students resigned from all provincial student advisory committees, and the minister of education, Bill Davis, wrote each university asking for replacements. Segal ended up on a student awards committee and met Davis six months later, when Davis and Ed Stewart came to a committee meeting. When Segal complained about the system and Davis told Stewart to respond, it was Segal's "first indication that when it comes to bad news, he doesn't like to deliver it himself."

He was elected national vice-president of the YPCs in 1971 and supported Davis at the leadership convention. His "campus sweetheart thing, a brief romance" with Maureen McTeer fell apart when she supported Bert Lawrence, although "her strong Catholicism was another reason." A year later Segal ran in Ottawa Centre against Liberal Hugh Poulin, and Davis appeared at McNabb Arena at an all-Ottawa rally for him. Tory officials had wanted Davis to attend the rally in Peter Reilly's Ottawa West riding, but he insisted it be in Segal's area. "It saved my ass. It took me from a guy who might have lost his deposit to a guy who lost by one thousand votes in a riding that had been Liberal for fifty years."

Segal became research assistant for left-wing Tory MP David MacDonald, then junior appointments secretary for Stanfield, moving over to communications director for the party when he ran again, and lost, in 1974. He had just returned to Carleton University to study international economics when Hugh Macaulay and Ross DeGeer asked him to be secretary for the 1975 provincial campaign. At a reception that week, Davis came over to Segal and said he needed his help. "Shit, I was twenty-four, came from poor immigrant parents from Quebec, and here was the premier of Ontario saying he needs me."

After two years as Davis's secretary, he left in 1977 to become director of corporate affairs for John Labatt Ltd. in London but returned in 1979 when Davis asked for help in planning for the Quebec referendum. In 1981 he became associate secretary of cabinet for federal-provincial relations, playing a major role in constitutional discussions, but he left in late 1982 to work for Norm Atkins. "One more pinko out of the picture," he joked at the time, adding quickly, "but there are many more around."

✻   ✻   ✻

A few days after the call to Segal, Davis appointed veteran Bob Welch as his house leader, a tricky job in minority (as the late Walter Baker found out for the federal Tories in 1979) demanding not only knowledge of the system but respect from caucus and cabinet. Minorities inevitably mean more legislation because the opposition can't be routinely outvoted, and for their part the NDP countered with Ian Deans as house leader, the Liberals with Jim Breithaupt — two of the more able parliamentarians. "It was a constant, day-to-day thing," says Welch. "Every issue, every piece of legislation, had to be scrutinized with a view to whether it could provoke an election or not. It's fun, challenging, but doesn't leave a lot of room for relaxation."

It was made even more challenging by changes in procedure. In the 1960s and earlier, opposition members would give ministers written notice of questions, a system that made it easier to get an answer, but one that was less politically useful to the opposition than questions sprung on the government with no notice at all. That changed in the 1970s, when the opposition was also given more office space, researchers, a longer question period (an hour rather than forty-five minutes), and changes in the composition of committees to reflect the make-up of the legislature. That meant the government lost its majority on committees as well as in the House.

Every government move during that minority period had one goal — regaining the majority. The Tories rammed through rent controls, of course. Despite private opposition from most party members, the government was in no position to tangle with Opposition Leader Lewis on that one. But there were no dramatic initiatives, no passionate debates.

In January, 1976, Davis, having earlier lowered the drinking age from twenty-one to eighteen, dispatched MPP Terry Jones to study the age question. Sure enough, after the dust cleared the drinking age was raised to nineteen, where it remains.

In April Treasurer Darcy McKeough released eight bulky government reports setting out ways to deal with a population that was supposed to increase from eight million to twelve million in the next twenty-five years. The idea was to generate growth away from Toronto while saving farm and recreational land. Once the problem had been stated, that was the end of that.

Davis was just grinding along, day by day, bringing in a bill to legalize the federal anti-inflation plans for Ontario civil servants, welcoming Liberal defector Marvin Shore (who had beaten Gordon Walker, then lost himself in the next election), fighting off Lewis over mercury pollution in the English-Wabigoon river system, watching as Bob Nixon stepped down as Liberal leader and

Montreal-born sex therapist Stuart Smith took over, and slowly regaining a lead in the polls. By October, 1976, Gallup put him at 40 per cent, 10 ahead of the Liberals and 12 in front of the NDP.

The universe, it seemed, was unfolding as it should. There was a problem with the separatists in Quebec, and the constitutional talks were heating up, but speculation began in earnest that the Big Blue Machine was getting ready to roll again. Journalist Eric Dowd wrote in December, 1976, that Tory MPPs should be happy for Christmas because, besides a card from Davis and the kids, "each will receive a dandy new guide, fully illustrated and with complete instructions showing how to assemble a winning election campaign in jig time."

In February, 1977, Davis held a two-day summit at the Hilton Harbour Castle called "Partnership for Prosperity," claiming it had nothing to do with politics but was "of crucial importance" to the economy. Naturally, something that crucial couldn't be left to chance, so Transmedia, the party's propaganda arm, filmed and recorded the whole thing. The Tories had also rented sixteen vacant offices and stores in Metro on four-month renewable leases.

In March Davis dropped the overdue but controversial property tax reforms, despite a report released the same day by a government commission calling for a detailed overhaul. The commission had been studying property tax reform for ten years, but Davis and McKeough said the proposals needed more study. It was just too close to campaign time to deal with that hot potato.

On March 16 a Gallup poll showed Davis had regained public confidence. Asked which party leader would make the best premier, 59 per cent said Davis, compared with 28 per cent for Lewis and 13 for Smith. "The problem was, there was no issue," says Sid Handleman. "We'd sit in meetings talking about what could be an issue, but there wasn't anything."

Re-enter rent controls. In what became known as the "two per cent solution," the Tories said the 6 per cent ceiling on rent increases was too low; it had to be 8 per cent. The Liberals and NDP said 6 was fine. Landlords could charge more anyway; they just had to go through rent review. It really was a minor dispute, but Handleman met Goodman at the east door of Queen's Park one day just after the opposition parties had said they would vote against the higher ceiling. Handleman kidded about the ceiling being an election issue, and Goodman said, "You mean to say both parties are going to vote against us?" and with that rushed off into the building. The next day Tom Wells sent a letter to the house leaders saying rent controls were now a matter of confidence. "I'd been telling everybody it was simply a housekeeping matter. I was as surprised as the opposition to find out it was a confidence matter." The proposed ceilings were duly rejected.

In his kickoff speech on May 3 for the June 9 election, Davis, defining the target for the campaign, said the NDP would turn a profitable province into an "industrial wasteland" and that this was "the most important election we have ever faced." He may have thought it was, at least for him.

The Tories spent $2.5 million on the campaign, and everywhere Davis went, he took eighteen assistants with him. Lewis usually had four, Smith about six. To bring out the crowds, the NDP had two advance men, the Liberals six, the Tories about thirty. At party headquarters it was the same story: The NDP had eleven staffers, the Liberals twenty, and the Tories fluctuated between thirty-five and seventy under campaign manager Ross "The Boss" DeGeer.

Davis travelled aboard a custom-built bus with color TV, microwave oven, shower, refrigerator, couches, and a duplicating machine. Rented from a Cambridge man, it carried a small sign, "God Bless Our Camper," hard to see beside the emblazoned Tory campaign slogan: "Your Future, Your Choice." He was always followed by a press bus and an unmarked OPP car, and, unlike his two opponents, he enjoyed several police escorts to and from the main highways — just another perk of power.

In an echo of the previous election, during the second week of the campaign Davis named Mr. Justice Samuel Hughes to conduct a judicial inquiry into a 1974 donation of $35,000 to the Tories from a garbage disposal firm that was seeking government approval of a landfill site. The donation, from Disposal Services Ltd., was made a few months before approval of the site, and the *Wall Street Journal* had quoted a memorandum from the parent firm saying the donation was for political reasons. No evidence of wrongdoing was found.

The two per cent solution aside, it was still an election in search of an issue, and Davis tried out stances on a number of them, sometimes on both sides. He tried to set himself up as the best hope to save Confederation, a stance the Liberals' Smith found "nauseating." But after Revenue Minister Margaret Scrivener accused the NDP of being sympathetic to the Parti Québécois at the St. David riding nomination in Rosedale and the media dumped on her for quoting New Democrat Jim Renwick out of context, Davis dumped on her, too, telling her not to use the separatist issue as a divisive one. Noble sentiments aside, he had known what Scrivener was going to say; her speech had been distributed to the press from his office.

Even worse was the May 19 unveiling of the sixteen-point "Bramalea Charter" written by Segal, promising 100,000 new jobs and 90,000 housing starts each year for the next decade. The document, printed on stiff buff paper and resembling a heraldic scroll, promised lower municipal taxes for seniors, more sales for Ontario goods abroad, two trees for every one harvested, a balanced budget by 1981, fewer strikes, and a series of individual rights covering work, family, and recreation, "personal fulfilment, growth, and self-improvement." (Two years later a review of the charter found, to no one's surprise, that few of these great pledges were ever kept.)

Two days before a TV debate with Lewis and Smith, Davis was crossing Toronto harbor by boat when he was struck square in the back by a bird dropping. "The NDP will stop at nothing," he quipped. But then, neither would the Tories in their quest to derail Stephen Lewis.

His big setback occurred midway through the campaign, when the Tories upstaged him over his attacks on mercury pollution north of Kenora. Lewis, who had hammered away at the issue for years, hired a larger plane than usual to accommodate all the television crews covering his flight north. When he stepped off the plane in Kenora, a Tory advance man handed him a speech delivered that day in Sudbury by Resources Minister Frank Miller, accusing native peoples at White Dog and Grassy Narrows of being unco-operative and listing in painful detail all the proffered government help they had refused. So instead of being on the attack at his Kenora press conference, Lewis was reduced to reacting to Miller.

But things got worse. Everybody headed to what was to be an

emotional town meeting at Grassy Narrows, but the NDP people decided to visit Minaki on the way, site of a lavish lodge into which the Tories had poured about $20 million, under harsh criticism from Lewis. The cavalcade came over the hill at the edge of the village to see two OPP cars parked at the side of the gravel road. The reason soon became apparent. The entire village population was out in force, hanging an effigy of Lewis, chanting, shaking their fists, and being altogether inhospitable. Lewis tried to speak, but the crowd wouldn't let him, and he had to quickly retreat to his bus. The demonstration made great television, and while Lewis and some print media people carried on to Grassy Narrows, the TV crews headed to Kenora to ship their film for the evening news.

Lewis later called it his worst day in politics and accused Northern Affairs Minister Leo Bernier of setting it up; Minaki was in his riding. Bernier denied it. He was smiling at the time.

When the votes were counted, the Tories had gained seven seats to 58, the Liberals had dropped one to 34, and the NDP had slipped five to 33. It hardly seemed worth it. Eddie Goodman, who admits the whole thing was his idea, says even though the Tories missed a majority, they gained "some distance" from the other two parties. But at what cost? Taxpayers spent $20 million simply to put the NDP back into third place and restore the Liberals as bridesmaids to the ruling Tories.

During six weeks and sixty thousand miles of campaigning, Davis had increased his popular vote by four points to 40 per cent, but it wasn't enough. A 1980 study by National Polling Trends Ltd. concluded, based on elections since Drew came to power, that the Tories need about 42 per cent to form a majority. They consistently get between 5 and 6 per cent more seats than their popular vote would indicate, while the Liberals get fewer; the NDP get about what they deserve, except in 1975, when they won thirty-eight seats with 29 per cent of the vote, largely on the strength of rent controls.

Having twice been given the message by the electorate, Davis never again tried to tinker with rent controls, opting instead to entrench them as a permanent fixture in the province, despite their destructive influence on apartment construction and the continuing problems of supply. But then, critics of the earlier mid-campaign decision to introduce controls had repeatedly pointed out that once controls were in place, it would be almost impossible to get rid of them.

Nor could Davis get rid of his minority, at least not for another few years, and the first thing he did after the 1977 campaign was promise to serve a full four-year term.

CHAPTER 11
GRACE RESTORED

———————— ☙ ————————

The Bill Davis of 1977 was certainly different than the Bill Davis of 1971. His dark hair had turned to silver, his chubbiness was gone, and he now smoked a pipe constantly, puffing on a cigar only occasionally. After six years in power, he had become very much the political pro, comfortable in office and confident enough to follow his own instincts. The advice of others was still welcome, but after the Fleck-Rowan fiasco and the two per cent solution, the decisions were his alone to make.

The opposition soon looked different, too. With the Liberals now back in their customary second spot and the NDP in third, it wasn't long before Stephen Lewis decided to quit. Lewis, whose oratory used to draw crowds into the public galleries, had always been a Davis favorite, and he was soon active on provincial labor relations tribunals and as a radio and television commentator in Toronto until 1984, when Davis convinced Prime Minister Brian Mulroney that he would be a good choice as Canada's ambassador to the United Nations. He was followed as NDP chief by Ottawa academic Michael Cassidy, a sour, intense man who hung in for one election, was pressured out as leader, then left in 1984 to run successfully as an Ottawa MP.

If Davis was looking forward to four years of smooth sailing after the years of scandals and near-defeats, he was disappointed. The bulk of those years saw him drawn into some of the toughest, most bitter, and most important battles of his career, primarily over national issues such as the Constitution, the Quebec referendum, the oil-pricing wars, and two federal elections.

At home the years were marked by the day-to-day tasks of governing Ontario and developing policies to ensure the continuation of the Tories' hold on power. They were also marked by a withering of the opposition — neither the Liberals nor the NDP could find leaders of the stature of Nixon and Lewis — and, in the expectation that he would follow the pattern of his predecessors and stay in power for the regulation Tory decade, a very quiet jockeying for the succession to the throne.

The performance of Davis's fiscal restraint, including a specific timetable for balancing the budget by 1981, never matched his rhetoric, and Darcy McKeough, the proponent of restraint and the leading heir apparent, finally got tired of waiting and returned to the private sector. But unlike Pierre Trudeau, who discouraged most of his skilled ministers from exercising power in their own right, Davis did encourage those who were interested to stake out their own constituencies, hoping to build up an impressive stable of potential leaders when he finally did decide to retire. Senior ministers Roy McMurtry, Frank Miller, Dennis Timbrell, Larry Grossman, Bette Stephenson, Tom Wells, and Bob Welch were essentially given the portfolios they asked for and were allowed to sink or swim on their own merits.

Davis continued his policy of quietly extending bilingual services in areas of the province with significant francophone pockets, but most of the attention he garnered on that issue came from his perceived failure to provide French-language high schools in Sturgeon Falls, Essex, Cornwall, and Penetanguishene. René Lévesque, ridiculing Davis's pledges to fight to keep Quebec in Confederation, pointed to the school battles as examples of Ontario's alleged bigotry against franco-Ontarians, and the fact that the fights were over buildings, not education (which was provided by law), got lost in the heat of the times.

Two other issues were heating up at the same time, oil pricing and the Constitution, and before he was finished those fights, Davis made lasting enemies of fellow Tories Joe Clark and Peter Lougheed and earned a reputation, not entirely warranted, of being a willing bed partner of Pierre Trudeau's. While the constitutional issue would percolate off and on until well after the next provincial election in 1981, the oil dispute had a bearing on the 1980 federal election, with Davis caught in the middle between fighting for Ontario consumers and opposing the newly elected federal Tories. He opted for the consumers, a decision that cost Clark his government and ultimately his job as Tory leader.

Davis, as usual, campaigned hard for the federal Tories in 1979, and Clark won the contest in Ontario. But relations between Queen's Park and Ottawa quickly soured. Clark brought in his own advisers, and the Ontario crew, who had been an integral part of the federal Tory machine as well, were sent packing. Under Bob Stanfield, Davis loyalists Dalton Camp, Norman Atkins, and Eddie Goodman had considerable influence. Goodman chaired the leadership conference when Stanfield replaced Diefenbaker, and as one of the few Tory insiders of national stature who seemed to get along with all the internal warring factions, his advice was often sought. Both Camp and Atkins, of course, had worked for Stanfield since his early days in Nova Scotia, and Atkins was Stanfield's leadership chairman while Camp was national party president. Even Hugh Segal worked in Ottawa for Stanfield, albeit in a junior position, but it was enough to make him loyal to the federal leader when he became a force in Ontario politics.

Under Clark, however, all that changed, and during his short-lived government in 1979, he and Davis feuded publicly over oil pricing, culminating in John Crosbie's December, 1979, federal budget with its eighteen-cent-per-gallon excise tax on oil. Both Davis and Frank Miller, then treasurer, viciously attacked the plan, and when Clark's government fell immediately afterward, Davis was pointedly not asked to help Clark until the last few weeks, when it was already too late to salvage his campaign.

In 1984 Davis said his relationship with Clark was "always cordial," and he felt that the advice he was prepared to offer during 1979—"which was sometimes not sought"—was meant to be helpful. "Not that he should have accepted it, but I just think that side of our relationship could have been more positive, because maybe he felt that I had a particular Ontario provincial interest to promote. But I guess that I also had an understanding of the party in this province and that in terms of federal success, support in this province is very fundamental."

It "disappointed" him a bit that people believed his opposition to the budget meant he opposed Clark personally and wouldn't campaign for him in 1980. "Maybe they forgot that we were still in a minority situation here, and perhaps they had forgotten that we opposed the initial excise tax [imposed by Trudeau]. . . . He felt, and those advising him felt, that perhaps there was no need for premiers, not just myself, but premiers generally, to be as involved."

After the 1980 federal election, Davis began thinking seriously of a campaign of his own, a quest to regain his lost majority. Speculation about an election was growing in late 1980 but virtually exploded on January 27, 1981, when Davis unveiled a glitzy, $1.5 billion, five-year economic blueprint for Ontario called BILD (Board of Industrial Leadership and Development). Liberal Pat Reid immediately dubbed the scheme BILGE, a recognition of the fact that the Tories simply compiled a series of existing programs, dreamed up a catchy name, churned out fancy press releases, and called it industrial planning. The largest single item in BILD, for example, was $125 million for highway improvements that would have been made anyway. But Davis, perched high on a platform behind Tory-blue tables, surrounded by eight cabinet ministers sitting in front of giant-sized blue-and-white-trillium logos, presented the package as his own Brave New World.

Davis dismissed opposition claims that the BILD spectacle was simply a pre-election ploy, but he added that should an election just by chance occur, "I'm prepared to defend this document on any platform anywhere in the province of Ontario."

A few weeks later he suddenly discovered that the people of Ontario really did need an election. Buoyed by favorable polls, six years of making minority government work, and a typically catchy but meaningless slogan — "Keep the Promise" — Davis headed off in search of his March 19 majority, driving the Big Blue Machine for the final time to a crushing 70-seat win, with 44.4 per cent of the vote. It was the twelfth consecutive Tory election win since 1943, the fourth for Davis. The Liberals, under Stuart Smith, stayed at 34 seats, while the NDP under Cassidy collapsed 12 seats to 21. It wasn't long before both Smith and Cassidy were gone, the Liberals choosing London businessman David Peterson, who finished second to Smith in the 1976 leadership race, and the NDP picking their federal finance critic, Bob Rae.

The 58 per cent turnout was the lowest since the Second World War, but it was still enough for Davis to claim his fall from grace had ended. In 1984 he said his re-established majority was "important both for the party and to me in a personal sense. I was anxious to accomplish that. . . . I probably started thinking a little bit about [retirement] after that election. . . . There wasn't any conscious decision made then, but to say that I didn't give it some thought would be wrong."

* * *

After the 1981 campaign a young Toronto lawyer, John Tory, was invited to join the Tuesday morning breakfast club. Not long after that Hugh Segal and Ed Stewart invited him to breakfast at the Park Plaza's prune danish lounge and offered him Segal's job as principal secretary to Davis. The appointment was announced formally in December, 1981, and he began on March 1, 1982, as the youngest member of the Palace Guard.

While Segal is noted for his spontaneous humor, John Tory is not. One of those people who is exceptionally mature at eighteen (read stuffy), Tory was described by Bruce McCaffrey as one of those perennial Young Progressive Conservatives: "Some of those YPCs don't grow up; they just seem to get taller." But Tory says, "Any stuffiness on my part was more nervousness I had when I arrived. . . . I'm not as outgoing and gregarious as, say, Hugh [Segal] or Sally [Barnes], but caucus members think I'm older than I am. They think maybe I'm thirty-five because I've been around, and thirty-five doesn't sound as young as twenty-seven."

Tory seemed particularly concerned about suggestions that he was a Rosedale prototype. "I cannot deny the fact, nor would I ever want to, that I came from a background most people, including myself, would consider a very privileged upbringing. . . . But I'm not from Rosedale. That carries with it the connotation somebody is rich, fat, waspish."

Now that that's cleared up, Tory's great-great-grandfather and two brothers were born on a backwoods farm in Nova Scotia. One of the brothers was Dr. Henry Marshall Tory, founder of the University of Alberta and former head of the National Research Council. The second brother, James C. Tory, was a Liberal cabinet minister before becoming Nova Scotia's lieutenant-governor.

The third brother, John A. Tory, was the first Toronto manager of Sun Life of Canada, building it into the largest life insurance operation in North America at the time. His son, John's grandfather, was J. S. D. Tory, a prominent corporate lawyer who founded the law firm that both John and his father (also named John) eventually worked for, the prestigious firm of Tory, Tory, Deslauriers and Binnington. His father is also president of the media, oil, and just-about-everything-else conglomerate, Thomson Enterprises. "There's no question they've been successful people, and if you're trying to define where they fit in, they were people who might fit that category of Rosedale. I don't like to sound like I'm defensive about this, because I don't apologize, and I don't feel I have to, for where I come from."

John Tory was born in North Toronto and has spent his entire life within a two-mile radius of his current home. He went to Bedford Park Public School until Grade 7, then moved on to the private University of Toronto Schools. "People have said to me, 'You mustn't have had any adolescence because you started in politics at fourteen or fifteen.' In fact, I think I did. The fact that I had an adolescence is evidenced by the fact I almost got kicked out of UTS in Grade Ten for causing trouble and almost failing. . . . As I think back on it, that must have been my adolescent period. I was badly behaved, being disruptive in class and doing practical jokes. . . . But I think I had a perfectly normal period of teenage years and did all the things normal teenagers do, except for the fact I lived where I did and lived how I did and got heavily involved in politics by the time I was sixteen."

His first formal involvement came in 1969, when a friend sold him a one-dollar membership to show up at the York Mills PC Association and vote for the riding executive. A year later he became recording secretary of the association and, like so many people who prospered under Davis, worked for Allan Lawrence in the 1971 leadership convention. He was president of the Ontario YPCs from 1974 to 1976.

Tory went to the University of Toronto from 1972 to 1975, then to Osgoode Hall law school until 1978, where he was student council president. Even as a student in 1973 he accused the Toronto media of being "unfair" to Davis over the series of mini-scandals, telling Scarborough Kiwanians that instead of criticizing, "newspapers might serve a purpose in society if they concentrated on explaining the policy of all governments to the people." The same attitude cropped up periodically over the years, and in September, 1983, as principal assistant to Davis, he complained about reporters covering a party think-in because they had described the Benmiller Lodge near Goderich as "posh." At the time party officials were roughing it in $150-a-night rooms in a majestically restored old river mill nestled on the banks of a spring-fed watershed. They were discussing government restraint.

Tory ran David Crombie's mayoralty campaign in 1976, author Austin Clarke's losing campaign in York South in 1977, and Susan Fish's successful aldermanic campaign in 1978. In 1979 and 1980 he ran Ronald Atkey's federal campaigns against John Roberts, winning the first and losing the second, and in 1981 he managed Fish's successful provincial campaign and became campaign secretary for the provincial party, another old job of Segal's.

When he was appointed to the premier's office, Tory said it was "a healthy thing" for Davis to have such a young adviser because his age was "representative of the bulk of the population." And John Tory is, after all, just your average young Ontarian. Certainly not one of those Rosedale types. Just ask him.

*   *   *

After what Davis liked to call "the realities of March 19," he was deeply entrenched in power in the finest Ontario Tory tradition. The Tories have maintained the longest-running regime in the western world by acquiring a not always deserved reputation for quietly competent management of the province's affairs, helped along considerably by the vagaries of a three-party system. Drew and Robarts, especially, endured by raiding the opposition's platforms and walking off with popular planks. Davis did, too, and it is a measure of how thoroughly he undercut the opposition's strength that when other, less laudatory features of previous Tory regimes — abuses of power and a tolerance for a police state mentality — were reprised under him, the harshest criticism came from within his own party.

During the late 1970s, for example, relations between Metro Toronto police and militants in the expanding East and West

Indian communities were rapidly deteriorating. In 1977 Attorney General Roy McMurtry had pushed the court of appeal into establishing tougher sentences for racially motivated assaults after a series of such assaults in Toronto. The actual cases of abuse were rare, but they happened often enough and were so widely publicized that the Davis inner circle saw an opportunity to capitalize on the issue in search of ethnic votes. So in 1979 Davis established a race relations division of the Human Rights Commission and began the process of strengthening the existing Ontario Human Rights Code. It was a move the bulk of his caucus privately opposed but could do nothing to stop.

In June, 1980, proposals to revamp the Code were introduced by Labor Minister Bob Elgie, easily the most left-wing idealogue in the Davis cabinet. Elgie, both a lawyer and a neurosurgeon whose father Goldwin was a Tory MPP for Toronto-Woodbine during the 1930s and early 1940s, was elected in 1977 and named labor minister the next year. From the beginning the NDP regarded him as one of their own in Tory clothes, and he was quick to prove that their faith was not misplaced, introducing mandatory checkoff schemes for all employees in unionized plants. When he was shuffled to Consumer and Commercial Relations, one union activist hugged him and praised him for his fine work on their behalf.

His proposals for the Code were greeted with outrage by people worried about the extraordinary powers given to human rights workers. The proposals gave them more power than the police had to search for and seize private documents without a warrant. The proposals contained no provision for punishing frivolous complaints (later added under protest by Elgie), attempted to muzzle a free press and free speech by extending government censorship powers, and imposed awesome hardships on employers and landlords by making them responsible for the discrimination of employees or tenants.

Typically, not wanting to fight an election on a police state law, the issue was temporarily set aside until after Davis regained his majority, but after months of controversial committee hearings on it and some modest harnessing of human rights workers' powers, Bill 7 gained approval on December 7, 1981.

Next up was cavalier treatment of labour union members' rights to strike and to believe that legally negotiated contracts meant something. Actually, throughout his career Davis had periodic labor relations disputes with two prominent groups, doctors and the Ontario Public Service Employees Union (OPSEU), and during his second majority both disputes came to a head.

In his first throne speech in 1971 Davis promised to end the practice whereby doctors charge more than the schedule of fees set out under medicare, and by October, 1980, he was still saying he found extra-billing "unacceptable." During the 1981 election campaign, shortly after 2,500 low-paid hospital workers were suspended and twenty-eight union leaders fired for taking part in an illegal, eight-day hospital strike, he said, "We don't support extra-billing, but we're not prepared to legislate every doctor into OHIP." Then in January, 1982, he called the doctors "irresponsible" for a series of rotating one-day walkouts to back their demands for a 31 per cent fee increase over two years plus a cost-of-living increase. They had already turned down a 10 per cent increase that would have given them an average $95,273 in take-home pay. But for all his tough talk doctors got a 14 per cent increase in April, 1982, and were promised another 11.75 per cent in two stages in 1983.

In the meantime the Tories introduced their own wage controls, which rolled back contracts negotiated between the government and civil service groups, restricting most to a 5 per cent wage hike. Doctors were exempted. Davis asked them to voluntarily comply with his restraint bill, but the Ontario Medical Association simply ignored his requests. That didn't seem to bother him, though, because in December, 1983, he suddenly said he supported extra-billing, calling it "a policy that has worked," and urging the federal Liberals to drop their plans to ban it in the new Canada Health Act. In an attempt to force Ontario to stop the practice, the federal government currently withholds transfer payments equal to the amount of the extra-billing, about $53 million.

His support for the public service unions, however, was not quite so touching. Hardest done by was the Amalgamated Transit Union, Local 113, of the Toronto Transit Commission, whose members have the legal right to strike but who were legislated back to work in both 1974 and 1978 when they exercised that right. In 1984 Davis introduced a new twist, legislating them back two weeks before a strike even began. It was set to begin on September 12, two days before Pope John Paul II arrived in Toronto, but the planned legal strike was summarily cancelled in a one-day special legislative sitting.

OPSEU always wanted, but never won, the right to strike. In 1974 it took a stand on the issue and ran a hard-hitting, $250,000 ad campaign attacking Davis, but during the 1975 election Davis hit back with his own advertisements saying public servants should not have the right to withdraw their services and that they "must be neutral, non-partisan, and impartial." At the same time the Tories forced Hamilton property assessor Brian Charlton to either resign as president of the Hamilton Mountain NDP Association or be fired from his civil service job. Charlton ran and lost for the NDP in 1975 but won in 1977. While the Davis advertisements argued for civil servants' impartiality, head civil servant Ed Stewart actually appeared in Tory campaign advertising.

When the federal Liberals imposed wage and price controls in 1975, after campaigning against them the year before, Davis objected strongly, then locked Ontario into the scheme, even using Anti-Inflation Board guidelines as an excuse to impose rent controls. In July, 1976, the Supreme Court of Canada ruled that Ottawa had acted legally but that Ontario was wrong to impose controls provincially without legislative approval. In 1981, a year after hinting he was thinking of introducing his own controls, Davis wrote a six-page letter to Trudeau asking Ottawa to do so. In January, 1982, however, Davis categorically ruled out wage controls for Ontario's public sector employees, even though two weeks earlier his treasurer, Frank Miller, had said Ontario should take a hard look at them. Eight months later Davis recalled the legislature to authorize a 5 per cent wage limit on over half a million public workers and restrictions on fees and prices set by provincial agencies.

Sean O'Flynn, the prickly president of OPSEU, violently opposed controls, arguing that they were illegal because they ripped up legally negotiated contracts. He also declared that if there were going to be controls, then doctors should be included along with everyone else earning their keep from the tax coffers. He led a group of two hundred angry supporters who were tossed out of the public galleries for disrupting the legislature during debate on the measures. O'Flynn, a hard guy to like, had a slogan — "Make the Bastards Pay" — that wasn't destined to elicit public sympathy since the "bastards" were the taxpayers, but he had a point.

He didn't get any support from the Tories over the doctors, but in October, 1983, the Ontario Supreme Court ruled that the part of the restraint package that removed the right to strike over non-monetary issues was unconstitutional. Mr. Justice E. E. Smith wrote that the right to strike is "a necessary corollary" to freedom of association under the Charter of Rights, adding, "No one escapes the force of its dictates. Sovereignty of Parliament as we have known it is a thing of history." Even Davis must have winced. He had expressed such fealty to parliamentary traditions while at the same time pushing hard for the Charter, and now his two-sided activities had come home to roost.

A month later Larry Grossman said Ontario's 680,000 public sector workers would be allowed an average 5 per cent wage hike under a revised restraint package that partially restored collective bargaining, and this time he included the doctors. He also ordered arbitrators to take into account an employer's ability to pay when setting new wage levels, adding that no award would be allowed unless it had a clear statement of the arbitrator's estimate of the cost. What it meant was that transfer payments to local governments were restricted to 5 per cent, but their employees could bargain for more. It removed the pressure from the province and placed it on the municipalities, the same technique Ontario had fought when Ottawa cut its transfer payments and put the onus on Queen's Park to either raise its own revenues or cut services.

While the restraint package cavalierly discarded legal contracts without so much as a by-your-leave, it stands as a model of deportment compared to Davis's seizure and sale of more than $2 billion in assets of three trust companies in January, 1983. The firms — Seaway Trust Co., Greymac Trust Co., and Crown Trust Co. — had been involved in financing a controversial series of transactions covering almost eleven thousand Toronto apartment units. In an unprecedented action, Consumer and Commercial Relations Minister Bob Elgie announced that the government had seized the firms and put their assets under provincial trusteeship, a move aimed mainly at financier Leonard Rosenberg, who had bought control of Crown three months earlier and planned to amalgamate it with Greymac, which he bought in 1981.

The apartments, originally owned by Cadillac-Fairview Corp. Ltd., were bought by Greymac Credit Corp. for $270 million in September, 1982, in a deal involving twenty-six parcels of land containing sixty-five apartment buildings, the largest transaction of its kind ever made in Canada. The sale touched off a flurry of tenant concerns about what would happen to their rents under the new ownership.

The original closing date was November 16, but this was advanced to November 5 because of concern that the government might intervene. Late on November 8 Greymac Credit resold the properties to Kilderkin Investments, owned by William Player, another controversial financier, for $312.5 million. The next morning Kilderkin, in turn, resold them for $500 million to fifty numbered companies, believed to be Saudi Arabian. Government officials, who believed the apartments weren't worth more than $300 million, discovered Greymac and Crown had advanced substantial mortgages on the properties to facilitate the transactions, meaning that the apartment "flips" appeared to break statutory lending limits, specifically that no more than 75 per cent of the value of properties should be mortgaged.

Elgie seized the firms on the strength of a law that was approved in one day just a few days before the Christmas break. The Tories were being hammered by opposition criticism, particularly from the Liberals, that the mortgage flips could mean higher rents. In fact, Cadillac had studiously avoided rent review for years, and tenants were already enjoying rents well below market value. But with so many tenants involved the Tories were not willing to take any chances. Davis invited Liberal Leader David Peterson and NDP Leader Bob Rae into his office individually, wooed them into agreeing to a dangerously open-ended law, and rammed the bill through the legislature. It gave the government power to seize companies on the vague pretext that "there exists a practice or state of affairs . . . that is or may be prejudicial to the public interest." Even Peterson, who supported the bill, admitted that it gave government "very broad [powers]. . . . They can do it almost on a whim."

Late in January the government announced it was selling the solid assets of Crown Trust, even though Rosenberg, who owned those assets, had not even been charged with any criminal offence, let alone convicted. As of early 1985 he still hasn't been charged, yet his companies have been sold, and he has been banned from the trust business in Ontario. Crown was sold to Central Trust, Seaway is being wound down over five years by Midland Bank Canada, and Greymac will be wound down within five years by Standard Trust.

In November, 1983, Elgie released a white paper containing a set of tough proposals to crack down on similar problems *before* they occur, not after, an acknowledgment by the Tories of the flaws in their own regulatory system.

Tenants, of course, were pleased because part of the deal was to guarantee continuous below-market rents. The political flak, which threatened to hurt the Tories for a while, disappeared as quickly as it had exploded into the headlines several months earlier. But the stench from the government's blatant abuse of its powers to seize private property without due process lingered on.

*   *   *

During the machinations preceding the federal Tory leadership contest in June, 1983, Bill Davis received more media attention for several months than the actual contenders as he tried to decide whether or not he would take a run at the job. In the end, of course, he decided he wouldn't, part of the reason being that even then he was seriously considering his retirement from politics.

Davis will not say whether he supported Joe Clark or Brian Mulroney in the end, although you could safely put your money on Mulroney. With Clark gone the bitter wounds that had ruptured the two branches of the party were quickly healed, and in the federal election a year later Norman Atkins took temporary leave from his duties for Davis to run the Mulroney campaign, while Eddie Goodman joined other senior businessmen, including Darcy McKeough, on a policy advisory committee established by Mulroney.

When Davis's Brampton riding association held a testimonial dinner to celebrate their man's twenty-fifth anniversary in political office in May, 1984, Mulroney was there as a guest speaker. And when Mulroney entered his first campaign as Tory leader a few months later, Davis was there with his Big Blue Machine from start to finish, helping to fashion one of the largest landslides in federal political history.

On election night, September 4, 1984, Davis, most of his Palace Guard, and their wives gathered in the Park Plaza suite to watch the results on television before heading downtown to Tory headquarters, then on to a gala at the Royal York Hotel.

About fifteen minutes after the polls closed Davis, who had the remote control channel switcher, chanced upon a New York Yankee-Cleveland Indians baseball game on a Buffalo channel and watched the game for about twenty minutes while everyone else squirmed, desperately wanting to know specific electoral results but not wanting to offend their premier by asking him to switch back to the election.

For Davis it might be that he didn't really want to watch the results at all. Certainly he wanted the Tories to win, and certainly he was glad they did, but he knew the huge Mulroney majority ended forever his hopes of leading the federal Tories. He also knew, although it took him a month to decide for sure, that his own time had ended.

On the surface it all looked so terrific for him. He had just ridden through a $10 million public relations masterpiece called "Ontario's Bicentennial," ostensibly a celebration of the two hundredth anniversary of the arrival of the bulk of United Empire Loyalists from the U.S. While the historical purity of the event, blatantly expanded into a general multicultural extravaganza, was open to serious question, there was no doubt it had been a hit with the thousands of municipalities and organizations that had happily accepted provincial handouts to finance their historical or multicultural activities.

He was in complete charge of his own party and light years ahead of the opposition in the polls, having recently extended aid to separate schools to strengthen his support among the growing number of Catholic voters. A Gallup poll that month showed his Tories at 56 per cent, the highest level of popular support of his career. The Liberals, at 24 per cent, had never been in worse shape, having dropped 13 points in the Gallup, and worse, having lost eight of their members since the 1981 election through either retirement, the federal election, or crossing the floor to the Tories. The NDP had gained three points but was still only at 19 per cent. The election hawks, this time his entire inner circle, knew if he didn't go to the polls it meant the end of the road, the last thing they wanted either for themselves or for the party.

Speculation had been intense for weeks that Davis was waiting for the Queen to complete her Ontario visit before calling a fall election. There had been stories that he was going to resign, but the bulk of media attention, and opposition preparation, was aimed at the election call. After all, even the Tories had hired election staff and ordered Bell Telephone technicians to install telephones in their downtown headquarters on Thanksgiving Monday, the last day Davis had to announce a November 22 election. So certain were most people that the machine was about to be thrown into gear that many candidates had paid between $500 and $2,000 to rent campaign offices, among them Bob Elgie. The Liberals were poised to move into rented quarters on Bloor Street West, the text of David Peterson's kickoff speech had already been stuffed into media kits, and on the holiday morning a rented Liberal campaign bus was parked and ready. The NDP had prepared signs and campaign literature and were holding a final election preparation meeting at Queen's Park the same day.

Joan Walters, Davis's press secretary, had told reporters to expect a Monday announcement, although she didn't know what it would be either, and the press gallery lounge, normally closed on holidays, was opened when veteran steward Jim Boyd volunteered to help with the anticipated crush of reporters.

But up in Georgian Bay it had been raining hard all that holiday Sunday. Bill Davis, his family, and his sister Molly's family puttered about their Townsend Island cottage getting ready for their traditional Thanksgiving turkey dinner. And somewhere between the main course and the dessert Davis told his family simply, "I've decided to retire." They had half expected it but, like everyone else, couldn't be sure. There was an awkward silence before Kathleen, Molly, and several others began to cry, as much from relief as anything else. His children had mixed feelings; they were happy for him but would miss the excitement and competitiveness of political life.

"The actual decision was made that weekend," says Davis. "I had begun to think about it seriously on the night of the federal election, but I hadn't decided for sure. There isn't any one thing which made me suddenly decide; it was a culmination of many things. When I told my family, it was a bit of an emotional fifteen or twenty minutes. Then it became, after it got emotional . . . sad is not the right word. I can't describe it, but things picked up and we all started to have a good time and talk about the things that we might all be able to do."

The next day he headed to Queen's Park. The second-floor lobby outside the premier's office was jammed with print, radio, and television reporters and technicians when Davis, Kathleen, and eldest son Neil arrived at about 2:30. Looking relaxed but saying nothing, Davis disappeared into his office, broke the news to about a dozen of his closest staffers who'd come in for the occasion, then telephoned Brian Mulroney in Florida and G. Emmett Cardinal Carter, assuring him that public funding of separate schools would not be abandoned. Afterward he went into cabinet, taking his family and staff with him, most of them for the first time, for what was described as "an emotional" event. Only about half the cabinet had come in, mostly because they believed Davis had called the special meeting simply to announce the election.

At 3 p.m. Davis walked briskly along the second-floor corridor, down the red-carpeted grand staircase, and into the packed media studio while a few dozen Liberal candidates milled around outside, waiting for the expected election pep rally.

He made his announcement in his opening paragraph: "I have today written the president of the Ontario Progressive Conservative Association, David McFadden, and informed him of my decision to step down as leader of the party effective the next leadership convention . . . "

And that was it. He went on to thank Ontarians for their support, to talk about the resilience of Ontario's economy, the strength of his party, his desire to spend more time with his family, his view that it would have been "less than honorable" to run unless he was "personally committed to serving a full term," and his hopes for his own future and "the importance of continuity." He had to stop reading twice, momentarily, to regain his composure, and emotions ran so deep in the room that when he finished his statement about half the media applauded, likely the only time that ever occurred at Queen's Park.

After a series of questions Davis returned to his office, poured himself a rye and soda, and celebrated for about an hour with his staff. Then he, Kathy, and Neil left the building through the east door, hopped into their waiting limousine, and headed directly back to Main Street, Brampton.

*   *   *

In his office a few weeks later Davis said he was deeply moved by the general reaction to him. "I think I always try to appear cool, calm, and collected . . . but I'm not a totally unemotional person, and it just made it a lot tougher."

He said that after the federal election, when he "started to think in a more conscious fashion of what my own plans should be," he had only the two options of retirement or a fall election. "One of the questions that would have been raised with me was, in light of the speculation, 'Are you going to stay a whole term?' Well, I could have rationalized that two and a half years or three would have been enough, but I could not have run and six months or a year thereafter, in my own conscience, say, 'That's enough to satisfy that commitment.' "

But he conceded that someday he may regret his decision. "I honestly believe we could have won an election, but I made the decision and did it in conscience. Some of the party still don't agree with it, and that's flattering . . . but I don't think anybody will ever accuse me [as many did Trudeau after the federal election] of leaving the party in a downward trend or at the low end in terms of public support. I think had the polls been down and it looked like a very tough election, or even if we had been behind, I don't know what I would have felt then. . . . I'm still a competitive soul, and I probably would have stayed.

"I don't have any misgivings . . . but to say I'm not going to miss this place — well, I will miss the House. There are some days you don't miss it at all, but I really do enjoy question period. In particular, the last six or seven years have been mentally stimulating. I get a kick out of it. It's a great institution."

Not surprisingly, Davis said the hardest part of public life for him was the price it exacted on family life. "Sure, there was some economic penalty to a certain extent, but if people in public life don't want it, they don't have to do it, so I've never complained about that part of it and never would. But the only regret, I guess, or negative part, is . . . what I have missed in terms of the family growing up. In the economic area maybe you can recapture some things. . . . But in terms of what you have missed with the children, those days you just can't. Those happened, and you were either there or you weren't. . . . Any advice I give to a young person going into politics is: 'You have got to know what you're going to miss.' That would be my only advice to Neil," who is expected to follow in his father's footsteps.

He said he looked forward to the pressures of public life being removed. "Listen, it will be kind of fun for Kathy and I to go out and watch the movies. I will look forward to at least some degree of anonymity. I have been in a public position, obviously, but I am, and I tried very hard to be, a private person. Even you will not really know all the things that I think and feel, or my private experiences."

Already there had been regular speculation about Davis becoming an ambassador to Washington or London, and he said he "would not be adverse to doing something in the public arena part-time that would be creative," but he wouldn't discuss speculation on anything else.* One of his closest personal friends, however, said, "Can you really see him going off to the airport to pick up a minister of the Crown and taking him to tea? Not likely." He could always return to law. "That's the one obvious thing . . . but I haven't really decided what I'm going to do. Anyway, there is no great hurry."

Asked what he will be remembered for as premier, he said, "I don't ever enumerate accomplishments. . . . You can go through a list of things we have done, and you may not agree with them all, but I don't think anyone can accuse us of being passive. . . . There's a whole list of reforms in the last fourteen years. I guess people are interested in how history will perceive them, but I guess that I'll never get into a list or discuss our main accomplishments or errors. That's what historians do.

"I really don't know what I want to be remembered for. Hopefully as an individual with, I think, or I like to think, a measure of sensitivity. A person who attempted to govern with conscience and a sense of what was right and wrong. I'll leave it for others to enumerate the charters, the college systems, this thing, that thing. Because that isn't my style."

---

*At the Mulroney-Reagan Shamrock Summit in March, 1985, Davis was named a special envoy to look into ways Canada and the U.S. could control acid rain.

PART TWO
PREMIERING ONTARIO

───────── ❦ ─────────

Behind that benevolent face is the partisan Bill Davis, a fiercely competitive man. Part Two reveals that partisan as premier, a Bill Davis who could be kind and sensitive but who could also be ruthless in dealing with cabinet ministers. It takes us into the bowels of the longest-running political regime in the western world, probing the Davis management style, how Ontario changed under his rule, and how he and his party adapted to retain power, monitoring the public mood and satisfying public expectations with their never-ending polls.

It describes his disdain for the right wing of his party, his prolific use and abuse of patronage, his approach to the issues of transportation, women, and ethnicity, his remarkable about-face on public funding of Roman Catholic separate schools, and the failures and successes of his strategy of creeping bilingualism. The latter illustrates the quintessential Davis formula of orchestrated change, appearing to be a conservative while acting like a liberal, all the while making sure not to fall out of step with his voting public.

Three weeks after announcing his retirement in October, 1984, Bill Davis said, "I honestly don't know what I'm going to do. This has been my life. Politics. I practised law for all of two and a half years, so I know nothing other than public life. . . . I do have to earn a living. I will find something, but I don't kid myself, either, into thinking that I won't miss what, apart from the family, has been my life for twenty-five years."

CHAPTER 12
KING BILLY

— ☙ —

The ancient king Charlemagne, in addition to having nine
wives, surrounded himself with a group of brave and loyal
knights called "Paladins," a word derived from Latin meaning
simply "one of the palace; a high dignitary." Things haven't
changed much. Current leaders may not have nine wives, but
they do have their own Paladins, or Palace Guard, who while
not literally standing by to don armor and charge onto the battlefield in defence of their king, certainly are allegorically. King
Billy Davis was no exception. If anything, his Palace Guard was
more influential than most.

Parliamentary democracy was never meant to operate this way,
but it always has. The idea was that to control kingly despo-
tism, the good citizens had to have a voice in choosing their own
palace representatives, and to some extent, of course, they get
that opportunity with each election. But more and more the people
they elect have less and less to say in the decisions of government, having been replaced by the powerful Palace Guard, the
guys with the muscle. As Bruce McCaffrey puts it, "I think there
should be muscle in the system, but I think it's not an inappropriate idea that elected guys have some of it."

* * *

When the regular Tuesday morning breakfast at the Park Plaza suite wrapped up, usually before 10:30, Davis and his gaggle of insiders would head down the elevator to their waiting limousines to be whisked the two minutes down Queen's Park Crescent to the legislature. Davis would arrive at the east door of the building, along with Ed Stewart, two OPP bodyguards, Bob Guay and Peter Balog, and his driver, Tim Turner. Tuesday is traditionally caucus day, so all the backbenchers and lesser cabinet ministers would have already begun to gather on the second floor in the large, nondescript caucus room distinguished mainly by the absurdity of heavily frosted windows on the two doors. The windows were installed on Davis's orders, after some rowdy caucus meetings in the mid-1970s, to stop reporters from peering into the room over the third-floor marble railing diagonally above it.

The massive, Romanesque, pink-sandstone Queen's Park squats at the head of University Avenue — Norman Webster once likened it to "a giant toad" — adjacent to the sprawling University of Toronto campus. Appropriately enough, it was once the site of an insane asylum. It has been the home park of the Ontario government since 1893, the most permanent in a series of seven parliamentary buildings that preceded it. (Davis convened a cabinet meeting in October, 1984, just after announcing his own retirement, at Navy Hall in Niagara-on-the-Lake, where the province's first parliament met on September 11, 1792, called by Governor John Graves Simcoe.)

It took six years to build Queen's Park and another year to paint and furnish it. It was designed to house the entire legislature and civil service, and when Sir Oliver Mowat rode his carriage up to the front door for the official opening on April 4, 1893, he said to his clerk, "Well, Joe, we built it. How are we going to fill it with people?" Today's public service employs over eighty thousand people, but then, writes Eric Arthur, it was just "a few hundred — only one of whom, a Miss Cowper, was a woman. When it was discovered that she was there, orders were given that no more women were to be employed." The order didn't stick: Women now make up 42 per cent of the Ontario civil service, although the bulk of them, like Miss Cowper, are in secretarial positions.

Mowat, seventy-three, had been premier eleven years at the time. His cabinet had eight people, and his operations budget was about $200,000. In Bill Davis's last year, his cabinet numbered twenty-nine, and his spending pushed $30 billion.

Mowat predicted it would take one hundred years to fill Queen's Park with people. It took thirty. We can only wonder what he would think today to see not only that building but also a huge colony of government office towers covering several city blocks nearby, one even named after him, and others bearing the names of premiers Hepburn, Frost, Macdonald, Whitney, Drew, and Ferguson. And that's but a fraction of the government office towers in Metro Toronto and elsewhere.

Legend has it that besides being plagued by politicians, Queen's Park is haunted by four ghosts, one an old soldier in full regimental dress, the other three women inmates of the asylum. One is dressed in white, with streaming hair; another has a checked dress thrown over her head. The third, perhaps anticipating the political madness that was to come, hanged herself on a basement hook.

The H-shaped building measures 480 feet across and 294 feet deep. It has five storeys, the top one added after a 1909 fire destroyed the west wing. It was supposed to provide more office space, but the added floor has never been used.

The legislative chamber itself, in the centre of the second floor at the top of a sweeping, red-carpeted Grand Staircase, is designed after the Westminster model, with the Speaker's chair at the south end, the government benches to its right, and opposition to its left. Mitch Hepburn rearranged the seating plan to a U.S.-style horseshoe in the 1930s, but that was quickly changed when the Tories took power under George Drew in 1943.

The lieutenant-governor's suite is located on the first and second floors at the northwest corner of the building; there's also an outside entrance, a red-carpeted, canopy-covered stairway leading up from the west driveway. The Speaker, who used to occupy what is now the lieutenant-governor's space, has a two-bedroom apartment, complete with kitchen and formal dining room, in the northwest corner of the third floor, a floor also occupied by various MPPs, *Hansard*, the press gallery, and assorted government offices. The Speaker's office is off to the right of the main lobby, with the clerk's office to the left. Clerk Roderick Lewis, and his father before him, have held that post since 1926.

The Liberal leader's office is tucked into the southwest corner of the first floor, next to his caucus room. The NDP leader is stuck in the far northeast corner of the north wing, with his MPPs and research staff occupying the entire floor. Liberal MPPs and researchers are the first ones you run into if you enter Queen's Park through the back door.

The basement, which houses a cafeteria, tuck shop, dining room (plus a cabinet dining room), barber shop, security office, and maintenance and food services offices, is connected by tunnel to the complex of buildings across the street. The media studio and three committee rooms are all on the ground floor.

The premier's staff occupies the entire east side of the second and third floors and much of the fourth floor as well. In 1970–71, the last year John Robarts was premier, his office operation cost $384,000. It was called the office of the prime minister then, but when Davis took over he changed it to the office of the premier, saying there is just one prime minister in Canada. The pretentious title, however, was the only thing he cut back on. His first year in office saw expenses leap to $428,000, then to $1,863,000 the next year. To compare how things grew like Topsy in twelve years, Leslie Frost spent $74,672 on his office during his final year, compared with Davis at $995,000; the main cabinet office under Frost cost $74,548, while under Davis twelve years later it cost $658,000. By 1984–85 Davis's estimates were $4.1 million — $1.64 million for the cabinet office, $2.46 million for the premier's — about eleven times what Robarts spent in his last year.

Located adjacent to the cabinet room, the premier actually has two offices, one for normal business and the other, which contains a dining table, for meetings over meals. There's a Polish Corridor arrangement joining his office area to a side door next to the government members' lounge just outside the legislative chamber. To use it, Davis would pass directly through the offices of Ed Stewart and his executive assistant, Ray McNeil, two of the small army of quietly competent people who make the day-to-day machinations of government work.

After Stewart was drafted by Davis in 1974 to rescue the office from the administrative excesses of Jim Fleck and Malcolm Rowan, he was in charge. Period.

An affable, straightforward Scot, Stewart was not noted as a big spender; his idea of ordering dinner in for staff was Big Macs without the fries. His one extravagance was his three-piece suits, with matching accessories, immaculately made up by his tailor, who went to his office for fittings. A fastidious man of habit, Stewart arrived regularly at 7:00 a.m. except on Wednesdays, cabinet day, when he would go to Brampton, then drive back with Davis discussing the agenda. He brushed his teeth several times a day but always at 1:50, when he could be seen heading to the Davis washroom carrying his toothbrush. When the legislature was sitting, he'd then wander down the Polish Corridor to the Tory lounge, pour himself a free coffee, take it back in a styrofoam cup, and light a cigar. At about 2:35 he could be seen butting the cigar into a sand-filled ash tray in the hall outside his office.

The truest measure of Stewart's influence was the fact that he had his own key to Davis's en suite office washroom. Officially, he was deputy minister in the premier's office, secretary of cabinet, and clerk of the executive council, but he was much more. He was the man who held the key not only to the washroom but to the entire government bureaucracy as well.

He was a civil servant but appeared in campaign commercials and was more openly partisan than some cabinet ministers, things other civil servants have been fired for. Opposition politicians complained about Stewart's partisanship, and they had a point, because it is illegal for civil servants to be actively involved in politics in Ontario. But Stewart simply rejected the view that senior bureaucrats can be pristine purists whose only interest is administration, saying he wouldn't have been much use to Davis if he hadn't been part of the discussions leading to the ultimate political decisions. "If you're caught up in the old traditional textbook notions which mean that politicians are here, the civil service is over there, and they both have quite separate functions and don't overlap, I guess the way we run our operation would be quite bothersome. I say those textbook notions don't apply any more . . . particularly in the premier's office."

More legitimately partisan was the other holdover from Davis's days in Education, his executive assistant, Clare Westcott. If he was busy, you could bet his business was being conducted on the telephone. The iconoclastic Westcott regularly juggled three and four calls at the same time, and he had a phenomenal network of contacts around the world, even in the 1960s. When the favorite granddaughter of then British prime minister Harold Macmillan came to Toronto to get away from it all, Macmillan called Westcott and asked him to keep an eye on her. He did. And when Premier John Robarts suddenly decided during a tour of Italy that he'd like an audience with the Pope, he too called Westcott, and with the premier holding on the line, the Protestant West-cott called a Vatican contact and arranged a papal audience on the spot.

Davis badly underestimated Westcott's value, yet over the years he built more personal credits for Davis than any of the Palace Guard. He was the Mr. Fix It of the operation; the common phrase was, "Got a problem? Call Clare." But he lost the personal influence he had with Davis when they were turning education on its ear in the 1960s and developed a love-hate relationship with his boss. One minute he would be the greatest politician in the world, the next an unfeeling cad who couldn't get to the bathroom without his advance men. Westcott resented those who joined the inner circle later — "They're all mercenaries, all of them" — because they undercut his clout.

Across the hall from Stewart, the public engagements section sifted a mountain of requests for appearances, about four thousand in 1984. Lyn Hilborn, who ran Davis's Brampton constituency office from 1975 to 1977, was the public engagements director until late 1984. Known internally as "One Car," a joking reference to an inability to organize a one-car funeral, Hilborn was a studiously efficient but amazingly personable time accountant who accepted about 10 per cent of requests, which means he said "no to 90 per cent of them, not always an easy thing to do." Davis would attend events outside Queen's Park about two hundred days a year.

Press secretary Joan Walters was located next to Hilborn's offices. The former Queen's Park bureau chief for The Canadian Press joined Davis in February, 1984, and managed to maintain the respect of both politicians and press gallery members, a tribute to her competence. Much of her time was spent checking the newspapers and wire machines to make sure Davis quickly learned of breaking stories, deflecting media requests for interviews, getting comments for questions, and keeping a watchful eye on the opposition.

Most Davis days were simply a long series of meetings, largely private, with personal and party operatives, businessmen, labor representatives, visiting heads of state — you name it. During the sessions his time was broken by the daily question period in the legislature, a partisan sport he delighted and excelled in, and by the inevitable scrums with reporters hoping against hope that some day he would complete a sentence and give a straight answer to a straight question. And, of course, there was the regular Tuesday caucus meeting and the meetings with cabinet, normally every Wednesday, when the ministers would pile around the coffin-shaped table, the premier in the middle on the west side, to spend two or three hours shuffling papers and arguing positions.

According to the textbooks, these meetings — in the legislature, the caucus, the cabinet — are where policy is decided in democratically elected governments, where the leader hears out the people's representatives, weighs their concerns, then defines the consensus that will lead to legislation.

Without exception the Davis inner circle raved about his patience, his willingness to let people ramble on about their own views regardless of how silly or whether he agreed. "Bill Davis is, among other things, a very patient man," said his deputy premier, Bob Welch, a bubbly little guy who is Ontario's answer to Hubert Humphrey. "I have never felt at any time that Bill Davis has discouraged anyone from expressing their point of view. . . . I sometimes think he's overly generous." Both Roy McMurtry and Larry Grossman claimed that Davis listened to everyone while remaining beholden to none. He could maintain that "core of people around him," said McMurtry, "without creating the image of cronyism." Grossman added that he never made "anyone feel less important because of their education or cabinet portfolio."

Maybe he was a saint, but several politicians outside the magic tent who were not afraid to speak told a different story.

Jim Taylor, the former cabinet minister who is famous for his 1979 comment, "I walked in the so-called corridors of power only to be mugged in the back alleys of bureaucracy," said, "When I first got elected [in 1971], I thought caucus was where the power was. After all, that's where all elected government representatives meet to debate. Well, I soon found out the power wasn't in caucus, so I figured it must be in cabinet. Then I found out it wasn't there, either. It's in the premier's office, essentially."

When Davis walked into the legislature on June 12, 1984, to reverse 117 years of history, not to mention his own position, and extend full public financing to separate schools, caucus had been called into special session just fifty minutes earlier, totally unaware that history was about to be made. There's some question that Education Minister Bette Stephenson knew much sooner, but Davis and his Palace Guard, armed with statistics showing immigration to be largely Catholic, simply changed sides. It didn't matter what caucus thought; it was told, not asked. Caucus had even less warning in 1975 when Davis imposed rent controls late in the election campaign without even consulting the two cabinet ministers directly responsible, Don Irvine and Sid Handleman. And when he announced shortly after the 1981 election that he was buying 25 per cent of Suncor, a caucus veteran described the "discussion" this way: "It was like a papal encyclical, a flawless decision from an infallible guy who'd just won his majority. And that was that."

Debate in caucus was often heated, but few MPPs believed it changed anything. Morley Kells, for example, said, "I think caucus collectively can rise up in anger and stop things occasionally. We can amend, but we don't do much initiating. I guess caucus stopped reassessment [property tax reassessment in Metro], but it doesn't happen often." He also complained that there was never a strong minister to whom caucus members could go. "There's nobody to look after the boys. Nobody. You soon learn around here not to have too many opinions, and the big thing is to find out what's going on around you so you can be onside."

Kells spoke of the experience of promising backbencher Ross Stevenson at a 1983 summer caucus at Toronto's Four Seasons Hotel. "It's known as the day Ross shot himself in the foot." Bette Stephenson had announced that the government was dropping its statutory restrictions on French-language education so that instead of needing a certain number, all elementary and secondary French-speaking kids would be guaranteed education in French even if they were the only ones in the district. "Ross had received some flack about that at home, and he gave this impassioned speech, and Davis felt he had to come to Bette's defence, if you can imagine, so he made one of those 'I'm almost too emotional to speak' speeches, and everybody said to themselves, 'Poor Ross.' He had been favored to get into cabinet the next shuffle, but he didn't make it."

Even if he had made it into cabinet, he wouldn't have fared much better at influencing policy. There, according to Davis's Resources Secretary Norm Sterling, if you fought for your beliefs, the insiders would "start to wonder whether they can manipulate you. Do you think that Eddie Goodman, Norm Atkins, and all those guys want me to think about anything? No. They want me to do their bidding. They don't want me to have one original thought. They want that for themselves. . . . I think there's a hardness in the group around Davis. They're damned tough guys, and that makes it hard on everybody."

Jim Taylor, who held the portfolios of social services and energy, described most of the Palace Guard as people who "couldn't get elected. They make the decisions. That's why democracy has broken down. . . . Here the problem is trying to make members feel they're participating. Ideas are still important, even if they do project the views of a dinosaur."

Added Sterling, "The problem with any premier who has stayed as long as he has, the same as some ministers like McMurtry, is you build up close connections, sometimes to your detriment. . . . The premier has this group of guys around him that you can't penetrate, and why should you have to if you're the elected person?" The best way to accomplish things was to champion an issue "which the Palace Guard isn't interested in. . . . You can always tell at cabinet when an issue has been vetted by the Tuesday group. There isn't much discussion. They only allow real discussion on things they don't give a damn about." Sid Handleman, who left politics in 1979 because he didn't want to "die of boredom," was customarily blunt about it. "Of course the decisions are made at Tuesday breakfast. At least all the big decisions are. The rest of the stuff is window dressing."

Bruce McCaffrey, who quit cabinet after being hit by a heart scare and a marriage breakup in 1983, said, "There's been a tendency over the years in the office of the premier to take all the ideas from the bureaucrats. They're fucking the system, cheating themselves. I don't know that it will ever change, either. It used to disappoint me, sitting in the cabinet dining room, and the boss would come in with the usual two or three people from his office for lunch. He sees these people all the time, but he couldn't manage to have a bite to eat with a cabinet minister or two who aren't on the inside. . . . I understand comfort, but I also understand if you don't keep in touch, you quickly forget why the others are there."

McCaffrey and other MPPs blamed the widespread use of polls for undermining the role of the ordinary MPP; things were so wild, even the NDP hired a pollster to help them decide on policies. "There are opinion polls on everything. The government sure as hell uses them, too. There's no meaningful dialogue on policy in the place, but why seek out opinions of elected members when you have an opinion poll? There's been a lot of shifting of power from the legislature and from cabinet to the premier's office, and much of it, too much, is because of the technology. If you can get two or three people in the premier's office to get the kind of information they used to rely on local members and party officials to get, it really begs the question of what the hell do you need the members for."

Eddie Goodman dismisses the bitchers. "Look, there is no doubt, if a guy wants to get out and scrap, he can push himself ahead. Larry Grossman pushed himself ahead without starting off with anything by working like a son of a bitch in committees. There are lots of those guys who sit back and instead of busting their ass and working on each problem, cutting out a niche, they just can't. No doubt under our system, if you're a backbencher you've got to work pretty hard."

You've also got to get elected, which is something the people Davis relied on most never had to do.

CHAPTER 13
KEEPING THE PROMISE

E very Thursday morning in the Davis years, if you were to park yourself outside the entrance to the private cabinet dining room in the basement of Queen's Park, you would notice a group of twelve people — ten men and two women — going in for breakfast. What would distinguish them from the others going in is that each would be carrying a large black binder. Inside would be the names of several thousand potential government appointees to about six hundred separate agencies, boards, and commissions.

The Thursday breakfast meeting, officially the Premier's Appointments Advisory Committee but more commonly known around Queen's Park as the "patronage committee," had a membership that did not represent a broad cross-section of society but did represent all views from the left wing of the Tory spectrum to the right wing of the Tory spectrum. The committee was chaired by Ed Stewart; Clare Westcott was vice-chairman; and Stewart's able assistant, Ray McNeil, was committee secretary. The other members were: Tom Kierans, a Toronto stockbroker; Dorie Dunlop, widow of the late Tory MPP Edward Dunlop; Senator Bill Kelly; Norm Atkins; Bob Harris; Brian Hamilton, head of the Tory caucus office; Eddie Goodman; Ruth Archibald, an official with provincial party headquarters; and John Tory.

Not all appointments were dealt with by the committee, but most were. The members would attend each meeting with their

list of names and a corresponding list of vacancies, kept scrupu-
lously up to date by McNeil, and in theory at least make their
recommendations to Davis. In practice, however, Davis never
got to see most of them, only the major ones.

The list of names essentially came from defeated Tory candidates, local party workers, or suggestions from MPPs and party
stalwarts all across the province. With about 3,500 appointments
involved, all of various lengths and compensation levels, it was
not always possible to get the best Tory available for the job,
and from time to time a known Liberal or New Democrat might
sneak in. But more often than not, if a Tory wasn't available the
appointment would go to someone who was non-partisan. And
the number of appointments available always seemed to grow.
During minority government in the mid-1970s, Davis introduced
a "sunset" law to get rid of agencies, boards, and commissions
whose usefulness had expired as a way of cutting government
spending. From the time that pledge was made to the end of the
Davis era, fifteen agencies were disbanded, but alas, twenty-five
new ones were created.

After 1971 the Davis Tories appointed several thousand people to hundreds of government jobs ranging from high-paying
positions on the Ontario Municipal Board (OMB) down to sitting on local commissions for the status it brings. There were
remarkably few problems in all that time, but there were some.

*   *   *

On January 5, 1983, the elevator door opened on the third floor
of Queen's Park; former Kitchener mayor Morley Rosenberg
glanced out, spied a reporter, and said, "I can't seem to escape
the media." Rosenberg was hoping to sneak in and out of the
building unnoticed, assisted by the premier's office, which did
not announce the fact that he would be dropping by to be sworn
into a cushy $60,100-a-year sinecure with the OMB. When the
elevator doors closed, Rosenberg went up one more floor, walked
quickly down the corridor to a remote office in the southeast
corner of the building, was sworn in, then immediately left the
building saying only, "I don't have any comments."

The Rosenberg case, you see, is one that gives the time-honored
practice of political patronage a bad name.

There are, after all, two absolute constants about patronage: First, every government does it, and second, every opposition party cries moral outrage. Generally speaking, the proposition is simple. The government either has a friend or patron looking for a job or has a job looking for a friend or patron. As retired treasurer Darcy McKeough once remarked, "You don't hire your enemies," and usually that's correct. After all, if two people seek an appointment and one happens to be of the same political cloth as the government, while the other works for the opposition, why not hire the friend? The problem comes, of course, when the friend of government is less qualified or when, as in the Rosenberg case, actions by the appointed one should disqualify him from public gain.

On September 21, 1982, just eleven days after the government had announced Rosenberg's appointment to the OMB, journalist Pat Crowe wrote a front-page, copyright story in the *Star* quoting a letter Rosenberg had written to Bill Davis on June 18, reminding the premier to live up to his 1981 campaign slogan: "Keep the Promise." According to Rosenberg, a former NDP candidate in Kitchener, his "promise" was that if he ran for the Tories in 1981 and lost, "I would be assured of a provincial judgeship, reasonably after the election and certainly before the end of my term as mayor." This "promise" had been made, he said, on behalf of the premier by Eddie Goodman and Kitchener lawyer William Hoskinson, the former riding association president. Both men emphatically denied it. Goodman said, "At no time was any promise made to Mr. Rosenberg," a bit of an overstatement that he later had to clarify. As for Davis, his reaction was that Rosenberg's claim was "not factually correct."

Rosenberg initially refused to comment, but two days later, although he kept himself hidden, he released a statement admitting he had lied about the promised judgeship. "Unequivocably and without question," he wrote, "I want to state there never was any commitment made to me, or any inducement held out to me, by any of the individuals referred to in my letter of June 18, 1982, nor by anyone at any time connected with the Government of the Province of Ontario." Before trying as a Tory in 1981, Rosenberg had lost three times provincially and twice federally as an NDP candidate and said he had been "frustrated" by his loss. As a lawyer he felt "qualified . . . to seek an appointment as

a judge" but admitted that his letter to Davis was "inappropriate, based on my personal assumptions, and was done totally as
a result of this frustration. I was in error, and I was wrong."

Liberal justice critic Albert Roy demanded that Rosenberg be
fired from the board and asked Davis how he could appoint him
to a quasi-judicial body knowing "he made serious allegations
that were unfounded. How does that make him an adequate candidate to dispense justice on the OMB?" adding later that Rosenberg "should have sufficient honor to resign himself." In his press
statement Rosenberg said he had "strongly considered" resigning, but "I honestly feel I can serve the people of Ontario in this
capacity, and accordingly I therefore will not be offering my
resignation."

Davis said he had no plans to review the appointment and
that he had been at Rosenberg's nomination meeting, where "there
was no discussion of that nature." Davis added he did not reply
to the letter and was "delighted" that Rosenberg had admitted
his allegations were untrue. McMurtry called the letter "obviously, to put it mildly, a very foolish" thing, adding that he hadn't
received any correspondence from Rosenberg, even though he
had, shortly after the election.

The matter was sent to the legislature's justice committee, but
on October 13 the Tories outvoted the opposition 7–6 to veto
the calling of witnesses to testify about it, prompting Liberal
Sean Conway to note, "They've drawn the wagons around this
wretched mess!" Brantford Tory Phil Gillies said there was nothing unusual or exceptional about the case; patronage was "something that's ongoing. I am not saying it is right. I'm not saying it
is proper. But I accept it as part of the system. I don't want to
pillory the mayor of Kitchener for taking part in the system."
And Goodman told reporters he had told Rosenberg that "the
premier never gave any commitments. But I told him subsequently
that if there were some appointments commensurate with his
abilities, I would support him. . . . I told him discussions about
provincial judgeships are just not had."

The Rosenberg story continued on into December only because
Davis refused to say whether he had ever read the June letter. He
had said earlier he hadn't replied to it but wouldn't say whether
he had known about it. McMurtry, however, told the justice committee, "I don't think the premier was aware of the letter." When

reporters asked Davis if that was true, he said he would "never hide behind not knowing about the letter" and that McMurtry "did not know whether I knew about the letter."

Finally, on December 10, nearly three months after the story broke, Davis admitted that, yes, he had read the letter but didn't feel Rosenberg's "significant error in judgment" should bar him from his appointment. "It's very simple—do you penalize a person because he made a significant error in judgment? Do you say, because of that, you are not going to carry out this appointment? And I made the decision, the government did, that we weren't going to do it that way."

Then, without any further ado, Rosenberg was sworn in as a member of the OMB.

*   *   *

After the 1981 election, Rosenberg wasn't the only loser to end up winning. A survey taken about a year later showed that eleven defeated Tories, or roughly 20 per cent of them, had ended up with patronage jobs.

Omer Deslauriers, former head of both the Association canadienne-française de l'Ontario (ACFO) and the Advisory Council of Franco-Ontarian Affairs and an electoral casualty, was happily licking his wounds as Ontario's agent general in Brussels, a job that pays over $52,000 a year plus a $6,500 special foreign allowance, a $16,500 annual rent allowance, and $2,000 for utility bills. Edward Browne lost in London North, but McMurtry gave him the lifetime job of master and taxing officer of the Ontario Supreme Court in London, a job that usually takes four hours a day, five days a week, and pays over $65,000 a year. And while Rosenberg's OMB appointment created a public stir, the appointment of defeated Huron-Bruce Tory candidate Gary Harron barely raised an eyebrow. He came within 224 votes of winning but ended up instead with an OMB term "at the pleasure of the premier," which could mean forever in Tory Ontario.

There were other, less profitable, appointments. Defeated Oakwood candidate Harriet Wolman was given a three-year stint on the Social Assistance Review Board at $115 per diem. Rainy River hopeful Jack Pierce and Renfrew North candidate Bryan Hocking both received three-year terms on local development corporations at $105 per diem. Scarborough West loser N. John Adams was named to the Ontario Status of Women Council for three years at $85 per diem, while Fran Baines, who lost in Halton-Burlington, became a three-year part-time member of the Board of Parole at the same rate. Kent-Elgin loser Wes Thompson, son of a former Tory cabinet minister, got a non-paying job on the Ontario Medal for Good Citizenship Advisory Committee, and London Centre candidate Russ Monteith was appointed to the Board of Governors of the University of Western Ontario.

This is not to say that these people weren't qualified for the jobs they got. Indeed, the record shows that most of them were. It's just to point out that one qualification that set them above the rest happened to be their politics. Even the one federal Liberal appointment at Queen's Park, Lieutenant-Governor John Black Aird, followed Aird's highly successful career in law, business, and the Senate, but he was singled out from other prominent Ontarians because he had been a successful Liberal bagman for years.

In November, 1973, the Liberals were screaming patronage when Davis hired former attorney general Arthur Wishart and party organizer Paul Weed and put them on the public payroll in his office. Davis said, "It's not negative to have someone in government who has a background in politics." The right kind of politics, of course, and what better proof of that than cabinet experience?

Wishart retired from politics in 1971 and was immediately appointed head of the Criminal Injuries Compensation Board, a post later held by veteran cabinet minister Allan Grossman, then granted in 1985 to demoted cabinet minister Margaret Scrivener. Grossman's cabinet colleague John Yaremko was appointed to head the Liquor Licence Appeal Tribunal and, in addition to that, was named chairman of the Commercial Registration Appeal Tribunal. Eric Winkler, the chairman of the management board of cabinet who was upset in the 1975 election, quickly recovered when he was handed a three-year term on the Ontario Highway Transport Board, and Bert Lawrence, who quit politics in 1974 after his trip to Cuba damaged his career, became chairman of the Ontario Heritage Foundation, to be succeeded eventually by former treasurer John White. William Stewart, who also retired in 1975 after eighteen years in the legislature, most

(*left*) With Vera ''Gramsy'' Davis and Grenville.

(*above*) Charting a course.

Surrounding the matriarch, Eliza Hewitson (*centre*), are Bill (*second row, third from left*), Molly (*front row, right*), Peggy (*back row, second from right*), and cousin Russell Cooper (*back row, second from left*).

Brampton High School, 1944–5.

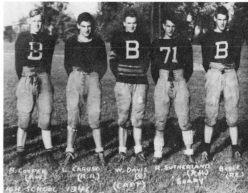

With the basketball team (*front row, centre*) and the 1946 football squad.

Davis (*No. 73*) and Roy McMurtry (*No. 31*) playing for the University of Toronto.

Bill and Helen
on their wedding day.

With Neil and the senior Davises and McPhees.

Cathy, Helen, Neil, Bill and Nancy.

With Grenville Davis in 1971.

Kathleen Davis.

From left: Ian, Kathleen, Nancy, Meg, Cathy, Bill, and Neil.
(*below*) Bill and Kathy with Gramsy on the night of the 1981 election sweep.

In his Brampton den (*top left*), playing football with the kids at 61 Main Street (*inset*), and with daughter Cathy (*plaid dress*).

Piloting ''Old Dutch'' in the bay.

The lifelong refuge, Townsend Island in Georgian Bay.

Daughter-in-law Ruth
and granddaughter Christine.

From left: Neil, Cathy, Kathleen, Nancy, Ian,
Meg, and Bill.

of them as agriculture minister, was named to the board of directors of Ontario Hydro, where he was joined a couple of years later by a new chairman, Hugh Macaulay, one of Davis's closest aides and personal friends.

Veteran MPP Leonard Reilly, who retired in 1975 to make way for Davis buddy Roy McMurtry — although everyone denies a direct connection — became chairman of the Ontario Science Centre after that election, replacing Matthew Dymond, a former cabinet minister who had been appointed in 1972 after retiring from office a year earlier. The day Reilly's appointment was announced, the premier's office distributed the news that Dymond had been named to the Workmen's Compensation Board as a commissioner; it later had to retrieve the notice because he hadn't accepted the post. The chairman of the WCB, incidentally, is former Hamilton Tory MP Lincoln Alexander.

Richard Potter, a controversial health minister in the early 1970s, was named Belleville coroner after his 1975 political retirement, and Fern Guindon, former labor minister, was appointed to the Ontario Lottery Corporation board of directors. Jack McNie, former minister of colleges and universities, found his services were suddenly required on the Conservation Review Board, while longtime cabinet minister Charles MacNaughton was named head of the Ontario Racing Commission when he retired. Then there is former treasurer James Allan, chairman of the Niagara Parks Commission, and former housing minister Donald Irvine, chairman of the St. Lawrence Parks Commission. Wilf Spooner, another former cabinet minister under Robarts, is chairman of the Ontario Northland Transportation Commission. When Environment Minister Harry Parrott figured he'd had enough, he became a commissioner on the Ontario Human Rights Commission, just after Hugh Segal's Ottawa friend Canon Borden Purcell found himself as the new human rights chairman, and eventually popped up as head of the Science Centre. And John Smith, former corrections minister, found himself on the Workmen's Compensation Board.

Bradford Bowlby, a former party organizer, is chairman of the Assessment Review Court, and George Nixon, a one-term Tory MPP, sits on the Social Assistance Review Board. Even High Park Tory MPP Yuri Shymko had a brief spell in a patronage position after he lost his federal seat in Parkdale in 1979 and was

quickly named to the Ontario Advisory Council on Multiculturalism and Citizenship. Former Liquor Licence Board chairman
Eber Rice was a former secretary of the Elgin PC Association,
and when his term ended he was replaced by former East York
mayor Willis Blair, the man Davis had tapped to do a property
tax review in the mid-1970s. In 1980 former Tory MPP Judge
Thomas Graham retired as chairman of the Ontario Police Commission, was replaced by Shaun McGrath, who has no particular politics except he was executive assistant to former cabinet
minister Jim Auld, and served on the Criminal Injuries Compensation Board before going to the OPC to join vice-chairman John
MacBeth, another former Davis minister.

When so many of the members of the Ontario Municipal Board
have Tory ties, there's no reason why the chairman shouldn't,
and sure enough, chairman Henry Stewart, onetime city manager of Mississauga, is a former Tory worker. Also counted among
party workers are businessman John Craig Eaton, a regular at
those twice-yearly Tory think-ins in various parts of the province, who is chairman of The Trillium Foundation, and H. Ian
Macdonald, a former deputy treasurer and president of York
University long closely associated with Davis, who is chairman
of the board of IDEA Corporation, an organization that grew out
of the campaign extravaganza called BILD — Board of Industrial
Leadership and Development — prior to the 1981 election.

In 1974 Davis named Ross DeGeer to the post of principal
secretary in the premier's office. DeGeer, who had been a key
worker along with Atkins in the leadership campaign of Allan
Lawrence and then hired on as executive director of the party,
did such fine work that in 1978 he was named Ontario's agent
general in London, England, a post eventually held by cabinet
minister Tom Wells. DeGeer replaced former "Hockey Night
in Canada" broadcaster Ward Cornell, a jovial man who worked
diligently for the party for years and who upon his return from
England was named deputy provincial secretary for social development, then deputy minister of municipal affairs.

When Davis appointed Bob Welch minister responsible for
women's issues, it meant setting up a women's directorate. To
lead it they chose Glenna Carr, the wife of former deputy minister Alan Gordon, who quit after the Wiseman Affair. Gordon, a

close friend of Ed Stewart, sat on the patronage committee himself in the late 1970s.

Stewart, of course, is not the only one with friends. Bhausaheb Ubale organized a successful trip to India for his pal Roy McMurtry and shortly afterward became Ontario's first race relations commissioner, despite the fact that he wasn't even a Canadian citizen at the time. Bill Davis's neighbor and closest friend, Joe Dobbs, found a spot on the Land Compensation Board after retiring early from his private industry job, and a couple of years later he, too, was named to the OMB. Former Peel chairman and longtime Davis supporter Lou Parsons is chairman of GO Transit.*

Just to show there is an element of fairness in all this, the Tories *did* appoint former deputy Liberal leader Vernon Singer to the OMB and former Liberal MPP and Toronto mayor Phil Givens chairman of the Metro Police Commission in 1978, a year after they retired as MPPs and their ridings turned Tory. In November, 1984, Davis named veteran Kitchener Liberal MPP Jim Breithaupt the $70,000-a-year chairman of the Ontario Law Reform Commission.

Former NDP leader Stephen Lewis, a great favorite of Davis, was made a labor representative on the Ontario Labor Relations Board, and in October, 1984, after Davis acted as the intermediary for Prime Minister Mulroney, he was convinced to become Canada's ambassador to the United Nations. Another former New Democrat MPP, Peterborough's Walter Pitman, became president of Ryerson after leaving his riding open in 1971, resulting in a Tory gain. Pitman was followed at Ryerson by Brian Segal — yep, Hugh's brother — and now holds the job of executive director of the Ontario Arts Council.

Odd how these cross-party appointments usually resulted in Tory gains. But while the Tories were always anxious to help open up opposition ridings, when they didn't want one of their own seats to become vacant, job opportunities could sometimes dry up. Sid Handleman, who was elected in Carleton in 1971, became housing minister in 1974, became minister without portfolio after suffering a heart attack, stepped up to Consumer Rela-

*Parsons later ran Frank Miller's successful leadership campaign, one of the few Davis confidants to show up in the Miller camp.

tions in 1975, and two years later, at his request, left cabinet to sit on the government back benches. Before he entered politics, he had built up his own business as a tariff consultant but soon lost his clients. By leaving cabinet he had "stepped down from $40,000 to $25,000 and was looking for a job after the 1977 election, when I soon learned the kind of hardball they can play from [the premier's] office."

He had at least twenty interviews for jobs for which he was qualified, but he kept getting turned down. "Finally a friend said to me, 'I can't tell you you're not qualified for this job, but I want you to know we checked with the premier's office, and we were told in no uncertain terms it would not be looked on with favor,' the fact that somebody would entice me away from the government. In other words, they were stopping me from getting a job [because] they didn't want a by-election." He did line up a job as a deputy minister in Alberta, but it was leaked to the papers. "I was quite upset. I phoned Alberta and told them to forget it, it was embarrassing to me and to them. I felt it was probably leaked from the premier's office."

Handleman insisted on meeting Davis and eventually did. "His first words to me were, 'Do you really want to leave?' I told him, 'No, but I'm not getting anything extra here,' and with my holdings in trust, I didn't have much. He said, 'Why don't we see what we can find you on the side.' That sounded reasonable to me, so subsequent to that I spoke to Pat Kinsella and Bill Kelly and said I wanted to get out and I needed a job. It all caught up to me, and in early 1979 I had two more heart attacks. While I was in the hospital, Pat [Kinsella] came to me and said, 'Look, those things you were talking about with the premier, nothing seems to be working out.' And they offered me . . . I have to call it a $10,000 slush fund to be our eastern Ontario public relations guy. I said, 'You've got to be crazy. This would create a scandal.' Basically, it was $10,000 out of party funds to avoid a by-election." When he left hospital, he told his riding executive to prepare for just that, and "Hughie Segal went crazy. He was furious. He came in the next day and told me a by-election would ruin Davis. That the Middlesex by-election [won by the NDP in 1969] had ruined Robarts."

Finally Handleman was offered a part-time job with Public Affairs Resource Group Ltd. by Torrence Wylie, a veteran fund-raiser for both Pierre Trudeau and John Turner. "People asked me why I went to work for a Grit. I said Tories wouldn't hire me." Ironically, the firm expanded considerably, and one of the three owners is now the brilliant Tory pollster Allan Gregg, a Davis confidant. One of the firm's biggest competitors is Hugh Segal's Advance Planning.

Appointments aren't the only form of largesse available to bestow on party stalwarts, of course. Late in 1974, when the Davis government was under constant attack following the stream of scandals and near-scandals, Winkler announced that the government was putting its advertising business on a tender system to avoid charges of political abuse. He promised to change the closed-door contracts, which the opposition charged went to government friends. The Liberals complained that Camp Associates, headed by Norman Atkins, was getting more than its share of advertising dollars, along with two other firms with Tory connections, Foster and McConnell. Ten years later there is a proposal system, whereby firms are invited to submit ideas for advertising campaigns and a committee of government officials chooses the best one. In theory it ends partisan considerations; in practice it doesn't. Camp and Foster still grab the bulk of the juicy contracts.*

In mid-December, 1984, three months before Camp Associates's tourism contract was set to expire and at a time when it seemed probable that Davis's successor would be Frank Miller, never a Segal fan, lo and behold Camp Associates again submitted the best proposal, winning a three-year renewal of the tourism contract worth $9.7 million, of which the company would keep $1.45 million.

Opposition politicians also accuse the Tories of funnelling more Wintario lottery money into Tory ridings. A report tabled in the late 1970s by the Metro Social Planning Council, which is itself suspect because of its blatantly left-wing bias, stated that the party's Toronto ridings came up lucky more often with lottery money, even excluding such big lottery fund-users as the Royal Ontario Museum (which is in a Tory riding), getting a per-capita allot-

---

*Speaking of Camp Associates, Tory guru Dalton Camp, although no longer associated with the firm, was picked by Davis, along with journalist Douglas Fisher and former Liberal leader Farquhar Oliver, to head the Ontario Commission on the Legislature in 1972.

ment of $31.30, while non-Tory ridings got only $10.35. Both
the Tories and lottery officials denied the accusations.

In 1980 Stewart said it was nonsense to suggest his committee
was dispensing patronage to the Tory faithful. "It wouldn't be in
our interest to appoint any but able people. The first criterion is
ability and experience." Perhaps, but political affiliation appears to
be a close second.

Westcott says the major problem with the system is that "they
often aren't diligent enough who gets appointed. Nobody was
paying attention when they got Walter Pitman into Ryerson.
Sometimes things get going and they can't be stopped, and often
it's done without Davis knowing anything about it." When Hugh
Segal's brother Brian became Ryerson president, the usual patronage stories appeared, and although Westcott denies it, a Ryerson
board member telephoned board secretary Jack Gorman, a former North Bay Tory candidate, and told him the best pick, politics aside, was Segal. Westcott thinks "it hurt Brian to be so closely
connected. They were paranoid at Queen's Park. They didn't
want to say anything for him or against him. He was a hell of a
good choice."

Westcott doesn't feel the same way about the decision to bring
the former high-profile federal Liberal mandarin, Bernie Ostry,
to Queen's Park. Ostry did not shine as deputy minister of industry
and trade and was later demoted to Citizenship and Culture. "He
wasn't a big noise in Ottawa any more. He was on his way out.
Why did we get suckered with him? I'll tell you why. He was big
socially, a hell of a nice guy, but it was Hughie [Segal] who phoned
up Brian Segal and said, 'You used to be a friend of Bernie's, you
used to do a lot of work for him, do you think he'd be interested?' Davis gets talked into that kind of stuff too often."

Eddie Goodman says Davis "sometimes gets himself into a
jackpot because he equivocates. He doesn't want to hurt people,
and because of that he'll leave a couple of guys with the impression they're going to get an appointment. I remember one appointment, a little thing like getting on the racing commission. A couple
of guys came to me and said the premier was supporting them.
Then another guy told me the premier was supporting him. So I
said to the premier, 'Now listen, just to help us, how many guys
are you supporting for this one application?' He said, 'Only two, I
think.' Then he told me he was in a bit of a spot. 'I didn't really

promise it, but I came close.' His problem is, he just doesn't like to say no to somebody."

Not all Davis appointments floated up from the Thursday morning group, and not all had political motivations. Personal favors were not unknown. Nick Lorito, who drove for Davis from 1966 until 1982, has no doubt how he became manager of the government auto garage, and he's thankful for it.

Lorito says Davis is the most generous man he has ever known, "but he has great difficulty saying 'Thank you.' Yet he can get most people to do any damn thing he wants. He would give me things at Christmas, hundreds of dollars, and he's not a wealthy man. He just knew that with a young family, money was the most sensible present to give. There'd be no hullabaloo or anything. He'd just hand me an envelope and say, 'Nicholas, perhaps you shouldn't lose this envelope.' This job is a thank-you. I was a very sick person when I came here. I was told by the doctor that if I like breathing, which I do, I'd better get out [of driving]. When I told him he was shocked, but he asked me if I had anything in mind. I found out later that Lloyd McWaters, manager of the garage, was taking early retirement, but the competition for the job was closed to MTC (Transportation and Communications) employees only. By some miracle it was re-opened and I was allowed to apply.

"Knowing how government works, a lot of people try to convince me I earned this job on my own, and I guess as a human being I like to feel that I did. Realistically, I think I'm proving I can do the job, but under the government system and without Bill Davis making a phone call, I wouldn't be sitting here today. That's reality.

"Now some people might call that patronage, Bill Davis getting a job for his friends. But I'll tell you, the fact he did what he did makes me work harder than I'd ever work under any other circumstance. Some people may see it as a free ride to a good job. Well, it wasn't free. I worked sixteen years before I got this. I enjoyed it, but it was hard work. Nothing's free."

CHAPTER 14
A WISEMAN FROM THE EAST

—————— ⚜ ——————

It was out in the gently rolling, rocky terrain of Perth, in deepest eastern Ontario, that the last fatal duel in Canada was fought with pistols, on June 13, 1833. Naturally, the fight was over a woman, Elizabeth Hughes, a teacher at Miss Ackland's School for Young Ladies. The combatants, both law students, missed their first two shots, reloaded, then fired again. Robert Lyon fell dead, shot by John Wilson. The site, snuggled beside the banks of the Tay River, is now a thirty-acre park and campground called, not surprisingly, Last Duel Park.

Just a short distance away, on a chilly evening on March 28, 1984, the final shots in another duel of sorts were fired by Bill Davis. He didn't use pistols, of course, but he used his verbal arsenal on over three hundred people packed into the Knights of Columbus Hall for the Doug Wiseman appreciation dinner. This duel wasn't fatal. Davis was decidedly off-target.

This is Tory country — real, down deep, heart and soul, capital-B Blue. The last provincial Liberal elected anywhere in Lanark won by eighty votes in 1902, but the current riding of Lanark, formed after redistribution in 1933, has never been anything but Tory.

They are polite people here, basic, God-fearing folks who would never be rude or throw buns at a speaker. But over his entire career, in the thousands of speeches delivered to partisan crowds, Davis never received a cooler reaction. They clapped but didn't applaud; they were respectful but didn't respect.

So deep was their quiet rage, their belief that Davis had betrayed their MPP, that they invited Frontenac-Addington Grit J. Earl McEwen (who crossed over to the Tories months later) and Cornwall New Democrat George Samis as dinner guests, the ultimate slight for such traditional partisans. Inviting a socialist to a Tory event in Lanark is akin to inviting a Presbyterian to celebrate mass. It's simply not done. "The last time I was at a PC event was when my father took me to a Diefenbaker rally in Montreal in 1958," said Samis. "This tells you how they feel."

Davis came to Perth not to bury Wiseman — he'd already done that politically by kicking him out of cabinet in July, 1983 — but not to praise him, either. He barely mentioned him. He came, although he denied it, out of a sense of guilt, and as Leeds Tory Bob Runciman puts it, "to smooth over the waters . . . a peace offering."

The fact that a Conservative premier would feel the need to make peace with such loyal subjects does not represent one of Davis's proudest moments. The Wiseman Affair was not a shining example of representative government in action. It was a shabby case of a bureaucrat with friends in high places out-muscling a man who wanted only to follow the rules and protect taxpayers' money. Wiseman, seen as a country bumpkin by Davis and his sophisticated sycophants, tried to fight his deputy minister of government services, Alan Gordon, and lost. Gordon eventually resigned, but long after Wiseman had been chopped, and not until Davis had publicly pledged to find him a comparable job and had offered fine words of praise for him. It left little doubt about who has the real power — politicians or senior mandarins.

One cabinet minister recalls the stormy events that burst into the open in the summer of 1983: "I don't think in retrospect they'd handle it that way again. The same thing could have been accomplished so much better. It's surprising. Davis is usually so sensitive to other people's feelings." Not this time. Even a year later, despite overwhelming evidence that the wrong guy had been victimized, Davis still refused to concede he had made an error. "I make mistakes, but I don't make that kind of mistake. I really don't."

The issue also underscored traditional feelings of resentment among eastern Ontarians, which they share with northerners, that they are taken for granted by Queen's Park at best and are totally ignored at worst. This, after all, is the Tory bedrock, the foundation that, through good times and bad, has kept them in power since 1943. With Wiseman gone, Davis had no one in cabinet representing a rural, eastern Ontario view. No one.

"They do take eastern Ontario for granted," says Prince Edward-Lennox MPP Jim Taylor. "They'd better get into the real eastern Ontario, not just Ottawa and Kingston. The ridings on each side of me fell in 1975 [Quinte and Frontenac-Addington]. You had two good Tory ridings that went down the drain. I can see an erosion of Tory strength, especially since the Liberals are to the right of the Tories. They're traditionally Conservative philosophically down here, but Bill Davis doesn't reflect that."

To hear head office tell it, you'd think Taylor was talking nonsense. After all, didn't Tory Noble Villeneuve win the Stormont-Dundas-Glengarry by-election by four thousand votes in December, 1983, just days after Alan Gordon finally resigned under fire over the Wiseman Affair? So what's the problem? Things are fine in the east, boasted Davis and other senior Tories, claiming the by-election win pooh-poohed opposition claims that Wiseman's unceremonial dumping (his riding is next door) would hurt Tory electoral chances in the region.

But when Davis became premier in 1971, the Tories held an astounding 19 of 21 ridings from Port Hope east to the Quebec border. Since then one seat has been added, and of the 22 seats, 15 are Tory (one of which was regained without firing a shot when McEwan crossed the floor in June, 1984), five are Liberal, and two are NDP. Still predominantly Tory, yes, but the slippage under Davis was irrefutable, a discomfiting fact for an area that has been to Ontario Tories what Quebec historically was to federal Liberals. When Davis steamrolled to a large majority in 1981, not one of the 12 seats he gained was in the east.

*   *   *

When Doug Wiseman was thirteen in Smiths Falls, he and his best friend, Bill Doland, hit on a plan. The two boys couldn't find a summer job, so they talked a local lumber dealer into giving them credit on enough wood to build a booth, convinced Rideau Canal officials to let them set up a business, and spent the summer at a nearby fishing and swimming hole, Poolimilee, selling hot dogs, hamburgers, and fishing tackle. After paying for the lumber and supplies, they each made $350 profit — big bucks for two kids in 1943.

Wiseman's formal education ended early in high school, but his entrepreneurial spirit didn't. He began working in a Smiths Falls shoe store and was then transferred to Perth. He rented farms, and each morning, hours before trudging off to sell shoes, he'd go out and look after his cattle. Eventually he built the largest cow-calf operation in the county. His wife, Bunny, a nurse, was working nights at a local seventeen-bed private hospital when the owner died and the widow wanted to sell. The Wisemans borrowed $1,000 from a relative, used it as a down payment for the $50,000 deal, and moved into a tiny cottage at the back of the hospital. Bunny ran the nursing side while Doug, still selling shoes and watching his cattle, was all-round handyman. They worked hard and soon started turning a profit.

In 1958, two years after buying the hospital, they scraped together a down payment for a Perth shoe store. A year later they bought their first farm. In 1969 they bought their current farm, a two-hundred-acre operation a few miles from Perth. They developed lots in the bush, and Wiseman, already into farming, the bull semen business, shoe retailing, and the hospital industry, moved successfully into real estate as well. Wiseman and his eldest son have now opened a chain of discount shoe stores — the first, C & M Discount in Perth, down the street from Wiseman Shoes, which handles only top lines — and are expanding to Smiths Falls, Brockville, and Kingston.

This is the man who was considered too dumb and unsophisticated to run the government services ministry.

Alan Gordon graduated from high school in Hamilton, took his BA at the University of Toronto, taught at Meaford District High School, and became assistant to the University of Waterloo president. There he was noticed by the assistant deputy minister of university affairs, Ed Stewart, and on April 1, 1967, when the minister, Bill Davis, elevated Stewart to deputy minister, Gordon was hired to take Stewart's old job.

From the outset the red-haired Gordon was outspoken. In March, 1968, as a panelist at a University of Guelph teach-in, he said teaching French in Ontario was about as relevant as teaching Swahili. "The government is introducing French because it is the thing to do," he said. "They aren't thinking whether it has any relevance. Everyone is jumping on this bandwagon . . . and the universities aren't doing anything to expose this quackery." The man leading the parade of French-language quackery was his minister, Bill Davis.

A few months later Gordon was applauded by one thousand delegates at a computer conference when he quit reading midway through a speech to spare them the "pain" of sitting through it. The thirteen-page speech had been written for Davis, but he was called away on business and Gordon was sent to fill in. Displaying the cavalier attitude that marked his public career, Gordon said, "If there is any real interest" in the speech, delegates could "read the rest of the five pages" in the local press.

In 1974 he became second assistant deputy minister in Community and Social Services. He made headlines in September, 1976, when he phoned a Wintario grants officer and asked him to speed up an application for a $104,333 grant for the Ashbridge's Bay Yacht Club. Gordon was a club member. The minister, Bob Welch, didn't see anything wrong with a senior civil servant calling his officials about a grant.

In May, 1978, Gordon's old mentor, Ed Stewart, brought him into the premier's office with a special assignment to cut government red tape and improve public services. There is precious little evidence that he accomplished much, but in July, 1978, Gordon said he wanted to improve the telephone directory listings; he later tried to accomplish this by approving a $617,000 contract for a computerized telephone listing without approval from management board and against direct orders from his minister, Doug Wiseman.

*   *   *

Wiseman was easily elected in 1971, replacing George Gomme, the silver-tongued lay preacher who spent several years in cabinet. Wiseman had chaired the Perth Public School Board for a decade and was active in a host of local groups. In November, 1975, he was made parliamentary assistant to Health Minister Frank Miller, and three years later he was sworn into cabinet as minister without portfolio. In August, 1979, he succeeded Lorne Henderson as government services minister.

Gordon and Wiseman never did hit it off. "For the first while I was with him," says Wiseman. "If things didn't go right he would always say he'd talked to Ed [Stewart], and this is the way it should be. I got fed up after a while." The situation worsened. Wiseman felt Gordon wasn't telling him what was going on in the ministry, so he set up meetings in his office with senior ministry officials. Gordon also had regular top-level meetings, but Wiseman was invited only once. "It got so bad that some of them [ministry officials] wouldn't come in the front door," says Wiseman. "They'd sneak up around past my secretary because if they were seen coming into my office they'd be questioned by him later. It was an awful way to live." At one point three senior ministry officials appealed to Clare Westcott to arrange a meeting with Davis so they could air their complaints about Gordon. Davis wasn't interested.

In February, 1983, Wiseman decided to confront Gordon. He reserved a table at the Westbury, and over lunch the two men had what one observer called "an old-fashioned donnybrook." For a while things improved. Wiseman credits Gordon with "a lot of good ideas . . . but I felt like I was in a boat which was filling with water. I'd work like hell to bail it out and get going, but I just couldn't do it in the atmosphere that was there."

Davis claimed he was unaware of the situation, but Stewart and Gordon were in constant touch about it, and other ministry officials, such as David Angus, Wiseman's executive assistant, and Fred Ross, communications director, spoke with John Tory and Westcott about it. Wiseman and Gordon also had an unprecedented open argument at a management board meeting over the telephone directory. Davis knew about all of this.

In March, 1983, Wiseman told Davis in the legislature he wanted to discuss his problems with Gordon, but Davis kept putting off a meeting until July. It was a week before the cabinet shuffle and a day before Wiseman was leaving for the Calgary wedding of the daughter of his boyhood pal Bill Doland. At this point Gordon's violations of contract rules were not public knowledge, but there can be no doubt that Davis knew — Stewart, Tory, and Westcott knew, and Wiseman had told Davis directly he wanted a meeting about Gordon. If Davis didn't know then, he could have asked Stewart what problems Wiseman was talking about. That's the way it works.

For the meeting Wiseman prepared a list of ten rules violations he believed Gordon had made, wrote them on a single sheet, and made a copy for Davis. None of the violations involved any personal monetary gain by Gordon. The issue was Gordon's penchant for proceeding on his own hook, often without required approvals, to dispatch large government contracts without tenders.

After a brief greeting in the office, Wiseman offered Davis the list. Davis refused to take it. "That hurt a little," says Wiseman. "He said he didn't want to talk about that, but he wanted to talk to me so he wouldn't have to call me back from the West and give me the bad news."

Davis fired Wiseman on the spot.

He said he needed room for three new ministers in the upcoming shuffle and Wiseman was being bumped because he was more financially secure than some of the others, and anyway, it wouldn't hurt politically in Lanark as it might in other ridings. Wiseman went back to his office in a state of bewilderment. He called in his personal staff to give them the bad news. "He was crying," one of them says. "Tears were streaming down his face. He kept saying, 'Out. I'm out.' He couldn't believe it. Neither could we."

Davis had told Wiseman he wasn't unhappy with his work. Maybe not, but the Davis inner circle said Wiseman was ineffective at best and downright incompetent at worst. Senior ministry officials say privately that Wiseman did a good job, improving staff morale that had sunk under Lorne Henderson. Fred Ross, Wiseman's former communications director, says some of the premier's aides were "uncomfortable" about Wiseman, seeing him as unsophisticated. "He would say, 'Well, you know, in the shoe store we do it this way,' and some people would say, 'How on earth does a guy try to compare a small-town shoe store to a multi-million dollar ministry?' But in effect the issues were the same. Whether you're talking about how to treat people who work for you, or how to treat customers or take inventory, Doug was taking the small businessman's approach to government, which, quite frankly, I'm not sure isn't a good idea."

Another senior official says he advised Stewart to "never piss on an angel. Whether he [Wiseman] should be an angel or not didn't matter. The fact is, he was perceived that way back home and in the media, and what comes out of that is a government which is getting too arrogant, too powerful, to worry about the feelings of an unsophisticated, rural guy like Doug."

The affair finally became public in the *Toronto Sun* on August 18, 1983, a month after Wiseman was fired. A day earlier the *Ottawa Citizen* had run a story from Renfrew North MPP Sean Conway, the Liberal deputy leader who did a masterful job pushing the issue, in which Gordon was accused of hiring Allan W. Foster and Associates at $900 a day without tender. The *Sun* account went much further, outlining three other apparent breaches by Gordon. Holidaying at the luxurious Minaki Lodge near Kenora at the time, Gordon admitted in a telephone interview that Wiseman "didn't know, and there were no tenders" on one of the contracts, an admission he later denied.

According to the manual of administration, which Davis always bragged was Canada's toughest government rule book, contracts over $15,000 should be tendered or, if not, approved by management board. In the Foster case neither had happened, and in what looked like a dodge around this rule, Gordon had Foster submit a series of ten invoices, each under $15,000. Gordon dismissed it as "strictly an administrative function. These people are experts, and that's the kind of fee these people charge."

Months later, testifying before the public accounts committee, Gordon claimed he was misquoted and said Wiseman did know about the contract. By then, however, a special auditor's report had criticized Gordon's handling of the Foster deal and other matters. Gordon had become too big a political liability to be protected by Stewart any longer.

After the contract disputes became public, Wiseman's successor, George Ashe, asked provincial auditor Douglas F. Archer to investigate four specific matters: the Foster deal; the development of a telephone data base (Telepac) and the summer, 1983, government phone directory; development of a computerized data base for legislation, with reference to a contract with Q.L. Systems Ltd. of Kingston; and consolidation of the ministry of muncipal affairs and housing in the downtown Toronto College Park development.

Archer found that Gordon had rehired Foster in eight successive phases covered by ten purchase orders. The contracts ranged from $900 to $15,000 each and totalled $81,300. The ministry denied trying to skate around the $15,000 rule, but Archer said it should have told management board about the deal "to avoid the appearance" of contravention. Later Archer testified at committee that "from a reasonable man's point of view," Gordon's contractual deal with Foster "certainly would have to be looked at [as deliberate]." Weeks later, when Gordon told the committee Archer had no basis for such a conclusion, Archer interjected that he had "internal ministry memos" to prove his point.

The Telepac project, which Gordon had dreamed up when he worked for Stewart five years earlier, cost $617,000 and entailed compiling the names of about 65,000 civil servants. Wiseman had ordered Gordon not to proceed with Telepac, and Archer said the submission to management board was withdrawn because the ministry knew it was "not acceptable to management board secretariat and . . . would not have been recommended to management board for approval." But Gordon had proceeded with Telepac anyway, even though there had been no feasibility study, a requirement for projects over $100,000, and no management board approval, also a requirement. "It appears they went ahead on their own," Archer testified.

On the contract with Q.L. Systems to computerize government legislation, Archer concluded that the ministry had complied with the manual, even though Gordon did hire the firm without tender. And on the housing ministry move to College Park, Archer found that the estimated cost had increased $2.1 million, from $1.6 million to $3.7 million, in three months — an increase approved by management board.

While this controversy was raging, the Tories tried to stonewall opposition demands for full disclosure. In August George Ashe, who had asked Archer to investigate, dismissed the original allegations, saying he'd checked them quickly, "and I don't see anything wrong with it at all." Stewart, on the other hand, who knew the situation, said, "I wish I could tell you all of these things were a crock, but I can't." He is a powerful man, Ed Stewart, but honest.

The auditor's report made it difficult to dismiss claims of contract abuse, but Ashe tried, saying they may have been "technical violations" by Gordon but nothing serious.

In November the *Sun* broke yet another tender tale of a $50,000, fourteen-month food services contract given by Gordon to Joe Dineley, a veteran Queen's Park vendor who had been on an annual $12,000 part-time consultant's contract for years. The ministry had issued a proposal call for the part-time job, and some proposals had been submitted, but Gordon had personally intervened, cancelled the proposal call, upgraded the job to full-time, and given the contract, without tender, to Dineley.

Both Wiseman and Sean Kelly, executive director of corporate services division, had flatly refused to sign the contract, worried about a possible conflict of interest because Dineley still had some corporate interest in a food company supplying the Queen's Park cafeteria. Gordon had ignored Wiseman's refusal to sign and simply awarded the contract under an internal food services policy, a convenient loophole in the rules. Again, both Ashe and Davis defended Gordon in the legislature.

When the Dineley issue came up at public accounts, Tory backbencher Alan Robinson (Scarborough-Ellesmere) broke ranks and voted with the opposition to order Gordon to explain the deal to the committee. Robinson's vote meant a 5–5 tie, promptly broken by committee chairman Pat Reid, a Liberal. As events unfolded, Gordon never did explain this deal. Christmas break intervened, and by the time the committee reconvened, Gordon had left the public service.

Gordon did appear before the public accounts committee on Thursday, November 24, 1983, however, and admitted to errors in awarding contracts without approvals but denied disobeying Wiseman. Asked if Wiseman knew about the $900-a-day management consultant contract, Gordon said, "He knew. The minister was aware at all times of what we were doing."

The gauntlet had finally been thrown down. The issue now became who was telling the truth, Wiseman or Gordon. The *Globe* headline read: "Deputy Says Ex-Minister Lied About Contracts." A senior insider said Gordon's testimony killed him. He said Wiseman "didn't know about that specific contract. That made it a choice between who was telling the truth . . . all the sympathy was with Wiseman. Some people may not have been impressed with his ability, but everybody saw him as honest."

Opposition MPPs grilled Gordon about his relationship with Stewart, but he repeatedly refused to discuss it, saying it was not a matter of public record. But if there were any doubts about how tight the relationship was, they were dispelled when Gordon left the committee and headed directly for Stewart's office for a debriefing that had been planned in advance. When it was reported the next day that Gordon had been "coached" for his appearance, Davis told Liberal Sean Conway that was nonsense. Gordon was not "coached . . . in my office. It is just factually incorrect." The denial was vintage Davis at his best, or worst, painstakingly measuring each word to avoid either telling a lie or telling the truth. True, Gordon had not been "coached" in the premier's office, but no one said he had. He had been "coached" by Stewart in his office and elsewhere, a chain of events, leading up to Gordon's Thursday appearance, that Stewart confirms:

On the Monday Stewart met management board secretary Robert Carman in his office about the case. Gordon phoned, and both men spoke to him about it. Stewart and Gordon had breakfast together Tuesday at the Park Plaza. Stewart was worried that the hot-headed Gordon would blow a fuse in public and make things look worse than they already did. They discussed Gordon's opening statement, and Gordon agreed to deliver a copy to Stewart the next morning. As promised, the statement arrived on Stewart's desk early Wednesday. Stewart read it, went over it with Gordon on the phone that evening, and asked Gordon to come to his office directly after his committee appearance the next day.

But Davis, trying to distance himself and his office from Gordon, said he wasn't "coached." And Davis is an honorable man.

The Tories were beginning to worry. At about the time Gordon was arriving in Stewart's office after his testimony, St. David Tory MPP Margaret Scrivener, an effective, obstreperous committee member, went to Wiseman's office and asked him to go away to avoid the press. "They [the premier's office] wanted me to go on a holiday," says Wiseman. ". . . She was really mad when I wouldn't. Then she didn't want me to appear in the House that day, but I'd never run from anything in my life, and I wasn't going to start now."

The issue had grown beyond a Wiseman-Gordon dispute, boiling over to the point where other people were being scalded, particularly management board secretary Carman and board chairman George McCague. Carman was dragged before the committee on December 1 and handled roughly and unfairly, particularly by Etobicoke NDP member Ed Philip, who was excessively hostile to the widely respected Carman. Carman's testimony proved embarrassing. He admitted that the system was "extensively self-regulating" and that he had no power to discipline deputy ministers who trampled the rules. He said he had known about Gordon's non-compliance in the Telepac contract in the fall of 1982 and had told McCague, adding that Davis had recently sent a letter to deputy ministers ordering "everyone who has the authority to acquire goods and services and engage personnel . . . to adhere to the provisions of the manual [of administration] without exception." It was the first indication that Davis's spirited public defence of the manual conflicted with his private views.

As management board chairman, McCague was the general manager of government. Yet when reporters asked what he did when Carman told him Gordon had broken the rules, he said, "I did not take any action. I never felt it was my responsibility to inform the auditor. It's up to each ministry."

Late in the afternoon of November 30, Davis convened a two-hour meeting in his office with Stewart, Treasurer Larry Grossman, and his deputy, Tom Campbell. "It had gone on too long," a senior official explains. "Davis knew it had. As circumstances unfolded, the inevitable conclusion being drawn was he was protecting Stewart's friend Gordon."

The four men agreed on a plan. First they'd announce a review of existing rules on government contracts, which Davis did the next day, naming Grossman and McCague to oversee the probe. They also agreed that Campbell would have a chat with Gordon, which he did, and early the next morning Wiseman was called into the premier's office and told that Gordon was resigning as deputy minister. In announcing Gordon's resignation, Davis said he'd find him a comparable job and praised him as a "very decent, honorable person . . . with seventeen years of very loyal and dedicated public service."

He never had such fine words for Wiseman. Indeed, before Wiseman could get Davis to even acknowledge his side publicly, he had to make some threats. Wiseman was angry that "it hadn't been cleared up once and for all who was lying," so he told John Tory he wasn't going back to the legislature until Davis agreed to straighten it out. True to his word, Wiseman skipped a no-confidence vote that night. Although easily won by the majority Tories, Wiseman's absence was loudly noted by the opposition. John Tory had told Wiseman that Davis would clear up the matter that day, but he didn't.

Wiseman was getting sick of this. "That was my credibility they were fooling with, my credibility back to my kids and going down in the records. It had to be corrected." He delivered an ultimatum: Either Davis would tell the legislature that Wiseman did not know of the contract, or Wiseman would rise in the legislature and read his own statement. At 2 p.m. the day before Christmas break began, Wiseman was talking on the phone in the government lounge when Davis tapped his shoulder and said, "I understand you have some doubts about whether I'll say that tomorrow or not." Wiseman told him, "If I have your word, that's good enough for me." The next day Davis did try to explain. "He sort of cleared my name, although it wasn't really black or white, a kind of half-assed apology. But I thought that was the best I could get." It was the last item of business before the break. Davis had delayed as long as he could.

The contrast in the treatment of Wiseman and Gordon — one was fired, the other promised a comparable job and given public praise — prompted Liberal Pat Reid to quip, "Heads roll uphill in this government." But two weeks after resigning as deputy minister, Gordon quit the public service, grabbing a private contract with Shell as a management consultant. Davis said he hoped now the issue "would be brought to an end." No doubt.

The Wiseman Affair raises several questions, not the least being just who is running the government.

Jim Taylor, former social services and energy minister, says, "Oh yes, there's no doubt deputies run the ministries. You can be stonewalled forever." Especially with backup from the premier's office. Sally Barnes says Davis "was advised badly on Wiseman. He was under pressure from Segal and Stewart to find new spots. . . . There are too few people trying to do too many things. There are so many deputy ministers who won't do anything without phoning Stewart."

But the Palace Guard insists that Wiseman's firing was unrelated to the problems with Gordon. Hugh Segal says Wiseman didn't say anything in cabinet. "Over the period of time he was minister of the Crown and a spokesman for rural eastern Ontario, he wasn't very strong on either account. I was at a lot of cabinet meetings dealing with issues of importance to rural eastern Ontario, and — silence. Total, absolute, and complete silence. He didn't say anything. Nothing."

In contrast, Lorne Henderson, Wiseman's predecessor who took over agriculture until he was dumped after widespread farm complaints, says, "Wiseman gave me as much opposition as any member of cabinet to some of my farm policies." He complains Wiseman said too much. "There's no doubt it was badly handled because Doug didn't accept the premier's decision. . . . He forgot he was a team player. . . . He was jealous of the minister of agriculture [Henderson]. He wanted that job. He couldn't accept the fact that the premier didn't want him any more."

Segal protested that he didn't want to talk about Wiseman because he couldn't "without reflecting badly on Doug. . . . Despite the confluence of events, it's my view the two events had no connection at all. There's no question it was not handled well. How could you look at it and come away with any other impression? Nobody was in a position to do anything about the unfortunate confluence of events, to stand back and say, 'Let's look at what's happening.' There was nobody in the process who could be that detached. Ed [Stewart] couldn't be for reasons already mentioned. The premier was not detached because he'd just be laboring with Ed's concerns and Doug's concerns. There just wasn't anybody who didn't have a strong feeling about either one of those guys who could stop it."

"To the guys in the game, it tells us how it's played," says Tory Morley Kells. "The guys with the lines through the civil service have more protection than the guys with the political lines because you can't get the political lines through to the top. Never mind getting to talk to Davis. You don't even get to talk to the guys who are close to him. Ed Stewart lives a block from me, Tom Campbell lives three houses away. I never see them. I think Davis demands the flow of party loyalty up the ladder through the system. He demands that. But I don't think he necessarily feels it flows back down the system, because if they have to sacrifice you they certainly will."

Clare Westcott says Wiseman's problem was "he's too honest. He doesn't know how to finesse these guys into a corner. He's just a kind of bungling farmer when it comes to doing something like this. He's a good minister, believe me. . . . If Wiseman had played his cards right, he could have manoeuvred Davis . . . where he would have had to go down there and say something. But you know, transcending all those personal values he [Davis] was raised with, is the fact he will never eat crow. No sir. He will not. He will tell me to my face an outright lie to try and rationalize what he's done. You know, I tell him something is going on in a ministry he doesn't know, but he wants to pretend he does. His favorite way out of tough spots is to say, 'Well, Clare, there are things about this I wish I could tell you.' He does that a lot."

Resources Secretary Norman Sterling says, "I don't know who screwed up, but it was arrogant. The part that bothered me more than anything with both Doug and Bruce [McCaffrey, his close friend, shuffled from Citizenship and Culture to make room for Susan Fish] is that I still find it hard to believe the premier could be that callous and insensitive. I don't even argue in terms of Doug's competence or incompetence, but I do know he was tremendously loyal to the premier and should have been given some time to find a nice way out. I find it hard to believe that was Davis's doing. Doug didn't speak up that often in cabinet, but he did speak sometimes. There aren't many guys who do oppose that much in cabinet period. Those who do don't help their careers."

McCaffrey agrees Wiseman "wasn't all that vocal . . . but he sure said things and was part of arguments when Lorne Henderson was agriculture minister. But I've heard that shit, too. They always bad-mouth the guys who get booted. Some say Doug wasn't all that bright. Well, that's their two cents' worth, but if you were to take an IQ test to get in there, there'd be a lot of empty seats. Doug made a lot of money. He must know something. What have most of those inside guys ever done?"

Hugh Macaulay says the problem "had something to do with the timing. There have been a lot of people leave cabinet. . . . The appointment of cabinet ministers is a very delicate business. A lot of people leave cabinet. Doug Wiseman was just one." The Gordon matter was "just a coincidence." Told it didn't look that way, Macaulay said, "I don't give a damn how it looks. I'm sure it was a coincidence."

Frank Miller recalls Davis told him privately "at least four times" it had nothing to do with Gordon. "I'm going to guess it had nothing to do with competence. Douglas was not a particularly good minister in terms of management of the ministry or the politics, but he was a lot better than some. I suspect with Doug, it was something on a personal basis."

Westcott told Stewart early on that Gordon was throwing his name in Wiseman's face whenever the two disagreed. "I told Stewart that. He said, 'Oh, shit.' I think Gordon assumed Ed would support him," says Westcott. "Here's Al Gordon. He bombed in our office, pissed off everybody, and yet they go to the wall with him. There's a kind of Rasputin effect over Davis by Stewart. It wasn't always there. . . . If you talk to some of the deputies about Gordon, some of the problems that guy caused, it's awful. Now there's a stigma on everybody."

"Gordon is the last guy I would have thought was getting into that trouble," says Eddie Goodman. "He was really trying to bring the whole system of rent and everything up to date. The things he did are done by every goddamn minister one way or another all the time. You know, the rules are there, but there's no doubt you can't always obey the rules. Ministers are delighted sometimes to have their deputies short-cut the rules. Unfortunately, he didn't obey the cardinal rule of making the minister, who wasn't too bright in my opinion anyway, part of the decisions." He was surprised at the strength of the perception that Wiseman was the good guy and Gordon the bad guy, with Davis protecting the bad guy. "It got to that largely because Gordon is not thought of as a bad guy . . . and there also can't be any doubt Wiseman was not contributing that much. So you have a tendency to down-play a guy who you don't think has done his job, and then another guy, who you figure is a pretty good deputy, you might overlook some things. And I suppose to some extent, Gordon was a friend of Stewart's. He had worked for Stewart. So you lose your perspective when you're dealing with fellahs you know well."

On February 8, 1984, Carman held a seminar to "boost awareness" of administrative procedures for three hundred senior officials from the management board secretariat, the Civil Service Commission, and the auditor's office. He said compliance with the manual was "generally high . . . and absolutely vital to the Ontario public service that this record be maintained."

Whether the message hit home or not, it's hard to say, but

some of the people who attended that seminar were at another one held four months later in Niagara-on-the-Lake for representatives of government, business, and labor. During one session at the week-long think tank, participants were asked by the group leader to name a personal "hero." One senior management person from the Civil Service Commission named Alan Gordon. Several other government people agreed, saying Gordon was martyred by the media and the opposition for trying to make government more efficient.

And Doug Wiseman, an uncomplicated, decent man who never claimed he would turn Queen's Park on its ear, doesn't smile as often as he did. "I don't know if he [Davis] still thinks I instigated the whole thing, but honestly, if I'd really wanted to be dirty and do him in, I would have walked out with the complete list and handed it to the press. Many things came out, and when they did I was asked if they were true. I tried to answer truthfully. I wasn't going to put myself in a box for him [Gordon]. That maybe bugged some people."

One of the people it bugged was Davis. In a July, 1984, interview he said, "It has bothered me in a personal way because I know Douglas doesn't accept this, but the decision was there well before any of this ever emerged as a problem. I have never gotten into a debate as to why I asked a minister to join cabinet or leave cabinet. Circumstances combined in the minds of some to make it appear we were holding a brief for Gordon. It's not true, but I'm not going to argue it didn't appear that way to some."

Perhaps he's right. Although it was his high praise and generosity for Gordon and prompt dismissal of Wiseman that created the perceptions, maybe it was simply a combination of circumstances.

One coincidence, however, was that one senior official in a position to know said that when Wiseman went to Government Services, "Stewart told Gordon not to worry, he wouldn't be there long, anyway." Then there was that odd coincidence in February, 1983, five months before the shuffle, when Gordon told some ministry officials at a Kingston workshop that Wiseman was on his way out. "Some of my officials came back and told me," said Wiseman. "That hurt a little. Nobody had said anything to me, but if he [Gordon] was saying that, I felt it was from a conversation someplace."

*   *   *

The Wiseman dinner didn't start well for Davis. It had been Wiseman's idea to invite him. "I told him I had worshipped the ground he walked on. I respect him now, but I don't worship the ground he walks on."

The Liberals had already asked Wiseman to run for them, but he said he was still a Tory. Feelings were running high. The *Perth Courier* ran a strong editorial that day calling Wiseman's demotion "a slap in the face, and the sting is still being felt by many here in the heartland of eastern Ontario. . . . What the Tory faithful of rural eastern Ontario want is a cabinet voice at Queen's Park. They want to know their faith is not blind. The citizens . . . want more than political rhetoric and kind words from Premier Davis."

They didn't get it. In fact, they barely got the kind words — just a couple of fleeting references by Davis to the hardship of politics, "the ups and downs" of political life.

George Gomme, the former highways minister and Wiseman's predecessor in the riding, introduced Davis in what became a speech in itself. In his haunting, melodic, evangelical voice, Gomme went on about Tom Kennedy bringing "this bushy-tailed and bright-eyed young man" to the legislature twenty-five years earlier. He told a few jokes to loosen the crowd, and for the only time anyone close to Davis can recall, Gomme stepped onto ground that is never mentioned, the "tragedy" Davis had suffered with his first wife's death, an intensely personal event that remains unspoken, at least in public. Yet Gomme did it with class, with amazing sensitivity. Davis, sitting beside the lectern at the head table, was visibly red-faced, decidedly uncomfortable, his eyes staring down at the table, rubbing two fingers beside his right eye, a sure sign, one of the few, of discomfort. Gomme delivered his lines beautifully, almost poetically, no doubt hoping to elicit sympathy for Davis from a hostile crowd.

But the personal nature of the introduction seemed to catch Davis off-guard. He seemed flustered during his opening banter. It simply fell flat, barely raising a titter from his audience. Davis, too, became unusually personal, almost funereal in tone, talking about the influence of his father, Grenville. He even trotted out his fail-safe "God, Queen, Country, and Morality" routine, which always sells, especially in rural Ontario. But this night they weren't buying. Davis desperately tried to reach his audience, but it was waiting for a good word on Wiseman, a job offer (which Davis would never do in such circumstances), anything. It simply wasn't to be.

Speaking in a serious, almost whispered tone throughout, it was often hard to hear what Davis was saying. But after invoking every sacred cow he could, he turned to Wiseman, thanked him for his service, and said, "While there are many opportunities, and you will assess them . . . I just happen to think you have a continued opportunity to contribute to public life. . . . And while my main purpose here tonight is to pay a tribute to you, it is only fitting I wish you well in whatever you choose to do."

Wiseman said later that Davis did not mend any fences that night. "I don't know what he expected, but it didn't work. He wasn't conciliatory. . . . It was like rubbing salt in the wounds because a lot of those people were really uptight about what had happened."

Davis, too, was uptight as he left the coolness of the crowd and dashed through the equally chilly night toward his waiting limousine, stopping only briefly when cornered by the press. "In my job you make your decisions," he said. "They are not based on some of the things you wrote about, but whatever I say will not change that. I do what I have to do. That's one of the tough parts of the job."

With that Bill Davis jumped into his car and sped off into the night, leaving behind the loyal Tories of Lanark. An old woman, her knitted wrap pulled tightly around her, hobbled down the front steps of the hall, leaning heavily on her wooden cane. She stopped to watch as Davis was whisked off, then turned to no one in particular and asked aloud what everyone was thinking: "What did Mr. Wiseman do wrong?"

CHAPTER 15
WRONGING THE RIGHT

————— ☙ —————

In a Quebec City speech in November, 1977, just after the RCMP had been accused of going beyond the call of duty in their pursuit of criminals, Bill Davis told the local Board of Trade that no nation could afford to be complacent about abuses to freedom, the perversion of law, or the inequalities that exist between peoples, saying, "Men and women of goodwill and courage will never tolerate such abridgments to our way of life and will move to expose and right the wrongs."

But that was before his own human rights bill institutionalized abuses to freedom, before his government carried out one of the classic perversions of law by seizing and selling multi-million-dollar private properties without bothering to lay a charge against the owners, and before his restraint package unilaterally wiped out legal, negotiated contracts with civil servants.

All these actions, and more — his mandatory seat belt legislation, rent controls, in fact, a whole series of measures — upset the right wing of his party, the *real* Conservatives, prompting many of them to leave politics in disgust.

Davis always insisted "this left-right thing" was greatly exaggerated and couldn't imagine anyone leaving the party because he was too left wing. But the long list of cabinet ministers who were fired or who left, disgruntled, over the years is made up almost entirely of those on the right. People like Jim Taylor, Bruce McCaffrey, Margaret Scrivener, Doug Wiseman, Sid Handleman, and Don Irvine represented a political viewpoint that did not find much favor with Davis and his Palace Guard, which with the notable exception of Bill Kelly was composed essentially of pink Tories. As Irvine said in early 1984, "Those on the right of centre don't seem popular. Policy-makers today seem to feel they're the ones they can do without."

*　*　*

In his first speech as premier, delivered on March 1, 1971, Davis told the Canadian Club of Toronto that his government would deal with specific problems, but "do not expect government to take over all of the responsibilities which each of us, as individuals, has to our fellow man. I do not want government to replace the individual."

Government has not, of course, replaced the individual, at least not completely. But Davis took a good run at it, becoming the epitome of big government and big brotherism. He claimed otherwise, especially during election campaigns or on partisan forays into bedrock Tory areas, but his record is one of government intervention, all in what he saw as the public good, of course, as well as the good of the Tory regime.

A constant irritation to the right wing of the party was Davis's tendency toward spending, spending, and more spending. He was never deterred from talking fiscal conservatism, giving hundreds of speeches on the importance of balanced budgets, for example, but he never had a balanced budget. Not once. After the 1975 minority, responding to widespread party criticism that he had strayed too far left, Davis and Treasurer Darcy McKeough did launch a highly publicized restraint package with a five-year plan to balance the books, but it never happened; his compulsive spending habits kept getting in the way.

It is true that running a government is not like running a business, and if people are hungry or poor or in trouble the government must help, but Davis was never one to stop at the necessities. Even when he was education minister in the 1960s, replacing one-room schools with large, regional ones, he overlooked the most simple economies. Some of the new buildings were virtual palaces, with marble imported from Italy, for example. Yet back then, even with the Davis spending machine in full flight as by far the largest source of government expenditures, Robarts still managed a balanced budget. As premier Davis was forever in the red.

In December, 1972, fresh from a record $519 million budgetary deficit, Davis said his recent "restraint" moves were unavoidable. "The province is sound. The credit of the province, for example, is very good. But we could see, in the future, if we didn't do something, it would be very serious." One of the things he did then was announce a $1.3 billion program for public transit, an amount far exceeding the scattered spending cuts he'd made. He also said, "The time has come when we must contain health costs" but a few years later announced a pre-election goody of free drugs to seniors, a program costing $15 million then and skyrocketing to $278 million by 1984–85.

In 1980 the legislature's public accounts committee criticized Davis and former treasurer John White for their 1974 landbanking scheme. By then Ontario had spent $35.7 million, or $2,775 an acre, for land at South Cayuga, near Hamilton, appraised at $850 an acre. The plan was to build a model town to cope with population increases, but the population didn't grow, and White's dreams, including a similar scheme for Townsend in eastern Ontario, turned into an $80 million nightmare.

In the 1974–75 budget Davis increased his spending by 24.7 per cent, the next year it went up 15.9 per cent, and in 1976–77, the beginning of McKeough's "restraint" package, it went up a modest 10.4 per cent, which still added $1.23 billion to the $1.9 billion debt he ran up a year earlier.

In the late 1970s Davis plunged headlong into a vulnerable game of bribing large auto makers with tax dollars, arguing, with some validity, that Ford and Chrysler would take up incentives offered by competing U.S. states if Ontario didn't reciprocate. Critics argued that it might be wiser to invest the money elsewhere, but it is unlikely that Ford would have built its $535 million engine plant in Windsor, rather than Ohio, without a $40 million federal grant and $28 million from Ontario, plus another $6.5 million spent by Ontario, without any announcement, on an expressway to the plant site. But there was no such rationale for his nonsensical purchase of 25 per cent of the oil company, Suncor, for $650 million in 1981.

In November, 1978, Davis told a Sault Ste. Marie by-election crowd that there was "too much government. . . . We have been spending too much . . . people feel it is essential we live within our means." If that's how people felt, then Davis continued to disappoint them because between 1975 and 1982, during seven years of what he called "restraint," his government's spending jumped 133 per cent, or about 16.6 per cent a year on average, well above real inflation for the period. Davis argued, again with some validity, that Ontario's per capita spending was lower than that of any other province, but to many on the right this argument was akin to debating the respective virtues of a $50 hooker versus a $100 one. He added that Ontario's expenditure growth was below the growth of its gross provincial product, but the right felt this was another curious argument, the implication being that the number of cars coming off an assembly line had some direct relationship to how much a government should choose to spend in its budget.

Thanks to fourteen years of such "government by Chargex," by 1984 Ontarians were paying about $7 million a day interest on the debt, without knocking a penny off the principal. Huge Davis deficits became so commonplace that Treasurer Larry Grossman was once moved to boast that an increase of $11 million in his predicted shortfall did not really mean a larger deficit because the total was still "within the original $2.7 billion range."

Yet at any given moment Davis could sound convincingly like a traditional small-c conservative. If you went with him to a local service club or riding association in deepest eastern Ontario, you would hear not the Bill Davis who racked up massive deficits, not the Bill Davis who bought Suncor, imposed rent controls, pushed the Charter of Rights, approved the Human Rights Code, or seized and sold the trust companies.

There you would hear the Bill Davis who was pushing 1984 as Ontario's Bicentennial — arguably two hundred years since the bulk of the United Empire Loyalists arrived from the U.S. to carve a country from the wilderness. But the Bill Davis speaking at the Cobourg Rotary Club, for example, would not say how the Bicentennial, which began as strictly a U.E.L. celebration, was changed into a $10 million multicultural extravaganza for fear that other cultural interests might be upset with his government for honoring the Loyalist tradition. Naturally, the advertising contract for the Bicentennial year went to loyalists of a different nature — Norm Atkins and Hugh Segal — but that seems fitting, for the celebration was aimed more at assuring an unbroken Tory future than at helping Ontarians appreciate their past.

Even friends of Davis's admit he's a paradox, a man who boasted of his respect for traditional values yet showed no compunction to discard them in favor of the latest trendy notion. His active support for the Charter of Rights is a case in point. He never tired of mouthing respect for the ties binding us to Britain, especially the tradition of parliamentary democracy, yet next to Trudeau he was the most vocal champion of the Charter, which undermines that tradition. Britain has no charter, and the conservative argument against it there and here is that it strips power from elected people and gives it to unelected, and largely untouchable, judges. Whether such a situation is good or bad depends upon your philosophy, but given Davis's stated love of the British system, even his friends were surprised by his passionate support of it.

Bette Stephenson, the "angry medicine ball" minister of education with impeccable right-wing credentials, admired Davis personally but didn't applaud all his views, especially on the Charter. She remained "convinced that most humane and free societies don't need anything down on paper, outside a Magna Carta. I'm also convinced you can have the most fascinating set of principles down on paper that mean absolutely nothing." But the problem Davis had, she said, was that once he finally made up his mind that a particular course was "the right thing to do, he has a hell of a hard time changing his mind. That unidirectional kind of thinking propelled him through the acceptance of the Charter of Rights as devised by Pierre Elliott Trudeau, which was certainly not the Charter he first espoused. A long way from it."

Tory Morley Kells agrees Davis is "kind of a paradox. You get cliché-ridden with him, but he'll be remembered for decency, family, a sense of protecting old-fashioned values that most Ontarians support. But there he is, standing straight up for those old-fashioned values, and at the same time he led the drift away into a whole series of government policies and government realities that don't serve that philosophy. He moved in the so-called human rights area much further than pressure dictated he had to." Indeed, there were few issues in the Davis era that angered the party's right wing more than Bill 7, the revised and often reviled Human Rights Code inflicted by Bob Elgie and pushed into law after the Tories regained their majority in 1981.

Ontario actually beat everyone else into the human rights game with the Ontario Racial Discrimination Act of 1944, four years ahead of the United Nations' Universal Declaration of Human Rights. Unlike the UN version, which many signatory countries ignore, human rights laws in Ontario have been accompanied by sanctions, including stiff fines and jail terms. But the revised Code took the legislation into new realms of enforcement.

Between 1978 and 1981 controversy over the Code raged, with Davis aides acknowledging that most Tories were opposed to the power it placed in the hands of human rights advocates. Under the original bill introduced by Elgie, for example, human rights workers acting solely on a complaint, whether legitimate or malicious, would have had more power than the police to enter a building and seize files without a warrant. That clause, at least, was moderated slightly, but rights officials can still grab anyone's files without a warrant under some circumstances, and what they might find in those files could lead to an arrest for thinking the wrong thoughts under a section making it an offence if "any matter, statement, or symbol is disseminated that indicates an intention to infringe the right or that advocates or incites the infringement of the right." It is up to human rights workers, of course, to decide what someone's intention is. But then, as commission counsel Thea Herman argued, intent to discriminate isn't necessary for discrimination to occur, anyway. Even well-intentioned people who innocently discriminate must be punished. What is worse, human rights tribunals have clearly established that in this business, once a prima facie case is established, it is squarely up to the accused to prove his or her innocence, another principle in direct opposition to our common law traditions.

The omnipotence of human rights legislation is such that even Canadian Civil Liberties Association counsel Alan Borovoy, normally a sensible man, appeared within a two-week period at both the Bill 7 hearings at Queen's Park and the federal investigation into RCMP wrongdoing in Quebec. To the federal politicians Borovoy said the police should not have the power to search and seize without a warrant; before provincial politicians he defended the principle of human rights officers being able to proceed without warrants.

Right-wing Tories were not only outraged over the enforcement provisions. Under the Code the only group in Ontario that can't be declared a designated disadvantaged group is that of white, Anglo-Saxon men between the ages of eighteen and sixty-five, providing they don't have a handicap or haven't been pardoned for a serious criminal offence in the past. Everyone else — women, blacks, Asians, you name it — are seen by the human rights industry as "disadvantaged," a notion that, if turned upside down, means that white, Anglo-Saxon men are not only advantaged but are the kind of people who take advantage of all other groups.

And while human rights legislation speaks of absolute equality, the law itself doesn't seem to afford equality at all. In November, 1982, for example, the Human Rights Commission got upset by a private scholarship fund set up in 1916 by Col. Reuben Wells Leonard. He died in 1930, and the Leonard Foundation offers three hundred scholarships, worth $550 to $1,150 each, to needy university students. To qualify, students must be white, of British origin, and Protestant.

George Brown, executive director of the commission, a black, labelled the Leonard scholarships "repugnant to the spirit of human rights legislation." But as some Tories were quick to point out, if the Leonard scholarships are bad, what about the Simon and Rosalie Halpern Memorial, restricted to Catholic or Jewish students, or the Murray Brooks bursaries for students from India, Pakistan, and Ceylon, or the McGill-Hellenic Club bursaries for students of Greek descent? Are they repugnant, too? Labor Minister Russell Ramsay, a much more sensible and considerably less left-wing person than Elgie, his predecessor, said he didn't see any problem with the Leonard scholarships, but the commission kept lobbying to have them banned. The issue has never been resolved, but most universities simply don't offer them any more.

This wasn't the only instance where some were more equal than others. Law professor Peter Cumming, a popular human rights advocate, wrote in the June, 1984, issue of the commission publication, "Affirmation," that while the basis of human rights legislation is to treat all people equally, "to treat all pregnant women alike is discriminatory" because pregnancy does not affect all women in the same way and therefore pregnant women shouldn't be treated as a class. How convenient. The law he and others ardently support specifically designates all kinds of people as a "class." But when it's inconvenient, the sacred principle of equality does not apply.

It was Cumming, by the way, who conducted a 1983 board of inquiry into the firing of a Metro police officer, Harjit Singh Ahluwalia. He said the police were not guilty of racism in the firing of Ahluwalia, but in his report he wrote that "circumstantial evidence" is crucial in discrimination cases because "discrimination is often difficult to prove by direct evidence." So is bank robbery, but the law requires evidence, anyway. He added that once a prima facie case is established by such circumstantial evidence, "the burden shifts to the employer to show non-discriminatory reasons for his conduct." Guilty until proven innocent.

* * *

Davis never avoided using right wingers as scapegoats to dismiss internal party criticism of his actions. In 1974, for example, at the peak of a controversy over a land speculation tax he was trying to impose, he said the problem was just with "some of my very right-wing Tory friends" who were accusing him of "interfering with individual rights." But the problem was widespread, and the speculation tax was later dropped. He similarly used the right wingers as philosophical scapegoats to smear genuine party criticism of Bill 7. But then, there were ethnic votes to win. Why worry about old-fashioned common law traditions?

As Morley Kells said in 1984, "The boss never talks about philosophy, not to caucus, anyway. He talks about the art of politics, the art of getting elected. He likes to be pragmatic and says if you can't get elected, you can't do what you want to do. He's not hypocritical about it."

Gordon Walker agrees Davis was "uncomfortable around people with definite philosophical views. He's not a man with philosophical views as such. It's not a religion with him, whereas my own views are a bit of religion. Sure, I compromise. You could not exist here if you didn't. . . . But I have an area on the spectrum, a range, beyond which I'm not prepared to go. I don't think Bill Davis has a position on the spectrum . . . he makes a strength out of it." Walker compares the Davis view to that of

Eliza Doolittle's father, who said upper-class morals are for them that can afford 'em. "If you're not in office, you haven't got anything to say. . . . That's why the premier is uncomfortable around people who do have a view. They have a philosophy, a strong set of principles, which is the answer to them, not necessarily the right political answer."

Like many on the right, backbencher Jim Taylor thinks "pragmatism is a serious threat to our parliamentary system." He says party politics is based on a set of beliefs that its supporters are prepared to fight for. "But if you're going to be simply responding to the current moods of the majority . . . you become a democratic dictator. If you don't have any philosophy, what you've done is undermine the party system, where you go to the people and ask them to choose. That bothers me because I guess you could stay in power forever. You become a mixture of everything. . . . These guys are modern-day revisionists selling out any philosophy they ever had. That might get you defeated at the next election, but so what? My reason is not to get elected [for] personal advancement. I feel I've made a sacrifice. . . . My prize is being able to speak my mind."

Taylor calls Bob Elgie a left-wing ideologue, who as such "is in vogue with the powers that run the place. If you're all sweetness and light and a champion of the weak and oppressed, then you're terrific. But if those ideals happen to be the freedom and integrity of the individual, some sense of self-reliance and self-sufficiency — not uncaring, but being fair, not homogenizing, not caring to make people wards of the state — it's wrong. . . . '"

Naturally, Davis's pragmatic approach has its defenders. Hugh Macaulay says Davis believes in "the balance of private sector-public sector that our present-day capitalism seems to indicate. Some people think we should go back to earlier things, the earlier principles of private enterprise and capitalism, free enterprise. . . . I don't think Bill Davis believes you can go back. You've got to go forward . . . accommodating present-day circumstances, not wishing it were 1920 again. . . . In that sense he sometimes aggravates people. . . . I don't see how we'd have gone as far as we've gone under any other kind of leadership because the 'do it my way and do it now' kind of approach won't work in Ontario. We've had a minimum of strife and a maximum of progress and change. That's his style. It sometimes doesn't please people, but it works. Is that a philosophy? Yes, I think it's a philosophy. He's a God-fearing, Canadian capitalist."

Others in the inner circle also object to the view that Davis would sell out his most fervent beliefs for votes. Roy McMurtry was bothered "that compromises are seen as being somehow dishonorable, indicating a lack of principle. He doesn't see it in those terms. He sees it in what is the most compelling argument . . . you can compromise without having to flaunt the dictates of your own conscience. If you have to flaunt your own conscience, you should get the hell out."

Davis is a fundamentalist about his own personal moral values, says Hugh Segal, "but he's more open to new ideas than anybody I've ever met. His approach to life is he'd always like to have more information. He fights his own rigidity." Imposing county school boards taught him "that things which appear to be right can offend people so much that they'll never be accepted, which . . . I think is his view of bilingualism. What he'll have difficulty with is people who are insensitive, whether left or right. Take Jim Taylor. He's a decent guy who should have been given a better chance than he got, but at one point he brought Margaret Birch to tears at cabinet over a senior citizens thing. He didn't mean to be insensitive . . . [but] she started to cry. Davis would develop a little hate in his mind for anybody who would do that to Margaret Birch and would never forgive him."

Frank Miller says a personal dislike and unforgiving attitude was true for Gordon Walker as well. "Gordon was the only guy I knew who the premier was down enough on to talk about it publicly."

Walker infuriated Davis by releasing his book, *A Conservative Canada*, in 1983, at about the time Davis was deciding whether to run federally, and admits he remained in cabinet only "because I had some geographic value." He says he liked Davis but knew the feeling wasn't reciprocated, blaming Hugh Segal and Larry Grossman for "a lot of bum raps put on me to the premier. . . . There's a certain abrasiveness about me, it's true. I'm straightforward, and they call that abrasive. Bill Davis is really a kind man. He doesn't harbor a Bobby Kennedy-type grudge; he turns more cheeks than they do in burlesque. But still, he does what he has to do."

Davis was never ecstatic about Ottawa's Claude Bennett, either.

Davis aides loved to give the impression their man was above personal animosity, but he tolerated Bennett basically because he was popular in Ottawa. On a trade mission to Japan during the minority period, however, the Davis group had got back on their tour bus after visiting an ancient temple when the Japanese guide noticed two people missing. She asked who hadn't returned for the three-hour trip back to Tokyo, and somebody said, "Claude and Claudette," the latter a joking reference to Bennett's wife, Deborah. Davis, sitting at the front of the bus, said aloud, "Good, let's go." The bus waited, but the point had been made.

Davis himself claimed he had "a few difficulties over the years, but very few with any ministers in terms of difference in points of view. Very few. I'm always intrigued by people who move from one ministry to another. You sometimes wonder if they're the same people," he said, refusing to be specific. "Sure, there is some right wing and left wing, but it's grossly exaggerated. People take on views to a certain extent which reflect their constituencies or their ministries." Certainly nothing personal.

And whenever Davis's defenders were asked why he disliked the right, they inevitably said it wasn't true and cried, "What about Frank Miller?" Well, what about Frank Miller? Did the strength of his personality, his affability, allow him to overcome his conservative philosophical affliction? Apparently so.

"We like each other," said Miller before he became premier himself. "That's one of the reasons we get along. I really do like Bill Davis, and I sense he likes me. He's never told me he does, but that's not his style." Miller said that as a representative of the party's moderate right wing, "They felt I should be there. . . . We can't afford not to have it represented. Politics really is brutal. You find you have to compromise to a far greater extent than you'd like to or you don't survive. . . . But even though you do compromise . . . if you have your oar in, you can effect change. That's pretty rewarding, even if the change isn't everything you wanted."

Sally Barnes calls Davis a "master at compromise. I remember him saying about [Sterling] Lyon that he was booting it. He might well have been sticking to his principles, but he was going to lose the election. . . . He loses patience, more so with the right wingers than the left wingers. He laughs off the extreme left but gets angry with the right wingers, and that's when he reminds them about Sterling Lyon. He's been through it all and knows hard-line views won't work in politics. By and large he's a tolerant person, but . . . he can't abide the far right politically, and he can't abide it personally. He feels right wingers are immovable . . . that's contrary to what he thinks is proper.

"There's no doubt [Davis] brought in measures he just didn't believe in. But the polls would show people wanted to do things. And he would."

CHAPTER 16
SOAP ON A ROPE

One of the first things Bill Davis did after beating Allan Lawrence to win the Conservative leadership was go out and commission a poll. Conducted by American Robert Teetor, it found that Ontarians had respected John Robarts but were in the mood for something different than his solid but predictable rule. That led directly to the dramatic decision to stop the Spadina expressway. It was a harbinger of things to come.

Davis and polls soon became synonymous, and by 1982–83, while civil servant salaries were kept to a 5 per cent increase under the government's restraint package, the Tories spent $632,142 on twenty-two polls, an increase of $140,000, or 30 per cent. The public paid for these polls, but Davis consistently refused to let anyone see the results. He did release a batch under duress during the minority period, but it was never the custom. Yet the Tories used these publicly funded polls to design policies for groups such as women, ethnic minorities, and Catholics, all of whose support is essential to the party's continued hold on power.

Naturally, the other side of the "politics by market research" coin got a boost under Davis, too. In 1982–83 the Tories spent about $50 million, up from $40 million a year earlier, on advertising and communications. In his 1983 report Auditor Douglas Archer said, "The government's reporting systems did not accurately disclose advertising costs," citing a $2.6 million campaign that had not been included in the totals.

When Davis became premier, Ontario was not on Canada's hit parade of advertisers, but by 1974 it was thirty-sixth nationally, spending $2.6 million, jumping to ninth the next year (an election year), and holding sixth spot since 1980. The big winners in all this, of course, were Foster Advertising, the government's agency of record since 1974, and Camp Associates, both firms being well represented at the Tuesday breakfast club and in every election campaign and strategy session. No doubt the advertisements were slick. The four famous programs that doubled the spending in 1980 to $16 million were the tourism promotion, "Ontario: Yours to Discover," "Foodland Ontario," with its trillium symbol, the "Shop Canadian" program, and the energy conservation promotion with its clever alliteration, "Preserve It, Conserve It," which, if you say it quickly, sounds suspiciously like "Progressive Conservative."

The benefits of fine-tuning the marketing of the political "product" aren't hard to find. Davis did stay in power for fourteen years and did capture his impressive last majority on the basis of a campaign almost totally devoid of content. But there's a down side to politics by poll, too. Policies announced not out of ideological principle or sincere belief, but out of the need for short-term political gain, tend to have unpleasant, long-term consequences that have to be dealt with sometime. Davis, however, the master procrastinator, certainly did his best to avoid dealing with such consequences, as he always avoided unpleasant tasks.

Clare Westcott says Davis hated sitting alone at his desk signing mail, "even to the point of hiding the stuff. . . . Maybe it's a great style, because it works. The guy has a lot of things he's good at, but he also has these terrible weak spots." Hugh Segal agrees that Davis's primary weakness was his "inability to confront unpleasantness. . . . His style is like a bar of soap hanging on a rope in a shower. It's a big problem, but after many showers it will get smaller and eventually disappear, and another bar will take its place."

For two of the major poll-inspired policies of the Davis years, however, the soap never got smaller. Rent controls, for example, which were supposed to be temporary, are still in place. Yet a 1984 study by the Canadian Institute of Public Real Estate Companies, albeit biased against controls, demonstrated clearly that they don't help the people they're supposed to — the poor — while benefiting those who could afford to pay more. There is no question that rent controls discourage development, so that instead of rental construction being largely private, government is forced to pay large subsidies to developers to encourage them to build. The result is that taxpayers end up paying to subsidize not only development but also the renters themselves, whether they need a subsidy or not.

The size of the taxpayers' contribution is enormous. The province spent $62 million in 1982–83 on one program alone, its renter-buy scheme, to encourage development, while on the other hand the Residential Tenancy Commission estimates it will cost $7.4 million in 1984–85 to subsidize renters. Yet while paying 30 per cent of income for mortgages or rents is the generally accepted norm in the real estate business, less than one-fifth of tenants pay that much. According to the province's own statistics, the median rent-to-income rate in Metro Toronto is just 18.1 per cent and even lower in Hamilton, London, Windsor, and Ottawa. Worse, over half the total benefits of rent controls go to the top 60 per cent of households by income.

To show that rent controls, which apply across the board, regardless of income, mean that those with a higher income enjoy more benefits, the Real Estate Institute of Canada published a case study of a high-rise apartment building in Toronto in 1983. The study showed that an interior decorator earning $35,000 a year paid 14 per cent of his income in rent, while a secretary making $13,700, while paying less rent, shelled out 35 per cent of her income for her apartment.

Yet controls, introduced in the heat of an election in a desperate bid for votes, are now so entrenched that to remove them would be, in the words of Davis's successor, Frank Miller, "political suicide."*

Typically, after imposing controls Davis didn't want to hear anything negative about them. "He [Davis] doesn't handle unpleasantness very well," said Sid Handleman, who fought controls in cabinet. "It just goes against his grain. He didn't want to hear what it was doing to the building industry. I mentioned that once, and of course it got a headline, and he said at cabinet we've

---

*As an election goody before going to the polls himself, Miller offered his own version of the two per cent solution, *lowering* the ceiling from 6 to 4 per cent. The change was announced by, of all people, Gordon Walker.

got to stop being negative about it. He never called to ask me if there was a problem with it. He didn't talk about it; he'd send somebody over, usually Stewart. I didn't even know about the Tuesday morning thing until well into rent review. I was called in and argued against it, but he didn't like it. I was called there three other times on the same topic. . . . When I first got there I looked around and said to myself, 'Who are all these people?' Darcy McKeough was there, but he knew when he'd lost because he went into a corner and started reading the paper. I didn't know enough to quit."

*   *   *

For an issue that neatly brackets the Davis era, however, it's hard to beat Spadina.

On October 19, 1984, just ten days after Davis announced he was retiring, Toronto New Democrat Ross McLellan rose in the legislature to ask Attorney General Roy McMurtry about the Spadina expressway. Nearly fourteen years had passed since Davis had exploited the issue to transform his stodgy, Establishment image into that of the modern sophisticate, a man for all trendies, ready to break with the past to preserve the cities and, just incidentally, win elections.

Davis, who had been in cabinet when the government had made the deal with Metro Toronto to build the expressway, became an instant hero to townhouse environmentalists in Toronto and to people across the province who are always pleased when Toronto is denied something. He was not quite such a hero to the truckers or commuters from North York who have had to fight their way through city streets ever since, wasting gasoline, clogging local streets, and spewing their exhaust through the neighborhoods. But then there was an election to win, an image to create, and, by God, the Spadina expressway was a symbol of urban sprawl gone berserk. Davis was not about to let that opportunity pass him by.

Why then would McLellan, an expressway opponent, still be complaining fourteen years later? Had not the premier kept his word and stopped Spadina? Well, not quite. He had stopped it for a while, allowed it to be extended a bit south, then in 1975, just in time for another election, promised it would never, ever,

ever be built any farther just as long as he was premier.

That's what worried McLellan. Davis wasn't going to be premier much longer, yet his 1982 promise to transfer the deed to a three-foot strip of land at the southern end of the expressway to block any extension forever had still not been fulfilled. He wanted to know when the surveys would be completed and the papers prepared to transfer the Spadina lands from Metro Toronto to the province, so that the government could then hand over the deed to the City of Toronto as promised. The problem, of course, was that the majority of Metro council politicians had always wanted to build the expressway into downtown Toronto, while the city politicians, or at least most of them, had fought it.

McLellan asked McMurtry "as one of the principal leadership contenders," why the promise of a deeded strip to block future extension hadn't been met. McMurtry said he didn't know but added, "I am confident that the pledge by the premier is going to be honored by whoever his successor might be." He had scant reason to be so confident. McMurtry and Treasurer Larry Grossman opposed extension, period. But Agriculture Minister Dennis Timbrell, one of the few North York aldermen to vote against it at the time, said that while he still opposed the expressway, if he became premier the municipalities would be given more power to determine their own fate, and if that meant Metro wanted to spend its budget allocations on the expressway, so be it.

As for the other contender, Industry Minister Frank Miller, the only non-Torontonian in the bunch, he said he'd review the entire matter if he became premier. And he did.

Like so many major issues Davis was involved in as premier, the Spadina decision in 1971 did not end the matter; it simply opened a new phase. On June 29, 1971, Davis dropped what was billed as the "other shoe" — his transportation policy. He upped municipal subsidies for road work from 25 to 30 per cent, but the major change was more money for public transit to "provide alternatives to the private motor vehicle and to encourage municipalities to view public transportation as a better alternative to spending ever-increasing funds for road improvements."

Despite such brave new world rhetoric, by the end of the Davis years the province paid a smaller share of the cost of major transit operations, such as the Toronto Transit Commission, than it did at the beginning of his regime, and all the while road build-

ing across the province proceeded unabated. In his 1984–85 estimates Transportation Minister James Snow, renowned for naming
a highway after himself, said the province would spend about
$372 million for municipal and provincial rapid transit systems.
At the same time Snow expected to spend over $1 billion on pro-
vincial and municipal roads, over three times the transit expenditures.

But back in 1971 the people couldn't have known that much
of the promise of Spadina would turn into a long and expensive
shell game, although they might have guessed when, just five
days before the 1971 election, Davis unveiled Project Spadina, a
$75 million complex he predicted would "make Toronto an exam-
ple to the world of what society can do to build communities
that enhance the natural environment rather than destroy it, and
what can be done to make urban living more enjoyable."

Famed American planner Buckminster Fuller was asked to
design a plan for the Davis Ditch, that conspicuous strip of
unpaved roadbed between Lawrence Avenue, where the pavement stopped then, and Eglinton Avenue, where it stops now.
Fuller offered a pie-in-the-sky design of apartments, commercial space, and parking, providing homes for twelve thousand
people in a forty-six-acre, climate-controlled apartment complex,
complete with terraced walls. "What is at stake in this issue,"
proclaimed Davis, "is the future of Toronto itself." Well, Toronto
survived, but Project Spadina was never heard from again, having never escaped Fuller's drawing board. But coming so close
to an election, the plan served its purpose, gaining Davis even
more adulation as the new urban man.

A year passed before the next post-Spadina transit spectacu-
lar was announced, this time a $1.3 billion scheme for urban
transit systems. Of that figure, $756 million was to build five
new intermediate-capacity transit routes in Metro Toronto, not
one of which was ever built. Davis said that within ten years —
that is, by 1982 — Torontonians would be whizzing between
home and office in driverless, push-button "people movers" without once stepping outside, all part of his futuristic transit scheme
that would see tracks for electric cars built into apartments, office
blocks, and shopping centres.

Davis then hired the German-based firm Krauss-Maffai to build
a $16 million elevated transit track around the Canadian National

Exhibition grounds. The track, scheduled to open by 1975, ran into a slight technical snag when the experimental vehicles wouldn't turn corners, but not to worry. In October, 1973, Davis was honored in Miami Beach by the American Transit Association as their Man of the Year. "By putting people first, Toronto created a breakthrough," said well-known American transit official James Haugh. "Toronto started it all." If only he knew the truth. Davis had certainly announced it all, but until then he hadn't started anything. All he'd done was stop an expressway and win an election. His promises to transit commuters hadn't begun to be met; only the voters had been taken for a ride.

The next post-Spadina guilt trip was to be taken on "futuristic magnetic cushion trains" developed by the province's new Crown corporation, the Ontario Transportation Development Corp. The trains were slated for service in Toronto by 1977, and in November, 1973, Davis grandly estimated the market for such trains at more than $5 billion in Canada alone. To show he meant business, he named a group of high-powered business executives to the OTDC board, including such notables as Paul Desmarais, president of Power Corp., Ralph Rowzee, chairman of Polysar Ltd. (and chairman of the OTDC), and Sonja Bata of Bata Ltd. They didn't quite turn the transit world on its ears.

The next initiative came in February, 1974, when Davis established the Toronto Area Transit Operating Authority to take over GO Transit, the provincial rail and bus commuter system and one of the few transit ideas that actually worked. The new agency covered Peel, York, and Durham regions, whose chairmen became directors, along with Metro Toronto Chairman Paul Godfrey. The men, solid Tories all, thought it was a terrific idea.

Not such a good idea was Dial-a-Bus, a system whereby a person could call a given number and a bus would show up at the door, then drop the passenger off at the nearest subway stop. Terrific theory, but hardly anybody practised it, and those who did complained of waiting up to an hour for their bus. In June, 1974, less than eighteen months after predicting that Dial-a-Bus would solve many of Metro's transit problems, Davis had to admit he'd dialed another wrong number. The scheme was dead. It was intended to be a three-year experiment, but after only eight months it had lost $616,073.

In September, 1974, the Alberta government and McDonnell

Douglas Corp. agreed to join a GO-Urban project, which also included Krauss-Maffai, and suddenly things were looking up. But only for two months, because the following November 13 Transportation Minister John Rhodes announced that the project had been scrapped.

Two months later Rhodes again — Davis only announced the good news — said the government was prepared to pave Spadina's unpaved Davis Ditch. But it wouldn't be an expressway, you understand; it would be a "four-lane arterial roadway" that just happens to look like an expressway, was designed as an expressway, has limited access like an expressway, but which was re-named the Allen Road after former Metro chairman William Allen. At the same time, however, the government promised it would never allow the pavement to proceed south of Eglinton, so the expressway to nowhere continued to loom menacingly over the Cedarvale Ravine, waiting patiently for a change of leadership to allow it to finish its trip down long-ago-expropriated rights of way to the city core. The $215 million Spadina subway line, which was to twin the expressway, did make it downtown, however, after being officially opened by Davis in January, 1978.

In May of that year the government's Urban Transit Development Corp., child of the unlamented OTDC, ran into some new difficulties, but for once the problems weren't technical foul-ups. A 1977 internal audit showed the money-losing corporation's president, Kirk Foley, a loyal Tory, was provided with a Mercedes-Benz, the UTDC maintained a luxurious Zurich apartment at public expense, and the corporation also paid higher moving expenses for its officials than the government's manual of administration allowed. By this time the UTDC had built a test track near Kingston, a one-and-a-half-mile subway in the sky, which, despite a series of embarrassing start-up problems, actually began to show returns when in December, 1980, after nine years and over $100 million, Foley sold a $290 million project to Vancouver and won a Los Angeles transit bid of $130 million. Buoyed by this success after nearly a decade of failure, Davis announced in January, 1981, a plan for an elevated transit system on the Toronto waterfront that would become a reality by 1983. The year came and went without it, of course.

In the meantime Foley, a super-salesman, was flying all over the world beating the bushes for the UTDC — and showing results.

He won a $90 million deal in Detroit, but for a time it was in jeopardy because of proposed budget cuts by President Ronald Reagan, prompting Davis to write letters of complaint to U.S. cabinet officials during the 1981 provincial election campaign. This escapade sparked a minor international incident because Davis had not cleared the letters through the Canadian Embassy in Washington, but then diplomacy wasn't his major worry at the time; he had another election to win. In August, 1981, the U.S. government agreed to some work on the Detroit deal, and at the same time the province twisted arms at the Toronto Transit Commission to impose a $130 million transit line from the end of the Bloor-Danforth subway system to the Scarborough Town Centre. In April, 1982, Foley did sign a $110 million deal with Detroit for a rapid transit system.

Davis talked constantly of an $8 billion, worldwide market for the UTDC product, but by the end of his time in office UTDC hadn't been successful in beating out the Japanese, French, Germans, or British for the big international contracts. As far as the potential Canadian market goes, there still isn't much of one, certainly not the $5 billion pie Davis had estimated a decade earlier.

In the meantime Ontario continues to have the finest network of highways and local roads anywhere, and with close to 25 per cent of the province's economy dependent upon the automobile industry, it is not surprising that Davis, beyond throwing millions into the development of magnetic cushion trains, did little to act on his pronouncements to get people out of their cars and onto mass transit in significant numbers. The wonder is how many people bought the rhetoric and joined in the applause for the only Canadian ever to win the coveted American Transit Association's Man of the Year award.

Meanwhile, back at the four-lane arterial road . . . In April, 1982, eleven years after Spadina was stopped, a poll showed that 54 per cent of Metro residents thought there should be more expressways, a sharp increase from a year earlier. On the other hand, support for more spending on public transit was at 58 per cent, down from 73 per cent a year earlier. Asked specifically about the Spadina, 60 per cent favored extending it to the downtown core, prompting one pro-expressway cabinet minister to quip, "Hey, the way he [Davis] responds to polls, we might get the damn thing yet." But Davis still said he would make good his first promise to the people, unpleasant as it might be for some in the party to accept and as hard as it might be for him to actually do it.

The retirement announcement came and went. So did his last day in the legislature, the leadership convention, the transition of power. It was February 7, 1985, and premier-designate Frank Miller's cabinet was slated to be sworn into office the next afternoon. Finally, even a dedicated procrastinator like Bill Davis couldn't put it off any longer. Literally hours before he left power, Davis announced that the province had given the City of Toronto a ninety-nine-year lease on a three-foot-wide strip of land just south of Eglinton Avenue, a lease that could be revoked by an act of any future legislature.

But at least he kept the promise.

CHAPTER 17
DISCOVERING WOMEN

—————— ❦ ——————

On May 27, 1982, Bill Davis and Ed Stewart stepped into an elevator in Toronto's downtown Four Seasons Hotel en route to a retirement lunch for a senior civil servant. At the second floor a beautiful, statuesque, blonde woman stepped in, accompanied by two other women and *Globe and Mail* photographer John Wood. Stewart immediately recognized her. Davis didn't, so Wood introduced them.

When Davis and Stewart got off at the eighteenth floor, Wood asked if Davis would mind having his picture taken with her. Never one to disappoint a potential voter, he agreed, but when the woman snuggled up to him and put her arm around his shoulders, he flushed and looked embarrassed. After she and Wood got back on the elevator, Stewart asked Davis if he knew who she was. He said no, so Stewart told him it was Shannon Tweed, Playmate of the Year and Hugh Hefner's girlfriend. Davis, expressionless, drew on his pipe, stared straight ahead, and gave an exasperated "Oh, oh."

The opposition parties, realizing his discomfort, twigged him in the legislature about it later that day, and Davis, his face scarlet, was at a loss for words, especially when told Hefner wanted a copy of the picture for what Liberal Jim Bradley dubbed "A Bedtime Tory." Hugh Segal got a copy, faked Tweed's autograph, and signed it "To Bill: Yours to Discover," mocking Ontario's tourism slogan. The incident, of course, was perfectly innocent, but it demonstrates that when it came to dealing with women in public, especially if even a hint of sex was involved, Davis was rarely at ease.

He was, after all, steeped in traditional family values where Dad worked and Mom stayed home to raise the kids, and his upbringing, dominated first by his grandmother, then by his mother, was exceptionally maternal. And, of course, he had two sisters, no brothers, and a quiet, unassuming father. As a young father himself, he never changed a diaper on any of his children, a fact he used to mention until it became unfashionable to admit such things. But at the 1984 softball game between his office staff and the press gallery, he saw a reporter changing his son's diaper and mused that now his own son Neil "does far more of these things than my generation ever did. That's sort of nice, really."

He remained uncomfortable personally about women working and leaving their children with a sitter or in a day-care centre but recognized the reality that 55 per cent of women do work and that the party must take what has become known as "women's issues" seriously. He was never chauvinistic or sexist about it, according to one insider. "He just can't understand why women want to work, except those who have to for economic reasons. . . . He has no personal reference point on that, but he's very genuine about the issues."

Until relatively recently such bewilderment about women's concerns didn't matter much politically, because most women toddled off to the polls to vote the way their husbands did. Fortunately that has changed, and while women, like men, do not vote in a block, Tory polls do show that women have a different perspective than men on certain issues; they're less risk-taking, for example, and more involved in environmental issues and anti-nuclear demonstrations, but there is no schism, no gender gap. Davis was popular with women because he was not seen as a risk-taker, maintaining instead a comfortable image as everybody's favorite uncle, and the Tories under his leadership got a fair share of their vote, except among Italian and Portuguese women, where they barely got a notice.

But while the Tories don't have particular problems getting women to support them (although to hear militant feminists tell it, you'd think any self-respecting woman would vote NDP), a host of issues have emerged that, while affecting men as well, are of particular interest to women. Any political party that cherishes survival can't ignore day care, equal pay for work of equal value, pornography, family violence, or sexual harassment on the job. The Tories have not retained power since 1943 by ignoring such things, and while there will always be some who accuse them of doing too little, or too much, they clearly understand the importance of the female electorate and have no intention of letting it slip away.

* * *

The history of women's participation in the legislature is pathetic. Since Confederation only fourteen women have been elected: six socialists, six Tories, and two Liberals.

The first two women were elected in 1943, when the current Tory reign began, both for the Co-operative Commonwealth Federation, forerunner of the NDP. In York East Agnes MacPhail took a seat that had belonged to former Tory premier George S. Henry, and in Toronto Bracondale Rae Luckock won by 286 votes, losing two years later and never running again. In 1967 Margaret Renwick won Scarborough Centre for the NDP but lost in the 1971 Tory sweep to journalist Frank Drea, who went on to become a colorful cabinet minister. The NDP didn't elect any women in 1971, but in 1975 they elected Evelyn Gigantes in Carleton East, Gillian Sandeman in Peterborough, and Marion Bryden in Toronto's Beaches-Woodbine. Sandeman lost in 1977 and Gigantes in 1981. Gigantes won another by-election in 1984, and Bryden won three straight, giving the six socialist women a total of eleven electoral wins, four behind the Tories and seven ahead of the Liberals.

Ironically, the first Liberal MPP was a lifelong Tory, Margaret Campbell, a Toronto municipal politician. When Allan Lawrence left to run federally in 1973, Campbell was interested in the Tory nomination for the by-election, but the Big Blue Machine bosses told her it was reserved for Davis's pal Roy McMurtry, so she got the Liberal nod and beat McMurtry by 1,800 votes, a riding Lawrence had won in 1971 by 9,500. Campbell retired before the 1981 election, but that year firebrand Sheila Copps won Hamilton Centre. In 1982 she became the first woman to run for the Liberal leadership, overcoming several veterans to finish a strong second. During her brief stay at Queen's Park, Copps was an effective, if somewhat erratic, critic, but she left in 1984 to win Hamilton East against the awesome federal Tory tide.

The first Tory woman elected was Ada Pritchard in 1963, also in Hamilton Centre. A veteran municipal politician, she was re-elected in Hamilton West in 1967 but retired before the 1971 campaign, when two Toronto women joined the Tories: Margaret Scrivener in St. David and Margaret Birch in Scarborough East. Davis promised to appoint a woman to his first cabinet, but when the shuffle came right after the election, neither of the two got the nod. Two years later, however, Birch was named minister without portfolio.

In 1975 Birch and Scrivener won again, and Bette Stephenson, former president of both the Canadian and Ontario medical associations, won York Mills. Birch was promoted to provincial secretary for social development, Scrivener was named government services minister, and Stephenson, one of only two people Davis ever elevated directly to cabinet (the other was Roy McMurtry), became labor minister.

All Stephenson knew about labor then "was having delivered five thousand babies and having had six of my own" but says Davis had three reasons for appointing her: First, the NDP had made occupational health a major issue, and her medical status would be an asset; second, "I was a woman, and he said there'd never been a woman labor minister; and third, he said all his advisers had advised him against it."

The three women were re-elected in 1977 and 1981, although Scrivener was turfed out of cabinet in 1978. They were joined in 1981 by Susan Fish, a Toronto alderman who won the downtown St. George riding and became minister of citizenship and culture two years later. In 1984 Ancaster Mayor Ann Sloat won Wentworth North for the Tories in a December by-election.

During the 1970s Davis took to including a few paragraphs about women in many of his speeches. When addressing businessmen, for example, he would encourage them to hire more women; when speaking to police chiefs, he'd remind them of the shortage of women on the province's police forces. He opposed legislating such things through mandatory affirmative action programs but constantly reminded various interest groups that if they didn't improve their ratio of women employees, government would eventually have to do it for them.

It was advice he followed within his own domain, even at the ceremonial top. In 1974 Pauline McGibbon became Ontario's twenty-second lieutenant-governor and the first woman to hold a viceregal post in Canada. Also the first woman member of the stodgy, seventy-five-year-old Canadian Club of Toronto, Mc-Gibbon once explained her membership in countless organizations by describing herself as "a girl who can't say no."

Somewhat lower down in the official pecking order, in September, 1973, he named Ethel McLellan, a career civil servant, executive co-ordinator of women's programs to increase the number of women within the civil service. He also said McLellan would sit on the soon-to-be-established Status of Women Council and not long after that appointed activist Laura Sabia the council's first chairman. He said he was "determined to see that every effort is taken to seek out qualified women. . . . This does not mean that special advantage or a quota system will be used to increase the number of women in any particular job category. That course, I am convinced, would be repugnant to everyone."

For International Women's Year the Tories spent $470,000 on a program called "Women on the Move — Equal Opportunity 1975," naming advisers to sixteen ministries to help promote women. There is little evidence that besides providing these women with jobs, the advisory positions made much of a difference, so in 1980, while Davis again rejected quotas for hiring women into the civil service, he ordered ministers to set yearly targets for hiring or promoting a minimum number of women to jobs where they were underrepresented. "I want to stress that these are not predetermined and inflexible quotas," he said, simply "a planned approach" to equal opportunity. By 1984 Labor Minister Russ Ramsay could boast that since 1978 the number of women in the public service had increased in 80 per cent of the employment groups where they had been underrepresented and that more women were moving into management, professional, and technical jobs. Perhaps, but at the time Ethel McLellan was the only woman deputy minister.

In 1975 Davis changed the law to give women the same access to credit that men enjoyed, and in 1978 Roy McMurtry's sweeping family law reform gave women for the first time a piece of the action, often half, in the family home or business in the event of marriage breakups. But the legislative agenda on women's issues was soon dominated by equal pay for work of equal value.

Liberal Margaret Campbell introduced a private member's bill in 1978 for the economic equality of women. A year later the NDP's Ted Bounsall introduced a bill calling for equal pay for work of equal value, a system whereby bureaucrats would determine the relative worth of different jobs. The law already required employers to give equal pay where men and women were performing "substantially the same work," and a 1984 amendment by Labor Minister Ramsay changed that to require equal pay under the Employment Standards Act among "substantially similar jobs," evaluated according to the four criteria of skill, effort, responsibility, and working conditions. That amendment came after all three parties had given unanimous approval in principle to a resolution by Liberal Sheila Copps calling for the equal value concept to be enshrined in law, but the Tories said that while they supported the concept in principle, practicalities made it impossible to implement effectively. A 1982 study of the concept by the labor ministry estimated it could cost up to $3 billion and would affect only a small portion of the wage gap between men and women.

During the 1981 election campaign, Davis said there was little hope of the Tories entrenching equal value laws. "We don't object to it in principle at all. I've debated this with my wife at some length . . . she has an understanding of the complexity of it. It's not a simple issue." He said it would be just too tough to administer because all jobs would have to be evaluated. Three years later he voted for the Copps resolution in principle, but Ramsay's bill was as far as he intended to go in practice.

During the constitutional wrangles of the late 1970s and early 1980s, Davis consistently said he favored enshrining women's rights in the Constitution, but when the crunch came he backed off in the interest of getting agreement on other points. Hugh Segal constantly told Sally Barnes, "Mark my words, Sally, there will be women's rights in the Constitution," but Barnes says that rather than open the whole constitutional package up again at the end, Davis "let that one slide. He just sat back in a Cheshire cat grin and let it go," even though he had assured her, " 'It will

come about.' Well, that was a matter of hours before we'd capit-
ulated, and we planned to all along." That should have been the
tip-off to Barnes that Davis's support of her views might be less
than whole-hearted.

In 1977 Davis appointed broadcaster Lynne Gordon head of
the Ontario Status of Women Council, much to the chagrin of
radical women's groups, who complained she was a "closet feminist," and he reappointed her in 1979. Then he replaced her in
September, 1982, with Barnes, a controversial appointment that
had some feminists screaming for her resignation before she could
get back to her office. Every mouthy militant in town dumped
on her, complaining she was too close to Davis to be effective.
But the critics overlooked the fact that she was also close enough
to him to have her message heard, even if the message wasn't as
militant as radical feminist groups demanded. Laura Sabia and
Lynne Gordon made considerable noise during their tenures, but
there is little to show for their efforts. Barnes, however, was instru-
mental in getting Davis to drop his veto of an amendment allowing women to drop out of the work force for up to seven years
without having that period included in the averaging of lifetime
earnings to determine Canada Pension Plan levels; she was also
the key person in setting up both a women's ministry and wom-
en's directorate.

Seven months after her appointment the Davis throne speech
promised a women's cabinet minister, and a month later veteran
deputy premier Bob Welch was appointed to the post. The first
thing he said was that the wage gap, whereby women earn an
average of 64 per cent of men's salaries, had to be lowered, and
he announced that all future cabinet submissions would be ana-
lyzed for their impact on women. A week later Welch named
Glenna Carr executive director of the newly created women's
directorate, the other Barnes coup.

Carr, a prissy, uptight woman with ten years' experience in
the public service, immediately set out to build an all-woman
bureaucracy of her own to promote equality. While Barnes and
her council limped along with a meagre budget, the directorate
quickly got into some real money. Even so, the council was constantly making news, while the directorate had little to show for
itself beyond some set-piece seminars. One of its few concrete
programs was launched in February, 1984. Called "Open Doors,"

it brought women in non-traditional jobs into public schools to encourage girls to plan their school curriculums around non-traditional career goals.

The 1982–83 council budget was $181,608, while Carr's group got $1,064,166. By 1984–85 the council was allocated about $268,000, while the directorate got almost $5 million, only $500,000 of which was earmarked for the provision of services for women. The rest went to salaries and wages, employee benefits, transportation and communication, services, supplies, and equipment, including a $400,000 advertising contract awarded to Hugh Segal's firm, Advance Planning.

The differences in style and approach were spotlighted in 1983 when Barnes and Carr were invited to a Tory think-in near Goderich. On the morning of their presentations, Carr showed up in the resort meeting room wearing a stiff business suit, her briefcase in hand, and took a seat near the front close to Davis. Barnes, relaxing in jeans, as were most people there, lounged casually at the back of the room until it was her turn to speak. One who witnessed the event said, "Glenna used every cliché and buzzword in the book. Sally spoke English."

As the months passed, both Welch and Carr maintained a discreet public silence on women's issues. Barnes, working long hours but earning a paltry $105 per diem, popped up everywhere making speeches about the inequality of women on the job. She constantly pointed out certain chilling statistics: The Ontario work force is 44 per cent women, 40 per cent of whom earn at or near the minimum wage; in the majority of families both partners work outside the home; 72 per cent of all Ontario women in the childbearing group (twenty-five to forty-four years old) and close to 55 per cent of all mothers of preschool kids are in the paid work force. All this, contrasted with the fact that women earn about 64 per cent on average of what men do (although in government it's 74 per cent).

Barnes conceded that there are reasons for some of this disparity: More women work part-time; women tend to follow their husbands during job transfers, thereby losing their seniority; and young girls have traditionally avoided the higher-paying professions. In a Kingston speech in May, 1983, Barnes talked about the need for girls to take maths and sciences and said, "Of all the

groups with whom I have met on the subject of women's issues
. . . the most discouraging are high school girls. Despite the soap
operas and the real-life situations they encounter, many are still
living in a dream world: They simply do not see their responsibility to themselves and their families in ensuring some security
through job training and so on."

Her musings about individual choices and responsibilities did
not sit well with the left-wing feminists who demanded legislated quotas and mandatory affirmative action, and the war of
words between Barnes and various women's groups grew hot-
ter. In the meantime Welch, Carr, and Davis remained silent,
happy to let Barnes burn while they fiddled at empire building.

Finally, in February, 1984, Barnes had enough, especially on
a part-time salary and with no support from Davis, Welch, or
Carr. She resigned and went home to Kingston, planning to be a
candidate in Frontenac-Addington. But early in 1984 the riding's
Liberal MPP, J. Earl McEwen, whose plurality had dropped in
three consecutive elections, crossed the floor to the Tories. Mc-
Ewen, rather than being given a sinecure, was nominated as the
Tory candidate for the next election, and Davis, who had made
endless speeches on the need for women in politics, refused to
lift a finger to help Barnes.

She says Davis is "a little uncomfortable now. . . . They all feel
they screwed me on that, and they did. They should feel uncomfortable. I don't see him as much as I used to. He doesn't appreciate it when you leave; he thinks you should hang in there. I
saw them at Kathy's fiftieth birthday party; she and I both got
bagged there. She gets bagged once in a while and tells him off,
but . . . she's really cowed by him. It's really awful."

On the other hand, she says that when she made her pitch for
the women's directorate at the Tuesday breakfast club, it was
Davis who backed her. "I was looking around that table and
said, 'Oh boy, I don't have much support here.' The guy who
turned that around was Davis. He turned it into a little harangue
about how he was going to become a grandfather and how Ruthie
[his daughter-in-law] and Neil [his son], if they were going to
have any hope of buying a house, both of them were going to
have to work. And who was going to look after the baby? You
could just see people's eyes open up. Not only the polls showed a

lot of people out there in a child-care dilemma, but his conversations around the dining room table with Neil and Ruthie made it something these guys should pay attention to."

Welch, conceding that Davis, ever the pragmatist, would do whatever he had to, said there was no question that Davis was committed to women's issues. "There's a certain inevitability over this whole issue now. It has gathered momentum. Things are going to happen . . ."

There is, it's true, some evidence of progress. In his November, 1984, estimates speech, Welch said the number of women in Ontario's public service had jumped nearly four per cent from 1974, to 42.2 per cent, and the wage gap had narrowed over 5 per cent to 23.2 per cent. Women's representation in jobs paying $32,000 and up shot from 5.1 per cent in 1974 to 16.1 per cent in 1984, even though the number of senior jobs was being reduced during that period. And at the administrative level the goal of increasing women's representation to 30 per cent by the year 2000 in all classes of occupations was reached sixteen years ahead of schedule.

In universities, too, statistics show that women are practising their own affirmative action to close the wage gap. In 1972 there were 72,446 men in full-time undergraduate studies at Ontario universities and just 44,898 women. By 1982 that had changed to 83,206 men and 72,617 women, a 14.85 per cent increase of men compared to a dramatic 61.74 per cent increase of women. The same applies to the total number of university graduates: In 1972, 19,440 were men; 5,737 were women. By 1982 the number of men graduates had increased by 0.81 per cent, but the number of women grads had skyrocketed by 115 per cent to 12,308.

In the natural course of events, numbers such as these will inevitably correct much of the male-female imbalance in higher-paying jobs. But waiting for nature to take its course is not dramatic enough for activist women or sexy enough for politicians who love to be seen to be taking action, whether the action is useful or not. The view that past injustices will disappear without legislation is a tough one to sell, particularly when the number of women in the highest-profile jobs remains miniscule. For example, between 1981 and 1982 the percentage of women executives in government increased from 6.3 per cent to 6.9 per cent;

there were just 44 women in the public service executive ranks and 598 men. This is hardly encouraging until you look one step below that rank, where women are rapidly closing the gap and working themselves into positions where executive promotions are more realistically obtainable. Even with the progress, however, in 1982–83, 71 per cent of women in Ontario's public service earned less than $21,000 a year, while 75 per cent of men earned more than that.

Education Minister Bette Stephenson, who has spent much of her life battering down traditional barriers, is "convinced, absolutely convinced, that given the appropriate period of time, the appropriate change of attitude on the part of both males and females, that women will come into their own full flower." Stephenson graduated from the University of Toronto medical school in 1946 and became the first head of the family practice department at Toronto's Women's College Hospital. She felt discriminated against only once, when she was blackballed by the Ontario Medical Association in 1961 after being nominated for its board of directors. But she made it onto the board the next year, became the OMA's first woman president in 1970, and was the first woman to head the Canadian Medical Association in 1974.

"It's difficult to anticipate all of that deeply ingrained socializing and attitude fostering that's gone on for six thousand years is going to turn around overnight. I understand the concern of those who feel it has to happen in a hurry. But I'm an evolutionary, not a revolutionary, and I just think it's going to happen anyway because women are innately superior to men." She says the "whole bloody argument about equal pay for work of equal value is specious because it will not benefit women. It will benefit men primarily. It will only have an impact on about five per cent of the area of difficulty as far as women are concerned. It's just a lot of bunk. It really is. It equates all kinds of employment. You can't limit it to female jobs only — not in our society — because you'd be charged with discrimination on the basis of sex if you did."

Stephenson agrees that the evolutionary argument is "tougher to make. It's a very simple argument to say we need equal value legislation . . . but I'd like to know who the Solomon is who's going to tell me how I measure the characteristics of all jobs in order to compare them accurately. It's a popular position, but it's wrong. As wrong-headed as it can possibly be."

She points out that politics was traditionally considered a man's game, just as medicine was. "For years very few women were allowed into medicine because the admission committees thought that women stopped practising and didn't use their medical knowledge after they graduated because they got married and had kids." Stephenson did a survey in 1952–53 and found as many women doctors using their medical skills for practical application as men. "We demonstrated that, and the admissions committees began to change their attitude and admit more women. When I started in medicine, the average admission rate was seven per cent women; now it's about thirty-eight per cent. The same thing is happening in politics. In the last ten years the number of women who are managers or campaign chairmen has tripled. That is going to have an impact on the number of candidates. That kind of experience is going to tell women they can do it if they really want to, and they will. But I don't think we can order them to do it or legislate them."

As women's issues became more prominent over the last of the Davis years, the Tories, as is their custom, got busy on other fronts. In July, 1984, Solicitor General George Taylor asked police to participate with Crown attorneys in a series of seminars designed to meet problems facing women who are victims of family violence. Police were told to lay charges in wife-beating cases, rather than wait for the victim to do it, thus sparing women their legitimate fears about brutish husbands taking it out on them for laying assault charges. That year Metro Toronto's first regional sexual assault treatment centre opened at Women's College Hospital, a twenty-four-hour-a-day, seven-day-a-week centre for both women and men who are sexually assaulted. Welch said that about one in ten women who is married or living with a man is battered, a staggering total of 200,000 Ontario women physically assaulted each year, and in response Attorney General Roy McMurtry appointed fifty specially designated Crown legal officers to deal with domestic assault cases. Welch also named a co-ordinator of family violence, and the province added $4 million to battle family violence and improve shelters for abused wives.

In a tough-sounding speech in August, 1984, to the Association of Municipalities of Ontario, Welch said the track record of Ontario's sixty-three largest municipal administrations in embracing affirmative action was "dismal." In 1982 only 5.6 per cent of senior municipal officials were women. He said women now comprise 10 per cent of senior executives in the Ontario public service, up from 3.9 per cent in 1977, and offered municipalities a $260,000 affirmative action incentive fund to help hire coordinators and establish local programs. And he told school boards to "significantly increase" the number of women in administrative ranks, although he didn't say what would happen if they didn't.

At the same time a host of cabinet ministers, encouraged by polls showing women were concerned about pornography and violence against women in movies, videos, and television, railed against the evils of pornography. The Ontario Censor Board was given more power to censor and classify videos, and even Liberal Leader David Peterson, whose party had wanted for years to disband the censor board, suddenly discovered that he, too, was "concerned" and called for even greater censorship powers.

Agriculture Minister Dennis Timbrell, not to be outdone, commissioned a study on women in rural areas and discovered that they worry about their finances and their children in much the same way urban women do.* And on the child-care front, spending for day nurseries by Social Services Minister Frank Drea was set at $89 million for 1984–85. Ontario has about ninety thousand licensed day-care spots and more government-subsidized day-care places than all the other provinces combined. In May, 1984, the budget added $4.8 million for fifteen hundred more full-time, subsidized spaces, and Drea announced plans to develop new rural child-care resource centres as well.

By 1984 women's issues had obviously arrived politically, as the federal parties discovered during the election campaign that year. The Ontario Tories had their own polls to tell them that, of course, but a not insignificant factor in the quickened activity was the arrival of a personal reference point for Bill Davis in the form of his first grandchild, Christine, in 1983.

Kathleen Davis has not worked outside her home since her wedding over twenty years ago because the pressures of political life are "very hard on families because of absenteeism. If the

---

*When Frank Miller became premier, he named Timbrell minister responsible for women's issues.

woman works, they have two separate lives. I haven't worked until recently because I have children and I'm perhaps old-fashioned, but when Billy isn't home, I feel I should be. That's partly why I haven't been active in politics. I felt somebody should be tending to what is happening in the home." She began taking some "just for me" courses at the University of Toronto — non-credit studies in Beethoven, for example. "I'm not desperate, though. I don't really need the money, and I'm busier now than I know what to do. I do look forward to the day when I can do something a little bit more meaningful."

As for Davis, he shares many of Kathleen's "old-fashioned" values. "I have to be very careful how I phrase this. Personally I have been very supportive of women pursuing individual professions. I also think we would be making a mistake to minimize or lose sight of the importance of the contribution a person like Ruth, who is pursuing a career on a part-time basis, the importance of her contribution being the mother of Christine. I think there is a balance. It has nothing to do with party policy."

Davis said before his retirement that his government would not take a back seat to any other on women's issues. "A lot of people will argue we haven't done as much as we should, but there are certain practical problems." He said Kathleen "feels very strongly" about this but would "also reiterate the importance, not just in a family sense, but in terms of society, of women's involvement with their children. What we have to find as we go through this is ways for women to maintain that and at the same time pursue their own careers, whether for purely economic reasons, which is the case in some circumstances, or whether it's a case of their own individual interests, which one has to encourage.

"I don't know what the solutions to all this may be, but whatever my traditional feelings are, they should never be construed as being anything less than encouraging for women to find alternate ways to involve themselves. I just hope we never reach the point where being — in quotes — a housewife or mother is not a very important part of their responsibility. I don't think many women's groups would argue that, but it is a growing matter of concern, not just for government, but for business and industry.

"I get a bit frustrated at some of the phrases, like 'equal pay for work of equal value.' Nobody is quarrelling. . . . The problem is in a pragmatic sense to get people to understand when you get into the other thing you're not talking male-female at all. You're trying in some way to equate different jobs, an extremely difficult thing to do. I'm not opposed to it in terms of the principle, but how in fact do you do it in a way that will work?

"I guess that I probably am more supportive of initiatives in this direction in a practical sense than a lot of people who go around talking about it a great deal. We just have to be practical about it, that's all."

An April, 1984, Gallup poll showed the Liberals slightly favored over the Tories among women, 29.4 per cent to 29.2. The NDP, which claims a monopoly on concern for women's rights, was floundering at 11.2 per cent.

CHAPTER 18
CHANGING FACES

❦

The first thing Bob Rae did when he breezed in from Ottawa in February, 1982, to take over Ontario's NDP leadership was accuse the provincial Tories of being racist.

Rae, a highly publicized federal NDP finance critic, had been seemingly preordained as the savior of a party desperately in need of divine intervention after four years of rudderless tutelage under Michael Morris Cassidy. He is a silk-stockinged socialist, raised with all the inherent and definitely unplebian privileges of a diplomat's son, such as being whisked off to private school in Geneva in a chauffeur-driven limousine. But here was this self-declared man of the people telling about two thousand socialists that the dreaded Tories were not only misguided, they were out-and-out racists to boot.

In his main convention speech Rae conveniently ignored the fact that there were less than a dozen non-white faces in the crowd and said he wanted to speak of two visions of Ontario: "Toryland and the real Ontario." He said many people from minority groups had been excluded from power because Toryland "is an Anglo-Saxon land; maybe that's why it's so bland. You won't see a black face or hear the Italian language or the Greek language or the French language spoken in Toryland. They'd rather those things were kept in some quaint little restaurant where they don't bother anyone."

Hugh Segal, doing television commentary for the convention,

246

called Rae's comments "the lowest political attack I've ever heard on any politician. To imply that somehow there is racial prejudice in any political party is not justifiable." Davis, too, was outraged, saying, "I think perhaps it's one of the first mistakes Rae has made. It indicates that he really doesn't understand the province yet. In fact, the Progressive Conservative party of Ontario is the most broadly based and representative party in the province."

Rae, rather than apologize for his silly claim, slid even deeper into the hole by telling the *Globe* that his remarks had been misinterpreted. "Toryland is not the Tory party. I was speaking of two visions of Canada." Asked what else Toryland could be if not the party, Rae launched into a rant about power not being evenly distributed in Ontario.

There is, of course, some truth to the charge that minorities are underrepresented in the Tory party.* But then, they are underrepresented in all three parties, despite the fact that they are a large factor in the electorate and are getting larger all the time. But to suggest that the Tories don't want them is absurd. Like any other political party, they want whatever votes they can get. Still, Rae's strategy to paint the Tories as anti-ethnic and the NDP as ethnic champions, however inaccurate and abusive, underscores the modern political agenda in Ontario, where the so-called ethnic vote has become a prize worth pursuing in the finest political traditions of unfettered viciousness.

Metro Toronto alone has about 400,000 people of Italian extraction, plus about 100,000 Portuguese and thousands more from every background imaginable. What was predominantly Orange Toronto a few decades ago is now close to 60 per cent non-WASP, and that trend continues. Until 1967 about 90 per cent of all immigrants came from the U.S. and European countries. Today, largely because of improved economic conditions in Europe, that is down to 40 per cent, meaning that 60 per cent come from Asia, the West Indies, and other essentially Third World countries. And about half of all immigrants to Canada head for Ontario. The 1981 census lists 4.5 million Ontarians,

---

* At the time Rae made his unfortunate remarks, incidentally, five of the twenty-one New Democratic Party MPPs (23 per cent) were from a non-anglo background, while fourteen of the seventy Tories (20 per cent) were of some other origin.

out of a total population of 8.5 million, as being of British origin. That's 52.6 per cent, light years ahead of the French at 7.7 per cent, Italians at 5.7, Germans at 4.4, Dutch at 2.2, Ukrainians at 1.6, Jewish and Portuguese both at 1.5, Polish and Chinese at 1.4, and Indo-Pakistanis, Greeks, blacks, and Yugoslavians all at 1.0 per cent.

Ontario governments have a long history of dealing with two minorities, namely francophones and natives, but the multicultural mosaic poses entirely new problems of cultural accommodation. And Bill Davis, leading a party that historically has exalted all things British, presided over a government faced with francophone militancy of national significance (see Chapter 20), the native rights movement, and the rapidly changing complexion of Ontario society.

*   *   *

While Davis was trying to win friends among various groups before the 1975 election, Polish-born MPP Ed Havrot, a brash, tactless, but hard-working man from Timiskaming, sprung into national prominence for angrily telling a *Globe* reporter that he could buy Indian chiefs off with "a case of goof. . . . These damn Indians have gone absolutely wild," he said, upset because their land claims were delaying a major development in his riding. "We should have given them a bunch of teepees and some cordwood and that's all."

Davis immediately fired Havrot as head of the Ontario Northland Transportation Commission and parliamentary assistant to Transportation Minister John Rhodes and ordered him to read a prepared apology to the legislature. Havrot was doing fine with his apology until he decided to mount an impromptu attack on NDP Leader Stephen Lewis for accusing him of racism, adding, "I might also add, Mr. Speaker, that my lifelong and best friend is Jewish; another is Estonian and is married to a squaw." Havrot claimed part of the problem was that big-city southern Ontarians don't understand northerners, who "are a little more open-minded and a little more outspoken than they are here. Up North, if you say the wrong thing in the heat of the moment and offend somebody, you apologize and it's all over." Havrot's constituents didn't agree entirely because they booted him out the next election, but two years later, after he had served his penance, they re-elected him.

While Havrot was doing his best to upset native peoples, however, Davis was doing his best to placate them. One of the major political issues of the mid-1970s was mercury pollution in the English-Wabigoon river system caused by the Dryden Paper mill, which was devastating the traditional fishing grounds, and hence the economic base, of bands on the reserves at White Dog and Grassy Narrows. An announcement by Reed Paper Ltd. that it wanted to develop nineteen thousand square miles of forest, an area the size of Nova Scotia, raised even more environmental and sociological fears used to good effect by Stephen Lewis and the NDP.

In early 1977, after considerable pressure had been exerted by local bands and after the NDP had prevented the minority government from signing a development agreement with Reed, Davis named Mr. Justice Patrick Hartt to head a full-scale commission of inquiry into northern development. Although it spent a lot of money, it never developed into much, but for Davis it took a troubling issue out of the political forum, where he was getting hammered, and put it into the hands of the commission, where it festered for years until as an issue it was all but forgotten.

Hartt grumbled about his job from the outset, but in April, 1978, after spending about $2 million, he issued an interim report. One of the things he recommended, and Davis accepted, was a moratorium on wild-rice licences. In fact it was a five-year ban against granting licences to local whites, a move that Davis's own Northern Affairs Minister Leo Bernier criticized as "counterproductive" and "reverse discrimination."

Hartt's argument was that native peoples "should be given the chance to show what they can do." The government was already supplying them with equipment and marketing help, but the fact that they were still not doing well harvesting the potentially lucrative wild-rice crop was not seen as a problem caused by them, but as a problem caused by whites who were outproducing them and probably exploiting somebody else to do so. As of early 1985 the moratorium is still in effect, with northern whites in the Kenora district still being denied new wild-rice licences. Bernier points out that Ontario has 19.2 per cent of the world's wild rice yet harvests only 7.1 per cent of the world crop. Minnesota, with a climate and terrain less suited to it than Northern Ontario's, harvests 64 per cent of the world crop.

In any event, even Hartt got sick of the inquiry and became Ontario's first native commissioner—a cushy job he himself had recommended—while mining executive Ed Fahlgren took over as head of the royal commission in August, 1978. Five years later the *Globe* took a devastatingly detailed look at the commission's record, discovering that its only major accomplishment was the $9 million tab it had chalked up, an Ontario spending record for that sort of investigation. By 1985 it was up to $11 million, with no report in sight.

In the meantime Davis and his unctuous natural resources minister, Alan Pope, a northerner himself, were busy secretly planning to give away massive fishing rights and land controls to native peoples. They reached a pact in late 1982 that was to be signed by Ottawa, the province, and five native organizations, but the federal government backed off at the last minute. When news of the pact came out, Pope tried to downplay the details but under questioning admitted it could have meant kicking whites off up to forty lakes or parts of lakes and giving enormous powers to bands to control fishing and set fees for non-native fishermen. The admission created immediate racial tensions in the North because local municipalities and tourist and outfitting organizations had not been consulted.

But Davis soldiered on. During the constitutional meeting in Ottawa with native leaders in March, 1983, he supported Pierre Trudeau's plan to recognize a form of native self-government. More sensible heads prevailed when most of the other premiers blocked the plan, and the conference ended with agreement only to pursue the issue in future meetings. But in December, 1983, the *Toronto Sun* revealed a secret cabinet document recommending that Pope turn over control of millions of acres of reserve lands to complete native control, giving them 100 per cent of mineral revenues and royalties instead of the traditional 50 per cent. And in March, 1984, speaking at another constitutional confab on the issue, once again Davis agreed with Trudeau, this time to a proposed constitutional amendment giving native peoples the right to self-government. Davis said many people find the term "somewhat intimidating," but the majority of the premiers said they weren't intimidated by the phrase; they just didn't know what it meant and thought it shouldn't be enshrined until its meaning was defined, a task that could take years. At the time Davis summed up his view of the issue and of the world when he said, "I am flexible." No kidding.

* * *

While Davis tried to appeal to every ethnic group imaginable, there was one exception — Arabs. Not that Davis had anything against Arabs per se, it was just that in a world of Arab-Israeli conflict, there was no middle ground, and Davis consistently opted to argue the cause of the Israelis and make dramatic, but often meaningless, gestures that won applause in Jewish circles.

In May, 1975, Davis raised the ire of the Canadian Arab Federation, which accused him of bowing to Jewish pressure groups, when he opposed the attendance of the PLO at a federally sponsored Toronto conference on crime and the treatment of offenders. Davis, in a letter to Trudeau, said Ontario would consider withdrawing its support for the conference if the PLO attended. The tactic succeeded, and the PLO, which had already been to the province twice before without incident, was not allowed in. He went after Trudeau again on the same issue in April, 1984, when he complained that Zehdi Terzi, the PLO's permanent observer at the United Nations, shouldn't have been allowed to speak to the Senate committee on the Middle East, saying the appearance was "inappropriate, given the involvement of the PLO in terrorist attacks and other violent activities."

During a trade mission to Israel in January, 1977, Davis announced that Ontario would refuse to give government business to companies complying with the Arab boycott against Israel and said firms that did comply would be named publicly and refused any financial support from the province. While the announcement won him headlines and sparked several demonstrations against him by angry Arabs, Davis certainly took his time matching his tough talk with legislation. He turned the matter over to then-backbencher Larry Grossman, who had introduced a private member's bill to prohibit boycott compliance. The bill died when the legislature was dissolved for the election, but that November, in a speech at the 1977 Negev Dinner sponsored by the Jewish National Fund of Toronto, Davis promised to take action within a month. He did, introducing the bill on the final day of the fall session in December, too late to do anything with it other than bask in the glory of some more headlines. Then in April, 1978, he said he would reintroduce the bill and send it to a standing committee of the legislature for detailed study. Those hearings finally began in September, and the Ottawa-based Council of Muslim Communities of Canada accused Davis, with considerable justification, of doing it as a way of winning more Jewish votes.

Finally, in November, 1978, just after Davis returned from his second visit to Israel, Bill 112 became law, the only anti-boycott legislation in the country. It provided for fines of up to $5,000 for individuals and $50,000 for companies caught entering into agreements to boycott Israel. While Arab officials here and abroad complained about the law and Jewish officials heralded it, there never was an occasion to test it in the courts. No one was ever charged under it.

But it served its purpose. Eddie Goodman, noting how the Tories do much better with second- and third-generation Canadians, said, "It's the same thing with the Jewish vote. As they became more integrated and more affluent, more a part of the mainstream, we did better. My father's family were the strongest Tories around, but most of the Jews were Liberals. But now we do very well. We're improving among the other groups, too, but you can't overcome these problems quickly."

Heaven knows they try.

*   *   *

In 1974 Davis went on a highly publicized, fifteen-day, sixteen-hundred-mile tour of twenty-one Italian towns and cities, including the Vatican, where he had an audience with the Pope. Enthusiasm was so high that some towns declared a civic holiday to mark the occasion and celebrate the historical ties between their homeland and the growing numbers of their relatives in Ontario. Upon his return Davis denied he was trying to curry political favor with the Italian community, saying only that he hoped the tour demonstrated to Italians "that the premier and the government feel they have an important place in Ontario and that we appreciate the contributions they have made to Ontario."

In the election that followed a year later, three prominent Italians who accompanied Davis on the trip became Tory candidates: Elio Madonia, a wealthy dairy owner and soft-drink bottler, ran in the downtown Toronto riding of Bellwoods; Joe Marrese, former chairman of the Metropolitan Separate School Board, ran in the west Toronto riding of Oakwood; and in Sudbury Mayor Joseph Fabbro, a former Liberal, got the Tory nod. All three lost badly. But that campaign did see the election for the first time of three men of Italian birth, all New Democrats: Odoardo Di Santo in Downsview, Tony Grande in Oakwood, and Tony Lupusella in Dovercourt. The socialists were not from the mould the Tories chose, the so-called community "leaders," the successful businessmen who'd come to Canada and made it big. Rather, they were essentially local union activists and community workers, much closer to their communities than the Tory big shots.

Madonia turned out to be a Pentecostal who liked making converts, hardly a political asset in a riding that was about 80 per cent Catholic, and even had the local priests angry with him. He finished a poor third in a downtown riding that had been held by prominent cabinet minister John Yaremko for twenty-three years. Millie Caccia, wife of federal Liberal MP Charles Caccia, finished second, while Ross McClellan, who pointed out to anyone who would listen that his wife had an Italian background, won the riding and quickly became one of the most effective opposition critics in the legislature.

John Nicholls, a former organizer who worked out of downtown Toronto Tory headquarters, moved on to the premier's office as executive officer responsible for multicultural liaison. When the position was created, Davis had been premier for a couple of years, and his officials noticed he was getting about three hundred invitations a year from ethnic organizations, and all but about ten were routinely turned down. At the same time they noticed that federal Liberals never missed any of these events, so they hired someone to co-ordinate these things, figure out which ones Davis should attend, and try to get someone to go to the others. A few years later Nicholls took over the job.

"To be totally crass about it, if you really wanted to turn those ridings around, you could spend millions on all sorts of programs," he says, but Davis was against that. He wasn't in favor of "a lot of expensive but token announcements." Personally, Nicholls finds the lack of support frustrating. He says a survey conducted in the 1981 election by MTV, Metro's multicultural television station, showed that about 15 per cent of Italian men in Metro supported the Tories, while just 5 per cent of Italian women did. "The survey wasn't scientific or anything," says Nicholls, "but that would be my sense of it."

For years the Tories have had the problem of getting candidates who may have impressed the Tory hierarchy but were not terribly representative of their actual community. "But no matter what we do, we don't seem to be able to win. We got Madonia and Marrese, and people say, 'Ah, the reason those people didn't win is because they're big shots who think they've got it made.' So in 1977 we had a woman social worker named Maria Sgro running in Bellwoods, and a young lawyer, Sam Stabile, who's a big shot now in Downsview, and then the word was that they weren't well known. So then in 1981 we got a couple of guys, like John Burigana in Dovercourt, just a nice young guy in his early thirties, and people say, 'Well, he's hopeless. You put him on CHIN radio and he's not very articulate.' We've tried every approach, and they don't seem to work. It's not that we want to dwell on the Italian community, it's just that it's so large, about 700,000 in Ontario. When you add the Portuguese, then we've got a problem."

Eddie Goodman describes the Tory success among Italian voters as "terrible. . . . We do well with the Ukrainians, and all right with the Latvians and Estonians, but basically we don't do that well with any Catholic group. The fact remains, there is still that sort of Anglo-Saxon feeling among people, even though it's not nearly what it used to be and not nearly what it is with the federal party. But there's no doubt the perception is there. It's sort of an historical thing. We're doing better, but it's slow."

Nicholls adds another historical dimension, seeing one of the difficulties Tories have with attracting Italian voters as stemming from the Second World War. "I'm not saying they hate the British, but I'm saying they're not big on the premier standing up and talking about the Queen and wrapping himself in the flag. That just reinforces their view this is a British party, so we're very weak among that group." Another factor is that Italy has twenty regions and a hundred provinces, which means they have a stronger central government. Because the Liberals have dominated Canada federally (until 1984, anyway), many immigrants feel warmly toward them but, not being used to strong regional governments, don't feel the same way toward the provincial Tories. "Also, many come from societies that are dominated by a small group of people, and in their homeland, 'conservative' tends to mean either facism or a small, elite group, so they instinctively don't like conservatives. And it's true in the past, they see us as a WASP, Protestant, Orangeman's party. I mean, our colors are red, white, and blue, the Union Jack and all that stuff."

As if those weren't problems enough, in 1979 Ed Havrot did it again, insulting some Italian MPPs during a late-night session. He called Tony Lupusella a "wop" and interrupted him several times to say, "This is the wop show" and "mama mia" and to tell the MPP he could "eat an awful lot of pizza ina five minutes." He even added, "Atsa nice. Good for Benito Mussolini."

Davis immediately ordered Havrot to apologize in person to the MPP, by letter, and in public in the legislature. The premier even invoked the Lord's Prayer in a statement asking MPPs to forgive Havrot. "One of the phrases in that prayer that we say every day relates to forgiveness. It relates to the human quality that I would hope is part of our being."

Havrot followed orders and said, "We tend on occasion to get a bit carried away from time to time in the cut and thrust of debate. However, I recognize that there is absolutely no excuse for the type of comment that I made . . . and today I want to apologize once more to the individuals involved and to the House in general." But the former Kirkland Lake reeve said later that that type of joking is normal in the North. "I get Polish jokes thrown at me all the time. I laugh at them. I think they're funny. I enjoy them." He said the press built up his comments "as abusive remarks. They certainly weren't. Pizzas — I love pizzas."

* * *

Way back in 1973 Davis set up an advisory council on multiculturalism to help minority groups preserve their culture and language. Davis said many times he was against the U.S. "melting pot" concept, and in addition to the council, which subsequently was expanded to the Advisory Council on Multiculturalism and

Citizenship, Davis appointed Attorney General Roy McMurtry head of a cabinet committee on race relations.

After the 1975 election the Tories set up an "ethnic centre" at St. Clair and Dufferin in Toronto, right around the corner from a similar one set up by the NDP. At a dinner of ethnic community leaders in April, 1976, to raise money for the centre, Davis warned ethnics to beware of socialism and the Liberal "comrades" in Ottawa, saying that both the other parties claimed to have ethnic voters in their pockets. "We make no such claim because that sort of claim is an insult, direct and mindless, to the people in this province of every ethnic origin."

But whether they like the claims of the provincial NDP and federal Liberals or not, the Tories envy their ability to attract ethnic voters to the detriment of the Tories. There remains an ongoing fight within Tory circles about how best to approach the problem, whether to tackle it with high-profile handouts and trying to match the Liberals by showing up at every ethnic event or with the slower, less public, but probably more effective route in the long run of simply plodding quietly along at the community level, the way the Ontario NDP have managed to build trust among ethnic sections of Metro.

"The traditional way has been to try to co-opt the leaders of the ethnic communities," says one senior party insider. "Or to buy a lot of advertising in their publications and go to a lot of their public events. I personally think that's a bullshit approach, not because of any moral dilemma on my part, but because it doesn't make sense. It's assuming the first frame of reference these people have is their ethnicity. That's a bizarre notion—that they think of themselves first as Italians and Portuguese or whatever. You don't go to the guy with the wool hat on the street and ask him if he thinks of himself as black. He'll say, 'No, but you do. . . .' You know, a lot of people in ethnic communities feel multiculturalism policies should not be aimed at ethnics, they should be aimed at non-ethnics. You don't have to tell Ukrainians they are good people, that their heritage is great. You have to tell the guy next door who calls him 'bohunk.' "

He concedes that the party has mistakenly concentrated on so-called "community leaders" in the past. "Most new Canadians don't look at self-appointed leaders of their communities at all. In the Italian community, for example, they have a history of that, which they want to get away from here. Their leaders are Tony down at the pool hall and Joe at the barber shop. And the real strategy is a community relations job. Go to these people and say, 'Look, your aspirations can be met with us.' It isn't going to be on the museum board, it's to assure that no one in class calls little Johnny a wop and that little Johnny can become president of the TD Bank if he does everything that anybody else has to do. Just assure them that the opportunity is there for little Johnny."

That's not the view from the top, however. From there the Palace Guard looked out over the sea of changing faces and charted a different course. But few of the people close to Davis had any personal frame of reference with ethnic groups, and Davis himself, growing up in Brampton, barely knew anyone who wasn't from the dominant anglo culture. While Brampton, too, has a large visible-minority population, most of it lives in the suburban areas of Bramalea and Heart Lake, far away from Main Street South.

The Bruce McCaffrey situation, more than anything else, underscores the often bitter and personal internal Tory dispute about the best way to combat anti-conservative sympathies in ethnic communities. In December, 1983, McCaffrey resigned as provincial secretary for social development shortly after suffering chest pains and collapsing while playing squash with a friend. A former high school teacher and investment broker, McCaffrey represents the wealthy north Toronto riding of Armordale. Elected in 1977, he was sworn into cabinet in 1981 as minister without portfolio, then became minister of citizenship and culture. A year later he was surprisingly demoted to the social development secretariat and replaced by Susan Fish, a trendy, former downtown Toronto politician whose municipal campaigns had been organized by Davis's principal assistant, John Tory.

McCaffrey says some people in the premier's office felt he "let down the team" because he wouldn't go to every ethnic event, but "that begs the question of just what is the team view of what multiculturalism is all about. Well, the team doesn't have one view, or they wouldn't be in such deep shit on the issue."

McCaffrey says the Tories have watched the federal Liberals enjoy massive support in the ethnic communities, which stayed relatively strong even in the 1984 Tory rout, "and after all this observing, what they have finally boiled it down to is this: Those fucking federal Liberals go around delivering cheques at Polish barbecues, Estonian dances, and Latvian fund-raising dinners. That's why they get the vote. You can see why they make that observation, but it doesn't take a genius to know why they're dead wrong. The federal Liberals have used those tactics to reinforce an existing strength. It comes from the fact they were in power when these people came to the country. It's not to create a relationship. You don't create a relationship with any human being by handing them a cheque, unless it's a hooker."

He says most of the Davis insiders had no idea about ethnic realities. "Well, John Tory, to be specific, and some of that ilk, people who have been exposed to an ethnic reality only when their car broke down, when they had to leave their BMW and take the subway once in the last ten years. These guys don't even know what an ethnic is. It's an insult to talk about using cheques to deliver the vote."

McCaffrey says his idea to open five new welcome houses for newcomers in the suburbs is far more useful than attending ethnic banquets and handing out cheques and that he still gets goose bumps walking into the Welcome House at University and Dundas, just south of Queen's Park, because he feels it is "one of the few government services where, if you walk in there, you can see it being of use to people right off the bat." He says governments are supposed to help people, "and by and large I think we've done a good job helping people the government is easily able to identify with, the north Toronto anglos, for example. Legitimately, we have an array of services for them, but I don't really believe we have an array of services for the ethnics."

He also doesn't think much of the belief that the party needs ethnic candidates to win ethnic ridings. New Democrat Fred Young represented the heavily Italian riding of Yorkview in northwest Metro for years before retiring, and McCaffrey used to say "at caucus and out-of-town meetings, 'In the words of that great Italian, Fred Young,' just to make the point that you don't run an Italian in a riding where there are Italians just because you think you're going to trick everybody. People are smart, whatever language they think in. They see shit for shit's sake."

But the ethnic candidate route is still favored by head office. Bob Harris, the party's executive director, says wooing the ethnic vote is "our biggest challenge. What we normally look for is somebody in the community who on his or her own is making a name for themselves. The difficulty we have in the west end of Metro is we don't have people at the municipal level or board of education level who are Tories. If you don't have those people, you have to run people with no past political experience, and whether they run a good campaign or not, they may be called a token, and they won't get a lot of votes." Harris's office has just thirteen full-time staff, with five organizers covering Metro Toronto, eastern, central, western, and Northern Ontario, but "for us to do the job we need to do, we'd need one person in every riding. The ethnic ridings take more work, too. There are more problems. You've got to spend more time there. There's no simple solution."

John Nicholls admits it is true that people grumbled about McCaffrey not attending enough ethnic events, although he's not convinced they're all that helpful, either. "But for those who were looking for a way to put a certain person with big glasses and shiny teeth in there, a female [Susan Fish], the piece all sort of fit."

Fish certainly gets her picture in the ethnic press more than McCaffrey did, but the importance of the newspapers has been largely taken away by CHIN radio and the multicultural television station, Channel 47. There are about 170 ethnic newspapers in Ontario, about 140 of them within easy driving distance of Toronto, but their total circulation is about 500,000. The biggest is *Corriere Canadese*, the three-time-a-week Italian newspaper with 25,000 circulation. "In most cases it's the old guard who are reading those newspapers," says Nicholls. "The Polish papers, for example, are mainly read by my wife's parents, who are Polish, but my wife doesn't bother ever to look at them. It's still a worthwhile audience, yes, but it's fragmented. You try to be nice to them so they don't speak out against you. I think the potential is there for them to do more harm to you." He points out that when the Liberals named black activist Anne Cools to the Senate, *Contrast*, a Toronto newspaper for blacks, "splashed the story and her picture all over the front page. But when we appointed Dr. Dan Hill as ombudsman, he got a little column inside."

Ontario also has about a thousand ethnic organizations. In the Pakistani community alone there are close to fifty. Part of

Nicholls's job is to make sure that when groups are invited to meet government officials, they don't invite people who have strong feelings about one another; for example, if it's a Filipino event, they don't want to bring pro-Marcos and anti-Marcos groups together.

The divisions within the ethnic communities are a constant problem for Nicholls. He concedes that Ontario's race relations commissioner, Bhausaheb Ubale, is not that popular even among his fellow Indians, "but it's hard to find somebody who is universally popular. Probably the safest thing to do in race relations or multiculturalism is to hire a sympathetic Anglo-Saxon because then people won't say you're favoring one group over another. I remember when we had Rocco Lafranco there as a so-called ethnic organizer. People of other ethnic groups said, 'He's really an Italian organizer,' and Italians said, 'He's from the south, he's really a southern Italian organizer.' In Ubale's case there is a lot of that. My sense of it is that part of the world is more stratified, and not always in a nice way. You get Hindus versus Muslims, Sikhs versus Hindus, and so on, one class of society against another class. . . . My guess is there are about 125,000 in Ontario from India, about 35,000 from Pakistan. Ubale is seen by these people as a Hindu from Bombay, and if other people from India have trouble relating to Ubale, what about somebody from Jamaica? But the problem politically is, the opposition would say, 'You have a position called race relations commissioner, and you can't even find a visible-minority person to put in there.' So politically it's imperative to have a visible minority in there, but the moment you do that, you get all the rivalries which have been brought over from their homelands with them."

Nicholls says Davis was very popular personally in the ethnic communities but didn't go to as many ethnic events as Nicholls would have liked. Outside the legislature he maybe went to eight or nine a year. In November, 1982, the South Asian community of Toronto held a testimonial dinner for Davis and Roy McMurtry, organized by Ubale and McMurtry. It was the only event Davis attended for people from India and Pakistan. The only "black event" Nicholls can recall Davis attending was a small dinner several years ago for McMurtry at St. Michael and All Angels Church near Bathurst and St. Clair. "The trouble is finding an event that is community-wide. You get Caribana, for example, which is big, but it's mainly for Jamaicans, but not other West Indians." This illustrates again the problem of viewing all blacks as one group. "We have some Canadian-born blacks and put them in high places, people like Lincoln Alexander [chairman of the Workers' Compensation Board] and Lloyd Perry [official guardian], and we think that's good, then some guy from Jamaica will come in and say, 'Yeah, but he's not West Indian.' There are times when you have to ask yourself what you have to do to win."

The ethnic vote is critical in about a dozen ridings in Toronto and Hamilton, and it is also significant in twice that many ridings where the majority is still Anglo-Saxon but where ethnics represent a sizable block of 20 or 30 per cent. "There's a concern over the long term that we really have to do something," Nicholls says, "but nobody quite knows what it is we have to do to make the lights go on." He believes Brian Mulroney is the first Tory leader who really seriously went after the ethnic vote. Davis didn't because he and Ed Stewart, not that they were anti-ethnic, they weren't, but they were just "not going to go to the point of almost pandering to new Canadians by promising them things that you really can't deliver on."

Nicholls found Davis to be "a little uncomfortable" around visible minorities, having grown up in "white downtown Brampton. He's reluctant to go to a lot of events, but once he gets there he gets warmed up and sometimes talks too long. I think he's liked because people see him as a humane guy with a social conscience, and in the eyes of many new Canadians they feel that's unusual for a Tory. They still won't vote for him, but they like him."

At a Tory convention in Quebec City in 1977, Davis inadvertently jammed his foot into his mouth when, joking about his long-suffering support for the Argos, he noticed Hamilton's Lincoln Alexander in the room, then Canada's only black MP. (Ontario has had just one, Etobicoke Liberal Leonard Braithwaite, from 1963 to 1975.) Davis quipped, "I see Linc Alexander there, and while the Argos might have their problems, Hamilton's got them in spades." Davis seemed surprised at the groaning and embarrassed titters; standing at the back of the room, Hugh Segal muttered, "Oh God, he didn't mean that."

No doubt he did not mean any racial slur; it just shows that in this area, as in others, his protected upbringing was a factor in his view of the world. He wasn't a total innocent, however, when it came to avoiding what he perceived to be ethnic slurs. A small but illustrative example of his attitude was his decision to send out only Seasons Greetings cards, not Christmas cards, to avoid offending any non-Christians who may have got one. The fact that he may have offended Christians by avoiding any reference to Christ never concerned him.

His son Neil says people really enjoyed getting the cards, but "there is no question there are some political considerations. John Prine calls it 'rape by the minority.' Certain things I do, too. We seem to compromise a lot just to have tolerance of other groups. I think we can have tolerance, all right, but we shouldn't offend people if we say who we are."

With no personal frame of reference on race relations, Davis increasingly deferred to others in the inner circle who supposedly understood such things, particularly Roy McMurtry. During the mid- and late 1970s, when controversies arose between the police and the black and East Indian communities in Toronto, a series of incidents, some major, some minor, were exploited by radical community representatives and left-wing Toronto municipal politicians to make it appear as if the city were on the verge of race riots. Race relations commissioner Ubale, who got his job after organizing a trip to India for McMurtry, actually predicted race riots. When a group of white youths beat up a Pakistani family, Ubale made headlines with claims of rampant racism; a few days later he said nothing when the reverse happened. Ubale prepared a report for McMurtry on relationships between the police and the ethnic communities, similiar to the one he had helped research when he lived in England; naturally, he painted a bleak picture. (Oddly enough, he was not concerned enough about his community to become a citizen before accepting his job from McMurtry; he took out Canadian citizenship only after negative publicity shamed him into it.)

There were several byproducts of this racial hysteria, including a Toronto study on racism by former NDP MPP Walter Pitman; a study by a provincial committee that concluded without any evidence at all that visible minorities were underrepresented in government advertising; and the establishment of a Metro police citizens' complaint bureau. By far the most horrendous byproduct of all this, however, was the draconian Ontario Human

Rights Code. There is scant evidence that the racial situation was the problem Davis and the Palace Guard claimed, but there is no doubt the main motivation of the expanded Code was an electoral appeal to the minorities.

Davis, who rushed to the aid of an embattled Elgie during the committee fights on the revised Code — criticizing largely his own caucus members for objecting to what they saw as a police state law — admits the Tory showing in ethnic communities is "of some concern, yes. I think we have been increasing our vote over the years, but there are certain traditions, particularly in Metro, some of it a carry-over in what has been a greater measure of support for the federal Liberal party than the federal Tory party.

"I'm concerned about it, although I'm encouraged because I think progressively we have been doing better. We wouldn't have had the figures in 1981 if we hadn't. How we sustain that and continue to improve that I don't have an answer . . . you just constantly work at it.

"I think the human rights legislation is helpful in that regard, and although I can't tell you if there's a direct relationship, a lot of them are separate school supporters. A lot of them," he repeated, just days after he extended full government aid to Catholic schools, a move that preceded by two months the historic visit of Pope John Paul II.

The Tories are already counting the votes.

CHAPTER 19
CARDINAL BLESSINGS

———————— ☙ ————————

In May, 1984, the Davis inner circle met for a strategy session on whether to call a snap election. The hawks wanted to pull the plug quickly because the federal Liberals were about to choose Pierre Trudeau's replacement and they wanted to beat the new guy (John Turner, as it turned out) to the punch. The Davis loyalists, afraid he might retire soon, also knew that if they could talk him into an election, there was no reason to think he wouldn't pad his majority and stay around for at least another three years.

What they didn't want was a divisive issue, say the question of aid to Catholic schools, blowing up just two months before the visit of the Pope.

It was at that session that Davis dropped a bombshell. Shortly after regaining his majority in 1981, he had held his annual pre-Easter meeting with Roman Catholic officials. What made that meeting different was that he had promised Cardinal Carter that during the life of the current government, he would end a 110-year-old dispute by extending public aid to Roman Catholic separate schools beyond Grade 10 to Grades 11, 12, and 13. It was ten years after he had won his only other majority, largely on the strength of his opposition to extending such aid. Uncharacteristically, Davis hadn't cleared it first with the Palace Guard. He had done it on his own.

"Everybody was absolutely stunned," says one of those at the meeting. "He'd done it completely on his own hook. So everybody convinces him he'd better go and see the cardinal and make him understand this isn't the time to do this at the start of a campaign because it could hurt him politically and could drive up sectarian divisions when the Pope was arriving. You know, the classic Bill Davis approach: 'We're making progress; it's the reality, not the smoke and mirrors, that matters.' "

So off Davis went to explain his predicament. But this time the cardinal, whom the opposition consistently accused of being too cosy with Davis, with considerable justification, wasn't buying. "He told Davis he was shocked he'd try to renege on a deal. He said he was a man of his word, a man of honor, and he couldn't believe he would back out. And then the cardinal hit him with the big stick and said, 'If you want to run an election without keeping your word, count on having opposition from every pulpit in every Catholic church in Ontario.' Well, Davis just folded like a three-dollar accordion. That's why there was no election. Nobody will talk about it, but that's what happened."

Indeed, within days of his meeting with Cardinal Carter, Davis ended the widespread speculation about an election by telling cabinet there would not be one. Six days after that he called an emergency caucus meeting fifty minutes before the afternoon session of the legislature to say he was going to announce the extension of aid to separate schools. "We were flabbergasted," says a caucus veteran. "Nobody had a clue. Sure, this issue had been discussed off and on for years, but to actually do it, just like that, wow." The legislature seemed to feel the same way because the announcement provoked the rare spectacle of a standing ovation by all three parties.

Davis denied that his decision had anything to do with politics, the upcoming visit of the Pope, any pressure from Carter or other Roman Catholic officials, or a lawsuit filed a week earlier by a group of separate school students and trustees based in Ottawa. "The decision was mine," he said. "I can no longer deal, in all conscience, with funding Grades Nine and Ten but not Grades Eleven through Thirteen." In his twenty-page statement, he quoted Sir John A. Macdonald speaking on the subject in his own day: "We do not want to stand on the extreme limits of our rights. We are ready to give and take. We can afford to be just, we can afford to be generous, because we are strong."

Thus ended the lesson.

*　*　*

Ironically, the dispute over religious school funding in Ontario originated with the Protestant minority of Quebec, which was fearful that the Catholic majority there would not allow it to operate its own school system. In 1841, when Upper and Lower Canada were united as the province of Canada, both the Catholic minority of Canada West (later Ontario) and the Protestant minority of Canada East (later Quebec) were given the right to establish their own schools. In 1867 this right was enshrined in the BNA Act.

That was fine for the times, but there were no public high schools to speak of then. There was a limited grade or common school system, but anything beyond that was the domain of the well-to-do in their private schools. Thanks mainly to the efforts of Egerton Ryerson, however, public high schools did arrive, and in 1874 the system was split into elementary and secondary levels. But the right to designate tax dollars for Catholic high schools was not extended, and the long fight for equality began.

The issue just simmered, and there was little tinkering with the system, although after 1886 corporations were allowed to contribute to Catholic schools based on a formula that reflected Catholic ownership of the firm. The growing complexity of corporations, however, made that provision more apparent than real. The Catholic system began doing more and more high school work, either through what was called "continuation," which meant Grades 9 and 10, or through private Catholic high schools, and the practice became so widespread that by 1915 the department of education began to be concerned that it was threatening the structure of common schools. It issued an edict forbidding any extension beyond the work of the fifth form. G. Howard Ferguson, premier from 1923 to 1930, was acting education minister at the time, and in response to outraged Catholic bishops said that the education department "never has, and, I venture to think, never will, change the well-defined, clear-cut, and well-understood line of demarcation between the work of our Public and Separate School and that of our Secondary or High School." During the war, however, Ferguson and Premier William Hearst agreed to leave the situation as it was and settle the issue in the courts once peace was restored.

But in 1919, after the United Farmers of Ontario under E. C. Drury won the election, the situation deteriorated. The Catholic authorities had conducted a widespread campaign to convince the press and public of the justice of their cause, but instead of winning public support, they stirred up public hostility, and Drury wouldn't bend. He decided to proceed with a "stated" court case, simply asking for a ruling, but according to historian Peter Oliver, the Orange Order preferred that a separate school board be forced to sue as plaintiff.

The Conservatives, now with Ferguson as their leader, regained power in 1923, and in what Oliver describes as a "virtuoso performance," Ferguson kept the issue from becoming a major political dispute by convincing Catholic authorities that "a friendly action" would indeed be better than a stated case and less likely to lead to outright hostilities. Ferguson also convinced them that he was well disposed toward their point of view but didn't want to get into it during his first term, when he was just getting established. The case did go to court and was restricted to the question of the right to do advanced work and to the dispute over the division of the legislative grant. The action was brought in the name of the trustees of the Roman Catholic Separate School for a section in Tiny Township. In May, 1926, the decision was brought down against the separate school petition. Catholic officials appealed, but that October the Ontario Appeal Court unanimously upheld the decision. The officials were angry, but they weren't angry with Ferguson, and funding for Catholic high schools wasn't much of an issue during the 1926 election or for a decade thereafter.

But on April 3, 1936, Liberal Premier Mitch Hepburn introduced the School Assessment Act, which gave the Catholic schools most of what they wanted. Its two major provisions obliged corporations (instead of giving them the option) to divide their taxes for school support in proportion to the faith of their shareholders, and if that was too complex, taxes would be split up in each municipality according to the proportion of Protestants and Catholics. To the outrage of the Conservatives and the applause of the Liberals, the bill was passed on April 9 at 5 a.m. after a bitter debate in front of packed public galleries.

The debate raged through the summer and fall of 1936, however, and newly elected Tory leader Earl Rowe accused Hepburn and his Liberals of being "tools of Rome." The issue was fought publicly in December of that year when a sitting Tory died and a by-election was called in East Hastings. The Tory had won by only 418 votes, and Hepburn, who campaigned personally on a regular basis, thought he could win the by-election. The separate school bill was the only issue, and Liberal cabinet ministers arrived daily in Belleville to fight the Tory Opposition. During the last couple of weeks Hepburn lived in the riding, travelling to every point and speaking to packed halls. On election day there was an 85 per cent turnout, despite such heavy snow that some voters had to ski to the polls. The Tory won handily by 1,136 votes, despite the $33,000 Hepburn had spent on his campaign, an enormous amount in the middle of the Depression. It was the first personal defeat of his political career.

The Conservatives promised to repeal the bill if they regained power, and soon even its supporters were disenchanted. For all its high-sounding rhetoric the bill had serious practical flaws, making it impossible to determine for assessment purposes just who the Catholic supporters in large corporations were. On March 23, 1937, Tory House Leader George Henry moved second reading of a bill to repeal the act, but instead of simply using his majority to vote it down, Hepburn surprised everyone by moving adjournment of the debate. That same night he rose to speak on the Tory motion and said that until the East Hastings by-election he had hoped the province would accept the legislation, but the bill was not working out, and "with a certain amount of trepidation tempered with regret" he was accepting the Tory motion. He then moved, and Harry Nixon seconded, that the question be put, effectively imposing closure on further debate.

At that point Tory Leopold Macaulay, outraged that he would now not be allowed to speak, shouted at Hepburn, "You may be a dictator, but you can't do this to us." The Speaker tried to keep order, but Macaulay — all five feet six inches and 126 pounds of him — moved into the aisle in front of his seat and shook his fist up at the press gallery, shouting, "Take this down, you fellows. It is the dirtiest, rottenest trick ever." He was literally dragged out of the chamber and ended up sitting in the press gallery. His son Hugh says the Liberals saw him sitting with a reporter, figured they might have been a bit hasty, and sent him a note asking him to come back; he sent them back a note saying, "To hell with you," after which a group of Liberal cabinet ministers signed their names on a brown bowler hat and sent it up as a peace offering. Hugh Macaulay still has the hat.

In any event, the bill was repealed by a vote of 80–0. Two days later Hepburn headed for Florida, and Catholic school officials headed back to square one.

During the 1940s and 1950s the issue merely percolated, but it gained renewed prominence in the late 1960s mainly because large numbers of immigrants, mostly Catholic, had come to live in Ontario and were upsetting the traditionally large Protestant majority that opposed extending aid to the schools. In 1969 separate school trustees, armed with facts about the growth of their system, met with the minister of education, Bill Davis, and officially requested extension of aid beyond Grade 10. (The system that had evolved up to then considered Grades 9 and 10 in the Catholic system elementary schools for grant purposes, so those two grades received partial grants. Schools up to Grade 8 got full grants, and Catholic high schools beyond Grade 10, of course, did not get any grants at all, which meant students paid tuition fees of up to $500 a year.) The minister said no.

In March, 1971, two weeks after he became premier, Davis said his government had not changed its mind but promised a definitive statement on the issue before the next election, adding that the decision wouldn't be "a surprise. I think most people already know what our answer will be."

The next month he was mobbed by angry separate school supporters while on an image-boosting trip to Windsor, one of the few areas where the Tories have been shut out politically. At the time 54 per cent of Windsor's student population went to separate schools, and 250 of them met Davis at the airport, chanting, "Save us, Davis, Save us, Davis, S.O.S., Save Our Schools." Nick Lorito recalls that night in the Cleary Auditorium, particularly the premier's nose-to-nose confrontation with a man with a pronounced Irish accent who shouted, "You've got to do something about it. If you don't we'll take to the streets. One more year of it and we will." He was still shouting and waving his fists as he moved from the fringe of the crowd to just inches from Davis. "We've got to rise up like they did in Ireland, like they did over there. It's not the BNA Act at all. It's just the goddamned Conservative government."

"The man literally had the wrath of God in his eyes," says Lorito. "But very calmly, Bill Davis looked at the man and said, 'Isn't that such a negative attitude. Really, you don't have to agree with what I'm doing or why I'm doing it, but wouldn't you feel better if you went out and helped elect somebody, rather than just attack somebody else? Because when you woke up the next day, you'd feel you'd accomplished something.' " The man stopped in mid-sentence.

Davis may have calmed that one man for the moment, but the onslaught continued. In May he was greeted by thunderous booing from five hundred demonstrators who had crashed Claude Bennett's Ottawa South nominating convention. The barrage of protests, aided by hand-held bullhorns, was so loud and so prolonged that Davis and other party officials were forced from the stage for about thirty minutes. YPC executive Hugh Segal was one of those forced off the platform. "I was bowled off my feet. In the back room there were various silly suggestions about how to handle the problem. Somebody even suggested getting the fire department to clear them out. But Davis said the only way to deal with it is to give them a chance to express their point of view and answer their questions, then ask them as citizens if they'd let us continue our meeting. He was superb. It could have been very ugly."

In June a group of fifty people representing the Ontario Alliance of Christian Schools presented Davis and Education Minister Bob Welch with a petition containing 120,000 signatures requesting extension of provincial grants to Christian and Jewish schools as well as Catholic schools — a still-unresolved side issue to the separate school debate that flared up anew after Davis's 1984 about-face. And in July the chairman of the Metro Toronto Separate School Board said he would try to encourage Ontario's two million Roman Catholics to oust the Davis government unless the Catholic schools "got what they asked for."

So the mood was set for a formal statement by Davis on August 31 at a press conference timed to guarantee that the issue would be a major one during the election that, not coincidentally, Davis officially kicked off two weeks later. He said extending aid would "fragment the present system beyond recognition and repair. . . . To embark upon such a policy could not be, in reason or justice, limited to some faiths and denied to others. . . . The government would be obliged to provide a system for Roman Catholic students, and a further system for Protestant students, another for Jewish students, and possibly still others."* He added that the decision was made "as much as humanly possible without regard to any political consideration, advantage, or disadvantage. Whatever the decision, it would almost certainly provoke vigorous dissent."

It did. Leading the dissenters was Liberal Leader Bob Nixon, whose father had seconded Mitch Hepburn's earlier repeal of the Liberals' own separate school bill. He was joined by then-Bishop Emmett Carter, who declared that Davis's refusal had made the matter an election issue and could lead to the closure of many schools. Later Davis told reporters, "I hope . . . I really hope that it won't be an election issue. At least not in the context of a religious battle."

Well, it was. Going into battle, the Tories were armed with Teetor polls showing that support for extension was limited, even among Catholics. Many Catholics felt that with government financing would come complete government control of their curriculum, thus removing the moral and religious milieu that is the main reason the schools exist. But everywhere Davis went in the campaign, he was met by protesting Catholic students carrying placards or coffins, chanting songs and slogans, a popular refrain being, "Uncle Bill went all uphill to cover the Catholic grants; Bill fell down and lost his crown, and equal rights came after." Bill, of course, didn't lose his crown at all. He romped to a one-sided victory, winning 78 of 117 seats.

There was some suggestion during the campaign that if Tory strategists weren't actually helping to organize the protests, they certainly weren't discouraging them. Charter Palace Guard member Tom Campbell, who travelled on the 1971 campaign, says, "There were people on the Tory bus in 1971 who would joke about hiring Catholic kids to come over with their placards. At first they didn't like the protests, but then they realized it was gaining them sympathy, even among Catholic voters. But I can't

---

*In 1984, just weeks after he reversed his stand, Davis said a request from Archbishop Lewis Garnsworthy for provincial aid for Anglican church schools was "comparing two situations which are not comparable. I get the impression perhaps he wasn't aware of the present status of the separate school system."

believe they organized that. Anyway, it would be too easy to get caught."

In a 1972 interview with the *United Church Observer*, Davis said he was "not completely surprised" that many Catholics supported his position. "I sensed then that there would be a number of separate school supporters who would be voting for the government. Quite honestly, I didn't expect that there would be as many as I now know there were."

So the issue was decided, although throughout the 1970s it would still flare up periodically. In September, 1974, for example, Rev. Patrick Fogarty, executive secretary of the English Catholic Education Association of Ontario, said Catholics were the "white Negroes" of Ontario, victims of outrageous discrimination by the provincial government. But stung by the 1971 results, Catholic officials and students alike barely raised the issue during the 1975 campaign, and in 1977 there were only a few protests, the largest in Guelph at a noon rally on the city hall square. Davis told the crowd he was opposed to further "fragmentation" of the school system. "Shouldn't we be doing our best to prevent fragmentation?" he asked, a question greeted with cheers from the audience.

*   *   *

The ties between Davis and George Emmett Cardinal Carter go back to the 1960s, when Davis was minister of education and Carter was deeply involved in the overhaul of the educational system in Quebec, where there were serious problems between church and state. Carter is given much credit by educators for convincing the Catholic church there that the state did have a strong role to play in overseeing education, and Davis was an important liaison when Quebec set up its first education department in 1964. For a while the two were in relatively frequent contact.

The charges of political partisanship against Carter began publicly in November, 1979, when a group of Liberal MPPs became outraged that he had thanked Davis for "consideration" for the separate school system during a speech at an Ontario government dinner in the cardinal's honor. Robert Nixon, who had more reason than most to be upset, said, "To use some of the terms His Eminence used seemed to me to show a devastating lack of information, or pure hypocrisy." Liberal MPP John Sweeney asked for a meeting with the cardinal — and got it — to have him explain his pro-Tory remarks, and Liberal Ron Van Horne fired off a letter expressing "absolute dismay and concern about your words of praise and commendation for a Conservative government which steadfastly refuses to extend support. . . ." Even retired Hamilton bishop Most Rev. Joseph F. Ryan complained that the Tories have "always denied our people the rights and means to educate their children as they see fit. . . . Is it suggested that we pay tribute to the premier of Ontario because he decided before the last election for political reasons not to extend aid to our Catholic high schools?" The *Catholic Register*, playing down the dispute, said Ryan didn't name the cardinal in his remarks, but it did not suggest who else he could possibly have been talking about.

The issue of their close relationship flared up again in November, 1983, prompting twelve opposition Roman Catholic MPPs to write the cardinal, complaining that he was too visibly identified with the Tories. The furor arose after a $200-a-plate dinner for Davis attended by two thousand Conservatives. Carter sat at the premier's right hand and offered blessings for the meal and particular blessings for Davis because of the heavy burdens of his office, no doubt a message to him to come clean on his secret 1981 separate school promise.

The next night Davis sat at the head table at a fund-raising event organized by the cardinal for Catholic charities. Liberal MPP Sean Conway, noting that Carter had also attended a fund-raising picnic in the summer for Northern Affairs Minister Leo Bernier, said, "This seems to be now a regular duet between the cardinal and the premier. But I would think the cardinal is being most unwise allowing himself to be involved in fund raising for the Progressive Conservative party." Even the NDP got edgy about the relationship. Downsview MPP Odoardo Di Santo said, "When the bishops issued their letter on the status of the economy, he [Cardinal Carter] said that it was too political and that it was not the role of the church to be involved in the political process. I think that it's a little bit contradictory when he attends Tory fund-raising dinners."

For his part, the cardinal dismissed the MPPs in a single-page letter dated November 9. He didn't really address the MPPs' complaints; he just criticized them for telling the media about them before contacting his office. "Under the circumstances, you will have no difficulty in perceiving why I consider your letter unacceptable and *non advenue*," he wrote, prompting Conway to say, "It sounds like it's coming from Cardinal Richelieu."

But if Carter was applying a little private pressure, public pressure was building in another corner of the province. In 1983 a small group of polite, well-dressed, articulate students from Ottawa, calling themselves the Ontario Students Association for Fair Funding, began showing up regularly at Queen's Park to lobby Davis, Education Minister Bette Stephenson, opposition party leaders, and other MPPs. President Richard Chiarelli, an Ottawa separate school trustee and student at Ottawa University, announced in June, 1983, that his group was going to court over the issue. Separate school boards across the province were not unanimous in supporting this move — although some did — fearing that it was too much of a risk and preferring the route of quiet negotiations. Chiarelli said the extension of aid would cost $175 million a year. The group got a bit carried away with itself, raving about a "fiscal holocaust," for example, and presumptuously giving cabinet a series of deadlines by which to enact parts of the proposals or else face court action. But overall it made a well-researched, intelligent case.

At about the same time the Ontario Association of Alternative and Independent Schools claimed that many cabinet ministers strongly supported funding of their schools as well, although many ministers listed as "very supportive" said later the association had misrepresented their views.

As if all that wasn't enough, there were, of course, the polls. Traditionally, Ontario Tories have run behind the Liberals in the Catholic vote, reflecting an historical antipathy toward the Conservative party among Catholics, who view it as the party of vested interests, the Establishment, and the Orange Lodge. It isn't any more, but it used to be, and old prejudices die hard on both sides.

On the other hand, party polls among Catholics showed Davis to be extremely popular, although that didn't always translate into support for the local Davis candidate. What was more worrisome to the Tories — and still is — was that the traditional demographics of the province were changing. The base the Tories have traditionally relied upon is no longer the majority, and the WASP component of formerly Orange Toronto is steadily diminishing.

Combined with a falling birth rate, the impact of immigration patterns on the education system has been profound. Until the 1970s the enrolment in the public system climbed steadily—sometimes marginally, sometimes dramatically. Then things began to change, and since 1970 elementary school enrolment in the public system has declined every single year, from 1,047,055 in 1970 to 787,486 in 1982. Enrolment in Catholic schools up to Grade 10, on the other hand, has increased, albeit marginally, from 418,433 to about 430,000 in 1984. Secondary school enrolment reached a peak in 1977 of 613,830 and now is also in constant decline, falling to about 500,000 in 1984. Catholic high schools from Grades 11 through 13 had about 45,000 students.

Davis, in his usual declaration of philosophical purity, says, "It's true the percentage of Roman Catholics has increased in the past fifteen or twenty years, but I don't know that it was a factor at all in the decision."

Education Minister Bette Stephenson, however, says, "Well, there's a lot of demographic reality involved in that. There's been a great shift in attitudes in the province. That demography had a great deal to do with the decision. The fact we now have close to 500,000 separate schoolkids in the province is a result of the federal immigration policies. We didn't have a lot of control over it, but they're there. That's reality. That's what it is." The ministry had been talking about it "very quietly" for about five years, she said, and it's true that cabinet "didn't know when the decision was going to be taken or precisely what it would be, but they knew about the issue. We had discussed it in caucus almost annually."

Davis said the subject was naturally discussed every year at his Easter meeting with the Catholic bishops. "I really had been worried about it ever since 1971. I felt while I was the minister of education that maybe the opportunity to have a single secondary system with panels, or something of that nature, was perhaps still achievable. I never got any encouragement for that view from any educators in the Catholic community, though, but I felt 1971 was not the time to move and we would wait and see if it was a possibility. Well, the separate school system continued to grow, and the logic of and the equity of things . . . well, we're at ninety per cent funding levels for Grades Nine and Ten. There's no way we could ignore that. The system was there. I just felt there was not going to be a single, secondary system, and the only logical thing to do was include the higher grades."

Under the Davis scheme the Catholic schools would establish a full range of elementary and secondary education with public funding, one year at a time, beginning with Grade 11 in September, 1985, and phasing in Grade 13 in 1987. He said the cost would be $40 million each year. He also said his decision would lead to the hiring of more non-Catholic teachers, although he was not sure how many — there already were a few — but declared, "This was understood by the church; this was part of the policy change." And in announcing that change, he set up a commission to examine the role of independent schools, to see if public funding "and its attendant obligations would be desirable . . . and compatible with the nature of their independence." He set up another commission to examine the whole question of educational funding, told it to report by May, 1985, and promised that the government would respond by January, 1986.

Two weeks before the announcement, a veteran party organizer who had worked in senior positions for Drew, Frost, Robarts, and even, briefly, for Davis, was bemoaning the Davis style of running government by polls. "But the one thing I did admire," he said, "was the way Davis handled the separate school issue [in 1971]. It's not a question of whether I agreed with it or not; it's that it was a strong decision. . . . I admired the way he said no. He didn't give them any sop or anything else. But that's an aberration for him, isn't it? I guess that's why it stands out."

Not any more.

CHAPTER 20
FORKED TONGUES

--- ❦ ---

The first embrace was embarrassing. Bill Davis and René
Lévesque were sitting side by side at a two-and-a-half-hour
private lunch in the stately Quebec legislative buildings on February 6, 1977, smiling and joking with reporters, simply agreeing to disagree about separatism. They even agreed that the level
of debate on separatism should be toned down, prompting one
Parti Québécois aide to say, "It was just what Quebec wanted,
to be seen to be conducting business as usual with mighty Ontario.
René was delighted. Absolutely delighted, as you anglos would
say."

Lévesque, playing the role of the reasonable separatist, said,
"There's no reason not to agree to disagree on the issue while
maintaining the best possible relationships and intensifying a lot
of things with Ontario on everything we can find common ground
about. And there are many things."

Davis acknowledged that maintaining close ties with Quebec,
while fighting it on separation, would be difficult. "It's a fine
line to tread, and I don't minimize it."

The next day there was an indication of what he would be up
against while treading that line. When Lévesque told the press in
English at a joint press conference that he and Davis had agreed
to "cool it" with respect to the separatism debate, it made headlines in English Canada, creating hope that things might not be
as serious as they seemed; the Quebec newspapers didn't even

report it. That night a group of English-speaking reporters were booted out of the Quebec Winter Carnival ball where Davis was guest of honor by the maître d' and a Quebec provincial police officer; the francophone reporters were allowed to stay. Such was the anti-English mood of Quebec, although to read the papers at the time, you'd swear it was the other way around — that English Canada was mad at Quebec.

Relations between Canada's two dominant cultures and between its two largest provinces have been tricky problems for every Ontario premier since Confederation. Quebec nationalism has had its ups and downs over the years, and pressure for recognition of language rights for Ontario's large francophone minority have plagued every provincial administration to some extent. But for Davis it was worse. The pressure for bilingualism was not only building within the province, but it was also being given added force by Ottawa's bilingualism policies and by the fact that for the first time an Ontario premier had to deal, face to face, with the reality of a Quebec separatist in power.

Being seen on stage acting excessively friendly with a separatist was not Davis's finest hour. But there were harder days ahead. As events unfolded over the next four years, the historical accommodation between the two cultures would be sorely tested and the relationship between Ontario's 500,000 francophones and the Davis government severely strained, forcing him to walk a linguistic tightrope by offering more French-language services without offending the non-French majority, all the while trying not to provide more fodder for the separatist assault on Canada.

*   *   *

The bilingualism dispute in Ontario dates to a day early in the 1911 session of the provincial legislature, when hostility over the Quebec nationalism of Henri Bourassa and widespread anger directed at Sir Wilfrid Laurier spilled over into the politics of what was essentially Orange Ontario. Education Minister G. Howard Ferguson introduced a motion: "That in the opinion of this House no language other than the English language should be used as a medium of instruction in the schools of this Province."

This was the introduction of the infamous Regulation 17. Although it was toned down before becoming law and compromises were made over the years, it became the Alamo for French-speaking Canadians in Ontario and Quebec and is still used in French-Canadian literature as a benchmark of Ontario's supposed bigotry against the French. Regulation 17 never did outlaw French in the schools, as separatists and radical franco-Ontarians still claim, but it certainly wasn't designed to enhance the use of French or to engender warm feelings between the two cultures.

That same year, on October 6, 1911, Laurier's Liberals were crushed by Sir Robert Borden's Tories, but nowhere was the rout more complete than in Ontario, where the language issue had become an obsession: The Tories won 72 seats to Laurier's 13.

That is the Ontario that even now Quebec schoolchildren learn about, while most Ontario pupils never do. But the events of those days, right up until the refusal by Davis to make Ontario officially bilingual, are at the root of a problem that, while being closer to accommodation, is still not completely resolved.

Ferguson's move was a predictable result of the rapidly escalating numbers of French-Canadians moving into several counties in eastern Ontario during the late nineteenth and early twentieth centuries. In 1885 the Liberal regime of Sir Oliver Mowat ordered that English be taught in every school in the province, and five years later this regulation was tightened up so that all instruction and communication would be in English unless children were unable to understand it. In areas where there were large numbers of French- or German-speaking children, however, inspectors were given the authority to allow reading, grammar, and composition to be taught in either of those languages if parents requested it.

The number of essentially French elementary schools remained high, and although they were supposed to be kept on a par with English schools, they were allowed to deteriorate. Few instructors had any formal training, most French-speaking children left school early, anyway, and those who did stay faced a linguistic minefield of all-English high schools and university entrance tests.

The Whitney government appointed school inspector F. W. Merchant to study the situation, and he discovered that many children in eastern Ontario were not being taught any English at all and that the level of French instruction was abysmal. These findings led to Regulation 17, enacted into law in 1912. It restricted the use of French for instruction and communication to

Form 1, although it could be carried further with the approval of the chief inspector if the pupils did not understand English; in practice it seldom went beyond that. French could also be taught as a subject in schools where it had formerly been offered, but for no more than one hour a day.

The regulation was slightly modified in 1913 to provide for better inspection of bilingual schools, but the Ottawa Separate School Board took legal action to have it rescinded altogether. During 1914, while awaiting the decision, separate schools there were closed for several months, stirring up more hostility on both sides. But the Ontario Supreme Court ruled that Regulation 17 was legal because the BNA Act protected education rights based on religion, but not on language.

The regulation was never rigidly enforced, and in 1927 Ferguson, now premier, ordered Merchant to study the situation again. At the time only one in ten pupils in French schools reached Grade 8, and only 13.5 per cent of their teachers held a first- or second-class teaching certificate; the others had basically no formal qualifications. It was Ferguson, who had introduced the regulation initially, who also killed it. He abandoned his effort to limit French to Form 1, established the University of Ottawa Normal School to improve French teachers' qualifications, and set up a committee to oversee upgrading of the French schools. By 1935 the situation had improved dramatically. Almost 60 per cent of teachers had first- or second-class teaching certificates, but even though more pupils were completing the high school entrance program in Form 4, they were not doing well because of their relatively limited skills in English, which were essential to proceed to the higher levels.

Things remained static until 1962, when Education Minister Bill Davis ruled that schools would be permitted, with ministerial approval, to teach Latin in French; three years later this was extended to history and geography. But the major breakthrough came later in the 1960s with the provision, in certain areas of the province, of a complete secondary school program in French, either in special schools built for the purpose or special classes set aside where numbers didn't warrant building a school. The Schools Administration Act, passed in 1968, made elementary French-language classes mandatory upon the request of ten or more francophone ratepayers where at least thirty French-speaking pupils were involved, and an amendment to the same act made French instruction in secondary schools mandatory under essentially the same conditions. It marked the first time franco-Ontarians had been guaranteed education in legislation.

There were already twenty French secondary schools operating privately, and the new policy essentially meant transferring them to the jurisdiction of individual high school boards. A year after the legislation was passed the number of private schools dropped to four.

On paper the legislation was terrific. It solved many problems, but it created many more. By 1971, when Davis left Education to become premier, tensions had escalated, largely because of the reluctance of school boards to build separate, French-only schools; they preferred to provide special classes for French-speaking students within existing schools.

This was the issue that would plague Davis throughout the 1970s, resulting in several well-publicized disputes invariably reported in Quebec as examples of anglo bigotry. And while there was some bigotry on both sides, the main objection was the cost, not the principle, of offering French-language instruction; the legislation at the time required French-language instruction if there were twenty-five French-speaking elementary pupils in a district or twenty secondary school students.

Tom Wells, education minister during much of the 1970s, points out that over three hundred French-language elementary schools were developed with no problem, and that the disputes were all "over secondary schools. Because of the size and complexity and, of course, the cost of secondary schools, a lot of them were not separate, and the francophones said they didn't want a wing of a school which was basically an anglophone school. They always believed the principal and administration and language of business of the school should be French. I think it's a reasonable argument from their point of view."

The first French high school was officially opened in Nepean in 1971 by Davis and the school board chairman, Sid Handleman. It didn't become an English-French showdown. Nor was there a problem later that year when Davis took a campaign swing through Kapuskasing to open Cité des Jeunes high school and was given a warm and enthusiastic greeting by more than five hundred students, parents, and community leaders. He reminded them of the French-language programs then offered at three Ontario universities, saying these expressed his commitment to assuring "that a dynamic French-Canadian society can feel at home in our midst."

But trouble was brewing due south in Sturgeon Falls, where a delegation of 350 local people had met him earlier in North Bay to demand a French school. The group had staged several walk-outs during the 1970–71 school year, arguing that while about thirteen hundred of the eighteen hundred students at their school were French-speaking, only three of the seventeen trustees on the Nipissing Board of Education were francophones. Davis told them it was under the board's jurisdiction but promised to speak to the education minister about it.

He then named Trent University president Thomas Symons as a commission of inquiry into the dispute. He was hardly a neutral mediator. Wells says, "Symons basically believed there should be separate French-language schools, and that's what he recommended."

*   *   *

While Davis's commitment to French-language education was open and forthright, there was always a large element of deceit in his approach to bilingualism. He steadfastly refused official bilingualism, yet he gradually expanded French-language services to the point where the 1983–84 budget just to operate them was almost $40 million, about $10 million of which came from the federal government.

In April, 1971, a month after being sworn in as premier, Davis flew to Montreal for a meeting with Quebec premier Robert Bourassa, arranged when Bourassa telephoned Davis after his victory at the leadership convention. After the meeting the two men predicted that relations would be strong between Ontario and Quebec, and Davis denied suggestions that there had been an anti-Quebec backlash after the kidnapping crisis in 1970, saying, "The people of Ontario feel close to Quebec."

In a question-and-answer session with the *Montreal Star*, Davis was asked if there wouldn't be political value in declaring official bilingualism and "being able to say that the French-speaking residents of Ontario have the same legal rights" as Quebec's English-speaking residents. "Let's get down to the practical application of it," he replied. "I don't believe in legislating something that you can't produce. Maybe I'm wrong in this, but I don't believe there is any point to it." Earlier, replying to almost the same question, he said, "You'd have to really determine whether you're talking about legal or constitutional rights, and to me that's an academic argument. I think it really is the spirit of the thing that matters. . . . I believe very sincerely that within the practical realities of our situation, that French-speaking citizens of Ontario are not in any way prejudiced because of language."

A month later Ryan Paquette, president of the Association canadienne-française de l'Ontario (ACFO), accused Davis of paying lip-service to bilingualism. "Last year the Quebec government gave more financial support to our projects than our own provincial government," he said. And in fact, in 1970 Quebec gave ACFO $13,000, while Ontario contributed $2,500 and Ottawa $185,000. But the question of Quebec's financial support of ACFO would become even more of a sore point as the decade wore on.

The same month, May, 1971, Davis set up a committee of six bilingual MPPs chaired by Tourism and Information Minister Fern Guindon to advise him on policy affecting French-speaking Ontarians. Guindon expressed the view that many Ontarians felt, and still do, that "it is not easy to implement bilingualism on the one hand in Ontario when you hear of people advocating unilingualism in Quebec. It makes our job extremely difficult."

In a major policy statement to the legislature, vetted first by the committee, Davis said he didn't oppose Ottawa's system of bilingual districts but felt they were impractical for Ontario's bilingual program. He promised to continue, without giving a time limit, a program to implement bilingual services in the lower courts in areas with significant French-speaking populations and said more documents would be made available in French as well. Trying to avoid the problems Pierre Trudeau had by force-feeding federal bureaucrats with his bilingual programs, he assured civil servants, "The future entry or promotion of unilingual persons into the Ontario public service will not be affected by our policy on bilingualism." Under a program begun by Robarts, about two thousand civil servants had received French-language instruction since 1968, the same year French was legally recognized as a language of the provincial legislature.

Davis's plan was essentially to set up a bilingual district where 10 per cent or more of the population was French-speaking. He promised bilingual birth certificates, driver's licences and instruction manuals, hospital insurance certificates, and other official documents. In addition, he said the Highway Traffic Act would be changed to permit municipal traffic signs in both languages, and subpoenas and summonses would be affixed with an information sticker containing the "essential details" in French.

Going into the 1971 constitutional conference in Victoria, Davis, speaking in Montreal, said he would not allow Quebec to be "isolated without friend or ally" at the meeting, then got swept away by the omnipotence of his bilingual policies when he said critics who "belittle the accomplishments and/or demean the effort . . . I consider such voices as spokesmen for an irreconcilable minority — the bigots on the one side, the fanatics on the other — to each of whom the attempt to co-operate is offensive and the success of it would be disastrous." Davis, typically, would not name names, nor did he ever say anything that strong about his critics while speaking in Ontario.

Relations were running so smoothly between the two provinces then that despite Bourassa's initial acceptance but final rejection of the Victoria Charter, Davis met him again in Montreal in July, 1972, at Man and His World, where the two leaders were seen quietly sipping champagne on the back porch of the elegant Hélène de Champlain restaurant. The two had been discussing strategy on getting Ottawa to give the provinces more money in direct transfers, and Bourassa described the meeting as having reached an "entente cordiale," which they were celebrating with champagne after a good meal.

After Trudeau barely won the 1972 federal election, beating Bob Stanfield by two seats but losing everywhere except Quebec, Davis was again playing his national statesman role, saying, "The vote pattern in Ontario was not, and I emphasize was not, dictated by any backlash or anti-Quebec feeling, and I want to make that categorical."

This is instructive for two reasons: First, Trudeau did win thirty-six Ontario seats, only four fewer than Stanfield; second, it demonstrates that the predominant mood of the 1970s was to measure everything that happened against Quebec, whether it had anything to do with Quebec or not. But once again, Davis

was commenting after a meeting with Bourassa. He was beginning to wear a path between Toronto and Montreal.

*   *   *

In 1973 Cornwall became the next Sturgeon Falls when 750 high
school students went on strike on March 14 to back demands
for an autonomous French high school. The principal of Cornwall's St. Lawrence High School, Jeanine Séguin, became head
of ACFO and was active years later in a similar dispute in Penetang.
As a result of the Cornwall fracas, Davis introduced legislation
guaranteeing franco-Ontarian students across the province the
right to an education in the language of their choice and setting
up the Languages of Instruction Commission. Ironically, the
Cornwall MPP was Fern Guindon, chairman of Davis's bilingualism committee.

The Stormont, Dundas and Glengarry Board of Education had
rejected the students' demands but agreed to a French school
beginning in 1974. That wasn't enough, however, so the province again dispatched Tom Symons to the rescue. At that time
Symons had other problems to contend with when the provincial auditor wanted to know why he had chalked up $3,200 in
cab bills while investigating the Sturgeon Falls dispute. Symons,
who became known as "Taxicab Tom" for a time, created such
embarrassment for Davis that the premier rose in the legislature
to defend him, saying there was a problem with the auditor's
terminology. It wasn't really a cab Symons used to zip about
the countryside in, one of those things "with a meter"; it was
simply a "rental arrangement." Alas, the non-taxi belonged to
Capital Taxi of Peterborough, a company owned by former Tory
MPP Keith Brown.

In November, 1973, having apparently solved all the bilingualism problems, Davis announced plans for trilingual high
schools, saying school boards could authorize the teaching of a
third language in the senior high school grades if there was enough
local demand. Speaking to the Second Ukrainian World Con-
gress at the time, he said it was a move "to encourage the preser-
vation and development of this province's multicultural heritage."

*   *   *

In 1974 County Court Judge John Matheson bent a provincial statute and allowed a French-speaking Ottawa woman to give evidence in French in an uncontested divorce case. It was almost three years since Davis had promised to allow French-language court cases, but Section 127 of the Judicature Act of Ontario still stated that all court proceedings must be conducted in English. An Ottawa Liberal MPP called it "idiocy" to pay to make many judges functional in French, then bar them from using the language.

Two days later, with a by-election approaching after Guindon's retirement, Davis met with ACFO president Omer Deslauriers,* a former Ottawa high school principal who was then superintendent of French programming for the Ontario Educational Communications Authority. Davis agreed to reinstate four employees of the province's translation bureau and promised to consider expanding it, even though demand for the eighteen-member, $300,000 bureau had dropped 45 per cent. The Tories lost the by-election, but in May, 1975, Deslauriers was named full-time chairman of the government-sponsored Advisory Council of Franco-Ontarian Affairs.

During the 1975 provincial election campaign, all three parties made an all-out effort to entice the franco-Ontarian vote with pamphlets and radio and newspaper advertisements in French and several bilingual candidates. And ACFO was busy getting political reaction to its demands for a French-only university, a French educational television network, and a call to make all government forms and publications available in both languages.

Le Droit, Ontario's only French-language daily newspaper, was not impressed with Davis's record, and in a pre-election editorial said he had promised many bilingual services, but while "the undertaking was formal, the results have been long in coming." The Tories countered with a message from Social Services Minister René Brunelle, saying the province had four thousand bilingual civil servants — out of seventy thousand — and had given $4.1 million in grants to post-secondary institutions for French-language programs. Also, bilingual enumeration forms, poll notices, and election manuals were available for the first time in ridings with significant French-speaking populations.

---

* Later a losing Tory candidate, then Ontario's agent general in Brussels.

(*above*) Queen's Park, Toronto.

(*left*) "Past, Present, Future." Davis with Tom Kennedy (*centre*) and Leslie Frost.

(*below*) Covering the massive riding of Peel by airplane in his first election, 1959.

(*above*) Popping up at schools all over the province as minister of education.

On the campaign trail.

Offering himself as ''A New Wave'' in the 1971 leadership campaign.

The final-ballot result is heard by the Lawrence (*above*) and Davis (*below*) cheering sections.

CANAPRESS

Campaigning in Brampton (*left*), the North (*above*) and in an ethnic neighborhood (*below left*).

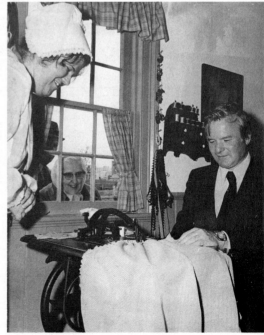

At Black Creek Pioneer Village.

(*above*) With Clare Westcott (*left*), Darcy McKeough, and the Krauss-Maffai elevated transit vehicle in Munich, 1972.

(*left*) The pro at ease with his audience.

With Helen Anderson (''Miss A'') and John Robarts.

In the legislature after the 1983 Grey Cup game.

(*left to right*)
Eddie Goodman
Hugh Macaulay
Hugh Segal

Ed Stewart
Clare Westcott

John Tory
Norman Atkins

With premiers Lougheed, Lévesque, Hatfield, Campbell, Moores, and Buchanan at the 1978 Grey Cup game in Toronto.

At the 1979 conference on the Constitution.

Watching the Queen, Trudeau, and federal Liberal ministers signing the new Constitution.

With Mila and Brian Mulroney on the Davis tribute night at the leadership convention.

Passing the leadership of the Tory Dynasty to Frank Miller, January 26, 1985.

Leaving the legislature for the last time as premier.

But election forms weren't enough. Prescott and Russell NDP candidate Raymond Desrochers, who had no chance of winning, managed to drum up some publicity for himself by refusing to buy his car registration stickers because the forms were only in English. During a post-election cabinet meeting in Welland, local ACFO director Jean-Jacques Fleury told Davis there was a crisis because eight people, including a Timmins bishop, had already spent a day in jail for boycotting English-only forms, and four more were going in that weekend. "Is the government waiting until thousands of francophones are behind bars before it takes some action?" cried Fleury. "The time has passed for pretty speeches. It is time for action."

ACFO's activities were obviously having some effect because after failing for the third time to become premier, Bob Nixon quit as Liberal leader, and three of the major contenders for the job — Stuart Smith, David Peterson, and Albert Roy — endorsed official bilingualism for Ontario, a position the party later softened. The fourth candidate, however, MP Mark MacGuigan, called a press conference in Sudbury to attack the notion of expanding French-language services in Ontario. He said he wasn't demanding a "purge" of existing services, but any further concessions would make the government vulnerable to "continually escalating demands. . . . Where do you stop? What about insurance contracts?" Yes, this was the same Mark MacGuigan who as federal justice minister a few years later attacked Davis for not making Ontario officially bilingual, took Manitoba to court for fighting bilingualism, and when running badly for the federal leadership, promised more bilingual services. He is now a judge.

Davis, in a 1976 speech to about one hundred YPCs, said he supported federal "constitutional recognition of both English and French"; supporting bilingualism was "the price we have to pay to keep Quebec in Confederation . . . [it is a] moral imperative in a free and pluralistic society." He referred to an incident at Maple Leaf Gardens, when some rude fans booed the bilingual announcer when he spoke French, adding, "Anti-French and anti-federal government feeling is running high, they say . . . there are votes to be won by being a little less co-operative," but he had "no interest in playing that type of politics on this type of issue."

He also again condemned bilingual critics — most of whom were francophones complaining he hadn't delivered on his promises—but did not mention Bill 22, Bourassa's highly publicized anti-English bill, a forerunner to Lévesque's French-only Bill 101, which was widely perceived in Ontario to be an attempt by Quebec to make English there a four-letter word. Again, this was a typical political response to the bilingualism issue, viewing it through a one-way mirror and dismissing all critics as bigots, something Davis bragged he never resorted to.

In October, 1976, an Ontario government task force on health reported that there was a terrible shortage of French-speaking doctors—there were only 505, and the report suggested the province needed at least another 319 — and that in some hospitals patients had to either learn English or rely on kitchen staff to act as interpreters. The task force accused the health ministry of acting under a "bilingualism façade" and said the "French fact is almost totally ignored," despite the 1971 and 1972 assurances from Davis. It concluded that the lack of progress "leads us to believe that [the government] fears the so-called English backlash." The fluently bilingual health minister, Frank Miller, promised to study its 130 recommendations.

This bubbling bilingual volcano finally erupted on November 15, 1976, when Lévesque led his separatists to a smashing win over Bourassa's Liberals. Davis said the win "does not constitute a defeat for Canada. . . . It is a time for calm and commitment to tolerance and understanding." The results gave both "cause to ponder . . . and cause for continued optimism and faith. . . . There is no gain to be made from promoting isolation. The Ontario position is simple. No province is our enemy." He also announced a speaking tour to promote national unity and said he intended "to seek normal relations" with Quebec and "pursue the national interest in that fashion."

The *Toronto Star* got so carried away with the election that it ran an absurd front-page editorial calling for a new coalition government to save Canada, but in a speech on November 29 provoked by the editorial Davis said, "For any newspaper or politician to be running about the countryside in sackcloth and ashes is for that newspaper or politician to proclaim their own insecurity about Canada and Canadians."

In this heavenly spirit of calm, reason, and co-operation, Davis blasted federal bilingualism programs during an angry exchange with provincial Liberals on December 15, blaming them for many of the French-English problems splitting the country. Davis said his own program "is working, it is not causing controversy, and if [the federal Liberals] had taken a somewhat different approach to bilingualism, there would be fewer issues existing in this country today. That's right."

Davis, who always loved to set up commissions and committees, couldn't resist the temptation here, and on January 14, 1977, he announced the formation of a special cabinet committee to develop Ontario policy concerning the prospect of Quebec separation. The seven senior ministers — Darcy McKeough, Roy McMurtry, Frank Miller, René Brunelle, Tom Wells, Bob Welch, and Davis as chairman — would be advised by another group of outsiders led by that perennial favorite, York University president H. Ian Macdonald.

After that Davis left town for a trade mission to Israel, and within minutes of landing at Ben-Gurion Airport near Tel Aviv, local reporters were grilling him about the Quebec situation; Jewish businessmen were concerned about what they called the "uncertain business climate" there. An Israeli official said they were concerned about the welfare of the Jewish minority in Montreal. "We're worried about what could happen to them in a separated state. Some of them aren't only concerned, they're panicky, and I don't blame them. Naturally, these concerns get translated back to Israel through family, friends, and business associates. . . ." He added there was also fear that some separatists viewed themselves as an emerging nation and as a result could be sympathetic to such groups as the PLO. Davis, as was his custom, simply skirted around the issue.

He returned from Israel to find yet another French-English high school dispute, this time in Essex, near Windsor. Newspapers were filled with reports of anti-French pamphlets being distributed there carrying such messages as, "What will they demand next: independent city-states? We must stamp out the subversive element which uses history to justify its freeloading on the taxpayers of Canada now." As often happened, the pamphlets were widely publicized; less well publicized was the discovery, well after the controversy died, that radical francophone activists had distributed them.

Lévesque and Trudeau were having a dispute of their own at the time. Davis told the Toronto Junior Board of Trade on February 1 that Trudeau had shown "immaturity" in his harsh reaction to a speech given by Lévesque to some New York investors a week earlier and that "the future of this country lies in the capacity of premiers and prime ministers to talk to one another, not yell at one another." Trudeau, outraged at Lévesque's insistence that Quebecers favored separatism, had challenged him to have an immediate referendum on it. When told of the Davis attack, Trudeau shrugged and said, "I hope for his sake [the unity debate] doesn't become a clash of personalities."

Two days later Davis said Ontario had to take charge from Ottawa as leader of the national debate to keep Quebec in Canada. Approaching an election of his own, he said Ottawa's relations were "clogged with by-elections and personality clashes" and that Ontario must not shrink from its "duty . . . by either emotionalism or pressure." Davis, having just returned from his friendly meeting with Lévesque, was feeling pretty chipper about things. He told twelve hundred YPCs in London he was "a clear and committed foe" of separatism, but Quebec was still part of Canada, "and irrespective of our disagreement with its long-term goals, it remains a member of our family and deserves the respect and civility others in our family receive."

Liberal Leader Stuart Smith, bilingual and Quebec-born, said Davis should "reject" Lévesque. "He is completely wrong when he goes to Quebec and acts in a friendly way towards Lévesque and says that Ontario and Quebec will always be closely linked, no matter what happens. He is only strengthening Premier Lévesque's hand." Many Ontario Tories agreed, although privately.

By this time the Essex school dispute had escalated from a local issue to a national one, widely reported in Quebec, usually as a struggle for French-language education rather than a fight for a separate building. It was also causing headaches at Queen's Park because while the three party leaders supported the francophone activists, each of their locally nominated candidates opposed building the school.

In Ottawa Marc Lalonde (then health minister) accused Davis of "trying to pull the wool over the Canadian people's eyes [by] pretending" franco-Ontarians had the same rights as Quebec anglos. He said even Bill 22, although Ottawa opposed it, "is

more generous than anything you will find in any other province
with regard to francophone minorities." Earlier that week Lalonde
had told the Canadian Institute on Public Affairs that Ontario
was only paying lip-service to bilingualism. Davis accused him
of "hatchet work." Things were heating up.

H. Ian Macdonald suddenly announced that what the country really needed was a unity conference, and Davis, hardly surprised by the call, said it was worth thinking about. Four days
later he announced that Canadians "from all walks of life" would
be invited to a June unity bash at York University for "an opportunity for people-to-people communication."

In the midst of all this breast beating the *Globe* reported that,
as everyone suspected, Davis had commissioned a secret, $60,000
opinion poll on the issue involving a forty-five-page, in-home
survey. "It has confirmed that Ontario people have a very positive set of attitudes," remarked Ed Stewart. "It may shape attitudes of the cabinet to some extent. It may change attitudes."

Specifics of the publicly funded poll were never released, but
it was reported that a 3–1 majority wanted Canada to remain
intact; a slight majority felt there was a good chance Quebec
would separate within ten years; an overwhelming majority, about
9–1, felt Lévesque's win showed dissatisfaction with Bourassa,
not enchantment with separatism; most thought Quebec would
suffer without Canada and Ontario would be worse off without
Quebec; and most felt French should be taught in schools to
promote national unity. The majority, however, did not favor
making all Ontario road signs bilingual.

There was certainly popular support for a unity crusade, but
donning the mantle was made a little more difficult when some
local councils, London and Burlington in particular, ran advertisements in Montreal newspapers promoting themselves as prime
locations for disgruntled Quebec industrialists. Between the election and the end of 1977, 118 federally incorporated companies
had moved their head offices from Quebec, fifty to Toronto,
twenty-five to Calgary, and thirteen to Ottawa. Davis sent a letter to all Ontario municipalities with a population over ten thousand, saying, "There regrettably appears to be a climate of
uncertainty in the [Quebec] business community. To take deliberate advantage of this situation can only hurt Canada in both
the short and long term."

He also moved in March to end some other bad press in Quebec. Education Minister Tom Wells told Essex school trustees he'd give them $4.8 million for the French school and up the provincial share to 95 per cent, compared to 75 per cent for English school buildings, and if the board still said no — it did, 12–5 — he'd have it built anyway. Davis suffered further embarrassment on April 26 when his bill to override local autonomy and force the school got bogged down in legislative wrangling and time expired before MPPs had a chance to vote on it. Davis eventually pushed it through, but he had wanted time for the issue to cool before the August, 1977, premiers' conference in St. Andrews, New Brunswick, where Lévesque planned to make minority-language education the main topic.

That March Quebec also opened the battle with Ontario on a new front, claiming Ontario was the main recipient of $4.3 billion "siphoned out" of Quebec between 1961 and 1973. That was the amount Ottawa supposedly received from Quebec taxpayers over and above what Quebec received back in federal transfers. A month later Davis responded with his own study showing Quebec had profited from Confederation, while Ontario had paid $26 billion more for redistribution to other provinces than it had received in transfer payments since 1961. Using Statistics Canada figures, Davis said the average subsidy from tariffs per job in manufacturing was $836 in Ontario, below the national average of $932 and well below Quebec's $1,111. Rather than losing money from Confederation, Davis said, Quebec had gained over $6 billion.

But the focus of debate soon shifted back from economics to language. Quebec's white paper on language, issued by Cultural Minister Camille Laurin on April 1, suggested, "Bilingualism will be replaced by a new state of affairs in which Quebec will be as French as Ontario is English," reflecting the still widely held belief in Quebec that Ontario offered few, if any, bilingual services. Laurin reinforced that view with a speech in Chicoutimi that month accusing Davis of defending the "privileges" and economic dominance of Quebec's English-speaking minority. Laurin said it was "impossible" for franco-Ontarians to study French past Grade 10, a charge that wasn't true but was widely reported in Quebec.

Once again Davis headed off for a national unity speech, this time to the Montreal Canadian Club. When he returned, he challenged Trudeau to take Quebec's proposed language charter to court, particularly the section restricting access to English schools for people moving into Quebec.

By this time Attorney General Roy McMurtry had opened bilingual courts in Sudbury, Ottawa, and L'Orignal, but any benefit was lost in negative publicity over a demand for a French-language trial from Gérard Filion, a prominent Quebec businessman who was among twelve people and ten companies charged in connection with dredging contracts in Hamilton and the Quebec towns of Beauport and Ile d'Orléans. McMurtry was pilloried in Quebec for refusing a trial in French, even though the demand from the bilingual Filion wasn't made until two years after charges were laid and several months after a thirteen-month, English-language preliminary hearing. McMurtry, calling the case one of the most complex in Canadian legal history, said he couldn't provide simultaneous translation services when it simply wasn't necessary. Criticism grew so pointed, however, that McMurtry went to Montreal the following July to explain his side to the media.

For his part, Davis was still trying to find a comfortable stance. On April 18, during a heated throne speech debate, Davis accused the NDP of being soft on separatism. NDP Leader Stephen Lewis said, "I can't credit it. It's not worthy of him." Three weeks later Tory cabinet minister Margaret Scrivener repeated the charge in an election speech, but Davis sharply rebuked her and warned his ministers not to exploit the Quebec situation in a partisan way. Davis appeared upset, but Scrivener's speech had been vetted by his office, distributed to the press gallery in advance from there, and he was at the event when she spoke.

What remained of the historical *bonne entente* between Queen's Park and Lévesque's bunker on the Grande Allée was shattered on April 21 when Davis told the Empire Club that under no circumstances would Ontario enter into an economic union with an independent Quebec. A public opinion poll in Quebec had shown that support for separatism there was tied to the province's ability to reach economic association with the rest of Canada. Davis said Quebec was "foolhardy" to expect such a deal. "As soon as doors are closed, debates are ended and discussions are terminated."

Undaunted, Quebec Intergovernmental Affairs Minister Claude

Morin opened a trade office in Toronto on May 6, telling a blue-ribbon audience of four hundred business and political leaders that "whatever happens, Quebec and Ontario will always be close together" because despite political differences, about $5 billion worth of Ontario manufactured goods were being sold in Quebec and Quebec products worth about $4.5 billion were being marketed in Ontario.

The same month Davis promised to hire a health co-ordinator for francophones and a few days later, flanked by Canadian flags at a campaign stop in London, told a thousand supporters that the "best and most able" Canadians should be brought together to work at saving Canada. He said the unity debate couldn't wait until after the Quebec referendum but "must go on now." At the end of the month he delivered four sentences of a speech in French in Kapuskasing, a town of 12,500 people, about 60 per cent of whom are French-speaking. The partisan crown applauded his efforts.

These gestures were by way of a buildup to late June, when 450 delegates gathered at York University for "Destiny Canada," a four-day, $250,000, whither-Canada extravaganza that included, as guests, Morin and Claude Ryan.

In July Ottawa launched its own unity road show, a task force co-chaired by John Robarts and Jean-Luc Pépin. In his first Commons speech in eight months Trudeau emphasized that English Canada must show more tolerance for the French language if Canada were to remain intact. NDP leader Ed Broadbent replied, "For God's sake, I wish the prime minister would get over his illusion that the Official Languages Act is a source of unity. . . . It is not. Whatever else might be said about the policy, it sure hasn't headed off the forces of separatism."

Trudeau wasn't the only federal Liberal given to lecturing. Davis and Supply Minister Jean-Pierre Goyer got into a bitter dispute over a decision by Davis to reject a low bid from MLW-Bombardier of Montreal for a $40 million streetcar contract, giving it instead to Hawker Siddeley Canada Ltd. of Thunder Bay. Goyer said it was "playing right into the hands of separatists." Davis said the decision had nothing to do with national unity but was made because of high unemployment in Northern Ontario.

He then got ready to meet the other premiers in St. Andrews.

Just before the conference Lévesque offered to sign reciprocal agreements with any province guaranteeing access to minority-language education. On the day Davis left for New Brunswick Tom Wells magically found $600,000 to subsidize French instruction in private schools.

Lévesque made his treaty offer, but Davis said franco-Ontarians were "unalterably opposed" to having their fate tied to "an agreement between two provinces . . . [when] the stated policy of one of those provinces is to separate from the rest of Canada." Lévesque left in a huff, but the nine remaining premiers signed a pact to "make their best effort" to provide bilingual school programs. Quebec newspapers gave front-page play to the refusal of the premiers to bargain with Lévesque, with *Le Devoir* the only major French-language paper to treat the alternative proposal seriously. And again, Essex was cited by Quebec officials as evidence of anglo bigotry and was widely reported as such. The fact that 100,000 franco-Ontarian students were learning in French-language classrooms was barely mentioned.

Not all franco-Ontarians were "unalterably opposed" to deals with Quebec. At an ACFO rally in Cornwall a working paper, "Un Nouveau Départ" (A New Beginning) urged more militancy, saying they'd been getting nothing but platitudes from Davis, and blamed franco-Ontarians for being apathetic to the issue. ACFO president Richler said they were "going to present a more militant and visible force" in Ontario, demanding language and religious rights. The group was still receiving financial support from the Quebec government, but during some of the French school fights, especially Essex and Penetang, Quebec was accused of sending not only money but also agitators to stir things up.

Denis Massicotte, a Quebec-born former broadcast journalist who worked for Tom Wells as intergovernmental affairs minister, then spent two years as Davis's press secretary at the height of the Quebec referendum and Penetang dispute, recalls, "There was a lot of ACFO activity against us. Those sons of bitches took advantage of the Quebec referendum to dump on Ontario and jump in bed with the PQ. ACFO's activities gave more weight to PQ accusations against us because they were saying we didn't care about franco-Ontarians. It was one of the most disgusting episodes in the history of French-English relations in Ontario. ACFO was giving news conferences with the St. Jean Baptiste Soci-

ety, which is as PQ as they come, denouncing the Ontario government, and some of their members even said, for the good of
the franco-Ontarians, Quebecers should vote 'Yes' [for separa-
tism]. They thought it would force realignment of priorities in
Canada if Quebec had a mandate to negotiate a new Canada.
They thought it would force English governments in Canada to
recognize the French fact in their own provinces. They just enjoy
making trouble."

Wells says he didn't think there was "much" separatist agita-
tion sponsored by the Parti Québécois during some of the school
disputes, "although there were some isolated incidents of offers
of help, if not from the PQ directly then certainly from separatists outside, and ACFO may have wrongly taken it, although I
don't have any documentation on that."

In September Davis said he would go to Quebec "to make the
case for Canada," despite any restrictions Lévesque tried to impose
during the referendum battle. A Southam Press national survey,
asking if people saw any political figures standing up for federalism, showed Trudeau first at 57 per cent, Diefenbaker second
at 17, and then Davis at 13, one ahead of Joe Clark. When people
were asked to name premiers who were fighting for unity,
52 per cent chose Davis first, with Peter Lougheed second at
11.4 per cent. Inside Quebec 6 per cent chose Davis.

In his brief to the Robarts-Pépin task force that November,
Davis said "different arrangements for various provinces within
Confederation" might help, adding that special relationships with
Ottawa should not create "barriers to mobility and development
across Canada." The next day ACFO said Ontario was "scoffing
at the future of the French fact," and if Davis were really concerned, "he would make French the other official language. . . ."

But he had no plans to do that. In February, 1978, Davis said
in Toronto he'd leave "self-serving proclamations of bilingualism to our federal friends. . . . Ontario has chosen moderation,
careful progress, and practical programming. . . . My government is not about to repeat the precise errors [of Trudeau's bilingual policies], errors this country is still paying for in more ways
than one."

Davis arrived in Quebec City on February 12 for a "goodwill"
visit, only to be booed by a large crowd at the Winter Carnival
after being introduced in French but speaking in English. A few

months later, when some fans at a Toronto Blue Jays baseball game booed a singer for singing part of the national anthem in French, it became a national incident, with cries of outrage from Trudeau, Lévesque, and Davis. Yet Davis's reception in Quebec wasn't even reported in most newspapers there and was deliberately ignored by many Ontario papers concerned about national unity.

In a Montreal speech a few days later Davis said he feared a political backlash if he made Ontario officially bilingual. "Symbols are important," he said. "But our symbol, our gesture of good faith and commitment, must be progress and performance." During that visit he tried to get across what that performance was by holding a series of private press briefings in his hotel suite with a steady stream of Quebec print and broadcast journalists, hoping to at least have his side of the argument reported there.

During the February throne speech plans were announced to translate Ontario laws and offer French-language jury trials, beginning in areas where lower courts were already bilingual, and McMurtry said amendments to the Juries Act and Judicature Act would give French a "legal basis."

Meeting in Montreal a few days later on language rights, the ten premiers adopted a strong stand to provide bilingual services, but it was left up to each province to determine how it would apply those rights and services. Davis called it "a step forward" when many provinces with no policies agreed at least in principle to minority-language education.

To prepare for that meeting the Council of Ministers of Education had written a report on the status of French-language education. "We presented it to the premiers," says Wells, "and Lévesque leafed through it, looked at Davis, and said, 'Well, this says practically everybody who is a francophone in Ontario is getting a French-language education.' So Davis said, 'That's what we've always told you,' and Lévesque replied, 'I know, but I didn't believe that.' He believed all those fights were not over schools, but over the denial of rights for French-language education! If he didn't know, how could we expect the people of Quebec to know?"

Maybe it sunk in a little bit, because in April Lévesque took an entirely new tack. He announced that beginning July 1, Quebec would not permit Ontario construction workers to work in

Quebec unless they had a thousand hours in the trade there. It didn't mean much because at the time about fifteen thousand Quebec construction workers were employed in Ontario, mainly in Ottawa and Cornwall, while only five hundred Ontarians worked in Quebec construction. The two leaders discussed the dispute on May 22, when Lévesque came to Queen's Park, but neither backed down. Lévesque said he was carrying on with his legislation, and Davis said he'd retaliate with a similar bill if he did.

Sally Barnes, Davis's press secretary then, says he was "incredibly uncomfortable around Lévesque. The prospects of separation really upset him. When he gets on the topic, he talks about his children and grandchildren being able to go to Quebec as part of Canada. After their meeting the two of them were waiting for their communiqué. They were standing there, not knowing what to say to each other. All the reporters were waiting outside, probably figuring the two premiers were holding heavy-duty discussions, when in fact they weren't even talking. It was embarrassing. I went over and started a conversation by asking about Lévesque's Wallabees. . . . At least it gave them something to talk about."

In July four Ontario construction workers were duly ordered off a work site in Gatineau. Davis said he wanted Trudeau to test the Quebec law in court, but when no action was taken, Labor Minister Bob Elgie brought in a similiar law on October 31, designating certain areas around Ottawa and Cornwall where Ontario workers would be given preference over non-resident construction workers.

Meanwhile a major furor over bilingualism began quietly on May 17, when Ottawa Liberal MPP Albert Roy introduced a private member's bill to guarantee certain French rights, falling just short of bilingualism. Roy's bill, adopted as official Ontario Liberal policy, would have set up a language service board to recommend areas requiring more bilingual services, provincially and/or municipally, and to suggest the extent to which French services should be provided in non-designated areas. The bill got off to a slow start when Roy declined to have it translated into French, complaining that the translation by the government bureau was literal and would mangle many of the intents of the bill. Still, it passed first reading and was set for debate June 1.

Then, in a statement minutes before the debate was to begin, Davis announced it would not be called for third reading, saying the decision was based on the "firm conviction that we have already in place a course of action that is consistent with the sentiments of the Ontario people and, equally important, the needs of our francophone citizens at this time."

The opposition was outraged. NDP Leader Cassidy accused Davis of acting with "arrogant disrespect" and moved adjournment of the evening session as a protest gesture. The motion paralysed the legislature for ninety minutes as the bells were rung calling members to a vote. When it came, however, the Liberals joined the minority Tories to defeat Cassidy's motion.

Francophone leaders across the province expressed anger, dismay, and disappointment, and Trudeau said he was "naturally disappointed that Premier Davis does not realize how damaging that can be to the rest of the country even from a symbolic point of view." In the lead editorial in *Le Devoir* journalist Michel Roy wrote, "What Mr. Davis said and did last week in Toronto is nothing less than an insult to Ontario's francophones." A week later French high school students in Toronto and Ottawa left their classes and staged a protest. The Union for the Defence of Franco-Ontarian Rights bought a full-page ad in the *Globe* to protest what they called "repeated insults and denials of justice since the cruel imposition of Regulation 17 by the Ontario government over sixty years ago."

Davis, striking back, told the Calgary Chamber of Commerce in July that the millions of dollars Trudeau had spent on his bilingualism program would have been much better spent and would have created less divisiveness had it been used to teach both official languages in the schools rather than to middle-aged civil servants.

At the same time Lévesque hosted about two hundred French-speaking people from other provinces and the U.S. for a three-day festival. He announced a $261,000 donation to help French-Canadians outside Quebec fight for French rights, the first instalment of a $500,000 budget for the year. Among the guests were twenty-five journalists from French-language publications, some from Ontario, whose expenses were all paid by Lévesque.

In late July McMurtry announced the expansion of French-language services in provincial court, family division, in Ottawa, and said criminal court bilingual services were now available in Ottawa, Sudbury, Prescott-Russell, Cochrane, Hearst, Horne-payne, Kapuskasing, and Smooth Rock Falls. He also promised to spend about $1.9 million to provide French versions of more than 150 of Ontario's 700 revised statutes over the next four years.

It all came to a head in November, when Lévesque published his white paper on sovereignty-association. Davis, delivering a scathing attack on it in the legislature, said Ontario would never negotiate it with Quebec because the concept was ". . . the most facile response, what some would call the ultimate cop-out, a self-imposed ghetto mentality, surely beneath the dignity of the French-Canadian people."

Unfortunately once again, Davis had a French high school dispute on his hands, this one in Penetanguishene, perfect timing for Lévesque's propaganda purposes. Two days after Davis attacked the white paper, Lévesque, referring scornfully to Davis in the Quebec National Assembly as "the minority premier of Ontario," said Davis was "in a panic" because of what Ontario would lose if Quebec pulled out of Canada and that he was hardly in a position to talk about a ghetto mentality when he was "a man whose government has just refused a school — a mere school — in Penetanguishene for the franco-Ontarian minority there. These are excessive words, essentially the kind of excessive language used by those who are in a panic."

Davis had said no to the school because of provincial budget restraints and declining enrolment in Penetang. The school board did offer to set up a French school within the existing high school, but French-speaking parents rejected it, saying that would not prevent their children from losing their ability in French. In May, 1979, Education Minister Bette Stephenson rejected enforced building of a French school — the Essex solution — saying a compromise could be worked out. At one point a group of students took over an abandoned post office building and set up their own French school to call attention to their demands. The government offered to erect a school on the grounds of an existing French elementary school, but the French Language Advisory Committee turned that down, too. The dispute dragged on and wasn't resolved until late April, 1980, three weeks before the Quebec referendum, providing a constant reference point for separa-

tists, supposedly showing how franco-Ontarians were being unfairly treated. The solution was to establish separate French classrooms in semi-permanent structures on the grounds of the English
high school, with a separate French-speaking staff and administration.

When the announcement was made Stephenson claimed, apparently seriously, that the timing had nothing to do with the referendum. She had said all along that unlike the other disputed school
sites, there weren't enough students to justify it. The Penetang
settlement, front-page news in Quebec for months, rated a four-
paragraph Canadian Press story on page two of *La Presse*. Other
Quebec papers didn't even report it.

When Lévesque released his white paper and announced the
referendum date, Massicotte was sent to the Quebec National
Assembly by Wells and Davis. "At that time it became obvious
that Ontario was a major participant in the campaign," he says,
"by virtue of the fact that the PQ decided we were a great target. All the ills of Confederation from before 1867 to today could
be blamed on Ontario, they said. In all the speeches by PQ members Ontario was a target for bigotry for Regulation 17 and for
all the other perceived grievances over the schools. We were clearly
the bad guys. And they also knew, if you attack Ontario, you get
great coverage and great sympathy out West as well, so Intergovernmental Affairs put a lot of pressure on the premier, who
had been willing to go to Quebec from the start if he thought it
would be useful."

As Lévesque and Liberal Leader Claude Ryan gathered their
armies for the referendum battle, Ryan made it clear he was issu-
ing a plan of his own for a "renewed federalism," and it was vital
that Davis and other leading English politicians accept it. Ryan's
officials were in constant touch with Wells and his officials, and
Wells even made a trip to Montreal to meet privately with several leading business people, academics, and political figures to
see what Ontario could do to help.

"Ryan really wanted us to do everything possible that we
could," says Wells. "He certainly wanted us to reply positively
to that beige paper he put out, and he got a positive response,
although we had some concerns. I recall Claude Forget, a former cabinet minister in Bourassa's government, and Claude
Castonguay, a former minister, visiting me in Toronto and phon-

ing me regularly. They were very persistent that we deliver a positive response. . . ."

Davis and Ryan met in Montreal on December 18 but had little to say after the hour-long meeting. But while they were meeting in one room at the Montreal Airport Hilton Hotel, Hugh Segal and Ryan's executive assistant, Pierre Pettigrew, met in another to discuss strategy. Ryan gave Davis an outline of what his January proposals would be, while Segal assured Pettigrew that Davis would respond positively to them.

When the proposals were released, Davis was holidaying in Florida, but Wells, as promised, supported them in public, even though Ryan's renewed federalism would have given Quebec a virtual perpetual veto and would have emasculated the federal government — the antithesis of Davis's consistent support for a strong central government — by giving the provinces powers over immigration and unemployment insurance programs.

In April, a month before the referendum, Ryan said publicly that the federalist forces could use the help of provincial premiers, particularly Davis and Lougheed. He said he wasn't in a position to ask them, but "it would be wonderful" if they came. He also said he guessed Davis was considering taking an active role in the debate. By that time, of course, the deal had already been struck between the two camps, and two days after Ryan's announcement Davis said he would indeed go to Quebec following a special May 5 national unity debate at Queen's Park.

The argument among Ontario officials was not whether Davis should go or not — everyone agreed he should — but how often he should go, where he should go, to whom he should speak, and whether he should stick to English and avoid his horrid French. Massicotte lost the battle there. "I didn't see why we should include a paragraph or two that he would massacre just to say he's sympathetic. He could say 'Bonjour' at the beginning and 'Merci' at the end and have the same effect." Massicotte also wanted Davis to go to places like Chicoutimi, rather than sticking to the anglo ghetto in Montreal. As a compromise, it was decided he would make a two-day trek to Montreal in early May, before the Ontario legislature's unity debate, meet with the editorial board of *La Presse*, hold private talks with the "No" side, speak to the Montreal Board of Trade and several invited French-speaking business people from other organizations, then hold a press conference.

While the Davis troops had the jitters, so did the federalist forces in Quebec, who held a meeting about it on April 20 in Montreal but never did decide whether the trip would help or hinder the cause. Lévesque, of course, was saying a Davis trip would help the separatists because of his record in such places as Penetanguishene.

When Davis finally did arrive, he told Quebecers there was more to unite the two provinces than to separate them and that Ontarians had a "compelling commitment" to Canada's survival. "We have too much to share in the future, too much to build, too much we can do, to turn away from our common destiny now."

In his hotel room before giving the speech, Segal and Massicotte rewrote the French portion several times. Davis "was very nervous about it," says Massicotte. He delivered three pages in French, spelled phonetically for him, "but he kept stumbling over, of all things, 'sovereignty-association.' We even practised it coming down in the elevator. He had it perfectly, but when he came to it in his speech he'd forgotten again, so he screwed it up and used the English pronunciation. But it didn't matter." The speech, to an audience split about fifty-fifty French and English, was well received.

At the press conference Jean-Marie Cossette, a militant member of Quebec's independence movement since the early 1960s, asked Davis, in French, why he had refused Lévesque's offer of a reciprocal arrangement on minority-language education. Massicotte sat with Davis to act as translator if needed, but Davis, who doesn't speak French but can understand it, responded without waiting for a translation, saying he wouldn't make deals with a separatist, thus avoiding what Cossette no doubt hoped would be an embarrassment for Davis.

If it was media coverage they were after, and it was, the trip succeeded. Davis appeared on the front page of most Quebec newspapers and was the lead item on many radio and TV newscasts for the two days of his trip. As for the senior federalist organizers who had worried the trip would boomerang, the *Toronto Star*'s Bob McKenzie wrote, "They needn't have worried. . . .

Davis proved he is a master of the undramatic, the matter-of-fact—the soporific turn of phrase that could make a declaration of war sound like the weather forecast."

Returning home, on the second day of a week-long "showcase" debate on national unity, when all three parties were hoping to portray a common front, the unusual all-party agreement was momentarily shattered when Davis announced he would not approve a separate French school board in Ottawa-Carleton because that would lead to the creation of a third school system. But when the debate ended on May 9, the members unanimously approved a resolution opposing negotiation of sovereignty-association and asking Quebecers to join other Canadians in drawing up a new Constitution. It was one of the few times in Ontario history that all MPPs have ever agreed on anything.

Not everyone liked what they were hearing, however. Quebec journalist, playwright, and actress Patricia Dumas, who moved to Toronto in 1977, says it was "difficult for French-Canadian reporters at Queen's Park during those years not to become raving separatists. . . . I remember when Davis gave his response to Lévesque—that 'ghetto mentality' stuff—it was so insulting, I had to walk for an hour and a half before I could sit down and write a story. To me this wasn't Davis. He was being so petty, so directly insulting. He doesn't do that. He usually circumlocutes around things, so he may be making you mad because he's not answering your questions, but at least he's not hurting your feelings." She maintains that Davis didn't have anyone around him who "had any sensitivity about what was happening in Quebec. Segal was supposed to be the guy, but he didn't answer our phone calls, so I wouldn't know. The French press had access to Don Stevenson [Wells's deputy], but he was much more an adviser to Wells than to Davis. The French press did not have access to Hugh Segal."

Four days before the referendum Davis and Trudeau met privately in Ottawa and agreed to a constitutional conference in July if the federalist forces won the vote. "I think that a sense of urgency, if I can use that phrase, is important," he said, adding that English Canada must not be complacent or assume the constitutional problems would disappear if the federalists won. And on the night of the vote, while the results were still being tabulated, Davis met the press at Queen's Park to pay tribute to "the courage and generosity" of Quebecers. Calling on Trudeau to organize a constitutional conference quickly, he said, "It is now our turn to demonstrate equal faith in Canada with commitment and goodwill."

While Davis sat behind the desk in the studio, surrounded by microphones, Dumas, whose sister Evelyn was a senior adviser to Lévesque, sat on the edge of the platform in front of the desk holding her tape recorder up and sobbing openly. Davis noticed it but didn't comment. "It was a very deeply sad experience for me," she says. "We were watching the results of the referendum with about as much interest as I'd watch a football game. . . . There was a party in the press gallery for something, and people were standing around the TV, laughing and drinking. Every Québécois, being there or not, had to think about it a lot. You were torn between nationalism and wanting to be at home and getting rid of these guys who never liked us anyway, and on the other hand really wanting to be part of this country which French-Canadians adore like everybody else. It was also the end of the Quiet Revolution and the end of so many dreams. People were watching it like it was just another event, and Davis was giving a press conference while Lévesque was on the air. It hurt. It's stupid, maybe. Just totally emotional and illogical, I agree. But I would rather have been in Quebec to cry than to have been in a place where people were saying, 'What's bothering you?' What was bothering me was that everybody knew, and I'm sure Davis knew but would never admit it, that Quebec had lost any kind of political power when they lost that referendum. You have ministers saying Quebec is just a big Newfoundland. It's the end of a long history of collaboration between Ontario and Quebec. That's sort of dead now."

The satisfying glow of victory was dimmed somewhat when Claude Ryan started taking all the bows. Massicotte says Davis took part in the campaign inside Quebec "because Claude Ryan asked him to, in fact almost begged him, and that lying son of a bitch, a day or so after the referendum, he said no, he didn't ask Davis to come."

Wells says that also puzzled him. "He went out of his way to say the premier had been no help. I'm sure the premier was hurt by that. Most of his staff just couldn't believe Ryan would make a statement like that. . . . Had he said nothing, that would be okay, but to go out of his way to say Bill Davis hadn't been any help when his people had spent time asking us to help and we had, well, that really disturbed a lot of people. Surely you can afford to be magnanimous in victory."

Massicotte says the request to Davis was delivered by Forget, a staunch federalist who was in constant touch with Wells. Massicotte also met in Quebec City with Ryan's executive assistant, Pierre Pettigrew, "and he reiterated the request from Ryan for the premier to come." Journalist McKenzie called Massicotte the day after for a reaction to Ryan's shot at Davis. "I called Ryan's office," says Massicotte, "and they told me, 'No, no, Ryan didn't say that.' Then I called McKenzie back, and he played me the tape over the phone. I couldn't believe it. . . . Ryan thought he was king. He was going to settle this and save Quebec like the hand of God. He hated Trudeau and couldn't stand Chrétien for showing up, although Chrétien did a hell of a job. Ryan wanted to do it all himself."

In September, during the third day of the federal-provincial constitutional talks, Davis again refused to back down on his opposition to making French an official language, despite an impassioned plea from Trudeau. Davis said he supported Trudeau on a Bill of Rights but refused to approve "institutionalized bilingualism" in Ontario. He agreed to enshrine language rights in education — Ontario's initial suggestion — but only "where numbers warrant."

Dumas was convinced Davis was going to accept official bilingualism. "Ontario is such a powerful province, it would have changed the whole political game so profoundly. Separatism in Quebec would have had a lot of trouble to carry on after that. After all, the courts here are bilingual, the schools are bilingual, they're starting bilingual services all over the place. . . . There is an openness to French and to people in general that wasn't here when I moved to Toronto [in 1977]. It is a very fair and generous society. Cold and reserved, yes, but fair and generous. When Davis got up around noon that day and said there would never be institutionalized bilingualism, it made me feel personally sick because I knew it was the backroom guys who were there checking the votes for the next by-election or whatever, and they didn't have the vision of the country."

In April, 1981, near the end of the special Commons debate

on the Constitution, Trudeau again called Davis and asked him to accept Section 133 of the BNA Act to institutionalize bilingualism. Davis, a month after regaining his majority in the provincial election, said, "That would not be possible. Winning a majority doesn't change our position."

But despite his intransigence, the pace of expanding bilingual services was maintained. In November, 1981, Roy McMurtry announced French-language services for civil court proceedings would be expanded to another dozen communities in Ontario, meaning that "a broad range of courts . . . from matters under the Highway Traffic Act to divorce proceedings, will be available to 83 per cent of francophones." And the following March Davis announced a provincial plan to allow municipalities to pass by-laws in both official languages. A year later the province decided to drop its numbers requirements—twenty-five elementary and twenty secondary students in a district—and provide French-language education to every French-speaking child in the province. Bette Stephenson said it would add only a thousand students who weren't already receiving French-language instruction under the old rules, anyway. She also announced that a minimum of four francophone trustees would be added to school boards with at least five hundred French-speaking students, or where they totalled 10 per cent of enrolment. But this initiative ran into opposition. It would mean, for example, that the Toronto Board of Education, with twenty-six trustees for 73,000 English-speaking and five hundred French-speaking students, would get four new francophone trustees, giving them 13 per cent of the school board votes for less than 1 per cent of enrolment.

In September, 1983, Trudeau met Davis at Queen's Park, then told a press conference he wanted Davis to announce official bilingualism before the next Quebec provincial election. Davis again said no, adding that "very real progress" had been made under his policy. Asked if he was afraid of a backlash, Davis said, "There would be some reaction."

On October 27, 1983, Roy McMurtry introduced legislation finally making French an official language in Ontario courts. Until then he had provided many bilingual court services, but the only official language under the Courts of Justice Act was English. McMurtry, however, was criticized by some of his own colleagues for having his aides telephone francophone reporters to tell them about the provision, while not telling anglophone reporters, then giving a lengthy statement in the legislature announcing a host of changes but never mentioning the French move. The complicated regulations containing the change did not arrive in the press gallery until the next day.

Even the soft-spoken Wells wasn't impressed. "I don't know why Roy decided to do it that way. I've never done that. I don't believe it has to be done without trying to announce part of it in an attempt to keep it quiet." McMurtry, as was his custom when asked embarrassing questions, simply refused to explain and walked off in a huff.

In December Stephenson told officials of twenty-one school boards that she would back off from her controversial francophone-trustee proposals and set up a committee of provincial and local school officials to study other options. Then in April, 1984, Tom Wells promised legislation guaranteeing French-language social services in the twelve regions of the province where most francophones lived, although it might take a few years because "in some parts of the province there is a shortage of [French-speaking] professionals."

In June, 1984, the Ontario Court of Appeal ruled that some of Ontario's education laws were unconstitutional — the result of a court challenge by some French-speaking teachers and francophone groups in Ontario — but it didn't change anything because the Tories introduced the changes promised earlier guaranteeing every French-speaking child an education in French. Stephenson said she still planned to allow minorities to directly elect trustees, but further consultation was needed first. And on July 1, 1984, she and Secretary of State Serge Joyal announced Ottawa would give Ontario $137 million over the next three years to help pay for French instruction. At the time 96,000 students were enrolled in French-as-a-first-language programs and about 896,000 were learning it as a second language.

Oh yes, on May 23, 1984, shortly before he retired, Trudeau tried once more, in a nine-page letter, to convince Davis to accept official bilingualism. In a six-page reply Davis again said "No."

*   *   *

Hugh Segal, who long favored official bilingualism but could never talk Davis into it, is firmly convinced, "If you were to take a poll in Ontario today, you'd find the majority of Ontarians think bilingualism is not a bad thing. But the minority would be about forty-five per cent, and we'd know them all by name. They'd be the people who come to Conservative meetings, the guys sitting in the legislature on the Conservative side. About sixty-four of the seventy would be part of the forty-five per cent."

Segal says Davis "always resented in a little way all the razzmatazz Robarts got for doing not very much. In the post-coital glow of 1967, taking a bunch of French-language Catholic schools and making them public schools when public dollars were already in them, and taking the press gallery to Quebec City, and the Confederation of Tomorrow Conference — that was it. Yet Robarts became the great savior of Confederation. Billy had to deal with all the Quebec nationalism, with guys like Bourassa and Lévesque who said language rights outside of Quebec didn't matter a shit. And Billy had to deal with Pierre Trudeau . . . [who] did more to destroy goodwill between English and French in this country than anybody else in our history by forcing things on the country nobody could accept. That's the mood Bill had to deal with, and he dealt with it damn well."

Wells agrees that Davis made tremendous advances in French-language services but "gets credit for zilch. . . . As the minister responsible for French-language services, I don't find that people in Ontario are greatly opposed to our policies. Some are, yes. But most Ontarians support it. It's the same as anything. Some people in the party violently object to anything and think Canada should be totally English. There are other people who want to go completely the other way and make it all bilingual . . . in-between the two are vast numbers of people who believe in the moderate view and in our step-by-step approach. . . . They're the ones you don't hear from, but they support what we're doing."

One of the Palace Guard who was "openly opposed" to institutionalizing bilingualism was Eddie Goodman, who said, "What makes it so important that 500,000 or 600,000 get written into the Constitution, which I think would cause more bitterness, more antagonism? It could have ripped our party into pieces. And for what? I never thought it meant a hoot in hell. We've got a policy that has been working, that is protecting all the legitimate needs of the population. Why change it? Sure, it would have made Davis look good in the history books. He would have come out of it a great Canadian in a bunch of people's minds, but it would have done a lot of harm to the province and the party. You don't get a lot of big support for bilingualism among the Italians or the Ukrainians, you know. They don't follow that argument too well. But the real point is, we're doing fine. We're giving these people what they're entitled to and more. Why would we rip out the guts of the Conservative party — although Davis wouldn't put it that way — for nothing?"

Frank Miller, one of the few bilingual cabinet ministers Davis had, said Davis never did what he really wanted to do. "I think Bill Davis, given his druthers, would have made Ontario officially bilingual, but he knows the people aren't prepared for that. If he thought it was salable, he'd do it."

And Denis Massicotte adds that "there is no need for Davis to apologize for anything. The fact is, his government has had the policy, and it has worked well. There was no need for him to change it because things had changed in Quebec. The policy is not for Quebec, it's for Ontario. . . . We have a lot more services in Ontario for our francophones than officially bilingual New Brunswick has."

For Patricia Dumas the Davis approach demonstrates one of the paradoxes "of this anglo government. There is this element of generosity in this part of the country, and there is also this feeling of moral duty towards promises they made. It's everything but giving the symbol of official bilingualism. They like to be seen as being so good to their French minorities. It's an attitude which says, 'We'll heal the sick, look after the poor, and all that, but we won't have any kind of symbol which says we have to do this. We're doing it because we are good citizens, good Protestants, good Loyalists. We are good. Look here, see how good we are.' All of which is fine with me. If they're good, I'll take it."

Throughout his years as premier, there were recurring rumors that Davis would ultimately make Ontario officially bilingual. After all, he changed almost every other policy, often more than once, why not this one? But shortly before his retirement he said, "No, I think the approach we are taking is right. It's been accepted, and it works. We never would have achieved what we did any other way. Certainly not with the relative harmony, anyway."

PART THREE
THE
NATIONAL MAN

———————— ⚜ ————————

Since the country began, Ontario premiers have been
power brokers, custodians of what they have believed
to be the national interest. It is an approach that infuri-
ates the other regions, for whom Ontario is the dreaded,
self-serving giant.

Bill Davis was no exception to the peculiarly Ontario
view that Ontarians, unlike other Canadians, are not
parochial, that however upsetting it may be to others,
it is generally true that what is good for Ontario is good
for Canada.

Part Three describes Bill Davis's attempt to maintain
that Ontario tradition in the face of growing wealth
and power in the West and the threat of separatism in
Quebec. It reveals Bill Davis as the loyal war horse for
his federal party whose loyalty was sorely tested under
the short-lived reign of Joe Clark, and it traces his bitter feud with Alberta's Peter Lougheed over oil-pricing
policies, his remarkable affinity to Pierre Trudeau, and
his personal obsession with the Constitution. It also
tells of his passion for federal affairs, his repressed
national ambitions, and the prolonged internal party
struggles over whether he should seek the federal Tory
leadership.

"It's never been a secret I've had more than a normal
interest in federal politics," Davis said in 1984. "I'll never
know whether I could have won a convention or not.

But when you have been premier of this province, the ambition to try to be 'on top' for the sake of being there starts to lose its relevance."

CHAPTER 21
CAPTAIN TORY

❦

Bill Davis is not really giving to boasting, but a little unchar-
acteristic bluster does show through whenever he talks of
his relationship with the federal Tories.

It was Bill Davis, he will remind you, who stood proudly on a
platform with John Diefenbaker at a rally in Hamilton late in
the 1965 federal campaign at a time when many Tories were
treating their losing federal chieftain like a leper. It was Bill Davis,
he will remind you, who worked in every single federal campaign since his own election in 1959, who in fact was headed for
a federal career until circumstances combined to change his
direction.

So it is one of the great ironies of his career that if you ask
many federal Tories even today about the 1980 election, it is
Davis they blame for their loss. How is it that such a party loyalist,
a partisan like Davis, could suddenly be seen as a Judas, a snake
in the grass who poisoned Ontarians against Joe Clark and cleared
the way for the triumphant return of Pierre Trudeau?

Like so many political truisms, the truth of the matter is not
what it's reputed to be. But that doesn't matter much, because in
politics perception is usually more real than reality, anyway. And if
there is just a bit of truth to the belief . . . well, that's all it takes,
especially when you don't win the election.

✳   ✳   ✳

The federal Tories have always suffered badly from their Grand National Delusion that they can't win without Quebec. The belief stems mainly from the great Diefenbaker sweep of 1958, when the Chief won 50 seats in Quebec and trounced the Liberals nationally 208–48. What is forgotten is that in that same election, Diefenbaker won 67 seats in Ontario while the Liberals, who won 25 in Quebec, won only 14 in Ontario.

A similar situation occurred in 1984 when Brian Mulroney won an astounding 211 seats, 59 of them in Quebec, as voters there, sensing a sweep, climbed on the Tory bandwagon as they had for Diefenbaker. Coincidentally, like Diefenbaker Mulroney also won 67 seats in Ontario, a gain of 29 over 1980.

Arithmetic being what it is, it is hard to win consistently without winning Ontario. In the fifteen elections since 1940, the winning party beat the loser twelve times in the province, and two of the exceptions to the rule were close: In 1972, when Pierre Trudeau beat Bob Stanfield 109–107, Stanfield *did* manage to take Ontario 40–36; Diefenbaker's narrow 1962 win (116– 95) was accomplished while losing Ontario 35–43. The only outstanding exception was the 1945 election, when the Liberals won 125–67, but the Tories took Ontario 48–34. So the Tories have won five of those fifteen elections and just missed winning another by two seats in 1972. In these six successful national outings, the Tories beat the Liberals in Ontario five times, four of them by lopsided margins.

But federal Tories, even those from Ontario, have always resented this fact and have tended to play ostrich in the province while focusing their attention on Quebec, where the odds against them are greater. And during most of those years, this attitude of neglect was returned by the provincial party. Between 1943, when George Drew kicked off the Tory regime, and 1971, when Davis took over, Tory premiers stayed out of federal campaigns, with one exception: Leslie Frost went all-out for Diefenbaker in 1957.

Davis, however, is a different cat. To him a Tory is a Tory. As Sally Barnes says, "He's fiercely partisan, almost to a point of fault. Maybe you've got to be in this business, but he just likes Tories better than other people. He believes they're nicer people. He really believes that. I think he's crazy, but he honestly believes that."

And so, when the 1972 federal campaign began, the first election after Davis became premier, he cancelled most of his Queen's Park appointments for a month, told his cabinet members and backbenchers to "be conspicuous" during the campaign, and became the first Ontario premier to campaign for a federal leader outside the province. He went to fall fairs with local federal candidates, went mainstreeting with them, dropped in to teas, and generally waged a highly personal campaign for Robert Stanfield. He said a party couldn't transfer its provincial support to the federal wing, "but what you can do is show voters our commitment and hope that it will help them decide in our favor at the polls."

Davis was so active for Stanfield, in fact, that it became a campaign issue. Trudeau said a federal Tory government would be indebted to Ontario because of the Davis contribution, but Stanfield denied that there was any deal with Davis and accused Trudeau of "trying to work both ends against the middle" by seeking to appeal to the national prejudice against Ontario.

Four years earlier the Tories had won just 17 of Ontario's 88 seats, but with the help of Davis and his Big Blue Machine, Stanfield won 40, a gain of 23.

After his loss to Tory Sean O'Sullivan in that election, Liberal MP Colin Gibson said he had scarcely noticed the Davis machine during the first half of the campaign. "But then, suddenly, I became aware of a flood of new Conservative literature, very well done and very persuasive. And from that time on I was under increasing pressure from the Conservatives." The Tory material was far ahead of anything the Liberals distributed. "It was slick, well done."

Two years later Davis again went all-out for the federal party. Two days after the 1974 election was announced, Davis went to Sault Ste. Marie with Stanfield for some pizza, pasta, and politicking at a local Italian festival. Davis, who was to leave for a tour of Italy in two weeks, practised his Italian and declined a "chicken catch-a-tory" offered by a decided Liberal. Later, surrounded by most of his cabinet, Davis again endorsed Stanfield for prime minister.

A week later the premier and five cabinet ministers attended the annual YPC conference, where he endorsed Stanfield's main campaign plank — and ultimate downfall — wage and price controls, declaring that such a measure wasn't "a long-term solution to inflation" but was better than Trudeau's "shrug of the shoulders" policy.

But this time the Liberals gained 19 Ontario seats for 55, while Stanfield dropped to 25, a loss of 15. Davis, who didn't deny the credit in 1972, wouldn't accept the blame in 1974, saying that the loss didn't reflect anti-Davis sentiment and adding that rejection of wage and price controls "was a very substantial part" of the Tory losses in Ontario. Nonetheless, Davis's key workers—Camp, Weed, and Atkins—had all been out working hard for Stanfield.

Diefenbaker blamed Camp for the federal loss and told Davis that if he didn't "get rid of" him as an adviser, he'd go down to defeat, too. "Dalton Camp is a self-appointed, would-be Warwick who has exercised an authority federally and provincially in the province of Ontario all to the detriment of the party," said Diefenbaker in a reference to the Earl of Warwick, also called Warwick the Kingmaker, who switched allegiance during the Wars of the Roses, who made and broke kings, and who came to an untidy end in one of the wars' closing battles when his earlier friends defeated his new-found ones. Davis said he had read Diefenbaker's remarks with interest but had no comment to make on them. Maybe not, but Camp was seen less and less frequently around Queen's Park after that. It wasn't long until he wasn't involved at all.

After the Tories' defeat in 1974, Stanfield's leadership was again called into question. And once again, as he had in 1972, Davis flatly denied any interest in Stanfield's job. "I'm quite content here in Ontario," he said. "It is quite demanding. I enjoy it, and I'm not giving any thought to the federal leadership."

In fact, Davis was having enough trouble keeping his head above water. Plagued by a series of mini-scandals and trailing in public opinion polls, it was hardly an opportune moment to go rushing off to Ottawa — particularly when the Tories had just been clobbered in Ontario, even with his much-publicized help.

Still, the question continued to be raised, and in July, 1975, after Stanfield had announced he was stepping down, a *Financial Times* survey of 211 readers showed that 48 per cent would choose Alberta's Peter Lougheed for federal Tory leader, with

Davis in second place at 18 per cent. Flora MacDonald was third and Claude Wagner fourth. Joe Clark wasn't even on the list.

At the beginning of the 1976 leadership contest, Davis telephoned Lougheed twice to say he would second his nomination. The Davis people were so serious about Lougheed—Davis having ruined his own chances with his minority government—that they even organized a dinner for Ontario and Alberta Tories to talk about his nomination. But it wasn't to be.

Officially, Davis stayed out of the contest and told his cabinet and caucus to do the same, arguing that involvement in the federal race might create rifts in the provincial party at a time when it could be facing another election. The Tories didn't obey, and most of them openly supported one of the candidates. Even Kathleen Davis came out publicly for Flora MacDonald, and Hugh Segal (for Wagner) and Roy McMurtry (for Mulroney) made no secret of their sympathies. Where Davis stood, no one knows for sure, but Hugh Segal says he'd bet Davis voted for Flora on the first ballot "because of Kathleen . . . and in the crunch I'd think he voted for Wagner."

In any event, Clark won the leadership race. Davis was initially supportive, but he never came to respect Clark, and the next few years provided a serious test of Davis's view that a Tory is a Tory is a Tory.

In 1977 Davis had another election of his own to contend with, but while Stanfield made a couple of appearances for Davis, Clark did not. The relationship had already begun to sour: The Davis Tories, used to running the federal party as well as their own, were upset that they were being shut out. And the Clark Tories, knowing that Davis was not enthusiastic about their man, wanted nothing to do with him.

In July, 1977, Clark dispatched his two senior staffers, campaign chairman Lowell Murray and chief of staff William Neville, to try to work out a peace. Meeting with them in the famous Park Plaza suite were Eddie Goodman, Hugh Segal, and Ross DeGeer. The sessions broke down and turned into slanging matches, each side accusing the other of the sins of the western world. Essentially, Clark's troops were told that their guy had better get his act together before he could expect the Big Blue Machine to do anything for him. Davis rode above it all, saying nothing about Clark. But his silence was in itself a far cry from the defence he used to give Stanfield whenever anyone criticized him within earshot.

While no one could ever accuse the Davis Tories of being humble, Clark had made some incredibly dumb moves, one of them being to bring in Albertan MP Harvie André to organize Ontario. Clark also embarrassed Davis by refusing to go to the Albany Club, the Toronto Tories' home away from home, because it didn't admit women members. (Just at that time Margaret Birch, Ontario's first woman cabinet minister, had applied for membership, and Davis was working quietly behind the scenes to correct the situation.)

Still, an uneasy alliance developed between the two Tory factions. As much as they may have disliked each other, they disliked the Liberals more.

In September, 1977, Clark, Davis, and three other Tory premiers — Alberta's Peter Lougheed, Newfoundland's Frank Moores, and New Brunswick's Richard Hatfield — met in Kingston and agreed that they wanted not just to amend the BNA Act but also to revamp Canada's Constitution. Clark read from a joint statement signed by the five leaders: "Dealing with Canada's major problems requires completely new attitudes by the federal government that go beyond reliance on legal changes to the British North America Act. . . . Our federal system must be modernized to recognize the cultural and economic realities of the 1980s. . . . This is the goal to which we are committed."

Clark may have been committed to a new Constitution at the time, but for Davis it was becoming an obsession, and Clark's refusal to deal with it seriously during his short term as prime minister ranks second only to energy as a sore point between the two men.

"The Clark government just didn't think that was a top priority," says Tom Wells, Ontario's reliable intergovernmental affairs minister. "It didn't meet with much favor as an issue. I felt they could have grabbed the initiative, but they probably didn't want to do it because Quebec wasn't in favor of patriating the Constitution. Bill Jarvis and I had great talks about it, but it never seemed to be a priority with them."

Clark made a few moves to heal the wounds in early 1978 when he supported Davis's bilingualism policy, stressing that it was more important to make practical language reforms than to pass symbolic declarations. "I can sympathize entirely with the Davis position," Clark said in an interview on his second anniversary as party leader. A month later Davis announced he was ready to do whatever Clark asked him to do in the coming election. Davis-watchers noticed the distinction between his pledge to do what he was "asked" and his aggressive, full-speed-ahead support for Stanfield. Still, Pat Kinsella, the party's executive director, said provincial party workers had been assigned to work on the federal campaign, including six full-time organizers at the provincial party's new headquarters on Dundas Street, just a few blocks south of Queen's Park.

The provincial party wasn't being exactly selfless, however. Party workers chose to work hardest in areas where Davis held seats or had a chance of winning them, rather than in areas more attuned to the federal party's plans. After all, contacts won during any kind of political organizing can be useful later.

Davis had yet another problem at the time. Just two months earlier, at a federal-provincial conference in Ottawa, he had agreed to a federal revenue-sharing scheme. When Finance Minister Jean Chrétien announced a sales tax cut in his budget, Ontario Treasurer Darcy McKeough called a press conference to endorse the idea, making it difficult for Davis to turn around a week later and attack Trudeau's fiscal policies.

Nevertheless, on March 11, 1979, Davis promised his "absolute, total, and overwhelming support" for Clark in the May 22 federal election. He told about 120 members of the Ontario PC Campus Association that the re-election of the Liberals would mean "four more years of indecision, inflation, devaluation."

On the other hand, Lougheed announced a few days later that he was willing to help Clark, but only in Alberta and only after a planned three-week holiday. "I've always taken the position that I'm involved in provincial politics, not federal politics," said Lougheed. This was a sore point with Davis loyalists, who maintain that everybody dumped on their man's lack of enthusiasm for Clark, while he did more for him than any other Tory premier.

And so Davis went out on the hustings, however reluctantly, and made speeches for Clark. He mainstreeted with a few federal Tories, and at a giant Hamilton rally late in the campaign, he clearly overshadowed Clark with a hard-hitting, ten-minute introduction to a speech by Clark that was downbeat even by *his* standards.

At a meeting of the Canadian Association of Broadcasters, Davis said in a fifteen-minute, Johnny Carson-style monologue that Clark was much like his beloved Toronto Argonauts — he may look like a loser, but he was betting on him, anyway. Davis explained later that he hadn't meant to slight Clark — although at the time the Argos hadn't won the Grey Cup in twenty-seven years — he had simply meant to illustrate his loyalty as a Tory team player. Indeed.

Clark won the election, albeit with a minority, and when the numbers were in it was obvious where the greatest support had come from: In Ontario the Tories won 57 seats, up 32 from 1974 (another seven seats had been added through redistribution), while the Liberals won 32, a drop of 23. And that's when the fight really began between Queen's Park and the prime minister's office. The Davis loyalists felt that even if they had had to hold their collective noses to do it, they had given Clark his victory. The Clark loyalists felt that may have been so, but now that they had power, they could solidify it themselves. They didn't have to worry themselves about the Davis people whom they didn't really like, anyway.

"The premier felt Joe lacked judgment and experience and was very mechanistic about the system," says Hugh Segal. "Clark seemed to believe government was committees and resolutions and meetings. He didn't realize it was basically people. Also, we were into our second minority, and they really felt we were on the skids but they were there for the duration. They held that energy conference just so we could express our point of view and save our ass politically; they really believed that. Jim Gillies and Bill Neville took Ed Stewart behind the curtains at that conference and said, 'We understand the soup you're in, but you guys can play your political games; we're here for the long term. We've got to start making decisions for Canada.' Stewart told them they were there until the next election—that's how it works."

Segal says they took themselves far too seriously. Take the case of MP David MacDonald, a United Church minister from P.E.I. for whom Segal had worked as a student in Ottawa. He had a rural charge and traditionally went home for three months every summer. "He'd just go home and he'd bury people, marry people, baptize people, counsel people. That's the best politics you can do — no politics. But Clark gave him a bunch of ministries, and he was so busy he said he wasn't going home that summer. It took his people at home about four days to say, 'I guess we're not important enough for him any more.' And that's the story for Tories right across Canada."

Eddie Goodman, who had run two national campaigns and three provincial ones, says, "It's not true at all that there was any personal bitterness . . . but Davis felt he'd been more loyal to Clark than Clark was helpful to him. I think there's no doubt that some people were pissed off. I don't think Clark's staff ran things the way they should have been run, and Hughie [Segal], of course, he'd go around occasionally sounding off. But it was more sound than fury. At no time when Davis wanted to speak to Clark did he have any problems. But they had a lot of guys pushing Clark then, and if I wanted to speak to him, or Hughie, they weren't jumping around. But then why the hell should they?"

Bill Kelly, only the fourth Tory Trudeau appointed to the Senate, said that his December 23, 1982, appointment would have been recommended by Clark to Trudeau, with "advice in a roundabout way through Billy, of course. . . . The relationship between Clark and Davis wasn't as good as it could have been, no doubt, but it wasn't as bad as some people think, either."

How bad was the relationship? "I don't think he [Davis] liked him," says Sally Barnes. "He didn't have a great deal of respect for him. He doesn't really like Trudeau, either, but he certainly respects him. Those little dinner meetings between the two — Clark would come in, and when he went away Bill would say, 'Well, we tried again.' And Clark would just nicely get back to Ottawa and the phone would ring and they had decided to do the opposite. His advisers there had got to him. I think it went to their heads, period. They had power; they didn't need Ontario. . . . It was a lousy way to treat their friends. They got what they deserved."

Attorney General Roy McMurtry says any comments Davis made about Clark in his presence "were always made more in sorrow. He just was troubled by the fact that Clark, or whoever was advising him, would be so unprofessional as not to take more seriously the concern we were expressing in Ontario. There wasn't any personal animosity. He wondered on occasion where Joe was coming from, and he'd try to tell them sometimes they were getting out of touch, but the response would be, 'Well, you know Ontario, but don't try to tell us about Canada; that's our field.' This Ontario tension is even reflected in the tension that is felt now for Norm Atkins [Mulroney's campaign chief at the time]. Certainly Brian doesn't feel that. He has no doubt in his mind. But part of the problem with Joe was I think he was just intimidated and felt uncomfortable in Ontario."

A senior party official, with direct ties to both the Clark and Davis camps at the time, says, "Like everything else, the attitude of the Big Blue Machine guys reflected Davis's attitude. He wasn't out to get Clark or anything, but he didn't have much respect for him. These guys say they got Clark elected. Fine. Does that mean they have to accept the blame for all the elections the Tories lost? Much of the animosity was personal jealousy. Under Stanfield those guys — Atkins, Segal, Goodman — ran the federal party as well. Clark shut them out. They were furious. Not only did they want Clark to consult with them before he made a move; they wanted him to consult only with them. They were outraged that Clark saw things differently than their view of the 'national interest.' . . . Davis is stand-offish. He doesn't involve himself in the day-to-day dirty deeds, but he allows them to happen. There are intense personal loyalties with his people which go far beyond making a living or playing power politics, although that's a part of it, too."

Despite their feelings for one another, Davis was Clark's first dinner guest at 24 Sussex Drive. It was June 13, 1979, the day before Clark officially moved into the prime minister's residence. In a prepared statement given after he returned to Toronto, Davis said he was "impressed by the prime minister's candor and his sincere desire to work together to resolve many outstanding problems."

The big daddy of all their problems was, of course, oil. Energy prices would not only split the two men, and make Davis and Lougheed bitter enemies, but also bring Clark's government tumbling down. Clark, an Albertan, was caught in the squeeze between the demands of Lougheed, the producer, to raise prices and the demands of Davis, the consumer, to keep prices down. There was not an awful lot of common ground, certainly none at all with Lougheed.

On the eve of the August, 1979, premiers' conference at Pointe-au-Pic, Quebec, Davis released an energy paper calling for a national pricing policy to keep the price of domestic oil well below the world price. The price of domestic oil was slated to rise a dollar a barrel in January, 1980, bringing it to $14.75, well below the world price of $23.50. Lougheed, of course, wanted the world price for his oil. Davis argued that if significant price hikes couldn't be avoided, Petrocan should remain and its profits used in a "reinvestment plan" to promote energy self-sufficiency. (This, despite Clark's announced intention to shelve Petrocan.) Davis also said that Ottawa should give tax credits to public transit riders and "low-income consumers" and allot more money for transit systems and grants for energy conservation.

The paper came just two weeks before Clark was planning to huddle with his cabinet at Jasper. Davis was clearly hoping to "cut him off at the pass" before Clark gave in to Lougheed's intractable demands for world prices.

It didn't work. Clark came out of the late-August Jasper meeting trying to take a middle road. But in effect he hinted at large price hikes — around $4 a barrel — and threw a little sop to Davis by saying that he hadn't rejected all the thinking behind Davis's oil profit-sharing proposal. Even that little sop outraged Lougheed, however, who viewed Ontario's proposal as an unacceptable attack on Alberta's resource rights and revenues, prompting Ontario Treasurer Frank Miller to call Lougheed a greater threat to Confederation than Quebec's René Lévesque.

The stakes were huge on both sides: For Alberta, every extra dollar would generate about $2 million a day in revenue; for Ontario, every dollar increase in the price of oil would mean a potential four thousand fewer manufacturing jobs.

Clark met privately with Lougheed in Jasper on August 31 and set a meeting with Davis at Queen's Park for the first week in September. On September 5 Davis huddled at Port Carling, a Muskoka resort town, with fifty-five senior cabinet ministers, civil servants, and private industry representatives to prepare his response to Clark's policies and get ready for the dinner meeting at Queen's Park. Coincidentally, the only other group at the luxurious Elgin House lodge that week was a clutch of British Petroleum executives and their wives.

Davis left for the dinner not terribly optimistic about winning

the battle, particularly when earlier in the week he had had dinner with Lougheed in Montreal and the mood, aides said, was
decidedly impolite.

Davis, a competitive man, loved to make bets of $1 and $2 on
football games, but he was not given to gambling more than that.
On the occasion of the Clark dinner, however, he lost $10 — the
largest bet he has ever made — when Hugh Segal wagered he
could prove that Clark was taking himself too seriously. The
dinner, with just the two men present, was held in what Davis
calls office number two, a smaller office next to his main one.
Segal told Davis he would "make the room look so bad that anybody with a sense of humor would dissolve the minute they saw
it unless they were so puffed up with themselves, that's the way
they think it should be." Behind Davis's chair at the end of the
table, Segal posted a huge Ontario flag. Behind Clark's chair,
kitty-corner to Davis's, he hung a giant Canadian flag. On a chair
between the two men, he plunked a large bust of Sir John A.
Macdonald.

"It was like a scene from Monty Python," chortles Segal. "There
they were, eating trout and discussing energy, and Clark never
said a word or let on he noticed the flags or the bust of Sir
John A. That was indicative to me of people who had lost their
perspective."

Davis and Clark emerged from the three-hour meeting saying
what everybody already knew: They had a problem, and they'd
try to work something out.

They never really did. In October the news leaked that Clark
was planning a twenty-three-cent-a-gallon increase in the price
of gasoline in John Crosbie's December budget. Davis was livid,
saying it would be "a wilful attack on the individual consumers
and economy of Ontario." In November Clark hosted a federal-
provincial conference on energy. Things did not improve. When
Clark asked Davis to address the conference, he introduced him
with a friendly "Bill." Once Davis had finished Clark gave a cool
"Thank you very much, Mr. Davis."

There was no turning back by either side.

On November 21 Davis surprised twenty-five hundred Tories
at a fund-raising dinner in Toronto by attacking Clark's energy
policies — and what's more, the crowd applauded. Clark and
Davis had spent forty-five minutes alone together beforehand,

but when Davis got up to speak at the $150-a-plate affair he declared, "There is no question that one and a half million Albertans must have their fair share, but you face the tough task of speaking for twenty-two million Canadians who also have their rights and expectations."

Clark, who seemed stunned by the unexpected attack, tried desperately to offer an olive branch: "It's clear that without the support of Bill Davis, we would not be a government, and I would not be here as prime minister." Then he turned to Davis and gave him a firm "commitment, as we face the complex decisions ahead, that we will bear in mind the interests of this province and this city — and we will bear in mind their historical role as an engine of growth for Canada."

The next week a small group of Davis aides, armed with province-wide polls warning Clark of the dangers of markedly higher oil prices, went to Ottawa to try to convince him of the political folly of his scheme. That didn't work, either.

On December 11 Crosbie revealed his budget containing an eighteen-cent-a-gallon excise tax, prompting Davis to complain, "Billions of dollars will be taxed from people across Canada and transferred to the treasury of the federal government and the governments of the producing provinces. . . . It will take more out of the pockets of consumers and place it primarily in the hands of government. This will exact a toll of higher inflation and fewer jobs." Asked if he planned to campaign again for Clark as he had earlier that year, Davis said, "I don't know when the next election is going to take place or what I am doing. I haven't crossed that bridge. . . . There is no campaign under way."

But there was soon enough. Too soon for Clark, as it turned out: Two days later his government lost a no-confidence motion in the House, the same day Ontario Treasurer Frank Miller delivered a blistering attack on the Crosbie budget.

Miller said the provincial Tories had not thought there would be an election. "We'd had a full summer of trying to offer our advice and experience, and while I had the greatest respect for John Crosbie, the relationship between Ontario and Canada during those months was really strained. We felt we had done our best to help them get in, only to find that the people who had been begging for our presence during the election found it very easy to dismiss us as provincial when we tried to offer our advice."

Ironically, Miller did not read the full text of his speech before delivering it. He had been at a Tory breakfast meeting in Don Mills that morning, along with John Crosbie. On the way back to Queen's Park Miller told his speechwriter, Sheila McVicar, that he wanted his response for the legislature to be "very hard and tough . . . midway through the morning Segal called and agreed that would be the tenor of Ontario's response. It was probably a little harsher than it would have been had I had time to re-edit it, but they were my words, and I was saddled with them."

Indeed, both Miller and Davis expressed their opinions so strongly that, come the election campaign, they found their views being used with devastating effect in Liberal campaign advertisements. One commercial began with a shot of Clark in the Commons; a male voice-over said it was the Tory budget that had caused the election, then went on to introduce what one prominent Ontarian thought of the budget: "This will exact a toll of higher inflation and fewer new jobs. . . . One cannot justify the large increase in excise tax on transportation fuels. . . . This will place a severe financial hardship on many people." The prominent Ontarian was, alas, Bill Davis, in a blue suit, standing at his desk in the legislature, while the voice told the people, "If Joe Clark's Conservatives let him down, think of what they'll do to you."

The other commercial began in much the same way, showing Clark in the House and giving voice-over comments about the budget: "Ontario will bear the brunt of these increases. . . . In 1980 it will cost $575 more for every Ontario household. . . . It will cost twenty thousand jobs." And there on the screen was Frank Miller, also dressed in a Tory-blue suit, sitting in a chair. The voice went on: "If the embarrassing Joe Clark budget worries him, what should it do for you? This is the time to vote Liberal."

Miller never saw the commercials, "but I don't think I'm ever going to have a seat in a Conservative senate, let's put it that way." Shortly after the campaign Miller was at a social function where Tory MP Gordon Gilchrest was chatting with Ontario Lieutenant-Governor Pauline McGibbon. "She saw me walk over, turned around, and said, 'Oh, Gordon, you know Frank Miller, don't you? He's also a Conservative.' Gilchrest said, 'Oh, is he?' and turned around and left."

Davis and Clark put on a brave front during the campaign. Davis called the election "unnecessary" but said he'd back Clark. "I am a Conservative. Mr. Clark is a Conservative. Mr. Stanfield was Conservative when he led our federal party. I have supported each and every Conservative leader who sought my support." And in Ottawa Clark told reporters, "I trust Bill Davis implicitly. I welcome his support."

First, however, Davis was heading off for his annual Christmas holiday in Fort Lauderdale. It wasn't until mid-January that Clark, starting to feel the wind against him, telephoned Davis and asked for help. Lougheed said he wouldn't be giving any media interviews until after the February 18 election, thank you very much, because of the "uncertainty of the federal political scene."

As for Davis, he agreed to help but made no plans to come back from Florida until January 21. Ontario Liberal Leader Stuart Smith meanwhile accused Davis of being "a first-class hypocrite" for giving Clark even token support. He labelled the Clark-Davis team "Wimp and Blimp," adding that an Ontario elector voting for Clark "would be like Anne Boleyn voting for Henry VIII."

In St. John's, Newfoundland, in early January, Clark told reporters he didn't have to rely on Davis as much as he had in the last election because he had his own "strong Ontario team" of federal cabinet ministers.

For his part Davis *did* come home three days early — to clean up "some personal matters"— and his troops *did* send out three thousand letters under the premier's signature to key Ontario Tory supporters, asking them to help re-elect Clark.

But Clark was getting desperate. He asked to meet with the Tory caucus at Queen's Park, and on January 23 he was welcomed by Davis like a prodigal son. Davis agreed to eight appearances in the remaining four weeks of the campaign, five of them with Clark as speaker. To get such a commitment, Clark offered Davis a voice in the redistribution of federal-provincial revenues after the election.

Davis made his first appearance on January 30 in Barrie, telling three thousand Tories that Clark "has my support and the total support of my government and my party." Nobody believed it, but there it was. And when the votes were counted on February 18, Clark had lost twenty-four Ontario seats and one job as prime minister.

Eddie Goodman, who organized federally when Frost was premier and was national chairman under Robarts, says, "I can tell you — Davis worked far harder than either Frost or Robarts, except Frost worked hard in 1957, but by and large Davis never turned down any strong requests from Clark. There was some feeling on the right wing of the federal party that Bill was too red, so to speak, but anybody who knows the facts knows how hard he worked. I know what the perception is, but it isn't fair. I don't deny that his position on oil prices hurt the feds a bit, but his first obligation was to his province. If Clark had taken the steps that were required, got the goddamn thing settled, and pushed Lougheed a bit, there wouldn't have been a problem. You know, Billy doesn't like that stuff. He doesn't like being cast as disloyal when he really is such a great loyalist. That really bothered him. No one was saying that any of the other Tory premiers were disloyal, premiers who hadn't worked or moved a finger for Joe."

Looking back at that time, Davis remarked, "There's a bit of mythology about that . . . part of it generated by the media. The truth of the matter was, when the election was announced I was away on holidays [not quite]. . . . I accepted the first invitation to help that was communicated to me, but the truth of the matter is, the federal party felt Joe needed some help the first time around, but he was going into this campaign as prime minister . . . the same measure of support wasn't necessary." Davis says people tend to forget that a year earlier he'd been equally critical about a Liberal government ten-cent tax. "I went to many meetings for Joe . . . but the truth of the matter is, we weren't asked as early."

At the time Davis said this in an interview in his Brampton home on July 8, 1984, Prime Minister John Turner called to say that the Queen's scheduled visit had been delayed because he was calling a federal election that day. "Kathleen won't be pleased," Davis said later. "She is out getting her hair done now for the Queen's visit. But whatever Brian [Mulroney] wants me to do I will do, you know. Within reason. But I'm not going to rush out and hire a hall here in Brampton on my own initiative and make a speech on behalf of the federal party. I'm going to be asked. This was the same with Joe. I may have missed one or two things they wanted, but not very many. I don't push myself where I'm not wanted, and we simply weren't asked, especially early in the game."

Davis, Kathleen, and his aides attended the Conservative leadership convention in June, 1983. But their luggage was in their cars parked outside the Ottawa Civic Centre, and they left for Toronto before the results of the final ballot were announced.

A few weeks later Mulroney showed up at a provincial Tory shindig at Toronto's Skyline Hotel, the same day he named Norm Atkins his chief campaign strategist. This was a sure sign that the war had ended and peace restored to the valley.

Mulroney even showed up at a dinner near the Toronto airport on May 25, 1984, in honor of Davis's twenty-fifth anniversary in elected office, saying, "We're doing something formally tonight that Progressive Conservatives have been doing informally for some years — paying tribute to Bill Davis." He added that Davis had "enriched the national political leadership in Canada, and this is why I can tell you quite simply tonight: I am honored to be in his company."

During the 1984 federal campaign, Davis certainly returned the favor as the Tories all went charging off to smash the dreaded Grits, putting their own battles well behind them.

When Davis went to party headquarters in Toronto at about 10 p.m. on September 4 to applaud "a new era in federal-provincial relations," he certainly had reason to be optimistic about Mulroney's overwhelming mandate: He had made nearly two dozen appearances on behalf of Mulroney and other federal Tory candidates, and almost the entire Mulroney campaign team had come from the Big Blue Machine.

Norm Atkins, of course, was the boss, and he'd chosen Bill McAleer, a close Davis supporter (who had also managed Joe Clark's leadership bid) to run the Ontario section of the campaign. Mulroney's campaign secretary, Paul Curley, was a veteran member of the Davis machine, and Pat Kinsella, former executive director of the Ontario Tories, was tour manager. Another Big Blue graduate, Jerry Lampert, who like Kinsella had gone to British Columbia, became Mulroney's director of provincial opera-

tions there. Another active Davis worker, Tom Scott, chairman
of Sherwood Communications, was named the campaign's advertising and communications director, and the director of operations, Harry Near, got his start in politics as an advance man for
Davis in the 1975 provincial election. Eddie Goodman and even
Dalton Camp also played senior roles in the Mulroney campaign.

Davis sent out a letter to thousands of Tories in the province,
urging them to "put their strength and experience solidly behind
Brian Mulroney." He had sent out a letter in 1980, too, asking
workers to support Clark, even though "while we disagree in some
areas, we have made some progress as well." In 1984 there were
no disagreements.

There were, however, some outstanding issues to be resolved.
But Davis, if asked about energy pricing and his disagreement
with the federal Tories over doctors' extra-billing, would always
avoid an answer by saying he wasn't discussing national issues.
He was just helping Mulroney.

The only deviation from this partisan love-in came early in
the campaign. Mulroney said he would try to persuade Davis
"in a firm and friendly manner to go further" and enshrine official bilingualism, but he backed off as soon as Davis declared,
"My position hasn't altered." The issue was rarely mentioned
again.

In mid-August, just before the premiers gathered in Charlottetown for their annual conference, federal Tory energy critic
Pat Carney said energy policy hadn't become an issue in the campaign because the Tory premiers had agreed that it was too touchy.
Davis, Lougheed, and the other premiers denied making any
"deals" not to discuss energy, but the fact remains that the issue
that had been so hurtful to Clark was successfully avoided by
Mulroney, deal or not. "Why provoke an issue?" Davis asked
reporters in Charlottetown.

In an interview with a *Toronto Star* reporter during a campaign stopover in Sept-Iles, Quebec, Mulroney said there was
some hostility between the Davis group and his own Quebec people at first, but "I had them brought to Stornaway one at a time
and ran them through. . . . That did it: no more fighting, a lot
more respect for each other. I knew how good they were — Bill
Davis's people, my own in Quebec. But I had to get them in the
same tent. We did it. And it really is a wonderful thing to behold."

John Turner, no doubt, would agree. But Turner had noticed how effective the machine was even before the votes were counted and, echoing Trudeau a dozen years earlier, told a Saskatoon audience on August 28: "I would be very concerned about whatever IOUs Brian Mulroney has had to sign with Bill Davis, because I can tell you they will be called upon to the detriment of Western Canada."

Indeed, the day after the election, Treasurer Larry Grossman dropped a broad hint of just what Ontario might seek from the Mulroney government. (Davis was too experienced to do that sort of thing himself, so he sent a chief lieutenant to do it for him.) Grossman told executives at a *Financial Post* conference that the province wanted new agreements on financing health and social programs, deficit cuts, better co-ordination on economic development, joint federal-provincial action to modernize Canadian (read Ontarian) industry, and an attack on government waste and program duplication.

With the end of the Ottawa-Alberta oil-pricing agreement and the extra-billing dispute, the unrepentant Tory love-fest may be marred by the odd spat, but it will never reach the same level of hostility as when Clark held power. "After all," remarked one senior Davis insider, "Clark wouldn't let our people in the door. Brian, on the other hand, has a room full of our guys. That can't hurt us, can it?"

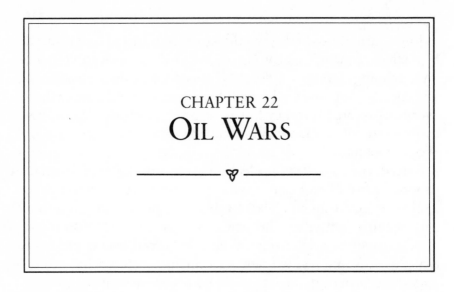

CHAPTER 22
OIL WARS

B ill Davis shocked the legislature, especially his own caucus, on October 13, 1981, with the announcement that he had bought 25 per cent of Suncor. The deal was supposed to give Ontario a "window" on the oil industry, but so far the window has been one-way glass. The government, peeking out, officially says it was a good deal. Everybody else, trying to see in, can't even figure the deal out.

The criticism and curiosity are not restricted to the opposition and the media. Many of Davis's own people, including some senior civil servants, think it was a mistake.

The $650 million purchase was announced just five weeks after Davis had abandoned his impressive five-year war on behalf of Ontario's consumers of oil and gas and about four months after Treasurer Frank Miller had introduced an *ad valorem* tax to make higher gasoline prices more profitable for the government.

But beyond the money, what was involved was Davis's pathogenic competitive instincts. A high-stakes poker game was being played with oil in this country, and Davis, tired of being a noisy spectator, wanted to be dealt in. What he was competing for was clout — a chance for Ontario to become a full partner with Ottawa and Alberta in the unending dispute over just what represents a fair price for Canadian crude.

As super-bureaucrat Malcolm Rowan told an international

energy symposium in Cambridge, Massachusetts, in April, 1981, the energy debate in Canada is not just about energy. "It is as much a debate about central government versus provincial powers, provincial versus national resource ownership and development, private ownership versus public ownership, centralization versus pluralism, western versus eastern commercial interests, the settling of old scores, the Canadianization of the petroleum industry versus its nationalization, constitutional change, the desperate need of the federal government for money, and the equalization of some basic governmental services across the country." The prize, said Rowan, is power.

The energy fight underscored both the greatest strengths and the greatest weaknesses of Confederation. It also pitted against each other the two most powerful premiers in the land in a struggle that ruined their personal relationship, changed the national government in 1980, but in the end moulded a unique Canadian pricing formula and swelled government coffers in Ottawa, Alberta, and, yes, Ontario. The fight drove up inflation and created unemployment, and while consumers accepted their fate with equanimity — a peculiarly Canadian trait — the governments and the oil companies laughed all the way to their vaults.

* * *

Ontario accounts for one-third of Canada's total energy consumption. About one-quarter of that comes from within the province, mainly from hydroelectric and nuclear power. But over 50 per cent of Ontario's primary energy requirements comes directly from Alberta, as either oil or natural gas.

Canadians have traditionally been the biggest energy gluttons among the industrialized nations, thanks to a cold climate, long distances between populated areas, high living standards, and a resource-based industrial economy. But beginning in the early 1980s, consumption began to drop. In 1982 alone, demand for oil in Ontario dropped 11 per cent as homeowners switched over to natural gas, electricity, and wood. Between 1975 and 1982 oil's share of Ontario's primary energy market fell from 40 per cent to 35 per cent, but it still is well out in front of second-place natural gas (at about 23 per cent), coal (16 per cent), uranium (13 per cent), and hydroelectric power (about 12 per cent).

Davis began to worry about energy prices in August, 1971, when Treasurer Darcy McKeough recommended an advisory committee be set up to study it. Queen's University principal Dr. J. J. Deutsch, appointed chairman of the committee, issued a fifty-four-page report in January, 1973, warning that "the period of seemingly unlimited abundance of cheap energy has come to a close." At that time 80 per cent of Ontario's energy came from outside the province.

About three months earlier McKeough had resigned as treasurer over a conflict of interest, but when the Deutsch report was released, Davis appointed him his parliamentary assistant on energy matters. (He became Ontario's first energy minister shortly after.) His first assignment was to accompany Davis to Alberta to meet with Lougheed, who was demanding that the price of wellhead gas double. Because 95 per cent of Ontario's natural gas came from Alberta, that meant big increases — about $100 million — in annual industrial, commercial, and residential fuel bills.

That first meeting with Lougheed, like most since, did not go well. Lougheed emerged from the two-hour encounter to say he did not intend to budge or even delay his timetable for doubling gas prices. But he told a *Globe* reporter that the meeting with Davis was historic. "So many times in Confederation and the history of Canada, the West, and Alberta in particular, we have been the ones seeking — we haven't been the ones holding the cards, if you like. We now *do* hold the cards in terms of energy. The visit of Premier Davis to Edmonton was significant in that it illustrated the changing nature of Confederation."

There was, even then, a lot more at stake than energy prices. There was Lougheed's own bizarre brand of western machismo. However, he did point out that he wasn't above accepting some Ontario greenbacks for the giant tar sands development. "Ontario being the financial centre of Canada, like it or not, the impact of an Ontario government blessing on investment in the tar sands would be of substantial benefit to Canada."

After this unsuccessful meeting, Davis told eight hundred oil men at a Canadian Petroleum Association meeting in Calgary that a coherent national policy, not individual provincial or federal action, was needed to solve Canada's energy problems. Davis met Lougheed again for thirty minutes at the Calgary airport, and the two agreed to ask for a federal-provincial energy conference, although Lougheed said later he wouldn't mind a conference but wasn't prepared to argue his price increases there.

Throughout the energy debates of the 1970s, Davis was accused by Lougheed and others of trying to block *any* price increases. The charge is not true. Even in 1973 Davis said, "Our argument is not with a change in price. Our argument is with the timing and with the ultimate extent of the price changes." Later on he also emphasized the importance of the distribution of the money from higher prices, arguing that the increased revenue should be used to help all Canadians, not just Alberta and the oil companies.

In April, 1973, Davis announced he was considering taking legal action against Alberta to stop Lougheed's proposed increases, and in June he said he was indeed going to test their constitutionality in court. At the same time he announced a $3.8 billion energy plan, including the construction of two nuclear plants, and the establishment of an energy ministry as proposed by Deutsch. He introduced legislation turning Ontario Hydro into a Crown corporation and also proposed an energy development fund for direct government investment in energy resources, if necessary, along with an emphasis on energy conservation and a comprehensive national energy plan.

In October Davis dropped the planned legal action when the Alberta Energy Resources Conservation Board ruled that Alberta could not interfere with a contract for the supply of natural gas to Ontario for a price lower than the new price Alberta had demanded.

Then in December Davis, who had been doing his best to stir up public concern, warned against creating panic and public fear. He repeated a theme he had used in a Canadian Club speech a day earlier that the worldwide energy shortage could actually be good for Ontario because the province had access to relatively secure supplies.

In late January, 1974, Pierre Trudeau and the ten premiers met in Ottawa. A month after his "don't panic, it might be good for us" routine, Davis told the conference that a rise to the world oil price could cost Ontario seventy thousand jobs and help push the increase in the cost of living to 10 per cent. So Ontario argued for oil prices "substantially" below world prices: Every increase of $1 would cost it $200 million.

While Trudeau told Alberta and Saskatchewan that they would have to modify their demands "to safeguard the interests of consumers of Canada," Davis proposed that the federal freeze on domestic prices, imposed by Ottawa in the fall of 1974 and scheduled to expire February 1, 1975, be extended until May and asked Ottawa to put more money into a pot to help hard-pressed eastern provinces hit by rapidly escalating prices for imported oil. He added that long-term pricing arrangements should be worked out, perhaps by a federal-provincial marketing board. Lougheed was not impressed.

At a follow-up conference in March, Davis agreed to higher oil prices than he would have liked to avoid a "serious confrontation" between the provinces. But the new policy meant that the price of Alberta and Saskatchewan crude would rise from the frozen level of $4.00 per barrel to $6.50 for one year, then be renegotiated. Davis wanted the price set at $6.00 for a two-year period.

When he returned from that meeting, Davis said he was relatively happy that the price increase wasn't worse. But to his great embarrassment, he soon discovered it *was* worse. During a shouting match with opposition critics in the legislature, McKeough claimed Davis had been misled in the oil talks. It seems nobody mentioned a twenty-cent difference between the wellhead price of a barrel of oil and the higher, citygate price. Davis had also "forgotten" the 12 per cent federal sales tax on oil, accounting for an increase of nine cents per gallon at the pumps instead of the seven cents he had announced after the conference. It was a $300 million oversight.

Trudeau opened the next energy conference in April, 1975, by saying that oil prices had to go up, but Davis—with an election just around the corner—warned him that Ontario consumers couldn't tolerate such a situation. He said an increase by Ottawa would be "directly denying thousands of people in Ontario the right to employment" and pointed out that a further increase of $1 would cost each Ontario family $100. The conference ended in deadlock, although Ontario's new Energy Minister Dennis Timbrell said, somewhat prematurely, "We've won."

Trudeau warned the provinces to agree on a price by July 1, or Ottawa would legislate price hikes unilaterally. On June 23 Finance Minister John Turner's budget contained a ten-cent-per-gallon excise tax on gasoline plus a $1.50-per-barrel tax on oil, which translated into five cents or more per gallon at the pumps. Five days later Davis summoned executives of seven major oil companies to his Queen's Park office and asked them to delay the increases until September 1 or face a temporary price freeze, and on July 3 he imposed a ninety-day freeze on gasoline and oil prices within Ontario. The oil companies screamed; the opposition and the public didn't.

One immediate result was a quick halt to the rally of prices of oil shares on the Toronto Stock Exchange. With oil company executives accusing Davis of imposing the freeze because of the impending election, the index of western oils dropped 11 points and refining oils 8; exploration oils, which had been booming the week before, also suffered losses.

In 1976 Davis and McKeough said again that expected oil price increases would halt Ontario's economic recovery and hurt its export industries. Davis also objected to Trudeau scheduling a private energy summit for May 6 at 24 Sussex Drive and fired off a telegram to the prime minister asking that it be held in public. Trudeau refused. He said that the summit would give "priority consideration" to pricing, while another meeting on June 16 would deal with shared-cost programs and the Constitution.

Two days before that conference, Davis and Timbrell released the province's "blended price" proposals, a scheme roundly criticized by the Ontario opposition parties, the provincial premiers, and the federal government. Ottawa wanted oil to hit world prices over a two- or three-year period to encourage exploration, but Davis argued that there should be a lower, blended price for old oil, which is cheaper to develop, and the more costly new oil.

The main justification for higher prices was to ensure more exploration and, therefore, security of supply. But in 1976 Liberal David Peterson pointed out that between 1972 and 1974, the combined revenue of Hudson's Bay Oil and Mobil Oil rose from $322 million to $604 million, an 87 per cent increase, and their after-tax earnings went up by 79 per cent. However, exploration dropped from $39 million to $38 million, or 2 per cent, during that time.

Once again the oil summit failed to reach a pricing agreement. Trudeau said he'd talk to Alberta and Saskatchewan to try to persuade them to ease their demands for an immediate $2.00-

per-barrel increase, and if he couldn't he would set the price himself under the Petroleum Administration Act. Two weeks later Trudeau said crude oil would rise $1.05 per barrel at the wellhead in July and a further $0.70 on January 1, 1977. Davis expressed "some satisfaction" that the increase wasn't higher, but NDP Leader Stephen Lewis called this reaction a "humiliating capitulation. . . . It is utterly disgraceful. . . . [Davis] calls it a partial victory when Alberta has come down twenty-five cents and Ontario has increased $1.56 a barrel from what it wanted." Davis, braving it out, said he at least didn't expect any more increases until 1978.

But in 1977 Ottawa was at it again. On its mad march toward world prices, it bumped the price by $1 in July, with another increase of $1 set for January, 1978. In a Kingston speech Davis said he'd continue his fight, even though "people have said there is no point. . . . But we have been successful in slowing down the increase."

In October, 1978, Lougheed released a document called "Harmony in Diversity," which he called "a confrontation document," arguing for control of resources, changes to the Supreme Court, and an end to Ottawa's jurisdiction over indirect taxation and interprovincial trade.

Davis countered a month later with a paper that declared Alberta's Heritage Fund was hurting national employment and price objectives because more money in the fund was being saved than was being invested. (At that time the fund held $3.3 billion and was expected to increase by more than $1 billion a year.) Lougheed told the federal-provincial economic conference in Ottawa that Davis was "simply wrong" in his facts. He said Alberta had set aside 30 per cent of the fund as "a savings fund for the future," but the money was being recycled. Once again the eleven first ministers wound up a conference without reaching an agreement on oil prices.

During the 1979 federal election campaign, Davis addressed the Canadian Petroleum Association again; this time he got a better reception than he had in 1973 because he attacked Trudeau, who had spoken to the Petroleum Club the day before. He accused Trudeau of fostering "discord and tension" between Ontario and Alberta, something Davis and Lougheed had been doing quite nicely by themselves for five years.

In July, 1979, after Prime Minister Joe Clark had increased prices because they had been "depressed," Imperial Oil and Shell Canada reported profit increases of 40 to 50 per cent for the first six months of the year. Imperial Oil's profit went from $146 million to $197 million, while Shell Canada suffered through the "depressed" prices by increasing its profit from $69 million to $98.7 million. Two weeks later Davis said part of such huge profits from domestic oil should be used to benefit all Canadians, not just the oil-producing provinces. Canadian crude had now reached $13.75 a barrel, up 362 per cent since 1973, and Clark had just told the Tokyo economic summit that Canada would move toward the world price for its oil.

Davis, on the eve of a premiers' conference at Pointe-au-Pic, Quebec, called for "a more equitable use of petro-dollars." The $2-per-barrel increase pushed by Clark meant that home heating would cost Ontarians $48 more and gasoline $40 more annually, add almost a full point to the Consumer Price Index, and retard the province's economic growth by 0.4 per cent. On the other hand, it would give Ottawa an extra $240 million, Alberta and Saskatchewan $880 million, and the oil companies $840 million. Davis called on Ottawa to set up a multi-billion-dollar national fund using oil revenues to finance such things as tax credits for transit riders, a temporary retail sales tax cut, and enriched grants for home insulation and other energy conservation projects. Lougheed told Davis to take a hike, saying he rejected the plan "as completely unacceptable."

Clark was in a bind. He was an Albertan who knew he owed his election to Ontario, and he simply couldn't make up his mind what to do. Under intense pressure from both camps, he held several meetings on the issue. Davis disagreed openly with Clark's scheme to sell Petro-Canada, at one point even offering to buy a share of it. In late October Clark and Alberta finally agreed on a $4-per-barrel wellhead increase, and Clark said his next step was to placate Ontario.

Lougheed warned Davis he was risking future oil shortages by his "misguided and short-sighted" policies and then, in an October 29 speech in Vancouver, said the oil taps could be turned off. "Within Alberta people will pay the world price for oil fairly soon," Lougheed said, "and if other Canadians want to pay the price, they can have some, too."

Clark called the ten premiers to Ottawa on November 12 for still another oil summit, where Davis failed to convince anyone to keep the 1980 increase to $2 per barrel. Everyone else wanted the increase to be $4, and Davis, looking slightly bewildered by it all, left early to return to Mississauga, where a chemical train had derailed, forcing the entire community to be evacuated. It was not his best day.

Ultimately, however, it wasn't Joe Clark's, either. John Crosbie's December budget tacked an eighteen-cent-per-gallon excise tax on gasoline, and both Davis and Treasurer Frank Miller bitterly attacked the move as a massive tax grab. When the government fell over the budget, the tax became the issue with Ontario voters, and out went Clark.

Oddly enough, during his brief sojourn in opposition, Trudeau had adopted the Davis blended-price formula that he and everyone else had scoffed at years earlier. And when Trudeau included a commitment to a blended price in his August, 1980, throne speech, it was the first real victory for Davis since the whole fight began.

Now, of course, it was Lougheed's turn to be outraged. He said the formula was an "attack" on western energy resources and a threat to Canada, and to show he meant business he announced a production cutback, forcing the East to import oil. A group of Alberta companies jumped in and announced a boycott of Ontario manufactured goods.

The federal budget in October, 1980, increased gasoline prices by 3.2 cents per gallon (nineteen cents less than what Clark had proposed nearly a year earlier), and in the same month Ottawa and Alberta signed the National Energy Plan, which set a blended price for oil in three categories: conventional old oil from pools discovered before 1974 (amended in June, 1983, to allow higher prices); oil discovered between 1974 and 1980; and oil discovered after 1980. While it was at it, Ottawa invented the Petroleum Compensation Charge, a tax to fund the blending of old, new, and imported oil prices into a single Canadian price, and in May, 1981, it brought in the Canadian Ownership Special Charge, a tax to finance increased Canadian ownership in oil and gas. Under the formula the industry gets 46 per cent, the producing provinces 32 per cent, and Ottawa 22 per cent—double what it used to get.

And so it seemed the war was over, at least until 1986 when the agreement expires. And Davis, having fought hard, was looking around for some new cards to play.

✻   ✻   ✻

For eight years Davis had stood alone against the combined might of the oil giants, Lougheed, and, to a lesser extent, the federal government. He had been castigated by his fellow premiers, ridiculed in the media for being unrealistic, and reviled in Alberta as a satanic curse. But in Ontario, where he was seen as the champion of the consumer, his personal popularity was so far ahead of the opposition's and his own party's that it barely hurt him when he abruptly changed his tactics in 1981.

Direct involvement by Ontario in the oil business was not entirely new. In 1975 Ontario put up $106 million for a 5 per cent share of the $2.4 billion Syncrude project, helping Alberta, Ottawa, and the oil interests get it off the ground when its future was in doubt because of escalating prices. Three years later Ontario sold its share for about $142 million (actually, $160 million, but it had six leases left over, paid interest on its debt, and realized about $36 million in profits). Shortly afterward Ontario invested in Polar Gas, a project that hasn't proceeded, but in which the province is still involved.

While Syncrude was Ontario's first venture into public ownership in the oil business, it was almost the second. In 1972, when Darcy McKeough was treasurer, he "took a good look at acquiring an interest in Gulf. Bill was aware of it. We called it Project Sutton, after [*Toronto Sun*] columnist Joan Sutton, although I have no idea why. But for $300 million, we could have bought 60 per cent of Gulf." The plan was to buy 20 per cent of the company and get one or two private investors to buy 40 per cent on the condition that the province would sell off its share to the public. "We asked Noranda and some others," said McKeough, "but we couldn't get enough interest in the private sector. That would have been a good deal, though, since 60 per cent of Gulf Canada now would be worth a couple of billion dollars."

But 1981 is to be remembered for two new initiatives. First, it was the year of the *ad valorem* tax on gasoline — a straight 20 per cent surcharge instead of a set price increase, meaning that the higher the price, the more the government would rake in. For every $1-per-barrel increase in price, Ontario would collect an extra $20 million, or about $1.7 billion during the five-year National Energy Plan.

In September, after Treasurer Frank Miller's budget had introduced this tax grabber, Davis suddenly praised the Trudeau-Lougheed agreement, even though the price of oil would jump $4.75 by January, 1982, another $6.25 by January, 1983, and $8.00 more by January, 1984.

People were just recovering from the *ad valorem* caper and the praise for the NEP when, incredibly, Davis dropped the Suncor bombshell. The *Toronto Sun* had reported three months earlier that the government was looking around to buy an oil company, but at the time the Tories denied it, the opposition didn't pursue it, and Davis became a mini oil baron.

McKeough said negotiations had begun about eight months before the 1981 election. He was out of government by then and was president of Union Gas, but he knew what was happening "because Noranda was trying to save itself from the clutches of Brascan." There had been meetings with Davis the summer before about a Suncor deal, and "it looked as if Noranda was going to go fifty-fifty with the province, but they backed off because the price was just too high."

Suncor was formed in 1979 by a merger of Sun Oil Co. Ltd. and Great Canadian Oil Sands Ltd. Commercially, it's best known through its Sunoco gas stations—553 in Ontario, 339 in Quebec, and two in Fort McMurray, Alberta, at the time of the sale. With assets of $1.7 billion, Suncor was the fifth largest oil company in Canada and the first one to get into the Alberta tar sands and launch a commercial project to exploit them. It also owns a refining company in Sarnia, has three producing natural gas wells in the Arctic islands, and is drilling there as well as in the Beaufort Sea and off the coast of Labrador. The province hired financial consultants McLeod, Young, Weir and Price to review the company before closing the deal, which allowed Ontario to negotiate for another 26 per cent of stock if Suncor couldn't find other Canadian buyers by 1986.

Officially, Davis gave three reasons for the government's 25 per cent investment in Suncor, previously 99.87 per cent owned by Sun Co. Inc. of Radnor, Pennsylvania: first, to participate in the federal government's goal of Canadianization of oil companies; second, to give Ontario the "window" on decision making in the industry; third, because it was a good investment with large future profits.

The province agreed to pay $325 million out of general revenues and borrow the other half from Suncor. The deal was made between Sun Co. Inc. and Ontario Energy Resources Ltd., a subsidiary of Ontario Energy Corporation, the fiefdom of Malcolm Rowan.

Rowan, still excited about the prospects, says, "Ontario was effectively being squeezed out of the picture. The feds and Alberta were saying, 'Why do we need all these other guys? Let's just sit down and divvy up the pie.' Part of the objective was to give us sensitivity in the oil business. That's really a euphemism for clout. It's big business. Suncor is profitable. It has always made a profit." He says a condition of the purchase was that an exploration company would be set up to Canadianize Suncor's frontier lands, and from January 1, 1983, to June, 1984, of the nine discoveries in the Canada Lands, "They've been involved in six of them" through Trillium Corporation (67 per cent of which is owned by Ontario Energy Corporation and 33 per cent by Suncor, giving Ontario 75 per cent ownership of Trillium).

Bob Welch, who was energy minister at the time, said in 1984 that Ontario bought Suncor simply "to take advantage of the cash that was available under NEP, to start giving leadership in the Canadianization of our industry. . . . All the reasons are still there. It's one company which is still making money. It's one of the success stories in terms of the oil industry on the market right now."

Suncor was known to a handful of Queen's Park insiders as "Project Phoenix," a rather fanciful name for what one senior bureaucrat involved in the deal called "a serious miscalculation. It was a bad decision, no question about it. Maybe if the market had gone the other way it would have looked brilliant, but the market didn't go the other way."

Indeed, the day before Ontario bought its thirteen million common shares in December, 1981, Sun Co. of Radnor, P.A., neatly awarded itself a dividend of $78 million. Ontario taxpayers weren't eligible because they had purchased Suncor stock one day too late. Welch explained simply, "It was part of the arrangement that they'd have an opportunity to declare a dividend." Some arrangement.

The three people pushing for the oil company purchase were Malcolm Rowan, Hugh Segal, and Eddie Goodman. Treasurer Frank Miller was opposed, and other senior people had mixed feelings. Once the decision had been made, Bill Kelly and financial adviser Tom Kierans were brought in to do the negotiating.

Kelly was one of the ones with mixed feelings. "If it weren't for the National Energy Plan, I wouldn't have thought it a wise move at all. But the federal government is offering returns up to eighty per cent for exploration by Canadian firms. I think that's an unwise route to go, but, nonetheless, the federal government has gone that route. But in principle I'm the last person ever to insist the government get into business. It will work out in time, I suppose. The whole scene changed right after. . . . No one is doing that well in the oil business today."

Even if it did make sense, those favoring the plan felt that Ontario should have had controlling interest, not just 25 per cent. When Noranda dropped out, negotiations took place for a while with Hiram Walker, but it wasn't interested, either.

"The feeling was, with that investment Ontario would gain access to an asset which over a period of time would pay back quite handsomely," says Segal. "I was in favor of making it Canadian completely, not just twenty-five per cent. At least fifty-one per cent. But the decision was made largely because the premier thought on balance it would be an important asset for the people of Ontario to have in the future. He was quite aware of what it would do to people in his own corps. They would not be happy with it. And he did not proceed without having approval from Lougheed. Sun Oil has all kinds of leases in Alberta, and if Lougheed felt it was a bad idea, it wouldn't have gone through. The premier called Lougheed and asked if there was any reason why we shouldn't do it. Lougheed is, after all, the landlord out there." He says people forget that the Liberals, who were apoplectic about Suncor, "had just come through an election where they were committed to a $650 million expenditure in methanol. That was the one campaign plank they had — $650 million for chicken shit."

Clare Westcott believes "it was a mistake, but they went in

thinking they were doing the right thing. They don't want to admit it now, but they had another buyer. They want to make it look like what they did was a good idea."

Former treasurer Frank Miller still doesn't know why the deal was made. "I've asked that question but never got an answer to it. There were those who truly believed we should do that for socialistic reasons; there were others who saw it as a necessary tool right then, as a political practicality. It's still the most common question we're asked at meetings. . . . I thought the deal would fall apart then in August when Noranda pulled out, but they were convinced they'd get another buyer for the other twenty-five per cent. I also sense that Suncor's American parent, like many companies, was so offended by NEP, they wanted to get some of their money out of Canada. And it had another benefit: If the company was Canadian, their forty-nine per cent was worth more, but because we never got the other buyer, that benefit never flowed to them." Miller believes the government will eventually get rid of Suncor. "There will be a time and place when it will be politically acceptable. It will happen some day."

Miller was so strongly opposed to the Suncor purchase that he almost resigned. On October 12, 1981, he says, Davis presented it to cabinet, "And there was such a shock around the table, we agreed to another meeting the next day. During that discussion I got up and left the cabinet table and went for a long walk in the park. Sally Barnes joined me. No matter how hard I'd argued, I hadn't gotten nasty or petulant, but I'd lost the battle and couldn't in my own conscience live with that one. I decided that day I was going to resign, so I wrote the premier a note in December telling him I would resign in late January. But on January 20 he called me in. We had a long talk. He said looking back, I'd got many things I'd wanted, but I can't win them all. He wanted me to stay."

As was usual with the big decisions, caucus didn't know about the Suncor deal until a few minutes before Davis made the announcement. There, and around the province, the Tories were universally outraged. Two weeks after the announcement, Davis tried to soothe three hundred party members at a London policy meeting by telling them, "I felt this was a valid investment." He said only four cabinet ministers knew of the deal until thirty minutes before the announcement — an account that doesn't square with Miller's — and said, "I don't regard it as contradictory to party policy." *What* party policy, one might ask?

Liberal Leader Stuart Smith, demanding details of the purchase, was continually rebuffed by Davis, who said the financial records were private. Finally, the Liberals began a filibuster to draw attention to the issue, and for the first time since 1874, the Tories invoked closure to end the debate.

By then Tory MPPs were complaining openly that everywhere they went, people asked them about Suncor, but they didn't know any details, either. In mid-November Welch promised caucus that he would explain the deal and table the final agreement on November 20. That agreement doesn't guarantee the province the right to buy the other 26 per cent of Suncor, even if it can find a buyer; it just calls on Sun Co. to enter into "good-faith negotiations" for a possible sale at "fair value."

Liberal David Peterson, who was running for the party leadership in December, 1981, said the deal would cost taxpayers $2.4 billion, not $650 million.

To make matters even worse for Davis, on January 28, 1982, Suncor reported fourth-quarter losses of $500,000 on revenues of $334.3 million, compared to $51 million earnings on revenues of $309.2 million for the same period in 1982. At the same time the parent company, which owns 74.87 per cent of Suncor's fifty-two million common shares, showed a tenfold increase in 1981 earnings.

Robert Brown, a partner in Price Waterhouse, said the company was asked to determine only a fair price, not how wise the purchase was. "It is still our view that it is a fair and reasonable price," he said. "Whether it is a good deal or not is a separate issue." Another company executive said the province won't begin to make profits for several years and may break even only by the end of the century, unless Suncor makes some new oil discoveries.

In October, 1983, the Liberals claimed that taxpayers had lost more than $494 million in the two years since buying into the company. David Peterson dramatically made the point that the value of Suncor shares had dropped by buying ten shares from a private investor at $15.00 each. The province had paid $49.77

each for thirteen million shares. Davis dismissed Peterson's claim as "grandstanding."

The Tories continually debunk their critics by pointing out that Suncor is a profitable company, not a money loser, as the opposition claims. Indeed, Suncor President William Loar told his shareholders on April 26, 1984, that Suncor's income had risen 80 per cent in 1983 — from $60 million to $108 million. Earnings per share were $2.06 compared with $1.13 in 1982. In addition, first-quarter earnings for 1984 were up 28 per cent over the same period in 1983.

Ontario officials quickly crowed that this showed what a great deal they had made. But the Tories' claim that the company is already showing a profit is true only if the actual investment plus interest is conveniently left out of the equation. It also ignores the basic question of why the government should be using tax dollars to speculate in oil in the first place, something that significantly increases the overall government debt and restricts spending on more traditional — and useful — services.

Still, Davis remained firmly convinced that Suncor "was a sound business deal." But was this a Conservative premier? "You know, this left-right stuff is really simplistic, overrated. That's not the way it works. It all depends on your perspective."

*   *   *

In mid-1984 the provincial energy ministry prepared a twenty-five-page analysis of the abrupt increases in oil and gas prices that occurred between 1979 and 1983 under the National Energy Program and that Ontario says cost the province ninety thousand jobs. During that period the wholesale cost to the province of crude oil and natural gas almost doubled, from $4.7 billion to $9 billion, reducing Ontario's real output by 3 to 4 per cent and accounting for one-third of its total inflation.

The Ontario brief, submitted to the Standing Senate Committee on Energy and Natural Resources, stated that while family income rose 40 per cent in Ontario during the period, retail prices jumped 130 per cent for home heating, 100 per cent for gasoline, and 90 per cent for natural gas.

Ontario argued that it had done everything it could as a con-

suming province to meet the objectives of NEP — conservation
and Canadianization — but still suffered because the program
did not include a revenue-sharing arrangement "which addresses
the needs of both the producer and consumer provinces."

It noted that the real winners were the federal government
and the petroleum producers. It claimed that the industry was
receiving more than two and a half times the amount it got
in 1979, while the producing provinces, although receiving a
larger amount in dollar terms, were getting a smaller percentage
of total revenues.

The paper was an early shot in the oil price dispute that will
re-emerge in 1986. It will then be seen whether ownership in
Suncor really does give Ontario more clout in the high-stakes
energy game. Under the Clark regime, of course, Ontario Tories
were not exactly welcome in Ottawa, but under Brian Mulroney,
all that has changed. "We don't find the prospects of real compromise as discouraging as we did in 1979," says one senior Davis
aide. "But we've been there before, and we know you can't get
too excited just because things look good." The provincial Tories are, however, allowing themselves to smile. Discreetly, of
course.

Lougheed, asked at the August, 1984, premiers' conference
in Prince Edward Island about the prospects of harmonious negotiations next time around, said he'd wait until after the federal
election to comment, but he was looking forward to "improved
relations."

Reminded that most of Mulroney's election campaign team
was made up of Davis loyalists, Lougheed quipped, "There's more
truth in that than I like to think."

CHAPTER 23
TIES THAT BIND

⸺⸺⸺ ۞ ⸺⸺⸺

The mythology is simple enough.

The final constitutional conference in Ottawa had broken down on Tuesday, November 5, 1981, and Bill Davis called for a temporary break in the action. It was during that one-hour break, legend has it, that federal Justice Minister Jean Chrétien, Saskatchewan Attorney General Roy Romanow, and Ontario Attorney General Roy McMurtry met in a fourth-floor kitchen in the refurbished railway station and hammered out an agreement to break the stalemate.

Canadians watching CBC television the night of November 6, after everyone but Quebec's separatist René Lévesque had agreed on a new Constitution, were treated to a staged re-enactment of the famous "kitchen meeting" and told it was the key. Print and broadcast commentators repeated the story, and it became thoroughly entrenched in Canadian folklore.

Unfortunately it's a fraud. Not that the three men didn't meet in the kitchen during the coffee break that day. They did. It's just that dozens of similar meetings were going on simultaneously, all of which were just as significant — some more so — than the celebrated get-together. The truth is, if any two people deserve credit (or blame) for Canada's born-again Constitution, those two are Pierre Trudeau and Bill Davis.

For all his work over a decade on the project, and for all the abuse he suffered from within and without his party, Davis is

349

rarely recognized as the ultimate deal-maker, the guy who even Trudeau says made it happen. In Ontario more people think McMurtry was the major player, although Davis, Tom Wells, and Hugh Segal all played more vital roles in the piece, and several other officials at least equalled McMurtry's contribution.

Yet the image that remains is of the three men in the kitchen, an image that not only says something about the media, especially television, but about Davis — his style, his quiet, behind-the-scenes, unemotional pragmatism that may make for good bargains, but makes for rotten TV.

"He was the glue that kept it together," says McMurtry, somewhat ironically considering his hamming for the cameras and his lengthy post-Constitution article in the *Queen's Law Journal* that mentioned Davis just once in passing. "His support was crucial. Trudeau said to me personally on more than one occasion that without that support, the whole thing would have been dead in the water. And Trudeau isn't exactly the kind of person given to making those sorts of statements voluntarily."

Nor did it help to highlight the role Davis played when, on national television, Queen Elizabeth and Pierre Trudeau, flanked by a host of Liberal cabinet ministers, signed the new Constitution on a huge stage in front of the Parliament Buildings. The image of Davis that remains from that event is him sitting forlornly in the pouring rain, his wife Kathleen wearing his top hat. It was a scene, Tory backbencher Morley Kells says, that "should never have been allowed to happen. It's not just him, or his inconvenience. He's representing us. I still wonder why he lets some things happen. All the work he did to help Trudeau, and all the flak he took for it, and that little pipsqueak André Ouellette is up there signing it, and Davis and his wife are sitting in the rain. That's just so damned insulting."

*   *   *

The first time Davis said anything about the Constitution as premier of Ontario was a month after he got the job in 1971. He told the legislature he was firmly opposed to any suggestion to drop the monarchy and switch over to a presidential system.

While his fellow Tories cheered and pounded their desks, Davis dumped on reports coming out of the joint Senate-Commons committee that such a move was being considered. Of course, the committee never recommended any such thing, but Billy Davis, monarchist to the core, wanted it to know what he thought about the idea, anyway. Years later, when Trudeau toyed with the same notion, Davis, in his unique verbal style, told a group of his close advisers it would happen "over my deceased body."

At every constitutional conference that decade, Davis was always the one to offer a compromise, to suggest a new wrinkle, to try to find a way to reconcile irreconcilable interests and personalities.

During the second day of the three-day Victoria constitutional conference in June, 1971, for example, it was Davis who proposed a combined federal-provincial guaranteed annual income plan, hoping to break a deadlock between Trudeau and several premiers. He suggested a tax credit system to finance a nation-wide minimum income plan, primarily to solve the impasse between Ottawa and Quebec over Quebec's demands for primacy in social welfare issues. The scheme, of course, never came to be, but it did get everybody talking again, and the next day they were able to announce tentative agreement on the Victoria Charter, a major breakthrough after forty-four years of constitutional wrangling.

The Victoria Charter would have brought the British North America Act home from Westminster with an amending formula for constitutional change, an entrenched Bill of Rights, provincial power to guarantee language rights (leaving it up to each to decide whether to become bilingual or not), and a system for appointing Supreme Court judges in consultation with provincial attorneys general. It would be ten years before the prime minister and the provincial premiers would agree on another system, a decade of acrimony and regional hostilities that, combined with the disputes over oil revenue sharing, shattered old alliances and shook the country to its core.

A few days after the Victoria conference, Quebec Premier Robert Bourassa announced that his province could not accept the agreement because it was unhappy with social and cultural provisions. The federal government and the nine other provinces had all approved the scheme. (Ironically, in 1981 Quebec again refused to participate, but Trudeau went ahead without it.) Davis met privately with Bourassa a month after Victoria, hoping to salvage the charter, but with no success.

Over the next few years there were periodic rumblings in Ottawa and the provincial capitals about the Constitution, but the first formal meeting after Victoria came during the August, 1975, premiers' conference in Newfoundland. There all ten premiers agreed to co-operate in preparing a detailed case for redefining federal and provincial government responsibilities to put to Trudeau. Davis darted in and out of the conference, arriving at midnight on the eve of the meeting and leaving late the next night to return to his struggling provincial election campaign. But he was there long enough to express concerns about duplicating government responsibilities and to extract general agreement that the issue would be discussed at a future constitutional meeting with Trudeau.

In April, 1976, Trudeau told the Commons that it would be worthwhile to patriate the Constitution with or without provincial consent. Most premiers were outraged by the statement, charging that it would create division, but Davis said a federal-provincial energy agreement was of more "pressing importance" than a constitutional agreement, and because of the "close inter-relationship between energy pricing and the future of federal-provincial arrangements," both topics should be dealt with at a single meeting.

Things started getting tougher for the champions of a provincial common front against Trudeau at the 1976 premiers' conference in Banff, where the ten first ministers failed to reach a consensus. Trudeau had set a September 15 deadline to reach agreement on domestic control of the Constitution — just three weeks after the August meeting — but the only thing the premiers could agree on was to hold more talks in Toronto in October.

Davis, ever the optimist, called this "progress." In fact, the talks had fallen apart because Alberta's Peter Lougheed, in a move to protect his oil and gas supplies, had surprised everyone by demanding the old Fulton-Favreau formula, worked out in the early 1960s, requiring unanimous consent for any constitutional change. That would mean any province, regardless of size, could veto any change.

The problem was that Trudeau had sent confidential letters to all the premiers the previous March, saying he would not entertain constitutional changes altering the distribution of powers. He had argued that a consensus on such changes would be difficult to reach and might delay patriation for years, contrary to his stated goal of bringing the Constitution home before the next federal election.

When the premiers met again in October, 1976, in Toronto, they were not surprised that Lougheed had not changed his mind. But now British Columbia agreed with him.

Still, Trudeau told the premiers in December, after the Parti Québécois had won in Quebec, he wanted the federal-provincial economic conference slated for later that month to deal with constitutional issues as well, adding that he hoped "final decisions" could be reached. They weren't.

During 1977 things went from the sublime to the absurd. Trendy Ottawa bureaucrat Bernard Ostry announced he'd managed to arrange the purchase of the American Freedom Train for $575,000. Used to promote the American bicentennial celebrations, it would be turned into a Canadian "Discovery Train," travelling coast to coast, its fifteen cars filled with museum pieces and arts and crafts, supposedly to promote a greater awareness of Canada among Canadians. But no idea could be too trendy for Davis (no bureaucrat, either, because Davis hired Ostry four years later as deputy minister of industry and trade, then demoted him after he bombed), so he agreed to contribute $200,000 toward the cost of the train. Other provinces, except Quebec, of course, kicked in varying amounts to get the train on the rails for 1978.

A Gallup poll in April, 1978, showed that 35 per cent of Canadians felt Ontario had benefited the most from Confederation, with Quebec and the West next at 16 and 15 per cent respectively. This was a reflection of the deeply felt bias of all regions against Ontario, historically the province most Canadians love to hate. Whether the view is valid or not—and it does conveniently ignore Ontario's contribution to Confederation — it hampered Davis in his role as peacemaker: The other premiers assumed he was interested in protecting the status quo simply because he had the most to gain from it.

Ottawa and the provinces went into 1978 still light-years apart

on constitutional reforms, but the allegiances that for a time would
isolate Davis and New Brunswick's Richard Hatfield were beginning to form. British Columbia was demanding status as a fifth
region, equal with Ontario and Quebec; Lougheed was hanging
in with his protective veto for each province; Saskatchewan
wanted to enshrine provincial ownership and taxation rights
over mineral resources; Manitoba's position was unclear, but
the province was making odd grumbling noises against Central
Canada. The Maritimes, worried about fat-cat Ontario, wanted
constitutional affirmation of the equalization principle, although
Hatfield liked Davis's constitutional proposals, and Newfoundland wanted the equalization measure, but was also demanding
complete control of offshore mineral resources. The chances for
harmony were remote, particularly since René Lévesque essentially wanted no part of the whole thing. He simply wanted to
opt out of Canada.

Trudeau finally introduced a constitutional bill in June, 1978,
about which Davis expressed his classic cautious optimism, saying
it was really too soon "to make a definitive statement" (something
he has never done in his life). The Constitutional Amendment
Bill was described as a "dog's breakfast" by constitutional expert Senator Eugene Forsey, a longtime fan of Trudeau's who
admitted that his ardor had become "less enthusiastic" with the
proposal to completely alter the Senate and downgrade the monarchy, making Queen Elizabeth Queen only when she was in
Canada and the rest of the time a deputy of the Governor General.

Two weeks later Davis also announced he would "vigorously
oppose" any lessening of the role of the monarchy in Canada; he
got himself into such a dither about it that he went to the premiers'
conference in Regina and presented a toughly worded position
paper telling Ottawa to practise what it preached and to stop
butting into provincial affairs. His ten-page paper on what he
called a question of "national revival" rather than "national
survival" accused Ottawa of dividing the provinces by getting
into areas, such as lotteries and land-use regulations, traditionally under provincial jurisdiction. Davis also pressed for minority-
language guarantees in a revised Constitution, "such guarantees
to be extended across the country in a true national context." This
was another idea that did not win him any ringing endorsements
from other provinces, with the exception of New Brunswick.

The premiers ended their meeting by demanding "significant concessions" from Ottawa, while offering few of their own. Even Davis, having earlier balked at the idea, signed the communiqué declaring that "the premiers firmly believe that significant constitutional reform should have the concurrence of all governments, recognizing the equality of status of all provinces in the process." They also rejected Trudeau's proposed two-stage deadline: July, 1979, for reform of the Senate and Supreme Court; July, 1981, for determining the division of powers.

Trudeau had scheduled a constitutional meeting for late October, and the provincial ministers responsible for constitutional reform — in Ontario Tom Wells and Roy McMurtry — were slated to meet a month earlier to draft a position.

By this time Davis had set up an advisory committee on Confederation under York University president H. Ian Macdonald, a former deputy treasurer of Ontario. Its members were given a cool reception in late August when they told the Senate-Commons committee on the Constitution that they wanted to scrap the Senate and replace it with a new parliamentary institution made up exclusively of provincial government representatives. This new "House of the Provinces," about one-third the size of the Senate, would have absolute veto over some legislation passed in the Commons and would include provincial cabinet ministers, perhaps even premiers. Senator George van Roggen of British Columbia told the twelve Ontario academics that their proposal reflected the naiveté of those who had never sat as members of government. "Premiers and elected members are very busy men," he said. "The best they could do would be to breeze through town and hold an airport press conference complaining, 'The feds are at it again.'"

Once more, Davis was the one who shook the October constitutional conference by breaking his earlier agreement with the premiers, which had been a backing-away from his previous position, anyway. He now demanded that minority education and civil rights be enshrined in a new Constitution. While the minority-education provisions were ultimately included and garnered Davis much favorable publicity, in fact their inclusion made no difference in Ontario, where they were already guaranteed by legislation.

Trudeau countered with a seven-point proposal to put limits on the use of federal spending and declaratory powers. Once again, everyone left the conference agreeing on only one thing—another meeting in February, 1979.

But again, Davis went charging off in another direction. In a sharp reversal of form, he called on the country's leaders to "bring the Constitution home to Canada." Davis, who had argued since 1971 that a formula for changing the Constitution had to be worked out before it was brought home from Westminster, now set that argument aside and said it was time to endorse Trudeau's position and "take, without further debate, the decisive step of patriating our Constitution." Davis was supported by Hatfield and British Columbia's Bill Bennett, but that was all. The proposal also put federal Tory leader Joe Clark in an awkward position because of the impending election: He had to determine which of his Tory premiers he should support and which ones he should publicly disagree with.

While Davis may have been genuine in his desire to get the stalemated process moving, he did contribute substantially to the growing resentment from the other premiers, and from his own Queen's Park caucus, over his "hopping into bed" with Trudeau. He tried to allay those concerns during an election appearance for the federal Tories in April, when he said Trudeau was "pitting East against West and sometimes French against English to win re-election," adding that if Trudeau won on May 22, it would be a "mandate of fear and suspicion."

Trudeau, of course, did not win. But a week before the election, after the televised leaders' debate, Davis was put in the embarrassing position of having to agree with Trudeau and disagree with Clark. During the debate, Trudeau and Clark had argued about whether the prime minister had Ontario's support in bringing the Constitution home unilaterally. Trudeau said Davis agreed, but Clark said he didn't. Obviously, Trudeau was right, although Clark could probably be forgiven for not being able to keep track of Davis's constantly changing positions.

When Clark won the election, the Queen's Park crowd was convinced that without Trudeau's prickly presence, constitutional reform was just around the corner. But as weeks and months passed and Clark showed no interest in the subject, they began to grumble aloud.

As if Davis hadn't upset enough Tories with his perceived tightness with Trudeau, on November 16, just a few days before he announced his first retirement, Trudeau told seven hundred Ontario Liberals that Davis was the only Canadian government leader attempting to speak for Canada. Trudeau said Davis was responsible for Clark's election because he had put his Big Blue Machine behind him, but "Canadians are beginning to be ashamed when the only one who is attempting to speak for Canada . . . is the premier of your province, Bill Davis."

Davis and Clark had a major disagreement on another important cog in the constitutional wheel when Davis attacked Lévesque's sovereignty-association proposals, saying he would never negotiate them. Clark initially said he would negotiate, then backed off, was criticized for being inconsistent, then said during the election campaign that he would negotiate.

Trudeau's November resignation, like Mark Twain's death, was highly exaggerated, but at the time Davis praised him for believing "in those things he attempted to do. One could not but respect his commitment to his view of Canada and the ideals he held and the tenacity with which he defended them." It seemed that Davis had lost his greatest constitutional ally. But by February, 1980, Trudeau was back in command and itching to resolve the constitutional impasse.

In May Davis told the Ontario legislature he had ten principles for constitutional change, a process he called urgent, so as not to betray the trust of Quebecers who had opted for federalism instead of separatism. His principles were not new, but he wanted to put them on the record. They included immediate patriation, provincial participation in appointing Supreme Court judges, Senate reform, minority-language education rights, entrenchment of a Bill of Rights, elimination of interprovincial trade barriers, and concessions for provinces, such as Quebec, seeking more power in areas like immigration.

Davis also excluded himself from a strategy session of premiers, organized by Newfoundland's Brian Peckford, on the eve of the June constitutional summit at 24 Sussex Drive. Ultimately, only six premiers met in Peckford's suite at the Skyline. Bennett and Hatfield did not attend, and Nova Scotia's John Buchanan missed the meeting because his plane was delayed by fog.

At the summit Trudeau offered some incentive to a quick resolution of the problem when he said he would be "anxious to retire" once a new Constitution was forged. But even that encouragement wasn't enough, because Lougheed, Peckford, and Manitoba's right-wing Conservative Sterling Lyon had all dug their respective trenches. While prepared to peek over the top at constitutional reform, they weren't ready to abandon their fortifications altogether.

Once again, no one could agree on much except the great Canadian pastime of calling another meeting, this one for September, giving officials the summer to meet and try to sort out some of the problems.

Tom Wells led the Ontario delegation in the constitutional road show — a group of officials from the eleven governments that met over the summer in Montreal, Toronto, and the West. He called a Queen's Park press conference to say that the western leaders had made "a veiled threat . . . that Confederation would crumble. It is hanging there as a spectre." In early July Lougheed and Bennett had issued a joint communiqué condemning Trudeau's suggestion that the federal government tax exports of natural gas, a move hardly designed to appease the provinces.

In the meantime Ontario's all-party select committee on constitutional reform, anxious to appear useful, set a budget of $94,000 for cross-country trips to the legislatures in Newfoundland, Quebec, Alberta, and British Columbia in August and September, hoping to get what New Democrat James Renwick called the "sense of alienation from Ontario to other parts of the country."

Davis arrived at the annual premiers' conference in Winnipeg and was greeted by his fellow premiers with all the affection of a leper entering a crowded swimming pool. By this time only Hatfield was supportive, while most of the others, especially Peckford and Lougheed, were openly hostile. Lougheed opened the conference by accusing Davis of being "in the lap" of Trudeau, but Davis wouldn't respond, saying he hadn't come to the two-day, closed-door session to fight with other premiers.

But even in that mood, the premiers appeared ready to be conciliatory toward Trudeau until news of a federal memo written by Privy Council Clerk Michael Pitfield appeared in the *Ottawa Citizen* on August 22. The memo showed Ottawa had already drawn up plans to bring home the Constitution, whether the premiers liked it or not. While even Wells was moved to complain that the memo "will cast a bit of a shadow over the talks," Davis said he would "be very surprised if [the story] is true." It was.

The Winnipeg meeting ended with Davis as the lone holdout, refusing to endorse the communiqué registering the premiers' opposition to any federal tax on the export of provincially owned resources and calling for a gradual increase in domestic oil prices. "You learn in this business," said Davis, "not to let things bother you. You deal with them as they occur."

Well, the next occurrence was the September summit in Ottawa, when Davis summed up the opening day rather sardonically: "It was a better day than it could have been." Indeed, at least everyone was still speaking, although eight of the other nine premiers — all but Hatfield — were openly critical of Davis. Even McMurtry was expressing doubts about a Charter of Rights that would take power from elected representatives and hand it to appointed judges. He said, "The concept does have a certain motherhood quality," but if legislation was inequitable, politicians could be pressured into changing it. "But how possible would it be to amend an entrenched Constitution?"

With Trudeau, Davis, and Hatfield lining up for a Charter, Lyon made a brilliant defence of the no-Charter position, pointing out that Canada simply didn't need one because individual rights, with few exceptions, were already protected under the existing system without being enshrined. Lyon pointed out that the office of the prime minister and the offices of the premiers were not enshrined either, but that didn't inhibit any of them. "We're all here doing a job for Canada."

Davis never addressed the need for a Charter of Rights. He saw it as a sexy political move, a trendy reform much easier to sell than the traditional conservative position that a Charter wasn't necessary. As noted before, under British parliamentary democracy, which Davis consistently supported — particularly during election campaigns and at political rallies in true-blue eastern Ontario — it is always assumed that a person can do something unless there is a specific law against it. Under a Charter or a republican system, there may be all kinds of things it is illegal to do, but no one will know for sure until unelected judges periodically reinterpret statutes approved by the people's representatives. It was always easier to understand Trudeau's support of the concept, because his background was in the French, rather than the British, tradition. But it was difficult to rationalize Davis's support of a system he was now actively seeking to discard.

The conference again ended in failure, with Davis actually supporting Trudeau's threat to simply bring the Constitution home regardless and Wells favoring Trudeau's suggestion of a national referendum as a way of circumventing elected governments.

Trudeau went on national television in October to unveil another set of constitutional proposals, and Davis urged Ottawa not only to ignore opposition from the other premiers, but also to discount the concerns of Joe Clark. "To do nothing at this point, not to seek patriation and reform, would be to admit a victory for those who say this nation is unworkable." Lévesque, of course, was the only premier saying that, but Davis, who never suffered criticism well, consistently used the technique of maligning his critics by either lumping them all together or simply tossing off broad, critical generalizations. He assumed that his own omniscience was beyond reproach, while those who disagreed were self-seeking louts.

But the opposition wasn't just from other premiers. Davis had become so shameless in his support of Trudeau that he was upsetting his Tory troops at home. The provincial party's executive director conceded that "the worker who works for both the federal and provincial parties is offended by the fact that the premier and Trudeau seem closer than the premier and Clark." The late Osie Villeneuve, a veteran Tory MPP from eastern Ontario, said at the time, "People are saying, 'What the hell is the matter with Mr. Davis? Why is he in bed with Mr. Trudeau?'" And Metro Toronto party organizer John Nicholls said, "Some of our people who work both federally and provincially have spent the last twelve years and five elections fighting Trudeau. They get tunnel vision, so all they can see is that son of a bitch Trudeau and Davis siding with him." Support from his own people, however, was never a big item on the Davis political menu, and he wasn't about to take advice from them or, for that matter, even seek their views.

In November a grateful Trudeau agreed to a suggestion from Davis to delay a referendum for at least a year to help placate those provinces that were worried that Trudeau would call a referendum without giving them a fair chance to negotiate. Five

premiers — Lyon, Lougheed, Bennett, Lévesque, and Peckford — were so upset by events that they launched a court action
to test the legality of Trudeau's plans for constitutional change.
The year ended the way it began — with everyone angry at everyone else.

Nineteen eighty-one did not begin auspiciously for Davis.
McMurtry, ever anxious to ride his own white charger, went to
England to say that Trudeau had mishandled the constitutional
package and should test its legality in the Supreme Court. Davis,
ambushed by reporters as he returned home from his annual Florida holiday, said, "Our position hasn't changed. There is no need
for it to be referred to the Supreme Court at this point."

While Davis was as usual outwardly calm, Ontario officials
were livid. Hugh Segal later explained, "You have a government
line on the Constitution, and you try to stick to it. We don't always
agree with each other, but we don't go out and knife each other
in public. Roy issued that statement long before anybody here
had decided on that Supreme Court route. Wells, and those of
us working on the issue, felt if that was the only way, fine, but
why would you put that card on the table before you see whether
it can be worked out politically or not? The other thing Roy did
was, during the constitutional process he wrote a letter to Chrétien
questioning the value of the Charter of Rights. That was discussed in cabinet, and as a government we were for a Charter.
McMurtry said he was mirroring police force concerns about
the Charter of Rights. He said the police made a good case against
it, and as chief law officer of the Crown he had a duty to pass
those views on. Well, if we all started serving separate constituencies like that, there'd never be a government view."

Segal says the strategy was: "Don't break ranks. . . . Davis
didn't seem upset by it. I guess you have to ask yourself, 'Is that
the kind of relationship that exists between Davis and some of
the guys in cabinet who feel they have more licence than other
guys do?' The feeling at the time was: We were taking a position
which wasn't popular with the rank and file, wasn't popular with
the media in Ontario, certainly wasn't popular among federal
Conservatives, was causing Billy all kinds of terminal difficulties in Western Canada, and then for Roy to say, 'I don't like the
Charter of Rights, either,' well, it's not the kind of thing William
G. Davis needed at that point in time."

During the March provincial election campaign, Davis trotted out his support for the Charter of Rights on occasions when he met multicultural groups. In Thunder Bay on March 1, for example, he said, "We must all appreciate that we live in a pluralistic society, made up of different ethnocultural groups whose aspirations to live and grow in freedom demand guarantees." Naturally, those opposed to the Charter were not disputing that, but Davis frequently stooped to hinting that the Charter's opponents had racist motives, ignoring the fact that the existing system already allowed for the freest society in the world.

In April Trudeau offered to test his constitutional package in the Supreme Court after provincial court rulings in both Manitoba and Newfoundland had muddied the waters even more. In Manitoba a court of appeal had upheld the legality of the federal proposals, although the ruling wasn't definitive, and in Newfoundland the court of appeal had ruled against Ottawa's package.

In a strongly worded telegram to Davis in early April, thirty-eight Tory MPs from the Ontario federal caucus urged Davis to help force Ottawa to put the constitutional question before the Supreme Court: "It is imperative to Canada that the province of Ontario, the cornerstone of Confederation, strongly support the rule of law as a Canadian concept," adding that silence by Ontario could be seen as acquiescing to Trudeau's "unseemly" strategy.

Wells had announced that the Newfoundland decision did not "in any way" change Ontario's support for the federal position, and when Davis arrived back from a Florida holiday on April 7, he huddled for over an hour with Wells and McMurtry to discuss the situation. The two cabinet ministers scurried away from reporters afterward, McMurtry literally running down a staircase to escape comment. Davis just stayed inside his office.

A day later Davis announced that Ontario would appear before the Supreme Court to defend the federal proposals, having filed an intervention to allow it to appear during Manitoba's appeal later that month. Manitoba and seven other provinces argued that the proposals were illegal. New Brunswick was the only other province that supported Trudeau.

While Davis was hotly defending Trudeau, Clark and the federal Tories were holding a two-week filibuster in Ottawa trying to stop him. The eight dissenting premiers, meanwhile, signed their own constitutional accord calling for patriation and an amending formula, but Davis, who at one point in the long-running debate had been prepared to settle for patriation alone, now said the Charter of Rights was "fundamental to our position." This was despite the fact that he had some "concerns" about some provisions of the Charter, particularly the search-and-seizure rights of police.

In June Davis and McMurtry even agreed to a secret request from Trudeau to dash off to Westminster to lobby senior British Tories on Trudeau's behalf, and Davis tentatively booked a flight, depending upon the timing of the Supreme Court ruling on the legality of the package.

In August, at the end of the annual premiers' conference in Victoria, the eight dissenting premiers met to discuss strategy. Davis and Hatfield were told they weren't welcome.

Davis had attempted to recoup some of his lost respectability by delivering a twenty-five-page speech on the economy that opened the conference, in which he attacked Trudeau's "anti-American trade policies," adding, "Responsible foreign investment is welcome in Ontario . . ." What Davis didn't say was that between 1971 and 1973, when the notion of economic national-ism was current, Davis was a leader in the movement to exclude American investors and "buy Canada back," even setting up a committee to study the idea and urging Ottawa to be tougher on foreign (read American) investors. The premiers weren't impressed.

In September, with both Trudeau and Davis out of the country, the Supreme Court, televised for the first time in history, ren-dered a decision that basically supported the federal package in strict legal terms, but not in convention or tradition. For the On-tario Tories, who constantly upheld the importance of tradition, it didn't matter this time. Tom Wells, openly gleeful about the ruling, told CBC's Peter Mansbridge, "I think we should move ahead." Mansbridge said, "In a way, that's the first federal reac-tion we've heard," underscoring the general feeling that Ontario was then so tight with Trudeau, it was being regarded more as a federal adjunct than Canada's most powerful province.

At the time Davis was resting up in Fiji after an Australian trade mission, and in a telephone consultation with McMurtry and Wells, he said Trudeau should now proceed at full speed with his package. Wells and Segal had already visited Westminster to lobby Tories there who were concerned about a Charter, something foreign to the British system. "We told them they should know that as Tories, there was another Tory government that had been around for thirty-eight years that didn't think the Charter was all bad," says Segal. "They were concerned about Trudeau, but we told them that whether they think he's a Commie sympathizer or not is another question; the fact is we supported the package."

On October 7 British Columbia's Bill Bennett met with Davis in Toronto for over an hour to try to reach a compromise. Davis said he'd consider "some refinement" of the Charter and be "flexible" in wording the amending formula, but that was it.

Later that month the ten premiers congregated in Montreal's Ritz Hotel. Davis, in a speech to the Ontario Progressive Conservative Women's Association just before he left, said the meeting was "almost like a football game, where you have two teams and we put on sweaters when we go to these conferences. . . . I would just hope that none of us put on team sweaters and that we don't go out there saying there are going to be winners or losers." Well, Davis went, but it was clear soon after he arrived that he and Hatfield were one team and the other eight premiers another. During the morning meeting, Davis and Hatfield left the "Gang of Eight" and met for two hours on their own. When Davis left that night, the eight dissenting premiers stayed another day and carried on without him.

On November 1, the night before the final constitutional showdown, Davis and Segal flew to Ottawa to sit on the back porch of 24 Sussex Drive with Trudeau and Michael Kirby and discuss the Constitution.

"The culture shock was amazing," says Segal. "Davis arrived wearing a blue blazer and grey pants, and Trudeau arrives at the door wearing a Peter Storm sweater, GWG jeans, and clogs. Kirby and I are there as note-takers, and at one point Trudeau lectures Davis on bilingualism, saying he knows Davis has problems with that, but it's important to keep the country together. And I'm thinking to myself, 'We're the last fucking friend on Omaha Beach the guy has, and he's lecturing us.' I'm thinking if we ever took a vote in our caucus, it would be sixty-nine to one against, or maybe sixty-eight, depending on whether or not McMurtry showed up. I had the temerity to suggest there were a lot of things everybody could be doing to make things easier, but Davis simply said, 'The point is, we should not find ourselves singing from different hymn books.' Which is as tough a statement as you're going to get from Davis."

Finally the big day arrived. Davis opened the conference by offering to surrender Ontario's veto powers under the 1971 Victoria Charter if this would assist compromise on the amending formula. Three days earlier Davis had denied news reports that he was planning to suggest that.

McMurtry had breakfast with Chrétien that day and later explained, "I urged him to bring whatever modest influence he had with the prime minister to prevent him from getting into this argumentative mood every time somebody wants to take a position contrary to him. Davis was always unfailingly courteous. . . . He believes strongly in the politics of reconciliation. You can always sense a great temptation to do battle, but he gives the impression of this inherent wisdom that there'll always be another day. Trudeau, at the drop of a hat, will always engage someone in an argument. Chrétien told me then, 'You know, Roy, he'd rather win an argument than anything else in life. You know, you win a lot of goddamn arguments, but you lose the war.'"

The second day began with the Gang of Eight meeting for breakfast, while Trudeau, Davis, and Hatfield had a breakfast of their own. The closed meeting began at 9:30 a.m., and the first ninety minutes were bogged down in what officials described as bitter, rancorous debate. Lévesque, Lougheed, Lyon, and Peckford lectured Trudeau on his proposals, and at one point the prime minister stalked out of the meeting, with Davis close behind trying to calm him down. It was after Davis returned with Trudeau that he made an emotional plea for acceptance of the dissenters' amending formula if they would accept a Charter of Rights.

The meeting broke at 12:45, and everyone ostensibly left for lunch with their own ministers and officials. But the formal meeting didn't resume until the next day. Bennett met with Davis over lunch to discuss a British Columbia proposal for a scaled-down Charter, and shortly after 2:00 the Gang of Eight gathered in Lyon's suite in the Château Laurier across the road from the Conference Centre. Davis joined them for an hour shortly after 3:00, then returned to the Centre to report to Trudeau. After that a subcommittee of three premiers — Bennett, Lougheed, and Buchanan — arrived to meet Davis and Trudeau, returning to the Château Laurier shortly after 6:00. Trudeau and Davis even exchanged heated words when Trudeau exploded because Davis was leaning toward acceptance of the modified Charter.

That evening the federal cabinet met for two hours and agreed to accept a compromise proposal from Davis that would enshrine a Charter but allow provinces to "opt out" of future amendments under the so-called "notwithstanding clause." Davis said that Ontario would not use the clause, that all rights in the Charter would apply to Ontario citizens. The new amending formula essentially said that any future changes must be approved by Ottawa and seven of the ten provinces, representing at least 50 per cent of Canada's population. It allowed provinces to opt out of change, a proposal Trudeau had dismissed a few days earlier as "incremental separatism," but which Davis had convinced him was the best they could hope for.

That night Davis and Saskatchewan's Allan Blakeney both ended up in the same Italian restaurant — by coincidence, they claimed — and sought a compromise. Blakeney, the only New Democrat in the bunch, was with the Gang of Eight in fact, but not really in spirit.

The next day, despite some progress, the whole thing almost fell apart and would have, had it not been for Davis. Indeed, at the press conference after ten of the eleven first ministers reached agreement (Lévesque didn't), even Lougheed said, "We did budge, friend Bill, and your persuasion was important to our budging." Lévesque, while not meaning it as a compliment, also underscored Davis's role by referring acidly to him having given a "hymn to harmony" at the conference. "I think the history books will show that he made the compromise possible," says Segal, who was not without influence himself.

At about 11:00 a.m. on the third day, Trudeau lost patience with the process and suggested they merely patriate and then put all substantial questions in a referendum. Lévesque immediately agreed, sensing this was a way to destroy the momentum of the issue.

"At lunch," says Segal, "Lévesque was jubilant, Trudeau was looking like the proverbial cat who just ate the mouse, and the rest of us were feeling that we got really screwed. Not us so much, because we were prepared to go the referendum route. Davis would have settled for patriation, period, at that moment in time. The guys who really felt screwed were the guys who'd been in there with Lévesque. They'd taken a lot of heat too about being in bed with the separatist government."

Lyon was opposed to a referendum because he believed in the parliamentary process. Lougheed didn't want one because he recognized the political difficulties of appearing to be fighting motherhood. "Those guys were really upset," says Segal, "which was really good, because for the first time they were beginning to see that those guys in Quebec were really in business for themselves, and they'd better start protecting their own asses, because Quebec couldn't be trusted."

During the lunch break officials had been working on the wording for a potential referendum. The debate rambled on until finally Trudeau asked who wanted a referendum. The yeas were four: Trudeau, Lévesque, Davis, and Hatfield.

Segal explains, "At that point Trudeau said, 'Well, we've tried everything, screw it. I think we should be prepared to meet the television cameras at five and tell them we couldn't agree.' That happened about three o'clock, and for the very first time, Davis got angry. He just waded in. We had thought the referendum was just a tactic to move Lévesque off from the others and open up discussions, but Trudeau comes in and says, 'Well, that's it, Bob's your uncle, let's go and face the cameras.' We still thought there was a way to save this thing, so Davis told Trudeau that facing the cameras would be premature and we should have a coffee break to consult and see if we couldn't come up with something more constructive, because there's always time to face the cameras."

Davis was telling Trudeau bluntly not to count on Ontario's support if he was going to end the thing like that. It was during this coffee break that the legendary kitchen cabinet meeting of Chrétien, Romanow, and McMurtry took place. "We all had our assignments to go and deal with the people we'd been dealing with during the negotiating period," says Segal. "The message was to be very clear: 'If you guys can't find a way to compromise, then don't count on us to be with you at Westminster.' Those were Davis's explicit orders to us all."

So Segal went off to give that message to senior Trudeau aides

Jim Coutts, Tom Axworthy, and Michael Kirby, while Wells spoke to Marc Lalonde and Serge Joyal; Ed Stewart told Michael Pitfield, and McMurtry spoke with Chrétien and Romanow.

"The feds were stunned," says Segal. "They just expected Ontario to sit there and accept everything. The break lasted about an hour, and when we all came back, Lougheed, to his credit, said to the prime minister, 'I think it would be premature to meet the cameras now. We have nothing to meet them with except failure, and we can meet them tomorrow with that.'"

Coming from the previously intractable Lougheed, that made Trudeau sit up and take nōtice. If Lougheed thought it was worth sitting another day, then why not? So they adjourned again with things still unresolved. But it was that night — not during the coffee break — that the agreement was finally forged.

As the meeting broke up, Davis and Blakeney spoke for about thirty minutes. They agreed, without telling the dissenting premiers, that Blakeney would go back to them and see if a compromise could be found, that Blakeney's people would work out a draft resolution and be in constant touch with Davis who, of course, was in touch with the federal officials and Trudeau.

Trudeau was told of the plan by Kirby, who had been filled in by Segal, and it was suggested by Ontario that Trudeau should call Davis later that night.

Davis and Blakeney spoke twice by telephone earlier in the evening, and at about 10:15 the phone rang again in the seventeenth-floor Davis suite at the Four Seasons Hotel. It was Trudeau. He had held a meeting at 24 Sussex Drive with Chrétien, Kirby, Pitfield, Axworthy, Deputy Attorney General Roger Tasse, Environment Minister John Roberts, External Affairs Minister Mark MacGuigan, Energy Minister Marc Lalonde, Treasury Board President Don Johnston, and Consumer Affairs Minister André Ouellet.

The Ontario crew had just ordered in Chinese food. Davis went into his bedroom, closed the door, and spoke with Trudeau for about twenty-five minutes. "Davis didn't tell us exactly what he told Trudeau," says Segal, "but I think he told him that unless he was prepared to be part of the compromise, don't count on his help. And you know, he came out and he said, 'Well, everybody, check your watches. It's ten-forty, and if there's going to be an agreement, this is it.' Then he picked up some

Chinese food and began eating and said, 'You know, I think the pineapple chicken is better in Brampton.' It was just like it was part of the same thought."

At about 3:00 a.m., the actual Saskatchewan document was written, but it became the Newfoundland document. "Blakeney was seen too much as a guy who had sat on the fence," says Segal, "and for someone like Peckford to do it made it more politic. They still wouldn't have known about Blakeney's go-between deal with Davis."

At 6:30 a.m. Kirby called Davis from 24 Sussex Drive and put Trudeau on the phone so they could review the details of the compromise, which Davis already knew through Blakeney. The peace was reached at about 10:30, although it took until early afternoon for the officials to draft the final wording. Davis was exhilarated, even more emotional than on the 1981 election night.

Because of limited space on the fourth floor of the Conference Centre, many of the Ontario officials were in a room on the first floor. On the way down to meet the media, Segal suggested that Davis drop in to see the staff. "He paced outside the door for a time, and only Tom Wells is capable of saying things, with the absolute best of intentions, in such a way as to make everybody too emotional to address it. When Davis walked in, Tom said, 'Ladies and gentlemen, we would not have been able to reach this point without the premier. We've all been through a lot together, but nothing is more important than a new Constitution for Canada, and without Bill Davis it never would have happened.' At this point I'm crying, which of course doesn't say much, but a lot of people were crying. The premier was just too emotional to speak. He just stood there and cried. Tears were running down his cheeks, and that produced a cheer, because everybody was so embarrassed they didn't know what to do. So we had three cheers, and a hip, hip, hurrah, and by the time he went down to meet the press he had regained his composure."

Wells says the kitchen cabinet performance happened at about 3:00 that day. "The thing was already signed, but the CBC, in order to liven up their presentation, was looking for some story that was going to give it a little zip. So they got those three guys to go up to this room and say, 'This is where the final agreement was made which set the thing back in motion.' That meeting never did happen the way the pictures showed it. Sure, they were talking, but everybody was. We were all milling around. I went from there into a meeting where Bill Davis and Trudeau were sitting, and I said we should keep the meeting going because there were some suggestions being made by Saskatchewan at the time. I'm not running anybody down on that thing, but anybody who was there knows it's just nonsense. You do get a little annoyed from time to time though, when you work hard and others are up front grabbing the credit. That's politics, I guess."

Wells says the main players were the eleven first ministers. "Everybody else was there to serve them. It wouldn't have mattered if any of the ministers had an agreement or not. The first ministers had to make the deal. All I know is, the credit for what happened should go to Davis. He's the one who was taking the flak and who set our course of action. And he built a backlog of credibility that allowed him to be the key at the end."

Even Davis, who rarely comments about this sort of thing, said in a 1984 interview that "it doesn't concern me. The kitchen meeting was not irrelevant, but it was not part of the final settlement. I'm not inclined to . . . Listen, Roy lived with this thing, he worked at it, but it was never part of the discussions between myself and the prime minister and Hughie [Segal] and Michael Kirby. I know roughly what happened, but I'm not going to diminish the feelings of others.

"Look, everybody played a part. I know the crucial points and when they happened . . . but it's done, and I think it's right. We're still sorting out some of the consequences, but the fact that we [meaning him] don't receive the degree of credit in some circles doesn't bother me. I would never take anything away from the attorney general. He was totally dedicated to it, but I know how things ultimately happened, and no attorney general or minister of justice was going to solve the impasse we were faced with."

Some of the jubilation began to wear thin in early 1982, when it became apparent that Trudeau was being excessively pompous, planning to bask in the glory himself while leaving the other leaders out of the picture.

"The premier became progressively disappointed with the lack of grace on Trudeau's part," says Segal. "Why wouldn't you have the premiers on the platform? How much would that have cost? If Lévesque wouldn't come, so what? He'd just look silly. But when you're trying to build bridges to the West, it doesn't cost you a thing to have those premiers there, who compromised a lot, instead of nineteen federal cabinet ministers, most of whom had nothing to do with it. Contrast that to Davis's statement when he met the press the day it was signed. Nobody, not even Trudeau, had been more machine-gunned than him. All those eight guys just hated him for his role, but he said something nice about every one of them, even Lévesque, on the assumption that now is the time you put those things behind you.

"That's the man-of-fair-play stuff, the decency and goodwill, small-town honor thing of his. It's a bit naive perhaps, but that's him."

CHAPTER 24
REACHING FOR THE TOP

———— ❦ ————

As usual, he procrastinated. While all about him aides were fur-
iously taking polls and flying from one end of the country to
the other to meet with provincial premiers, line up potential delegates, and build up a national organization, Bill Davis pondered.

"I have no plans to have plans," he would say, as weeks slid
into months. All the while the 1983 federal Tory leadership contest drew closer and closer, until finally, on May 4, less than five
weeks before the convention, Davis said thanks, but no thanks.
He was happy in Ontario.

He had come through the valley, walked to the bottom of
the mountain, and looked up. But despite his access to all the
necessary equipment, the icy slopes of federal politics — especially Tory politics — did not seem worth the climb. Worse, had
he weathered the frosty blasts of convention politics to plant his
banner at the peak, the big question would remain: How many
of his fellow climbers would join him, and how many would
simply wait down below until he was frozen out, fell off, or
slipped into a political crevasse from which there was no escape?

He didn't run, but for several months, while Joe Clark and
Brian Mulroney hammered away at each other and John Crosbie
tried to turn comic relief into delegate support, the eyes of most
Tories and much of the media were trained on Bill Davis. The
story was: "Will he or won't he?" Those who thought he should,
like those who thought he shouldn't, never tired of speculating,

never stopped encouraging or discouraging. And all the while the imperspicuous subject of all this attention did what he did best — nothing.

Had he run, he would have been bucking tremendous odds, and not only because of his controversial stature in some parts of the party or because he would have had to then defeat the entrenched Liberals. Canadian history has not been kind to provincial premiers who have decided to climb the mountain to Ottawa. Only two premiers have ever made it — both Tories — but they didn't hold power long. Sir John Thompson lasted just two years, from December 5, 1892, to December 12, 1894, then dropped dead at Windsor Castle, and Sir Charles Tupper lasted from May 1, 1896, to July 8, 1896 — two whole months — before Laurier's Liberals swept him out of power.

Many others have tried. Indeed, George Drew, who began the current Ontario Tory regime in 1943, left Queen's Park five years later to take over the federal leadership, only to be slaughtered twice by Louis St. Laurent. Bob Stanfield came within two seats of catching Pierre Trudeau in 1972, which is as close as any former premier has come to being prime minister in this century. But politics is not horseshoes, and close, alas, does not count.

Many thought it would have been different with Davis. The problem most premiers have is that if they are noticed at all in other parts of the country, they are believed to be regionalists. Davis was certainly known nationally and was admired by many across the country for his tireless efforts toward constitutional reform. But for every Canadian outside Ontario who admired him for that, at least one other despised him for his stand against world oil prices or — a fact of life in Canada — just for being from Ontario.

Could Davis have won the leadership convention? Even his own supporters are split on that question, although all agree that had he won, it would have been an easier task for him to win the country. But in the end, for better or worse, they were not going to take the boy out of Brampton.

*   *   *

Even in the 1967 federal leadership campaign, when Bob Stanfield replaced John Diefenbaker, a group of Ontario Tories, impressed with Davis's record as an innovative education minister, tried to convince him to seek the party leadership. But cooler heads prevailed—among them Eddie Goodman, who told Davis he'd be annihilated — and he didn't make the attempt.

But after Stanfield lost (again) in 1974, two names emerged most prominently as possible successors: Bill Davis and Peter Lougheed. The two were mentioned frequently again in 1976, although any aspirations Davis had were hurt badly by his embarrassing minority squeaker in 1975. At the time Davis tried to get Lougheed to run, even offering to nominate him, but Lougheed wasn't interested in federal politics. Davis was, but it's a giant step from interest to participation.

On the surface Davis and Lougheed should have been buddies. After all, they were both Tories, both prominent premiers since 1971 of Canada's two wealthiest provinces, both loved football (Lougheed played pro ball, and Davis played in university), and whenever they socialized together, they appeared to be having a swell time.

But the oil wars changed all that. Davis thought Lougheed was being parochial and malicious, while Lougheed thought Davis was being parochial and malicious. They were probably both right, but that didn't help the relationship.

In late September, 1971, two weeks after he became premier of Alberta, Lougheed and his wife, Jeanne, were weekend guests at the Brampton home of Bill and Kathleen Davis. Davis was in the throes of his own election campaign—he had been premier since March, but this was his first election — and Lougheed headed off to Environment Minister George Kerr's campaign room in Burlington, stood on a chair just vacated by Davis, and said, "I'm with you all the way. I'm thrilled to be a part of this very, very important election."

That night the two young couples—Davis was just forty-two, Lougheed forty-three — headed off to the Coal Bin, a swingles club on Wellington Street, to see how Toronto's young people were enjoying Davis's decision two months earlier to lower the drinking age from twenty-one to eighteen. A long-haired youth wandered up to their table and said, "Hey man, thanks for giving us the vote. And I like the beer, too." They had gone to the bar, a rarity for Davis, after watching the Toronto Argonauts defeat the Calgary Stampeders, 18–7. Davis won a dollar from Lougheed on the game.

The first serious personal falling-out between the two men came in February, 1975, in Winnipeg, when they were meeting with federal officials to try to shore up the giant Syncrude project. At one point Davis discussed the possibility of investing $50 million in the oil sands project. Lougheed scoffed sarcastically that he could have saved himself the airfare if that was all he could come up with and told Davis to take his assistants (two cabinet ministers, actually) into another room and come up with a serious proposal. Both federal and Ontario officials said later they were shocked at Lougheed's tone; yet before it was over, Davis had chipped in $100 million, or 5 per cent of Syncrude. When Davis said he would like to feel that his presence was welcome in the project, giving Lougheed a chance to be gracious, the Alberta premier was silent. Asked about it later by reporters, Davis would only say, "I always think there are two ways to do business."

They did remain on speaking terms, however, and were next seen at the Calgary Day dinner at Toronto's Canadian National Exhibition, exchanging pleasantries but nothing more. Davis was fighting another election and, unlike 1971, could have used Lougheed's help. But he didn't ask for it. Nor was it volunteered.

That dinner followed a federal-provincial conference where Lougheed, attempting to keep control of Alberta's oil, insisted that agreement of all provinces should be required before future amendments were made to the Constitution. In a campaign speech in Hamilton on September 15, Davis dumped on the proposal, saying it would make the Supreme Court of Canada more important than elected politicians. And in October Davis again criticized Lougheed, this time for "not properly" stating Ontario's position on bringing the Constitution home from Britain. Lougheed, as chairman of that year's premiers' conference, had written Trudeau on the matter.

And so it went, the two men fighting over oil and the Constitution — which to Lougheed, at least, was the same issue — and while they still kept appearing at Grey Cup games and making friendly wagers, they had become bitter political enemies.

Most of those closest to Davis liked to think that their man did not harbor hostilities of this kind. They were only too happy to talk about Lougheed's latest unfriendly act, but they said Davis did not indulge in such low-life behavior. Yet one of Davis's senior advisers later admitted, "The relationship between them has become pathological. The only real difference is Davis hides his feelings better than Lougheed does. Davis doesn't have to show how he feels about Lougheed; he's got Hugh Segal and those guys to do that. . . . It stems from their disagreement over oil prices, but it's even more fundamental than that. Davis sees himself — a mirror of Ontario in this respect — as a leader who puts the national interest first. He sees Lougheed as a parochial man first and foremost, and he has no time for that view. They sugar-coat their feelings with all that football-betting bullshit, [but] things got so partisan at one point that in the 1983 Stanley Cup, a bunch of us were watching it, and Segal cheered for the Islanders. Not because he liked them, but because he didn't want Edmonton to win anything."

In practical terms, Davis was back in the federal leadership picture after ending six years of minority rule — a politically weak situation that made it doubly difficult to step up — by leading his Big Blue Machine to a seventy-seat sweep in 1981, and it didn't take long for speculation to heat up again. Senator Keith Davey, part of a CBC panel analyzing the results of the election, said, "I shouldn't be giving you this advice, but you Conservatives will never win a federal election unless you've got a popular leader from Ontario. I'd say that if you're looking for a leadership candidate, you've got to look at Davis."

Davis said he was "a little reluctant to accept political advice from a very able political strategist who obviously doesn't have the interests of the Progressive Conservative party at heart." But Davey's comment was enough to spark a new round of stories on Davis's plans to take over from the faltering Joe Clark.

Eddie Goodman, who remained convinced throughout that Davis shouldn't run federally, told the *Montreal Gazette*, "It's simply not on his [Davis's] mind to run. . . . It's not a question of shortcomings. . . . He's best suited by interest and temperament for the role he's now playing." Goodman conceded that there would be great pressure from the party for Davis to run. "But I and his other close friends wouldn't dream of trying to make him change his mind, and even if we did it wouldn't do any good. Besides, anyone who tried to convince him to run wouldn't be a true friend."

Two years later two of his friends—Hugh Segal and Norman Atkins — were so persistent and so persuasive in their efforts that they came within an eyelash of convincing Davis to set aside his better judgment.

During all this time Davis consistently denied any interest in the federal job. His stock reply was, "I am completely engrossed in my duties as premier and am not giving any thought to entering federal politics now or in the future." But then, there was no federal Tory leadership contest coming up. There was, however, a subtle change in his response beginning late in 1981, when he told a year-end press conference at Queen's Park that he wouldn't take part in any movement to force a leadership review on Clark. But what would he do if that leadership review occurred and Clark lost? "You know me," he said. "I don't deal in hypothetical situations." When pushed further he would only say, "My prime adviser is my wife, and I know what her advice would be."

In May, 1982, Segal said he rated the odds at 75–25 against Davis opting to run federally. "For myself or Norm Atkins, because we know his bias is not to run, we're telling him not to decide. And I know his wife, Kathy, probably has a bias against him running. Hell, look at him; he's healthy, he's happy, he's a winner. Does he need the hassle?"

In November, 1982, Davis announced where he would stand at the party's leadership review in Winnipeg in January, 1983, telling 1,450 Tories at a $200-a-plate fund-raiser, "I'm a loyal supporter of Joe Clark."

A week before Clark's fate was sealed, a Gallup poll mysteriously showed up in a plain brown envelope at the Toronto office of The Canadian Press. The poll, which Gallup verified, had no admitted sponsor. It showed that Clark would easily defeat Trudeau in an election but would lose if John Turner became Liberal leader. It also showed that both Davis and Lougheed, as federal leaders, could beat Turner.

On January 28, 1983, Clark won the support of only 66.9 per cent of his own party delegates in Winnipeg, immediately recommended a leadership convention, and announced that he would be a candidate for his own job. Davis told a mob of reporters that he still supported "the federal leader," a typical Davis response ambiguous enough to mean anything.

The first thing Hugh Segal did after Winnipeg was hop on a plane and head to the Maritimes, where he met individually with the three Tory premiers — Nova Scotia's John Buchanan, New Brunswick's Richard Hatfield, and Prince Edward Island's James Lee. He didn't bother going to Newfoundland to see Brian Peckford because he was already committed to John Crosbie. "I just wanted to see what kind of support there was for Davis around the country," says Segal. "The premier never gave his approval or disapproval. I just said, 'I'm going out to see what's cooking,' and he said he hadn't decided on anything."

Segal was encouraged in the East — Lee said he'd nominate Davis, Buchanan said he'd be "totally supportive," and Hatfield even visited Davis himself to convince him to run.

Next Segal went west, first to see British Columbia's Bill Bennett. Although he's Social Credit, that's sort of Tory, and there were solid ties between his people and the Big Blue Machine: Bennett's chief of staff at the time was Pat Kinsella,* who had gone west after serving as executive director of the Ontario Tories; Jerry Lampert had left his job as eastern Ontario organizer for Davis to organize Bennett's Socreds in priority ridings; and Norman Spector, a senior Ontario civil servant, was Bennett's assistant deputy minister in charge of policy co-ordination. Bennett told Segal that although he wouldn't be involved in the leadership, the British Columbia delegation could be expected to be favorable. Even Manitoba's Sterling Lyon said he'd be hard pressed not to support Davis on the second ballot.

Segal and Norm Atkins next had dinner with Saskatchewan's Grant Devine at the Westin Hotel in Toronto, just a few blocks south of Queen's Park. "He laid out the problems Davis would have in Saskatchewan, the perceptions and concerns, but he said that while he was with Clark, he was prepared to be 'positively neutral' about Davis," says Segal. "So what that would have meant is we basically isolated Lougheed as a negative force. Everybody else had a purpose, which was to elect the candidate of their choice. There's nothing wrong with that. But Lougheed was the one person whose sole purpose in life was to destroy Billy Davis."

---

*Later campaign chairman for Premier Frank Miller.

Lougheed, of course, wasn't the only problem Davis had. The federal Tory caucus, or at least most of it, hadn't forgiven him for what it perceived to be his undermining of Clark in the 1980 federal election by his opposition to the Crosbie budget. It was a convenient excuse for the federal Tories, who had basically fallen on their own swords, but it still presented a problem for Davis. Early in February two dozen Tory MPs launched a draft-Lougheed movement. But Prince Edward-Hastings Tory MP Jack Ellis, then Davis's sole public supporter in caucus, said it was too soon to panic. "Bill Davis is still surveying his options."

The other hang-up Davis had was that his own version of party loyalty made it distasteful for him to seek the leadership when Clark — still the leader, after all — was in the contest. Segal and Bill Neville, a senior Clark strategist, had breakfast together in Toronto soon after the Winnipeg convention, with the Davis people hoping that if Clark's support started to go soft, maybe he could be convinced to step down so their man could jump in. They were dreaming in technicolor.

In late February, when the leadership convention was announced for June instead of the fall, as the Davis troops had hoped, Davis said, "I'm not running. I have no plans to run. I'm here trying to run the province of Ontario, and it's a very demanding task." As definite as that statement sounded, Davis was never definite, and even his deputy, Ed Stewart, who was opposed to the idea of Davis running — "What would he want to do a crazy, goddamn thing like that for?" — said he was "certain Davis hasn't made his final decision yet. I hope he isn't running, but I don't know. He's just standing back and letting this thing swirl around him, and in due course, as is his way, he'll make a decision."

Atkins said at the time that a fall convention "would have been easier to plan for, but if his [Davis's] inclination is to go, as I hope it is, I don't think it makes all that much difference."

Reporters later learned that Davis's comments came after a secret meeting with Clark at the Park Plaza Hotel. The Clark people said that Davis had pledged not to oppose their man, but the Davis people discounted that as "silly."

In early March, having failed to convince Lougheed to run, a small group of Tory MPs circulated a draft-Davis letter, but it never got more than half a dozen supporters. Naturally, a draft-

Davis campaign at Queen's Park, organized by Brantford's Phil Gillies, North Bay's Michael Harris, and Sarnia's Andy Brandt, fared better. Gillies told the *Globe* that the support was "overwhelming" but "bittersweet. . . . We would like to see him run because our party needs someone the voters can have confidence in . . . but we would reluctantly see him leave here."

On March 9, two weeks after Davis had declared that he definitely was not a candidate, he told reporters he had not set a deadline for making his final decision. Word went out from Queen's Park to elected and unelected Tory officials that until Davis had decided, they shouldn't make any commitments. The party's executive director, Bob Harris, said the question of a Davis run was "not a dead issue," and they were just telling other provincial Tories to "keep their powder dry." Throughout the whole thing, "It was never a case of the premier saying, 'I really want to run,' or 'I don't want to run.' What he didn't say was 'No.' Our best guesstimate was he'd get over fifty per cent of the Ontario delegates, but it was difficult to monitor from an organizational point of view because he wasn't a candidate."

Davis left for a Florida holiday on March 25, but Senator Bill Kelly flew down a few days later to urge him to run. "My chore is to persuade him that he is absolutely the right person to lead the Conservative party and become prime minister," Kelly said before leaving. "He has absolutely got to go; he's not just another candidate."

Clark, starting to worry, said in an interview with a Montreal radio station that Davis lacked national experience and would be considered a "regional candidate." Clark, who himself essentially ran on a platform of viewing Canada as a "community of communities," said, "A province is not a country, and there are a number of differences that one must face between Ontario and Canada." But then, Clark called Mulroney a regional candidate, too.

Political journalist Don Braid, who writes from the West and is attuned to western sentiment, wrote on April 3 that if Davis decided to run, "Lougheed will try to dump his bandwagon into the first ditch on the road to Ottawa." Quoting senior Alberta Tories, Braid continued that Lougheed would prefer to steer delegates away from Davis, but, if he felt he had to, he'd even enter the race himself to stop him. Albertans believed Davis was "a

Liberal in disguise," citing his support for Trudeau's oil and constitutional positions. Davis espoused both those views before Trudeau did, but that fine point was lost in Lougheed's bitterness.

Davis people say Lougheed resorted to carrying newspaper clippings around on what Davis had said about oil pricing, just to make the point with people how anti-Alberta Davis was. Ontario Treasurer Larry Grossman, who was industry minister at the time of the 1981 first ministers' conference on the economy, says Davis and Lougheed were still outwardly friendly at that time. Indeed, Grossman, Davis, and Lougheed left the Governor General's dinner and dance and went back to Davis's hotel suite to watch Monday-night football. (The hotel didn't have a cable converter, so Davis had brought his own from Brampton.) But later on Grossman went to Edmonton to discuss interprovincial co-operation and barriers to trade with his Albertan counterpart, Hugh Planch. "After we exchanged pleasantries, he said, 'How can you expect to come out here and do business with us when we read this kind of thing?' And he threw several Toronto press clippings on the desk about the oil stuff. I came out of that meeting stunned. I couldn't believe their attitude."

The Davis troops, although they would never admit it, commissioned a secret poll by Canada Facts in mid-March and leaked it to the *Toronto Star* on April 13. It showed that Davis would do far better nationally against John Turner or Trudeau than either Clark or Mulroney. The next day a Gallup poll conducted in early March gave Clark a clear lead on the question: "What one person would you like to see as leader of the party?" About 23 per cent said they preferred Clark (40 per cent among Tories), while Lougheed was next at 6 per cent, and Davis, David Crombie, and Mulroney were tied at 5 per cent apiece. However, 49 per cent were undecided.

In late April, after Lougheed had decided he would meet with the major candidates on their campaign swings through the West, Alberta officials said he hadn't ruled out the possibility of the party caucus voting en masse for a chosen candidate if Davis entered the race. And with seventy-five MPPs and eleven provincial appointees, Lougheed controlled the largest block of uncommitted Tory votes in the country, large enough, perhaps, to make the difference in what was expected to be a dogfight.

Not everyone in Alberta was anti-Davis, however. After

Lougheed declared he wasn't running, senior businessman Bob Blair came to see Segal and said that now that Lougheed was out, he would be delighted to encourage Davis. "But later on, when it got to the crunch, he didn't call directly, but somebody called on his behalf to say Lougheed was now pathological about Davis," says Segal. "There was some big fund-raising dinner out there, and Lougheed's people took Michael Meighen aside and said, 'You'd better let Davis know we'll be very tough if he gets in, and we'll stop at nothing to make sure he doesn't make it.'"

In late April Davis held a clandestine meeting at the Park Plaza with a group of twenty Quebec supporters of Peter Blaikie, the former party president, who had just pulled out of the race. Davis, who had thought the meeting was secret, was greeted on his way out by a Canadian Press journalist. He told her that he had explained to the delegation he was busy in Ontario, "although I am mindful of national concerns."

Segal, of course, was ecstatic. In addition to his problems in the West, the Davis people were concerned about their man's lack of ability to speak French and about his controversial disputes with franco-Ontarians over schools. The issue had received more publicity in Quebec than his program of whispered bilingualism. "They [the Quebec people] went out of their way to say that some people in French Canada, in the press, and in Liberal politics would try to embarrass him, but the vast majority of French-Canadians just want to know whether he's a decent guy who can create jobs. They had sixty delegates, all nominated. It ain't a lot, but it wasn't a bad start."

Also in late April Kathleen Davis had lunch with old friend, *Toronto Sun* columnist Joan Sutton. "She wasn't taking any notes," said Kathleen. "We were just talking. But she wrote some stuff down, and the paper took it out of her column and made it into a story. They took everything out of context. It upset me because it came at the worst possible time." Indeed, the headline announced: "Bill Has to Run: Wife," quoting Kathleen from Sutton's column: "I had the feeling at one time that he had definitely decided not to enter this race, but now I know there is a sense that whether he wants it or not, it is something he has to do." She said she thought he could win nationally, but winning the convention would be "a much more difficult thing," adding that the decision was tough because it meant "Billy has to decide what he wants to do with his life for the next ten years."

The story was picked up and run coast to coast, and when Davis came home that night he found Kathleen on their bed, weeping. "He said, 'What's going on here?' I said it was Joan Sutton's article, and he said, 'Don't cry about that. I don't care about it,' and I don't think he did. I just felt that I had betrayed him when he was struggling so hard with the decision."

Kathleen says she was quoted "out of context." Maybe, but Roy McMurtry says Davis came "closer than I ever thought he would to running, to the point where Kathleen told my wife she thought that they were going. Ed Stewart and I had lunch with her and gave her a copy of Maureen McTeer's book of famous Ottawa residences."

The game of hide-and-seek was getting ridiculous. Every day reporters would ask Davis if he was running and every day he would reply, "I have no plans, and no plans to have plans." In the meantime Segal, Atkins, Kelly, and others were frantically building a machine as if Davis were a candidate.

Just to give him some food for thought, *Calgary Herald* publisher J. P. O'Callaghan, in a signed editorial, said Davis would split Canada in two if he ran, adding that his "unremitting stance" on cheaper energy prices had driven Clark's Conservatives from office in 1980 and that he had "hopped into bed" with Trudeau on oil and the Constitution.

On Sunday, May 1, just weeks before the convention, Davis met with Kelly in his Brampton home. Kelly had polls and his own passionate belief to try to persuade Davis that he should run, and although the two men discussed the situation most of the afternoon, Kelly left still not knowing what Davis was going to do, although he expected the worst. "It was nothing specific that he said," Kelly explained to the *Star* a few days later. "With Billy Davis, you just know when his mind is made up. And you know when it's final."

Davis cancelled all his appointments for the next two days to think it all over. He spent part of the time helping his son Neil and his daughter-in-law Ruth paint a room in their house for the baby they were expecting in June (now granddaughter Christine). He spent hours on the phone talking to everybody involved, both hawks and doves. But a phone call he hadn't expected came from Saskatchewan Premier Grant Devine.

"Davis told us about it Tuesday afternoon [May 3] when we were out at the house," says Segal. "He told us Devine had said in sadness that he had to do what Lougheed had asked — oppose the premier — and Davis said that makes it more than a personal problem between Peter and him, it makes it a regional problem — the Prairies — and he didn't think he should consider getting into something that divisive." Segal argued that they shouldn't be intimidated by Lougheed and that they should "go and beat their ass." But Davis replied that he had to live with the nature of the campaign itself and what the situation would be like afterward. "He said the Tories on a good day are split nineteen different ways, and he didn't want another ten divisions attributed to him. And besides, he wasn't sure he wanted to leave Ontario. So he said he'd sleep on it."

Segal says Devine's decision really hurt because the Ontario Tories had helped him win his election. "We'd sent people out there, organizers, anything they asked for — and now this."

Westcott, Macaulay, and Goodman, none of whom wanted Davis to enter the race, left the Tuesday meeting early, but Segal and Atkins stayed on to convince him to run. "You could tell by the way he was talking he was close to making up his mind," says Atkins. "It seemed to me it was over. His style is not the politics of polarization." He says they had Clark on top on the first ballot, followed by either Davis or Mulroney, neck-and-neck. Atkins, Segal, and Kelly had argued that Clark's support was soft and would melt away and come over to Davis. Goodman disagreed. (And as it turned out, Clark did have considerable support through the entire convention.)

Goodman was against Davis running because "he wouldn't be happy. That is a zoo in Ottawa, particularly for Conservatives. He was really not considering it anyway until the others started to push and twist, and then he started to think about it against his best instincts and against what his wife wanted, but I felt for a while he was going to make a mistake. I think he finally said to himself, 'Why the hell am I going to fight like an s.o.b. for something which might well end up as a slap in the face and I don't want anyway?' I mean, how far does his obligation to the party go? I said to him, 'You owe those sons of bitches nothing, and if you win, you lose. It will be hell.' "

Atkins and Segal left about 10 p.m. that Tuesday evening, looking glum but unwilling to comment. As it happened, I had been waiting in the driveway outside the house, alone. When Davis opened the door for Atkins and Segal, he said to me, "I can't tell you a thing, but if you want to talk, come in." An hour later, after talking about his father and mother, the importance of his family, and his attachment to Brampton, all he would say about his decision was that "the process is not all completed yet." Then he said he had to speak with Kathleen. When I left she was in the kitchen making coffee.

"We didn't talk about it much during that time," she said later. "He wanted to know from me whether I would do that, and I said I would. I didn't want to be involved too much because I didn't want to feel myself responsible for any decision which he might regret later. . . . I didn't really know either until that night he came up to me in the kitchen and said, 'I don't think I'm going to do it.' That was all. You know how his mind works. He reserves judgment, he really does. He has this ability to set out a whole slew of alternative actions or solutions, and he simply doesn't give off any waves which way he's moving, one way or the other, until he finally knows what he's doing. Then he does it."

Ed Stewart arrived at the Brampton home at about 8:30 the next morning. The two men spoke about the decision, then walked out the front door to Davis's waiting limousine. On the way he ran into his friend Ron Webb. "I thought he was going to run," said Webb. "I saw him that morning. Spoke to him. He looked really troubled, far away, but he didn't tell me."

An hour later he told everyone at a packed Queen's Park press conference, "I honestly believe that I can make the best contribution to this country by serving as premier of this great province, and it is my intention to do so." He conceded that Lougheed "probably would not have been enthusiastic" and said he wouldn't support any particular candidate at the convention.

So what was it that finally tipped the balance against trying for what had once been his ambition?

"I think the bottom line really was the personal reasons," said

Bob Harris. "He really does enjoy Brampton, enjoy getting home every night. I think he gets a lot of strength from the fact he can get home. The other reason came from his press conference, when he said his political style is one of a conciliator, but the noise from the West made that difficult. I don't think it was a sure thing if he'd run, but he certainly would have had a great chance."

Bill Kelly said, "One of his big problems was he's Mr. Loyal, and he felt uncomfortable about running against his national leader. Isn't that strange? But there it was. If Clark hadn't run, I think Bill would have had less discomfort."

Frank Miller was "convinced the fact Lougheed would fight him plus the last-minute withdrawal of support by Devine did it. We don't know a heck of a lot about what his personal thoughts are, though. He's so private that we really don't know much, except I always sensed a real personal competitiveness between those two."

John Tory said, "I'm not sure he has a burning ambition to be prime minister. I think he felt it could be a self-defeating exercise. He was worried about his ability to unify the party. And he told us a few nights later at the Albany Club dinner [May 7], the culmination of the so-called non-campaign, that he has experienced everything that goes with holding high office and doesn't have any driving ambition to get the only office higher in this country than the one he has. And finally, he may have just decided that particular lifestyle, the rigors and disciplines and intrusions in his personal life, are not for him. You know, the 61 Main Street lifestyle which Kathy enjoys very much. Her ability to be able to go shopping in the local supermarket, to be able to go to the U of T and take courses and most people don't know who she is. She leads a very normal life, but when you become the wife of the prime minister, and it's not 61 Main Street, but 24 Sussex Drive, then all that changes. I don't think they really wanted that."

Ron Webb said the speech Davis gave to about a hundred supporters at the post-non-campaign Albany Club dinner was "the best I'd ever heard him. God, it was good. And nobody taped the speech. He was very emotional. He talked about how he would have split the party. He was surprised with the reaction to him from the West. He couldn't understand it. Neither could I. I mean, they had their differences over energy, which is very important to the West, but political differences usually aren't taken that personally—with that much hostility. It hurt and surprised him. Why didn't he run? Well, I'm reluctant to answer that. I don't want to embarrass him, but I think he worried whether he could win or not. He could win the country, but the convention was something else."

Davis's eldest son, Neil, said his father "obviously prefers to stay here and get to the Bay every weekend he can, but I think he had perhaps resolved the family problem. I don't think that is all that made the decision for him. It was a combination of his family feelings and, not just the problems from the West, but whether he was going to be accepted by the party and whether he wanted to devote that kind of time to it." He has noticed in the last two years that his father "gives everybody [family] a call every Sunday. He never used to do that. I think there's no question that his family has become even more important. . . . When I was younger we hardly ever saw him at night. Now he tends to be home three nights a week. I'm not sure if it's because he has a granddaughter or if it's just a stage."

Davis's sister, Molly Endress, said, "Family considerations were a major reason. He missed a lot of the kids growing up, you know. Kathy would have supported him; we all would have. But she was glad when he decided not to go." His other sister, Peggy Dale, said, "I thought there was a possibility he'd run. It was a plum which isn't offered to everybody, so it would be tempting. But I was glad he didn't. . . . I think he owes something to his wife and his family. You can't help but feel a little proud of what he's done. He did miss a lot with his own children, though. He's very proud of his granddaughter."

Segal is still more than a little upset about Lougheed, convinced that without his hostility they could have talked Davis into running. "Lougheed is hung up on that western thing; his father and his grandfather had property seized during the Depression, and he identifies Davis with the bad guys in the East. The assumption is that nobody lost their farms in Ontario during the Depression, that no stores were repossessed by the banks in Ontario. That's the whole psychology out there."

But Darcy McKeough believes the problems could have been ironed out had Davis personally made the effort. McKeough had coffee with Lougheed at the Edmonton airport during the "will he or won't he" episode, and "I got the impression that if Bill would kiss his ass a little bit, Peter wouldn't have been so negative. If Bill had just gone to, say, Lethbridge and talked to the fifteen delegates there, because Bill is good at that, I don't know if they would have voted for him, but they wouldn't have been as mad as they were. Bill just took too long to make up his mind. The longer it festered, the worse it got out there."

The day after the long-awaited announcement, Lougheed was in Washington on provincial business and was asked by reporters if he had heard about Davis's decision not to run. He had. Asked if he had any comment, he said, "No, I wouldn't make any comment on that." (Lougheed also refused to be interviewed for this book. Ron Leipert, his press secretary, took the request, called back a week later, and said, "The premier has nothing to say about Bill Davis." Asked if that showed what Lougheed thinks of Davis, Leipert said, "Yes, I think it does.")

And what does Davis say about Lougheed's attitude? Well, he says, there "may be more strains" from Lougheed's point of view than his. "I think the fact that Peter and I have our differences over oil policy on occasion, that the difference of opinion has been escalated in Alberta to the extent of using it for political purposes—you know, 'Central Canada gets everything, and we're paying the price.' But I guess that's politics."

Davis says he has been blessed "with a group of people who have always been pretty loyal. . . . I've appreciated that, but sometimes people who are enthusiastic about your political career sometimes may have greater ambitions for your future than you may have yourself. But that's human nature.

"I can't tell you whether my decision would have been any different if Peter had been at least somewhat supportive, or not negative . . . or if Joe Clark had decided not to be a candidate. I was not totally comfortable with that. And yes, there is something to your grandfather theory, no question. Part of the price paid are family considerations. I've been kind of fortunate to have the family I have, most of that because of Kathleen. But what I have missed is some of the things most parents enjoy. Things like the school concerts, the open houses. That's a part of it, no question. But there was no single reason."

In the middle of the interview in his Brampton den, his daughter-in-law Ruth and granddaughter Christine walked into the otherwise empty house. Christine, just over a year old at the time, was carrying some dandelions she'd picked for her grandfather. Davis got up from his chair, walked over to the little girl, and held out his hand as she gave them to him, murmuring something that passed for "Grandpa."

After they left, Davis settled back into his chair, lit his pipe, and said, "Yes, family was an important factor. No question."

*   *   *

On May 24, 1984, more than a year after Davis's decision not to run federally, and just a few months before he announced his retirement, the Tories held a huge party in honor of his twenty-five years in politics. Brian Mulroney was there, and late in the evening dinner chairman Ron Webb said he had several telegrams for Davis, but it was too late to read them all. So Mulroney was introduced, and Webb handed the telegrams to Davis.

Davis slowly looked through the pile of congratulations from all the other Tory premiers. Then he turned to Webb and said sadly, "There's one missing."

It was Lougheed's.

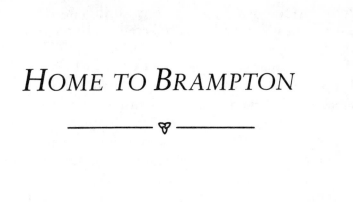

HOME TO BRAMPTON

Two days after he announced his retirement, Davis spoke to 3,200 Tories at a $200-a-plate fund-raising dinner at Metro's new convention centre. It was supposed to have been a campaign rally. Naturally, Cardinal Carter joined him at the head table and asked God to "bless our friends Bill and Kathy."

Davis talked of "new beginnings, new starts, new initiatives, the courage to work for the future without being imprisoned by the past" and warned the Tories not to get caught in "the ideological prisons of the left or the right. . . . That is not the kind of self-indulgence that the people of Ontario will tolerate from their party. I call it Ontario's party."

Speculation began immediately about his successor. At week's end Dave McFadden announced that the convention would be held January 24–26 at the Canadian National Exhibition's Coliseum and that the party had accepted Davis's suggestion of an October 8 deadline for eligibility to either become a delegate or be allowed to vote for delegates. The Tories were anxious to avoid the ugly spectacles that had marred two federal leadership races when campaign workers had dragged derelicts and young children in off the street in their anxiety to pack selection meetings for their candidates. The process for the Ontario Tories would be orderly, civilized, with the delegate selection meetings completed by the end of November and seven regional all-candidates meetings planned in advance. And to avoid a nui-

sance candidate, contenders had to post $10,000 up front, half
of which would be returned to them if they won fifty votes on
the first ballot. McFadden predicted a campaign would cost
$500,000, an estimate that quickly escalated to $750,000 or $1
million, ten times what Davis had spent in 1971.

For a couple of weeks it looked as if there might be a dozen
contenders. The media and party insiders spoke of Darcy Mc-
Keough making a comeback, of Bette Stephenson becoming the
first woman to seek the leadership, of the certainty of regional
right wingers Gordon Walker and Claude Bennett entering the
race, of Alan Pope's plans to go for it. As one by one these potential candidates fell away, party officials began to worry. All four
eventual contenders — Frank Miller, Dennis Timbrell, Larry
Grossman, and Roy McMurtry — wanted a fifth candidate to
give them more flexibility after the first ballot. Pressure was
exerted on Sarnia newcomer Andy Brandt; Hugh Segal, who was
promoting Grossman, telephoned him and tried to convince him
to announce. Brandt thought seriously about it but figured all
he could raise was $200,000 and about 150 votes, so he settled
instead for the job of keynote speaker at the convention, allowing him to remain neutral but affording him a high profile for
next time.

At that early stage Agriculture Minister Dennis Timbrell, who
had been quietly campaigning for years, had more than $235,000
in his war chest. Education Minister Bette Stephenson was next
with $95,767.93, Treasurer Larry Grossman third at $61,204.93,
followed by Justice Secretary Gordon Walker with $47,215.31
and Attorney General Roy McMurtry with $30,247. Well down
in the pack with $24,861 was Industry Minister Frank Miller.

*   *   *

Miller was first out of the gate, fifteen days after Davis quit.
Flanked by six decidedly right-wing ministers and with a dozen
caucus members cheering him on, the affable, bilingual Muskoka
businessman said he had decided to get out of the race in November, 1983, because "I had no enthusiasm for an undeclared race.
It was too covert for my liking."

Indeed, in an interview at his spectacularly refurbished Muskoka retreat the previous May, Miller said he had raised $200,000

from two fund-raising dinners but had spent it "on the countless small evening meetings in hotel rooms . . . paying people to fly to various spots to organize delegates, putting all the necessary information on computers," and had reached the point where he had to "get into the big time and set up a fund-raising organization. I thought about it and basically concluded I've had my time here; I just don't want to pay the price of leadership." Looking out the large window of his Acton Island home, he said he had enjoyed politics, "but I find I'm no longer fighting as hard as I should fight. What's more, I have a great view of the lake here, looking at the boats like the one that just went by, tending my garden, and playing with my grandchildren."

Five months later he told his wife, Ann, that if he didn't run, he'd spend the rest of his life second-guessing himself.

Calling himself "a moderate right winger," Miller's opening statement concentrated on his argument that a fiscal conservative "can also care about people" and on his experience as a chemical engineer, car dealer, teacher, and tourist resort owner. Miller was thirteen in 1941 when his father died and his mother, virtually penniless, moved her family of five from Toronto back home to Gravenhurst. At his press conference Miller, now a millionaire, told of working his way through school, sometimes holding down three jobs at once. "I know what it is to be poor and to want the better things in life."

Miller earned his chemical engineering degree at McGill University, married Ann Norman, and became bilingual while working for Alcan Ltd. in Quebec. Later he taught high school in Aurora, sold paint in Brantford, sold cars in Bracebridge, and ended up owning and operating family tourist resorts and Santa's Village there.

He was introduced to the party as a "token young PC in Muskoka" in the early 1950s. He was trying to sell cars, and Gordon Aiken, a Gravenhurst lawyer then and now chairman of Ontario's commission on election contributions and expenses, "called me in and said, 'Frank, I'll give you some good business reasons for being a Conservative. The OPP would do business with you if you're a Conservative, and others will too, and we need people like you. So why don't you join the party?' " He did.

In 1971 Miller had just lost his bid to become mayor of Bracebridge when the sitting Tory in Muskoka announced his retirement. One week before nomination day, Miller was painting his house when some friends asked him to run. Two days later he decided he would, and he went on to defeat a Huntsville businessman by nine votes, developing a folksy technique for which he has since become well known. Miller is also noted for his loud, green, Muskoka-tartan sports jacket and knitted (by Ann) yellow socks, although during the leadership contest he dressed in standard business suits.

During thirteen years in government, ten of those in cabinet, he was treasurer and minister of natural resources, health, and industry and trade. During his Health stint between 1975 and 1977, he tried to cut spending by closing hospitals, a bitter political fight that led to a heart attack and also pitted him against Larry Grossman, then a young backbencher fighting to save a hospital in his riding. They remained enemies ever after.

On his political philosophy Miller said, "I come from the right wing of the party. I'm the only one of the candidates who has run a business. In small business you become either a socialist or a capitalist; I'm a capitalist, and I'm proud of it."

* * *

Two days after Miller made his announcement, Agriculture Minister Dennis Timbrell invited the media to the basement of the Westbury Hotel, using the same room and the same kickoff-rally technique used by Allan Lawrence nearly fourteen years earlier. But then Paul Weed had helped organize them both. Weed, a surly former bill collector, was a major Lawrence operative but had a falling-out with Norm Atkins after the 1974 federal Tory loss when Atkins was at Ottawa headquarters and Weed was the chief Ontario organizer.

Timbrell's staff hoped the party atmosphere, the forced hoopla, and the canned cheers from supporters who had spent some time at the bar before the press arrived would overcome the natural stuffiness of Timbrell, a Davis clone in looks and style, a man whose main claim to fame was his safe, unimaginative, but competent running of several key ministries. He immediately announced he was the front-runner, and whether he was or not at that stage, the race was seen as being chiefly between Timbrell and Miller from the beginning.

Born in 1946 in Kingston, Timbrell was elected in 1971 after teaching at Don Mills Junior High School and after serving two years as a North York alderman. In 1974, at twenty-seven, he became the youngest cabinet minister in Ontario history, minister without portfolio responsible for the youth secretariat. In 1975 he became energy minister and two years later was elevated to Health. His switch to Agriculture in 1982 was the shocker selection of that cabinet shuffle, but Timbrell had asked for the post and Davis had agreed. "Sure, there were political considerations involved," said Timbrell, "the opportunity to meet people, a lot of whom will be Tory delegates. Look at it this way: Where was I going from Health? I knew damn well there was going to be a big change . . . so I was looking around at where I should go, and I obviously wanted it to be beneficial politically."

Timbrell, a grandfather at thirty-seven (he married Janet Sullivan in 1980; she had four children from a previous marriage, and they now have two more), is no urban cowboy but says he was well received in Agriculture. Prior to the campaign he downplayed his early rural experiences on a farm near Kingston, but during his leadership pitches he used his rural roots as a constant reference point, particularly when he spoke to audiences outside Toronto, trying to paint himself as a non-Toronto-Torontonian.

When he went to Agriculture from Health, he wasn't on the front pages or on the television news any more, and people began writing "Whatever happened to Dennis Timbrell?" stories. But that was just in Toronto. While Larry Grossman, considered his main rival then, continued to make a splash in Metro Toronto, Timbrell was out in the back forties meeting farmers and local councillors, annually attending 200 fall fairs, travelling close to 100,000 miles by car or plane, giving 150 formal speeches, and often appearing three or four times in local newspapers. He concedes he lost coverage in Toronto, but when he was in Health, "The only time people in my own constituency heard about me was when I was in trouble."

Timbrell says he became a Tory partisan during the federal pipeline debate; he was incensed at Liberal closure tactics — he was nine at the time — and licked stamps for federal Tory Frank McGee, a Diefenbaker minister, when he was eleven. He boasted that he "always resisted the extremes of the right or the left," adding that if some people view him as boring, dull, and bland, "Well, so be it. I am not now going to start to pretend to be something I'm not. I am what I am." Indeed.

*   *   *

Almost from the time of his election in 1975, Roy McMurtry was seen as a leading contender for the Davis throne. A brawling Irishman in style, McMurtry's penchant for bluster attracted constant headlines, prompting his media nickname, "Roy Mc-Headline." But as years passed and Davis stayed, McMurtry was mentioned less often as heir apparent.

In April, 1984, he said, "I expect I'll stay around here as long as he [Davis] is around. . . . I'd had fifteen years of law practice before I became a candidate. I was forty. Some people are determined to have a political career, and they don't give a goddamn who the leader is. . . . Had it not been for Bill Davis, I wouldn't be in politics. My personal relationship with him is immensely important. . . . If you play in team sport with a guy, you always remain on a friendly, unpretentious sort of relationship."

McMurtry became a federal Tory backroom boy in the 1960s and saw Davis periodically at party functions. He got deeply involved in Dalton Camp's failed bid to unseat Liberal Mitchell Sharp, and in 1971, after he'd overseen the dinner meeting that built the Big Blue Machine, Davis tried to talk him into running, but McMurtry said no. Davis even sent a government airplane to McMurtry's Lake Muskoka island retreat and flew him to Townsend Island for "a little word with the boss, a word of prayer, as he used to say." But McMurtry became the party's legal adviser instead. His father, Roland Roy, a prominent trial lawyer who raised his family in "a rather comfortable environment," was "intensely suspicious of politics. . . . I grew up with a very definite mind-bent against getting directly involved."

After an embarrassing 1973 by-election loss, McMurtry moved north to a safe Tory seat and was immediately elevated to attorney general. He stayed there, doubling as solicitor general between 1978 and 1982, never wanting another portfolio. During the all-candidates debates his lack of expertise in various fields showed, making him appear weak and unaware when responding to serious economic, environmental, or agricultural questions. He entered the race on November 2 after being convinced by Norm Atkins, his campaign boss, that he had the money and the votes to run a respectable campaign. An aide said he "had reached the point where he likely wouldn't have run again anyway, so he might as well go after it while the chance was there."

McMurtry always had a contradictory political image — a red Tory in many respects, a self-proclaimed civil libertarian but a strong law-and-order man who never hesitated to use the power of the state. He was the man responsible for the controversial raid by 150 Metro Toronto policemen on four steam baths frequented by homosexuals, resulting in 273 arrests. He was noted for attacks on drunk drivers, authored Ontario's first family law reforms, made Rosalie Abella a family court judge when she was thirty and seven months pregnant, yet supported tough censorship and opposed freedom of information laws that could hamper police intelligence work.

A sleepy-eyed man, he could be gentle one minute, quietly painting his well-known landscapes, then turn into a snarling grouch the next, storming away from reporters who dared question his wisdom. He once dismissed claims made against him by a defendant in a criminal case by calling him "a known con man," even though the case was before the courts at the time. He was considered the Number Four man in the race even before Treasurer Larry Grossman officially became the fourth candidate to enter.

* * *

Larry Grossman had never been shy before. He had been openly campaigning for the job for years, but suddenly, when it became vacant, he turned into a reluctant suitor, playing coy with the media and delaying his official campaign announcement until two weeks after Miller had kicked off the race.

At his press conference and at the all-candidates debates that followed, it was a different Larry Grossman, a soft-spoken, low-key man, constantly leaning forward, clutching the podium, and talking about the need for a man for the future, not a man for the past. He even talked right-wing, promising to balance the budget and raise tuition fees 10 per cent a year above inflation. But for all the efforts to present the "new" Grossman, the old one was still around.

For years the Tories had sloughed off critics of their fiscal affairs by boasting of Ontario's Triple-A credit rating. But in August a major New York investment firm, Standard & Poor's, was on the verge of dropping the rating to AA plus, a move that would add one-quarter of a percentage point on money borrowed by the Tories, about $75 million more. Worse, at least to Grossman, it would deal a mortal blow to his leadership hopes; it wouldn't have been his fault, but as treasurer he would have carried the can. Grossman asked Davis to go to New York with him and salvage the rating, mainly by pledging to keep the deficit under control in future budgets. Davis went, but when news of the meeting broke in October, Grossman denied the rate had been at risk and called the Davis visit "routine." It wasn't. It was the first time Davis had had to do that, and he even admitted to reporters he had appeared before an "appeal tribunal," prompting opposition critics to ask just what they were appealing if not the rating? Davis said he wouldn't call it "routine. . . . I cannot say it wouldn't have been changed if [Grossman] and I had not gone there." The next day Davis tried to "clarify" his remarks, but the damage to Grossman's credibility had been done. The issue itself faded, but the question of Grossman's trustworthiness didn't.

When he released the names of his leadership campaign staff, one conspicuously absent was Hugh Segal's. Segal had offended so many Tories during his years as a Davis power broker that it was thought best not to list his name. (One week before the leadership, Grossman finally included Segal in his campaign literature.)

Grossman turned eight the day his father, Allan, was elected a Toronto alderman in 1951. Four years later he worked for him in the bitter election in St. Andrew against Joe Salsberg, the last sitting Communist in the legislature and one the party didn't want to lose. Grossman's parents regularly received telephone calls at 4 and 5 a.m., their campaign headquarters was torched several times, committee room phone lines were cut constantly, and a round-the-clock police guard lived in the Grossman house during the entire campaign. "They had big thugs following my father everywhere he went. If he went to the corner for coffee, they'd go sit in the next booth just to intimidate him." Worse, they handed out what Grossman calls "a piece of sickening propaganda" showing his father with blood dripping down his hands, accusing him of complicity with the Nazis. "That was a heavily Jewish riding, and that stuff was just scandalous, outrageous, but my father didn't let it intimidate him. Our campaign manager was beaten up one night, and they poured sugar in the gas tank of my father's car, but Dad won by 114 votes." Allan Grossman served with distinction in the cabinets of Frost, Robarts, and Davis.

That initial campaign wasn't encouraging for a lad hoping to enter politics, "but we saw things from our side too which made it worthwhile. We saw hundreds of people who had come from behind the Iron Curtain, who were helping . . . fighting hard, motivated by the Communists. That spirit . . . was really stimulating. It's easy to get hooked on that." Grossman's father and Tory colleague John Yaremko took in dozens of Hungarian revolution survivors, feeding them, finding them jobs and housing. "It stirs you up, gives you a sense of what really counts."

It wasn't only his dad's campaigns that turned him into a scrapper. In his earliest days, "I was one of three Jewish kids in the class then. You had to fight your way to school. People would call you a dirty Jew, and being the shortest kid in the neighborhood didn't help."

In 1963 he was his father's assistant campaign manager and ran the campaigns in 1967 and 1971. He practised law for six years and became a member of the Metro Zoo board in 1974, eventually leading a revolt against a board "made up of many prominent people, some of whom haven't forgiven me to this day."

Sensing in 1975 that they were in deep trouble, the Tories wanted Allan Grossman to stay, but he told his son "words I'll never forget. He said, 'I'd rather leave when they want me to stay than stay when they want me to leave.' " They didn't want Larry to run, but he did — and won. He was named minister of consumer and commercial relations in 1977, of industry and tourism in 1978, of health in 1982, and became treasurer in 1983.

He wanted to be treasurer, despite the political risks, to show people "there's another side of me than being a pink Tory. I think I've done that with my last budget. That was one of my needs, just as it was Dennis's need to get out and meet those rural people." Several years ago a Toronto journalist said Grossman was "too

short, too Toronto, and too Jewish" to become premier. In an
interview before Frank Miller had reconsidered his decision to
get out of the leadership sweepstakes, Grossman conceded his
image was "a problem in the sense that no single one of those
things is a problem standing on its own. I don't think many Tory
delegates, if any, would not vote for me because I'm Jewish . . .
but what has to concern me is the package. Dennis, in his style
and manner, looks less Toronto than I do. I don't think it's because he's not Jewish or because he's taller than I am."

At his kickoff news conference Grossman was asked extensively about his religion, particularly because some of his supporters (although not he) were whispering to reporters that
Miller's dislike of him was anti-Semitic (which it isn't) and because Grossman himself, at a recent speech to Toronto's Prim-
rose Club, had made sure the man introducing him mentioned
that he was Canada's only Jewish cabinet minister. Grossman
said, "We believe Ontario has grown to the point at which religion is not a factor."

His office features a rare photograph of his political hero,
Benjamin Disraeli, Britain's Jewish-born prime minister. It is a
reminder of what can be done.

*   *   *

Bill Davis wanted the transition to be orderly, so after making
sure the delegate selection process and the all-candidates meetings would be tightly structured, he asked the four contenders not
to disagree publicly on rent control, Suncor, separate schools,
or bilingualism. A few days later Miller let the cat out of the bag.
Some say he put his foot in his mouth, others say he "goofed"
intentionally, but the deal was soon off, and it wasn't long before
everybody was promising to sell Suncor and keep rent controls.

Then Davis ordered the contenders and their campaign managers to a breakfast meeting in the cabinet dining room at Queen's
Park and told them not to use public officials, space, or equipment for campaigning. He also ordered them to appear regularly for question period. The order was virtually ignored, but
then Davis himself made only four legislative appearances during his final two months as premier.

On his final day in the House, December 14, the galleries were jammed with people who had come to witness an historic event. Davis was expected to deliver the traditional wind-up budget-debate speech, but instead he delegated the task to deputy premier Bob Welch. Davis spoke for only about ten minutes, saying little of note, and while Welch and the opposition leaders waxed on about the Davis era, he sat, silent and subdued, staring down at his desk. There was considerable speculation later about why he had chosen not to give a rousing wind-up speech. Some said he didn't want to show his emotion, others that he had lost his competitive edge and just wanted out. Davis, naturally, said nothing.

The fact is, he did not speak because he was an emotional wreck. The family had been up until after 2 a.m. that morning, devastated by news from Toronto's Hospital for Sick Children that for the second Davis granddaughter, born on November 21 to Neil and Ruth, there was no hope. She had suffered irreversible brain damage during delivery, and they had just learned she had cerebral palsy. Their choice: Either keep her institutionalized on machines or pull the plug and let nature take its course.

For anyone such a choice is tragic. But for Bill Davis, whose children and grandchildren had become increasingly important to him, it was all he could do to show up on his final day in the legislature. It was too much to expect more. Typically, he didn't tell anyone, not wanting to share his private grief, just as twenty-two years earlier he had asked his colleagues not to make a public show over the death of his first wife, Helen. He left Queen's Park telling reporters not to write off his political career just yet. "I still have a lot of things I want to accomplish," he said, refusing to elaborate.

It soon became apparent what those "things" were. On January 17, one week before the leadership convention, he announced the construction of a $150 million, 62,000-seat domed stadium, featuring the world's largest retractable roof, to be built on railway land at the base of the CN Tower in the heart of downtown Toronto. Scheduled to be completed for the opening Blue Jays game of the 1988 baseball season, the province will toss in $30 million lottery money, Metro Toronto $30 million, CN $10 million cash plus $20 million in land and services, and twelve major corporations $5 million each.

On Thursday, January 24, opening day of the convention, Davis sent a letter to the Opera-Ballet Hall Corp. pledging provincial help — a one-third share, with Ottawa and Metro splitting the rest — for a $90 million home for the Canadian Opera Company and the National Ballet of Canada. While he did not specify the exact site or size, it's expected to be built on about two and a half acres of provincially owned property at Bay and Wellesley streets, one block from the legislative building.

Early that afternoon Davis and Kathleen checked into the Royal York Hotel's Royal Suite, getting ready for the Davis tribute that night at the Coliseum, a horse palace on Toronto's CNE grounds. It was a disappointingly flat tribute, featuring swing music from the Spitfire Band, a boring video tribute of set-piece clips from a series of friends, and a number of jokes, apparently, from emcee Don Harron. With Prime Minister Brian Mulroney and wife Mila looking on, the delegates did come to life, waving thousands of "Thanks Bill" signs as Davis and Kathleen were finally called onto the stage.

Speaking without notes, Davis rambled on for about thirty minutes, touching on all his favorite themes — Brampton, his mother, his family, the Queen, and the Tory party. The Coliseum was only three-quarters filled, for which organizers blamed the snowy weather conditions outside and the boozy condition of some delegates prowling a host of candidate hospitality suites in several downtown hotels. Davis let his emotions slip twice, becoming noticeably choked up, even wiping away a tear, when talking about his family. "It is tougher to retire and leave than to assume leadership — nothing is so emotional or difficult." He said he had no advice to offer the four contenders. He praised them all, urging the audience to remember the words of Sir John A. Macdonald that he "not only needs Conservatives who support me when I'm right but Conservatives who support me when I'm wrong."

His aides said they'd never seen Davis so nervous as before the tribute. "He was just wishing it was over," said one. "You know how he is. The prospect of having to be emotional in public overwhelms him." The party had planned a more elaborate send-off, including a sit-down dinner, but Davis had asked them not to. However, after the tribute Darcy McKeough hosted a dinner at a classy Italian restaurant downtown with about 150 friends, staff, and former colleagues present.

With the new morning, his final day on the job before the new leader was elected, Davis was supposed to relax. Instead he spent the morning settling a twenty-six-day horsemen's strike, a $5.7 million dispute between harness and thoroughbred racers over post times. Drifting between officials from both sides, Davis ended the dispute by threatening to send the matter to binding arbitration if they didn't settle. It worked, and 650 Greenwood track employees, off work since January 1, were called back. "I hope people remember," he told aides, "that I spent my last day settling a strike."

That night he sat in his box, well up in the stands but directly in line with the Coliseum stage, listening to the leadership speeches, habitually switching channels on the television set in front of him. Within minutes of a top-level deal between Grossman and Timbrell that whoever finished third would join the other to stop Miller, he was informed by John Tory (who in turn had learned of it from Segal), which indicates which way Davis's sympathies went. Davis, of course, won't say, but it's clear he voted McMurtry on the first ballot and Grossman on the next two. After all, in their two camps were numbered his entire Big Blue Machine, and while he didn't openly politick at the convention, he was kept constantly up to date as he stayed in Eaton's Royal Winter Fair suite in a Coliseum annex, watching television, chatting, and nibbling on finger food.

On Saturday, voting day, Grossman and his wife, Carole, who stayed in a Royal York suite just down the hall from the Davises, dropped by briefly to say hello before they all left for the convention. Davis arrived at his box at about 1 p.m. and, on impulse, decided to visit each candidate's box, prompting one of his advance men to mutter, "Goddamn it, it's just like Mulroney." Davis went to McMurtry first, then to Grossman (who wasn't there), then to Timbrell, and finally to Miller, offering a handshake and a brief word of encouragement to each. When voting began, thirty minutes late, Davis was whisked along a VIP route to vote, then retired to his suite to await the results.

Miller had been the favorite all along, and he was expected to get at least 650 votes on the first ballot. Every poll placed Timbrell a strong second, Grossman third, and McMurtry a poor fourth. Davis had told friends that he hoped McMurtry wouldn't be embarrassed, and when the first-ballot results were announced and McMurtry had a surprising 300 votes, Davis's daughter Nancy leaned forward and patted her father on the back. Davis said later of McMurtry, "If he'd had more time, then maybe it would have been better." Miller led with 591, then came Timbrell with 421 and Grossman with 378.

McMurtry immediately went to Grossman's box, and the two men embraced, sending chills through the Timbrell supporters, who like most people had expected their man to face Miller on the final ballot. An aide said Davis would have picked Timbrell as his fourth choice. "He wouldn't have been demolished had Dennis won, but he worried about him. . . . He said it bothered him that unlike the other three, Dennis didn't have any close personal friends in cabinet. He worries about things like that."

He needn't have, for when the second ballots were counted, Grossman squeezed by Timbrell by six votes, 514–508. Miller had 659. Timbrell demanded a recount and got one, but it didn't change anything.

It meant that the final ballot was a showdown between the Establishment and the non-Establishment, the Big Blue Machine and Miller's Tartan Train, the Palace Guard against the disenchanted and the disaffected from the right. For there behind Grossman, literally or figuratively, were all of Davis's people — Macaulay, McMurtry, Atkins, Segal, Goodman, Tory. No doubt Davis was extremely popular within the party, but as with the popular John Robarts at the end of his rule, the party did not want more of the same. Grossman's loss not only underscored the end of the Davis era; it also meant the power structure had gone with him. When the dust had settled a few weeks later, the only Davis confidant to retain influence in Miller's Ontario was that old survivor, Eddie Goodman.*

---

*Macaulay disappeared from public view; Tory remained in the premier's office as associate secretary to cabinet for federal/provincial relations (a job held by Segal in the years when it meant something); Segal was out of favor; Kelly remained ensconced in the Senate; and Atkins was asked to be campaign chairman but would come on board only if Segal came, too. (Miller's response was to appoint Pat Kinsella as chairman and Bob Harris as campaign manager.) Roy McMurtry announced his retirement from politics on

It was 10:47 p.m. before it ended, with Miller winning by just 77 votes. When the results were announced Davis rose in his box, clapped, pulled a Miller button from his jacket pocket — leaving the Grossman button inside — and pinned it on his lapel.

After things calmed slightly, David McFadden introduced the contenders one at a time and invited them and their wives onto the stage. Then Bill and Kathleen Davis fought their way across the concrete floor, stopping constantly to shake hands or exchange a friendly word, smothered by television cameras and guarded by a phalanx of burly party workers and security personnel. To the end he remained reserved. Each of the four candidates had shaken hands on stage and kissed each other's wives; when Davis came up, Kathleen kissed the men, but he shook hands with both the men and their wives.

When he reached the top step leading to the stage, where Frank and Ann Miller were waiting for him to make his final speech and introduce his successor to the delegates, he congratulated the winner, offered his help for the future, and asked, "Aren't you glad you took my advice and stayed in there?" (Six months earlier Miller had decided to tell his riding association he was retiring before the next election, but Davis told him to wait and see what happened.) In his last hurrah Davis congratulated the party and congratulated the candidates, urging them to work together. Then he watched proudly as his children and granddaughter Christine came up onto the stage.

After Miller's brief victory speech Davis turned to leave, at which point his two veteran police bodyguards — Bob Guay and Peter Balog — split, Guay staying on with Davis, Balog going to Miller. Seeing that, Kathleen, who'd kept her composure until then, rushed over to Balog, hugged him madly, kissed him, and rocked back and forth sobbing as Davis stood awkwardly by, tears welling up in his eyes. "It really hit them then that it was

---

January 31 and on February 4 was appointed High Commissioner to the United Kingdom by Brian Mulroney. Ed Stewart remained in the premier's office on an interim basis, and Clare Westcott made ready to join the Metro Toronto Police Commission on April 1, 1985, with a view to becoming chairman. Under a supplementary benefit fund for the pensions of deputy ministers set up by order in-council signed by Davis on February 5, 1985, Westcott, in addition to his $70,000-a-year police commission salary, will collect an annual government pension of $55,000 rather than the $40,000 he could expect under the previous system.

over," said an aide. "We were all crying then. Peter had been part of the family, and now he'd gone to Frank. It was a small thing, but symbolic."

Premier-designate Miller, surrounded by his security, was taken out behind the stage, while Bill Davis was led off behind a barrier. He did not go back to his Coliseum suite. Instead he headed off under the stands and through a huge staging area with Kathleen, Guay, and Bob Harris, discussing the convention and the coming transition.

At the main door next to the Royal Winter Fair's executive office, Davis shook hands with Harris, took Kathleen by the hand, glanced quickly back toward the main convention hall, then walked briskly to his waiting Tory-blue Oldsmobile 98. His coat was already in the back seat, and their bags were in the trunk.

He helped Kathleen in, hopped into the back seat beside her, then leaned forward to his driver and said, "Let's go home to Brampton."

Index